D1252392

PROXIMATE SOLUTIONS

PROXIMATE SOLUTIONS

". . . democracy is a method of finding
proximate solutions
for insoluble problems."

—REINHOLD NIEBUHR

Case-Problems in State and Local Government

EDITED BY

G. THEODORE MITAU

James Wallace Professor of Political Science, Macalester College

AND

HAROLD W. CHASE

Professor of Political Science, University of Minnesota

CHARLES SCRIBNER'S SONS, NEW YORK

A–12.63[V]

Printed in the United States of America

Library of Congress Catalog Card Number 64-10216

TO

Charlotte and Bernice

Preface

At a time when there is no shortage of excellent texts in a particular field, a new entry requires some explanation. A new text can be rationally justified either on the basis that it is somehow better or somehow different from all others. We feel that ours is different.

The idea of the law-case book is not new. Not only has it been used almost universally in Constitutional Law courses, it has also been extensively employed to supplement regular texts in American Government courses. It is surprising, therefore, that no one previously saw fit to use the approach to supplement the regular texts in State and Local Government courses. Perhaps, the best explanation for the lack of a law-case book in this area is that it is difficult in a limited number of cases to demonstrate adequately what state and local law is on important subjects, for we deal with a large number of jurisdictions in such courses as contrasted to the one jurisdiction which is the focus of American Government courses. But such an explanation does not do justice to the approach. One of the chief virtues, if not *the* chief virtue, of having students read law cases is that it is an extremely fine way to introduce them to living problems and issues in government.

Our important issues and problems seem, sooner or later, to find their way to the courts for judicial resolution. In order to become the bases for legitimate cases or controversies, these issues and problems must be shaped precisely by the contending parties. For those who seek an understanding of them, the cases provide well-reasoned arguments as well as a rationalized decision on certain of these issues.

What we have attempted to do here is to bring together cases which describe and illustrate some of the important and interesting problems and issues in state and local government. The essay which precedes each set of cases is designed to provide a basis for intelligent reading of the cases by the students. Also, the essays raise questions about the cases, aimed at pointing up the complexities involved in resolving the problems and issues. In addition to providing students with some understanding of the enormous complexities of state and local government, we think that a reading of the selected cases will excite their interest in the subject matter, because it is presented not as academic questions but as actual controversies. Further, students will have the opportunity to obtain the benefits generally derived from the study of law cases. Hopefully, they will learn a great deal about the law, particularly as it pertains to the subject matter of state and local government. Secondly, they will be subjected to the discipline and precision of thought required in the proper study of law cases.

It is suggested that students first read the appropriate chapters in an expository textbook. Then, when they return to this volume, they read carefully the essay preceding the cases, taking notes, and paying particular attention to the questions raised. These questions can also be made the basis for fruitful classroom discussion.

A word of explanation is in order regarding our editing of cases. We have omitted multiple citations of cases because we felt they served no useful purpose as far as the students were concerned. When a citation is followed by ellipses, no substantive material has been deleted. We have also deleted footnotes and paragraph numbers. Our own editorial comments added to the cases themselves are set in italics and enclosed in brackets. If, in any quoted material or cases, we have used italics for emphasis, this use has been indicated by the following phrase: [Italics supplied—*Eds.*]; phrases that are similarly worded are an integral part of such quoted material and/or cases. Finally, in an effort to retain the authenticity of the cases, we have reproduced them as they appear in the original. Therefore, the student will find certain inconsistencies in punctuation, spelling and capitalization.

We would like to thank Professor Terrance Sandalow of the University of Minnesota Law School for his patient and incisive review of some of the essays, and Professor David Danelski of the University of Washington for thoughtful suggestions as well as Bernice M. Chase for her help in preparing the manuscript.

We alone bear responsibility for any errors of commission or omission.

G. Theodore Mitau
Harold W. Chase

ST. PAUL, MINNESOTA
MINNEAPOLIS, MINNESOTA

Contents

PROXIMATE SOLUTIONS

CHAPTER ONE

Intergovernmental Relations

At this point in your studies you undoubtedly have a good general idea of the relationships among the multitude of governments in the United States. In conveying this general picture of our complex system, your professors and textbook writers have given you in digested form analyses of governmental relationships based upon intensive study of our history and the resolutions of specific problems. As a result, you may have received the impression that the system is more simple than it actually is. In addition, you may have mistakenly assumed that *all* the problems involved in intergovernmental relations have been settled. The relationships among our governments are constantly changing as indeed they should for at least two reasons. First, it is wise to constantly reassess old problems in the light of new conditions. What was a good arrangement in the nineteenth century might not be very effective in the twentieth. Second, even when conditions do not change, our notions of what is good and true often do.

In this connection, Reinhold Niebuhr's idea that "democracy is a method of finding proximate solutions for insoluble problems" has special appeal. The inference is that we must make decisions about government and public policy as we progress, but that it is the mark of wisdom to understand that in a democratic society we never resolve our problems once and for all. Rather, we resolve them for the present, and when and if conditions change or we see the problem differently, we should be prepared to seek new solutions.

With these considerations in mind, we want to share with you a feeling for the complexity of our governmental system as well as an understanding of some of the major problems for which we have as a society achieved some "proximate solutions." We invite you to evaluate these solutions carefully. There is nothing sacred about them. Perhaps, you in your own good time will reach better ones. After all, in a few short years, the responsibility for maintaining the old consensus or achieving a new one on these matters will fall to your generation. Before you jump to the conclusion that some of these issues have been resolved badly, as indeed they may have been, be certain you have a good understanding of the factors involved.

A. *Some Problems in the Relationship Between National and State Governments*

It is a well-established principle that when Congress passes a law in consequence of its constitutional power, a state cannot successfully challenge the validity of that law nor can a state pass legislation in conflict with it. Chief Justice Marshall stated this clearly in 1819 in *McCulloch* v. *Maryland*, 4 Wheat. 316:

> If any one proposition could command the universal assent of mankind, we might expect that it would be this—that the government of the Union, though limited in its powers, is supreme within its sphere of action. This would seem to result, necessarily, from its nature. It is the government of all; its powers are delegated by all; it represents all, and acts for all. Though any one state may be willing to control its operations, no state is willing to allow others to control them. The nation, on those subjects on which it can act, must necessarily bind its component parts. But this question is not left to mere reason; the people have, in express terms, decided it, by saying, "this constitution, and the laws of the United States, which shall be made in pursuance thereof, . . . shall be the supreme law of the land," and by requiring that the members of the state legislatures, and the officers of the executive and judicial departments of the states, shall take the oath of fidelity to it. The government of the United States, then, though limited in its powers, is supreme; and its laws, when made in pursuance of the constitution, form the supreme law of the land, "anything in the constitution or laws of any state to the contrary notwithstanding."

The general proposition that laws passed by Congress in accordance with its constitutional powers are supreme is clear enough, but, unfortunately, it is not always clear whether acts of Congress actually bar or supersede state laws in the same subject-matter area. *Pennsylvania* v. *Nelson* (p. 11) demonstrates the difficulty of deciding in some cases whether or not Congress in a specific piece of legislation meant to preclude or supersede state law. This case also demonstrates why and how allegations that a state law is invalid come to the courts for resolution. In our system of government, any one who feels that he has been convicted or otherwise hurt by a state law may challenge the validity of the law in the appropriate court(s). This, of course, is much easier for an individual or a group to do effectively in most situations than to attempt to achieve legislative action or to convince administrators that a "proper" interpretation of the law makes it inapplicable in his or its case. The *Nelson* case is important, too, because it illustrates how the Supreme Court determines whether or not a congressional act supersedes a state law. When you read the case, note how Chief Justice Warren, speaking for the Court, tries to make clear the bases upon which the courts have made and should make such a determination (pp. 12–14).

For a proper understanding of the *Nelson* case, it must be remembered that Congress can generally, if it so wishes, expressly permit the states to legislate in any area where Congress has apparently been granted exclusive power to legislate by the Constitution.[1] Also, Congress can close out possible ambiguities by expressly forbidding the states to legislate about matters which constitutionally come under the jurisdiction of Congress. But as a matter of actual fact, Congress usually does neither when it legislates. This is not generally an oversight. Rather, there is a consensus in and out of Congress that in most cases it would not be wise to include or exclude state action in a particular area without having some actual experience to go on. It is considered preferable to see what the states will do and then let the courts resolve the problem on a case-by-case basis. If, in a particular area, national and state law result in conflict or prove impractical or if the dual laws result in inconclusive or conflicting interpretation by the courts, then it is time for Congress to decide whether or not it wants to grant or withhold power for the state to legislate in that area. The best recent example of this kind of process has been congressional action explicitly granting the states limited power to deal with labor relations in businesses in interstate commerce. This was done after Congress became dissatisfied with the manner in which the Supreme Court had in a case-by-case approach determined that Congress' power in the field as to most matters was exclusive. In an effort to be brief (we do not want to explore that story further here), we heartily recommend to students who are curious about the process that they explore the issue more fully on their own, for it is a fascinating story.

In light of the preceding, it is interesting to note that some congressmen were convinced that the Supreme Court had made a grave and dangerous mistake in *Nelson* in deciding that national legislation had superseded the state action under which Nelson was originally convicted. Instead of attempting to pass specific legislation granting the states power to legislate in this one area, thirty senators in the course of a few years joined Senator McClellan in introducing a bill which, as he described it, would do two things:

> First, acts of Congress would not repeal State laws or nullify them, or preempt a field of legislation unless Congress specifically so provided.
>
> Second, State laws would not be declared by the Supreme Court as being ineffective and incapable of enforcement, unless they were in irreconcilable conflict with the Federal law.[2]

Despite stout support, the bill never became law. Nor should this be surprising. Such a broad law would have created great confusion about all legislation in which Congress had been silent about the question of state power. In some of these areas Congress may not want to allow the states to act. If Congress wants to clear up all ambiguities about its intent, it would literally require canvassing all applicable legislation now on the books. The

[1] For an exception to the generalization that Congress can delegate power to the states see *Knickerbocker Ice Co.* v. *Stewart*, 253 U.S. 149 (1920).

[2] 105 *Congressional Record* 256 (1959).

magnitude of such a task would be enough to frighten even those who are most concerned over the problem. In addition, as indicated previously, there are many who feel that it is a matter best left to the courts. There is nothing to prevent Congress in future legislation from indicating what role it wishes the states to play. And finally, since Congress did not pass the legislation suggested by Senator McClellan, the *Nelson* decision remains the law of the land. This means that it will still be the prerogative of courts to resolve questions of preemption and supersession where Congress has been silent and that the courts will use as the criteria for making their decisions those laid down in the opinion of Chief Justice Warren.

Conflict between state and national law may arise even when the state legislature does not legislate precisely on the same subject matter and in the same manner as Congress. State legislatures have frequently passed laws which have a direct effect on interstate commerce. Yet interstate commerce is subject to the exclusive control of Congress, if Congress so desires. As Chief Justice Stone stated in *Southern Pacific Co.* v. *Arizona* (p. 25): "Congress has undoubted power to redefine the distribution of power over interstate commerce. It may either permit the states to regulate the commerce in a manner which would otherwise not be permissible . . . or exclude state regulation even of matters of peculiarly local concern which nevertheless affect interstate commerce." Consequently, it becomes a real problem where Congress has not indicated precisely how it wishes to handle specific aspects of interstate commerce. Historically, some of our Supreme Court justices have taken the view that, in lieu of congressional action precluding it, the states should be free to legislate "on matters of peculiarly local concern" even when the legislation affects interstate commerce rather markedly. Other justices have taken the opposite view that the states cannot, even when Congress has not acted, pass legislation which affects interstate commerce only remotely. But the Supreme Court as a whole has taken a middle view described by Chief Justice Stone in *Southern Pacific Co.* v. *Arizona.* The states should be permitted, he wrote, a "wide scope for the regulation of matters of local concern, even though it in some measure affects the commerce [*sic*], provided it does not materially restrict the free flow of commerce across the state lines, or interfere with it in matters with respect to which uniformity of regulation is of predominant national concern." Who is to determine the extent of local regulation? In Stone's words, the Supreme Court, "and not the state legislature, is under the commerce clause the final arbiter of the competing demands of state and national interests. . . ." It is not easy to determine whether or not state legislation which affects interstate commerce is permissible under the standard laid down by the Court. Based upon your reading of *Smith* v. *Alabama* (p. 18) and *Southern Pacific Co.* v. *Arizona* (p. 24) what is your decision with reference to this problem?

In the former case, the Supreme Court upheld a state law requiring the examination of railroad engineers who operate trains in the state, including those just passing through; in the latter case, the Supreme Court struck down a state law limiting the length of trains operating within the state. Are these decisions compatible with each other? The Court professed to see a difference in principle between the two cases in its opinion in *Southern Pacific Co.* v. *Arizona.* See if you can understand and accept the Court's distinction between the two cases. After that, see if you can reconcile the decision in *Southern Pacific* with *South Carolina State Highway Department* v. *Barnwell Bros. Inc.* (p. 33).

Another fascinating conflict problem arises out of situations where the states in exercise of their taxing power pass legislation which affects interstate commerce. In this area, too, final resolution is made by the courts. We have reproduced two cases, *Alaska* v. *Arctic Maid* (p. 40) and *Michigan-Wisconsin Pipe Line Co.* v. *Calvert* (p. 43), for the purpose of illustrating the difficulty in resolving the issue in specific cases. Notice that in one case the Court upholds the state tax and in the other it does not. Again, see if you can understand and accept the Court's distinction between the cases.

B. *Problems in the Relationship of States to Other States*

Two fundamental problems arise in any federal system composed of states, whatever the number, which have their own comprehensive body of law and their own judiciary. Briefly they are (1) What effect must state agencies (including courts) give to the judgments of courts of another state? (2) What effect must state courts give to the laws of other states in deciding a case where it is appropriate to consider the law of other states? Evidently, the framers of our national Constitution endeavored to meet these problems, although it is not clear from the records of the proceedings exactly what they had in mind. They wrote in the Constitution that "Full faith and credit shall be given in each state to the public acts, records, and judicial proceedings of every other state" and they empowered Congress to "prescribe the manner in which such acts, records, and proceedings shall be proved, and the effect thereof." The First Congress accordingly passed an act in 1790 which read in part that judicial proceedings which have been authenticated in a prescribed manner "shall have such faith and credit given to them in every court within the United States as they have in law or usage in the courts of the State from whence the said records are or shall be taken." Here, too, the intention of those who framed the proposal cannot be determined by reading the debates on it. Outwardly, it would appear that state courts were required to accept without question the judgments of other state courts. But early in the nineteenth century at a time when states' rights sentiment ran high, the Supreme Court decided in *M'Elmoyle* v. *Cohen,* 13 Peters 312 (1839), that in a case involving a judgment rendered first in another state, a court could in some special circumstances (at least the special circumstances of that case) apply the law of its own state rather than the law of the other state. To do so may, of course, mean giving a different effect to the judgment and to the extent that a court gives a different effect to the judgment of another state's court, it is obviously not granting full faith and credit in the strict sense of the words.

An intriguing mystery of the Act of 1790 is whether or not the word "acts" was deliberately or inadvertently omitted from the sentence requiring that court records and judicial proceedings be given full faith and credit. Did Congress feel that, since the constitutional clause already required it, there was no reason to require it again? But could not the same be said for judicial records and proceedings?

Patently, the vagary about the meaning of the full faith and credit clause and the Act of 1790 has given wide scope to the judiciary to develop their "real" meaning. Congress has been reluctant to provide direction for the courts even when the Supreme Court partially nullified the Act of 1790 in *M'Elmoyle.*

From 1790 until 1948, Congress did virtually nothing regarding full faith and credit. In 1948, Congress amended the 1790 law to require that acts of state legislatures receive full faith and credit in the courts of other states. It has been suggested that even here Congress was merely codifying court-made law on the subject and making no substantive changes. In sum, it is clear that the courts have played the leading role in attempting to resolve the two fundamental problems described. However, according to a former justice of the Supreme Court, the courts have not successfully resolved these questions. Justice Jackson wrote in 1945:

> To a foreign observer the United States may well appear to be "a nation concealed under the form of a federation." However true this may be as to political power and economic controls, it is far wide of the truth as to the administration of internal justice among our forty-eight state legal systems. Indeed, today in respect of our legal administrations we have not achieved a much "more perfect union" than that of the colonies under the Articles of Confederation. *We have so far as I can ascertain the most localized and conflicting system of any country which presents the external appearance of nationhood. But we are so accustomed to the delays, expense, and frustrations of our system that it seldom occurs to us to inquire whether these are wise, or constitutionally necessary.*[3] [Italics supplied—*Eds.*]

Nor has the situation changed much since Jackson wrote those words.

1. FULL FAITH AND CREDIT AS TO JUDGMENTS

In order to understand the immense complexity of the problems involved in determining how much full faith and credit state courts should give to the judgments of other state courts, we have reproduced the critically important decisions of two divorce cases: *Williams* v. *North Carolina* (p. 46) and *Armstrong* v. *Armstrong* (p. 57). This is not to imply that the problem only arises in divorce cases. But since divorce cases dramatically illustrate the problem and are substantively important because of the high incidence of divorce in our society, there is justification for their inclusion here. In reading them, bear in mind (1) that laws respecting divorce vary from state to state; (2) that in some states it is a very easy matter for a person to ac-

[3] Robert H. Jackson, "Full Faith and Credit—The Lawyer's Clause of the Constitution," 45 *Columbia Law Review* 1 (1945) p. 17. Reprinted with permission.

quire "residence" for the purposes of divorce and thus to come under the jurisdiction of that state's courts, even though he or she is in actual fact a resident of another state; (3) that when a court takes jurisdiction in the *initial* divorce proceeding, it will decide the case in accordance with the law of its own state.

In the *Williams* case, the Supreme Court upheld a conviction for bigamous cohabitation in North Carolina of a couple who had obtained divorces from their respective spouses in Nevada. This decision of the Court brought forth violent protest. To many, it seemed foolish to abide a system in which it is possible for individuals to obtain a divorce in a *bona fide* court in the United States, to have every reason to believe that they have been legally divorced, and then later to be imprisoned for bigamous cohabitation upon remarriage. It is not surprising, then, that the Supreme Court has modified its approach since *Williams*. Since that decision the Supreme Court has evolved the concept of the "divisible divorce." The essence of the divisible divorce concept is as follows: A court can consider the divorce itself, *i.e.* the rending of the marital status, as one matter, and support, property settlement, and child custody as a separate matter, if their disposition by the other state court is challenged. Consequently, a court will only rarely countenance a challenge to another state court's judgment as to the divorce itself. As to the whole host of issues which inhere in divorce cases, such as alimony and child custody, a state court which has reason to take jurisdiction will not grant full faith and credit to another state court's disposition of these matters. This, of course, in effect is a denial that the other state court had jurisdiction as to these matters.

The rationale of the Supreme Court for the divisible divorce was first provided in a case involving support, *Estin* v. *Estin*, 334 U.S. 541 (1948). In that case, the Court said that since the abandoned spouse was a resident of the second state that state "was rightly concerned lest the abandoned spouse be left impoverished and perhaps become a public charge. The problem of her livelihood and support is plainly a matter in which her community had a legitimate interest." The Supreme Court hailed its own wisdom in splitting divorce down the middle: "The result in this situation is to make divorce divisible—to give effect to the Nevada decree insofar as it affects marital status and to make it ineffective on the issue of alimony. It accommodates the interests of both Nevada and New York in this broken marriage by restricting each State to the matters of her dominant concern." The fact remains, however, that the husband obviously went to Nevada only to obtain the divorce. Under those circumstances what was Nevada's interest other than maintaining a profitable divorce mill? Of course, Nevada would have a real interest where the party seeking the divorce really came to Nevada to live.

As you read over the divorce cases, consider this question, Is this the best conceivable approach to the problem of how much faith and credit one state court should accord to the judgment of the court in another state? Bear in mind that one special feature of divorce as contrasted to other judgment problems may make the divisible idea seem more attractive than it actually is. Human nature being what it is, it is rare for a spouse to want to stay married to someone who no longer wants him or her. Hence the real contest is not over the marital status but rather over such issues as division of property, support, and child custody. Also, bear in mind that the Court seems to have resolved some of the practical difficulties regarding the validity of divorces, but in so doing it has cleared the way for the growth of the "quickie" divorce business. For one can now be reasonably certain that such a divorce obtained in a divorce-mill state will enable a man or woman to rid himself or herself of an unwanted spouse, even though the questions of alimony, child support, and the like may not be resolved. This means that people still flock to the divorce-mill states for the purpose of escaping the "tough" divorce laws of their own state. Should that be permissible in a nation like ours?

In the last analysis, you may feel that the Supreme Court has done about as well with the problem as could be done. Nonetheless, you might find it exceedingly interesting to explore with your professor other possible ways for dealing with the other-state judgment problem generally and the divorce problem specifically.

2. FULL FAITH AND CREDIT AS TO LAWS

The choice-of-law problem is well-illustrated by the facts in the interesting case, *Alaska Packers Ass'n* v. *Industrial Accident Commission*, 294 U.S. 532 (1935). An employee had entered into a contract for employment in California and then went off to fulfill that contract by working in Alaska. The contract contained a provision stipulating that the employer and employee would be bound by the provisions of the Alaska Workmen's Compensation Law. Later, the employee came back to California where he applied to the appropriate agency for compensation for injuries received in Alaska. The stipulation in the contract binding employer and employee to use Alaska law was meaningless under California law because California's Workmen's Compensation Act provided that (1) the California Commission "shall have jurisdiction over all controversies arising out of injuries suffered without the territorial limits of this state in those cases where the injured employee is a resident of this State at the time of injury and the contract of hire was made in this State, . . ." and (2) "no contract, rule or regulation shall exempt the employer from liability for the compensation fixed by this Act." But, despite California law, the injury did in fact occur in Alaska and a good argument could be made, and in fact was made by the employer, that the law of Alaska should be accorded full faith and credit in the California courts and applied in this case. In short, there was in this case, as in many others, legitimate grounds for the court to apply either one of the conflicting laws of two jurisdictions. Under the circumstances of this case, which law should the California courts have regarded as controlling? Eventually, the Supreme Court of the United States had to supply the answer. The Court said that ". . . the conflict is to be resolved, not by giving automatic effect to the full faith and credit clause, compelling the courts of each state to subordinate the statutes to those of the other, but by appraising the governmental interests of each jurisdiction, and turning the scale of decisions according to their weight." Applying this principle, the Court concluded that because the employee was a California resident, California's interest was greater "than that of Alaska, of which the employee was never a resident and to which he may never return."

It is important here to observe that Congress on the basis of the power granted in the full faith and credit clause probably could constitutionally define in legislation how the courts should resolve the choice-of-law problem. For example, as to the situation involved in the *Alaska Packers* case, Congress could pass a law requiring that the law of the state where the contract was made would apply or, conversely, that the law of the state where the accident occurred would be given full faith and credit. But Congress has chosen to let the courts develop the law in this area on a case-by-case basis.

It is also important to note that the choice-of-law problem becomes more important as Americans become more mobile. As far as business and travel go, we as a people are little inhibited by state lines. It is commonplace for contracts to be made in one state and to be executed in another state. Our national penchant to travel about the country gives rise to choice-of-law problems. One such complex problem arose when a widow, whose husband had been killed in an airplane crash in Massachusetts, was granted a $160,000 award by a jury in a New York court. Although the crash occurred in Massachusetts, the husband had bought the ticket in New York and the plane had taken off from LaGuardia Airport in New York. Since a Massachusetts statute limited recovery in such cases to $15,000 at that time and New York's law did not, the airline appealed the decision on the grounds that Massachusetts law should have been controlling in this case. Obviously, to the widow and to the airline it was more than an academic question as to which state's law should be applied. A United States court of appeals upheld the $160,000 award. It cited with approval the reasoning of a lower court in a parallel case: "An air traveler from New York may in a flight of a few hours' duration pass through several commonwealths. His plane may meet with disaster in a state he never intended to cross but into which the plane has flown because of bad weather or other unexpected developments, or an airplane's catastrophic descent may begin in one state and end in another. The place of injury becomes entirely fortuitous." *Pearson* v. *Northeast Airlines*, 309 F. 2d 553, 561 f.n. 15 (1962). Interestingly enough, the United States Supreme Court refused to review that decision.

Another such complex problem is highlighted in *Hughes* v. *Fetter* (p. 61) which you will read shortly. As you read the case, try to determine for yourself which of the opinions, the majority or the dissenting, constitutes a better solution to the problem.

C. Problems in the Relationship of the Cities to the State

One of the most widely held mistaken conceptions about our system of government is that our cities have the same legal position to the states as the states have to the national government. In reality, nothing could be further from the truth of the matter. *Trenton* v. *New Jersey* (p. 65) reaffirms the doctrine long held by the Supreme Court that cities are legally the creatures of the state and subject to the absolute control of the state. This formulation does not mean, however, that the state legislature can do anything it pleases with regard to the cities in the state. The state constitution may restrict the state legislature's power over the cities but where it does not, the legislature can do as it wishes. As the Supreme Court wrote in 1907 in *Hunter* v. *Pittsburgh*, 207 U.S. 161, ". . . the State is supreme, and its legislative body, conforming its action to the state constitution, may do as it will [with respect to cities], unrestrained by any provision of the Constitution of the United States. . . ."

In recent years, there has been an increasing tendency for the cities to feel that they can obtain a more sympathetic response to their problems from the national government than they can from their state governments. The reasons are threefold. First, in the states containing the largest cities, the legislature tends to be controlled by the Republican Party. However, cities tend to be strongholds of the Democratic Party. Therefore, when the majority in Congress and the Presidency are held by Democrats, there is a political affinity between city and national government. Second, and dependent upon the preceding, the cities have in the past been under-represented in the state legislatures, and it is probably true that in most state legislatures the cities have not been accorded fair and sympathetic treatment. Third, only the national government under the present tax structure has the resources to provide the vast sums needed to help the cities solve their housing, slum clearance, transportation, and other problems. As a consequence, a working relationship has arisen between cities and the national government which threatens to preclude the states. This problem is well-illustrated in *City of Tacoma* v. *Taxpayers of Tacoma* (p. 68) involving an arrangement between a city and the national government which did not meet with the approval of the state government. The interesting question raised by the decision in this case is, Does it modify the old doctrine that cities are creatures of the state?

PENNSYLVANIA v. NELSON

UNITED STATES SUPREME COURT

350 U.S. 497 (1956)

Nelson, an acknowledged member of the Communist Party, was convicted in a Pennsylvania court for violating the Pennsylvania Sedition Act and sentenced to twenty years in prison and a fine. He appealed the conviction to the supreme court of Pennsylvania alleging that trial errors and conduct of the trial court had been such as to deny him due process of law. The Pennsylvania supreme court decided the case on the narrow grounds that the Smith Act passed by Congress had superseded the state law. This meant, of course, that Nelson's conviction for violation of a law which had been superseded could not stand. In the name of the Commonwealth of Pennsylvania, the state attorney general brought the case to the United States Supreme Court seeking to reverse the decision of the Pennsylvania supreme court. Significantly, many state attorneys general and the solicitor general of the United States appeared as amici curiae *(friends of the court) for the petitioner.*

Mr. Chief Justice WARREN delivered the opinion of the Court.

. . . .

. . . BECAUSE OF the important question of federal-state relationship involved, we granted certiorari. . . .

It should be said at the outset that the decision in this case does not affect the right of States to enforce their sedition laws at times when the Federal Government has not occupied the field and is not protecting the entire country from seditious conduct. The distinction between the two situations was clearly recognized by the court below. Nor does it limit the jurisdiction of the States where the Constitution and Congress have specifically given them concurrent jurisdiction, as was done under the Eighteenth Amendment and the Volstead Act. . . . Neither does it limit the right of the State to protect itself at any time against sabotage or attempted violence of all kinds. Nor does it prevent the State from prosecuting where the same act constitutes both a federal offense and a state offense under the police power, as was done in Fox v. State of Ohio, 5 How. 410, and Gilbert v. State of Minnesota, 254 U.S. 325, relied upon by petitioner as authority herein. In neither of those cases did the state statute impinge on federal jurisdiction. In the Fox case, the federal offense was counterfeiting. The state offense was defrauding the person to whom the spurious money was passed. In the Gilbert case this Court, in upholding the enforcement of a state statute, proscribing conduct which would " 'interfere with or discourage the enlistment of men in the military or naval forces of the United States or of the state of Minnesota,' " treated it not as an act relating to "the raising of armies for the national defense, nor to rules and regulations for the government of those under arms [a constitutionally exclusive federal power]. It [was] simply a local police measure * * *."

Where, as in the instant case, Congress has not stated specifically whether a federal statute has occupied a field in which the States are otherwise free to legislate, different criteria have furnished touchstones for decision. Thus,

> "[t]his Court, in considering the validity of state laws in the light of * * * federal laws touching the same subject, has made use of the following expressions: conflicting; contrary to; occupying the field; repugnance; difference; irreconcilability; inconsistency; violation; curtailment; and interference. But none of these expressions provides an infallible constitutional test or an exclusive constitutional yardstick. In the final analysis, there can be no one crystal clear distinctly marked formula." Hines v. Davidowitz, 312 U.S. 52, 67.

And see Rice v. Santa Fe Elevator Corp., 331 U.S. 218, 230–231. In this case, we think that each of several tests of supersession is met.

First, "[t]he scheme of federal regulation [is] so pervasive as to make reasonable the inference that Congress left no room for the States to supplement it." Rice v. Santa Fe Elevator Corp., 331 U.S. at page 230. The Congress determined in 1940 that it was necessary for it to re-enter the field of antisubversive legislation, which had been abandoned by it in 1921. In that year, it enacted the Smith Act which proscribes advocacy of the overthrow of any government—federal, state or local—by force and violence and organization of and knowing membership in a group which so advocates. Conspiracy to commit any of these acts is punishable under the general criminal conspiracy provisions in 18 U.S.C. § 371, 18 U.S.C.A. § 371. The Internal Security Act of 1950 is aimed more directly at Communist organizations. It distinguishes between "Communist-action organizations" and "Communist-front organizations," requiring such organizations to register and to file annual reports with the Attorney General giving complete details as to their officers and funds. Members of Communist-action organizations who have not been registered by their organization must register as individuals. Failure to register in accordance with the requirements of Sections 786–787 is punishable by a fine of not more than $10,000 for an offending organization and by a fine of not more than $10,000 or imprisonment for not more than five years or both for an individual offender—each day of failure to register constituting a separate offense. And the Act imposes certain sanctions upon both "action" and "front" organizations and their members. The Communist Control Act of 1954 declares "that the Communist Party of the United States, although purportedly a political party, is in fact an instrumentality of a conspiracy to overthrow the Government of the United States" and that "its role as the agency of a hostile foreign power renders its existence a clear present and continuing danger to the security of the United States." It also contains a legislative finding that the Communist Party is a "'Communist-action' organization" within the meaning of the Internal Security Act of 1950 and provides that "knowing" members of the Communist Party are "subject to all the provisions and penalties" of that Act. It furthermore sets up a new classification of "Communist-infiltrated organizations" and provides for the imposition of sanctions against them.

We examine these Acts only to determine the congressional plan. Looking to all of them in the aggregate, the conclusion is inescapable that Congress has intended to occupy the field of sedition. Taken as a whole, they evince a congressional plan which makes it reasonable to determine that no room has been left for the States to supplement it. Therefore, a state sedition statute is superseded regardless of whether it purports to supplement the federal law. As was said by Mr. Justice Holmes in

Charleston & Western Carolina R. Co. v. Varnville Furniture Co., 237 U.S. 597, 604:

> "When Congress has taken the particular subject-matter in hand, coincidence is as ineffective as opposition, and a state law is not to be declared a help because it attempts to go farther than Congress has seen fit to go."

Second, the federal statutes "touch a field in which the federal interest is so dominant that the federal system [must] be assumed to preclude enforcement of state laws on the same subject." Rice v. Santa Fe Elevator Corp., 331 U.S. at page 230, citing Hines v. Davidowitz, supra. Congress has devised an all-embracing program for resistance to the various forms of totalitarian aggression. Our external defenses have been strengthened, and a plan to protect against internal subversion has been made by it. It has appropriated vast sums, not only for our own protection, but also to strengthen freedom throughout the world. It has charged the Federal Bureau of Investigation and the Central Intelligence Agency with responsibility for intelligence concerning Communist seditious activities against our Government, and has denominated such activities as part of a world conspiracy. It accordingly proscribed sedition against all government in the nation—national, state and local. Congress declared that these steps were taken "to provide for the common defense, to preserve the sovereignty of the United States as an independent nation, and to guarantee to each State a republican form of government * * *." Congress having thus treated seditious conduct as a matter of vital national concern, it is in no sense a local enforcement problem. As was said in the court below:

> "Sedition against the United States is not a *local* offense. It is a crime against the *Nation*. As such, it should be prosecuted and punished in the Federal courts where this defendant has in fact been prosecuted and convicted and is now under sentence. It is not only important but vital that such prosecutions should be exclusively within the control of the Federal Government * * *."

Third, enforcement of state sedition acts presents a serious danger of conflict with the administration of the federal program. Since 1939, in order to avoid a hampering of uniform enforcement of its program by sporadic local prosecutions, the Federal Government has urged local authorities not to intervene in such matters, but to turn over to the federal authorities immediately and unevaluated all information concerning subversive activities. The President made such a request on September 6, 1939, when he placed the Federal Bureau of Investigation in charge of investigation in this field:

> "The Attorney General has been requested by me to instruct the Federal Bureau of Investigation of the Department of Justice to take charge of investigative work in matters relating to espionage, sabotage, and violations of the neutrality regulations.
>
> "This task must be conducted in a comprehensive and effective manner on a national basis, and all information must be carefully sifted out and correlated in order to avoid confusion and irresponsibility.
>
> "To this end I request all police officers, sheriffs, and all other law enforcement officers in the United States promptly to turn over to the nearest representative of the Federal Bureau of Investigation any information obtained by them relating to espionage, counterespionage, sabotage, subversive activities and violations of the neutrality laws."

And in addressing the Federal-State Conference on Law Enforcement Problems of National Defense, held on August 5 and 6, 1940, only a few weeks after the passage of the Smith Act, the Director of the Federal Bureau of Investigation said:

> "The fact must not be overlooked that meeting the spy, the saboteur and the subverter is a problem that must be handled on a nation-wide basis. An isolated incident in the middle west may be of little significance, but when fitted into a national pattern of similar incidents, it may lead to an important revelation of subversive activity. It is for this reason that the President requested all of our citizens and law enforcing agencies to report directly to the Federal Bureau of Investigation any complaints or information dealing with espionage, sabotage or subversive activities. In such matters, time is of the essence. It is unfortunate that in a few States efforts have been made by individuals not fully acquainted with the far-flung ramifications of this problem to interject superstructures of agencies between local law enforcement and the FBI to sift what might be vital information, thus delaying its immediate reference to the FBI. This cannot be, if our internal security is to be best served. This is no time for red tape or amateur handling of such vital matters. There must be a direct and free flow of contact between the local law enforcement agencies and the FBI. The job of meeting the spy or saboteur is one for experienced men of law enforcement."

Moreover, the Pennsylvania Statute presents a peculiar danger of interference with the federal program. For, as the court below observed:

> "Unlike the Smith Act, which can be administered only by federal officers acting in their official capacities, indictment for sedition under the Pennsylvania statute can be initiated upon an information made by a private individual. The opportunity thus present for the indulgence of personal spite and hatred or for furthering some selfish advantage or ambition need only be mentioned to be appreciated. Defense of the Nation by law, no less than by arms, should be a public and not a private undertaking. It is important that punitive sanctions for sedition *against the United States* be such as have been promulgated by the central governmental authority and administered under the supervision and review of that authority's judiciary. If that be done, sedition will be detected and punished, no less, wherever it may be found, and the right of the individual to speak freely and without fear, even in criticism of the government, will at the same time be protected."

In his brief, the Solicitor General states that forty-two States plus Alaska and Hawaii have statutes which in some form prohibit advocacy of the violent overthrow of established government. These statutes are entitled anti-sedition statutes, criminal anarchy laws, criminal syndicalist laws, etc. Although all of them are primarily directed against the overthrow of the United States Government, they are in no sense uniform. And our attention has not been called to any case where the prosecution has been successfully directed against an attempt to destroy state or local government. Some of these Acts are studiously drawn and purport to protect fundamental rights by appropriate definitions, standards of proof and orderly procedures in keeping with the avowed congressional purpose "to protect freedom from those who would destroy it, without infringing upon the freedom of all our people." Others are vague and are almost wholly without such safeguards. Some even purport to punish mere membership in subversive organizations which the federal statutes do not punish where federal registration requirements have been fulfilled.

When we were confronted with a like situation in the field of labor-management relations, Mr. Justice Jackson wrote:

> "A multiplicity of tribunals and a diversity of procedures are quite as apt to produce incompatible or conflicting adjudications as are different rules of substantive law."

Should the States be permitted to exercise a concurrent jurisdiction in this area, federal enforcement would encounter not only the difficulties mentioned by Mr. Justice Jackson, but the added conflict engendered by different criteria of substantive offenses.

Since we find that Congress has occupied the field to the exclusion of parallel state legislation, that the dominant interest of the Federal Government precludes state intervention, and that administration of state Acts would conflict with the operation of the federal plan, we are convinced that the decision of the Supreme Court of Pennsylvania is unassailable.

We are not unmindful of the risk of compounding punishments which would be created by finding concurrent state power. In our view of the case, we do not reach the question whether double or multiple punishment for the same overt acts directed against the United States has constitutional sanction. Without compelling indication to the contrary, we will not assume that Congress intended to permit the possibility of double punishment. . . .

The judgment of the Supreme Court of Pennsylvania is affirmed.

Mr. Justice REED, with whom Mr. Justice BURTON and Mr. Justice MINTON join, dissenting.

The problems of governmental power may be approached in this case free from the varied viewpoints that focus on the problems of national security. This is a jurisdictional problem of general importance because it involves an asserted limitation on the police power of the States when it is applied to a crime that is punishable also by the Federal Government. As this is a recurring problem, it is appropriate to explain our dissent.

Congress has not, in any of its statutes relating to sedition, specifically barred the exercise of state power to punish the same Acts under state law. And, we read the majority opinion to assume for this case that, absent federal legislation, there is no constitutional bar to punishment of sedition against the United States by both a State and the Nation. The majority limits to the federal courts the power to try charges of sedition against the Federal Government.

First, the Court relies upon the pervasiveness of the antisubversive legislation embodied in the Smith Act of 1940, . . . the Internal Security Act of 1950, . . . and the Communist Control Act of 1954. . . . It asserts that these Acts in the aggregate mean that Congress has occupied the "field of sedition" to the exclusion of the States. The "occupation of the field" argument has been developed by this Court for the Commerce Clause and legislation thereunder to prevent partitioning of this country by locally erected trade barriers. In those cases this Court has ruled that state legislation is superseded when it conflicts with the comprehensive regulatory scheme and purpose of a federal plan. Cloverleaf Butter Co. v. Patterson, 315 U.S. 148. The two cases cited by the Court to support its argument that the broad treatment of any subject within the federal power bars supplemental action by States are of this nature. In our view neither case is apposite to the Smith Act. The Varnville case dealt with general regulation of interstate commerce making the originating carrier liable to the holder of its interstate bill of lading for damage caused by a common carrier of property. This Court held that the section through the federal commerce power superseded a state right of action against a nonoriginating carrier for damages and a penalty for injury occurring on another line. The pertinent section, 34 Stat. 595, § 7, expressed a controlling federal policy for this commerce. The Rice case dealt with regulations of warehouses. We barred state action in that area because the Act declared that the authority it conferred "shall be exclusive with respect to all persons securing a license" under the Act. . . .

But the federal sedition laws are distinct criminal statutes that punish willful advocacy of the use of force against "the government of the United States or the government of any State." These criminal laws proscribe certain local activity without creating any statutory or administrative regulation. There is, consequently, no question as to whether some general congressional regulatory scheme might be upset by a coinciding state plan. In these circumstances the conflict should be clear and direct before this Court reads a congressional intent to void state legislation into the federal sedition acts. Chief Justice Marshall wrote:

> "To interfere with the penal laws of a State, where they * * * have for their sole object the internal government of the country, is a very serious measure, which Congress cannot be supposed to adopt lightly, or inconsiderately. * * * It would be taken deliberately, and the intention would be clearly and unequivocally expressed." Cohens v. Commonwealth of Virginia, 6 Wheat. 264.

Moreover, it is quite apparent that since 1940 Congress has been keenly aware of the magnitude of existing state legislation proscribing sedition. It may be validly assumed that in these circumstances this Court should not void state legislation without a clear mandate from Congress.

We cannot agree that the federal criminal sanctions against sedition directed at the United States are of such a pervasive character as to indicate an intention to void state action.

Secondly, the Court states that the federal sedition statutes touch a field "in which the federal interest is so dominant" they must preclude state laws on the same subject. This concept is suggested in a comment on Hines v. Davidowitz. . . . The Court in Davidowitz ruled that federal statutes compelling alien registration preclude enforcement of state statutes requiring alien registration. We read Davidowitz to teach nothing more than that when the Congress provided a single nation-wide integrated system of regulation so complete as that for aliens' registration (with fingerprinting, a scheduling of activities, and continuous information as to their residence), the Act bore so directly on our foreign relations as to make it evident that Congress intended only one uniform national alien registration system.

We look upon the Smith Act as a provision for controlling incitements to overthrow by force and violence the Nation, or any State, or any political subdivision of either. Such an exercise of federal police power carries, we think, no such dominancy over similar state powers as might be attributed to continuing federal regulations concerning foreign affairs or coinage, for example. In the responsibility of national and local governments to protect themselves against sedition, there is no "dominant interest."

We are citizens of the United States and of the State wherein we reside and are dependent upon the strength of both to preserve our rights and liberties. Both may enact criminal statutes for mutual protection unless Congress has otherwise provided. . . . In Gilbert [Gilbert v. State of Minnesota] the federal interest in raising armies did not keep this Court from permitting Minnesota to punish persons who interfered with enlistments . . . even though a comprehensive federal criminal law proscribed identical activity. . . . We do not understand that case as does the majority. In our view this Court treated the Minnesota statute only alternatively as a police measure. . . . Minnesota made it unlawful to advocate "that men should not enlist in the military or naval forces of the United States." It was contended, . . . that the power to punish such advocacy was " 'conferred upon Congress and withheld from the States.' " This Court ruled against the contention, saying:

> "An army, of course, can only be raised and directed by Congress; in neither has the state power, but it has power to regulate the conduct of its citizens and to restrain the exertion of baleful influences against the promptings of patriotic duty to the detriment of the welfare of the nation and state. To do so is not to usurp a national power; it is only to render a service to its people, * *." . . .

Thirdly, the Court finds ground for abrogating Pennsylvania's antisedition statute because, in the Court's view, the State's administration of the Act may hamper the enforcement of the federal law. Quotations are inserted from statements of President Roosevelt and Mr. Hoover, the Director of the Federal Bureau of Investigation, to support the Court's position. But a reading of the quotations leads us to conclude that their purpose was to gain prompt knowledge of evidence of subversive activities so that the federal agency could be fully advised. We find no suggestion from any official source that state officials should be less alert to ferret out or punish subversion. The Court's attitude as to interference seems to us quite contrary to that of the Legislative and Executive Departments. Congress was advised of the existing state sedition legislation when the Smith Act was enacted and has been kept current with its spread. No declaration of exclusiveness followed. In this very case the Executive appears by brief of the Department of Justice, *amicus curiae*. The brief summarizes this point:

> "The administration of the various state laws has not, in the course of the fifteen years that the federal and state sedition laws have existed side by side, in fact interfered with, embarrassed, or impeded the enforcement of the Smith Act. The significance of this absence of conflict in administration or enforcement of the federal and state sedition laws will be appreciated when it is realized that this period has included the stress of wartime security requirements and the federal investigation and prosecution under the Smith Act of the principal national and regional Communist leaders." . . .

Mere fear by courts of possible difficulties does not seem to us in these circumstances a valid reason for ousting a State from exercise of its police power. Those are matters for legislative determination.

Finally, and this one point seems in and of itself decisive, there is an independent reason for reversing the Pennsylvania Supreme Court. The Smith Act appears in Title 18 of the United States Code, 18 U.S.C.A., which Title codifies the federal criminal laws. Section 3231 of that Title provides:

> "Nothing in this title shall be held to take away or impair the jurisdiction of the courts of the several States under the laws thereof."

That declaration springs from the federal character of our Nation. It recognizes the fact that maintenance of order and fairness rests primarily with the States. The section was first enacted in 1825 and has appeared successively in the federal criminal laws since that time. This Court has interpreted the section to mean that States may provide concurrent legislation in the absence of explicit congressional intent to the contrary. . . . The majority's position in this case cannot be reconciled with that clear authorization of Congress.

The law stands against any advocacy of violence to change established governments. Freedom of speech allows full play to the processes of reason. The state and national legislative bodies have legislated within constitutional limits so as to allow the widest participation by the law enforcement officers of the respective governments. The individual States were not told that they are powerless to punish local acts of sedition, nominally directed against the United States. Courts should not interfere. We would reverse the judgment of the Supreme Court of Pennsylvania.

SMITH v. *ALABAMA*

UNITED STATES SUPREME COURT
124 U.S. 465 (1888)

The State of Alabama enacted a statute in 1887 requiring the examination and licensing of persons who are "to operate or engineer any train or engine upon the main line or roadbed of any railroad in this state. . . ." The petitioner, Smith, was a locomotive engineer who operated a train between points in Alabama, Missouri, and Mississippi carrying United States mail, passengers, and freight. He was arrested for failing to comply with the statute. He sought to be released from the custody of the county sheriff upon a writ of habeas corpus *on the grounds that the state law was unconstitutional because it contravened that clause of the United States Constitution which conferred upon Congress the power to regulate interstate commerce. Smith lost the case first in the city court of Mobile and later on appeal to the Alabama supreme court. At that point he brought the case to the Supreme Court of the United States.*

Mr. Justice MATTHEWS delivered the opinion of the Court.

. . . .

THE GRANT of power to congress in the constitution to regulate commerce with foreign nations and among the several states, it is conceded, is paramount over all legislative powers which, in consequence of not having been granted to congress, are reserved to the states. It follows that any legislation of a state, although in pursuance of an acknowledged power reserved to it, which conflicts with the actual exercise of the power of congress over the subject of commerce, must give way before the supremacy of the national authority. As the regulation of commerce may consist in abstaining from prescribing positive rules for its conduct, it cannot always be said that the power to regulate is dormant because not affirmatively exercised. And when it is manifest that congress intends to leave that commerce which is subject to its jurisdiction, free and unfettered by any positive regulations, such intention would be contravened by state laws operating as regulations of commerce as much as though these had been expressly forbidden. In such cases, the existence of the power to regulate commerce in congress has been construed to be not only paramount but exclusive, so as to withdraw the subject as the basis of legislation altogether from the states. There are many cases, however, where the acknowledged powers of a state may be exerted and applied in such a manner as to affect foreign or interstate commerce without being intended to operate as commercial regulations. If their operation and application in such cases regulate such commerce, so as to conflict with the regulation of the same subject by congress, either as expressed in positive laws or implied from the absence of legislation, such legislation on the part of the state, to the extent of that conflict, must be regarded as annulled. To draw the line of interference between the two fields of jurisdiction, and to define and declare the instances of unconstitutional encroachment, is a judicial question often of much difficulty, the solution of which, perhaps, is not to be found in any single and exact rule of decision. Some general lines of discrimination, however, have been drawn in varied and numerous decisions of this court. It has been uniformly held, for example, that the states cannot by legislation place burdens upon commerce with foreign nations or among the several states. . . .

[*As the Court said in* Sherlock *v.* Alling, 93 *U.S.* 99]:

"General legislation of this kind, prescribing the liabilities or duties of citizens of a state, without distinction as to pursuit or calling, is not open to any valid objection because it may affect persons engaged in foreign or interstate commerce. Objection might, with equal propriety, be urged against legislation prescribing the form in which contracts shall be authenticated, or property descend or be distributed on the death of its owner, because applicable to the contracts or estates of persons engaged in such commerce. In conferring upon congress the regulation of commerce, it was never intended to cut the states off from legislating upon all subjects relating to the health, life, and safety of their citizens, though the legislation might indirectly affect the commerce of the country. Legislation, in a great variety of ways, may affect commerce and persons engaged in it, without constituting a regulation of it within the meaning of the constitution. * * * And it may be said, generally, that the legislation of a state, not directed against commerce or any of its regulations, but relating to the rights, duties, and liabilities of citizens, and only indirectly and remotely affecting the operations of commerce, is of obligatory force upon citizens within its territorial jurisdiction, whether on land or water, or engaged in commerce, foreign or interstate, or in any other pursuit." In that case it was admitted, in the opinion of the court, that congress might legislate, under the power to regulate commerce, touching the liability of parties for marine torts resulting in the death of the persons injured, but that, in the absence of such legislation by congress, the statute of the state, giving such right of action, constituted no encroachment upon the commercial power of congress, although, as was also said, . . . "It is true that the commercial power conferred by the constitution is one without limitation. It authorizes legislation with respect to all the subjects of foreign and interstate commerce, the persons engaged in it, and the instruments by which it is carried on."

The statute of Indiana, held to be valid in that case, was an addition to and an amendment of the general body of the law previously existing and in force regulating the relative rights and duties of persons within the jurisdiction of the state, and operating upon them, even when engaged in the business of interstate commerce. This general system of law, subject to be modified by state legislation, whether consisting in that customary law which prevails as the common law of the land in each state, or as a code of positive provisions expressly enacted, is nevertheless the law of the state in which it is administered, and derives all its force and effect from the actual or presumed exercise of its legislative power. It does not emanate from the authority of the national government, nor flow from the exercise of any legislative powers conferred upon congress by the constitution of the United States, nor can it be implied as existing by force of any other legislative authority than that of the several states in which it is enforced. It has never been doubted but that this entire body and system of law, regulating in general the relative rights and duties of persons within the territorial jurisdiction of the state, without regard to their pursuits, is subject to change at the will of the legislature of each state, except as that will may be restrained by the constitution of the United States. It is to this law that persons within the scope of its operation look for the definition of their rights and for the redress of wrongs committed upon them. It is the source of all those relative obligations and duties enforceable by law, the observance of which the state undertakes to enforce as its public policy. And it was in contemplation of the continued existence of this separate system of law in each state that the constitution of the United States was framed and ordained with such legislative powers as are therein granted expressly or by reasonable implication.

It is among these laws of the states, therefore, that we find provisions concerning the rights and duties of common carriers of persons and merchandise, whether by land or by water, and the means authorized by which injuries resulting from the failure properly to perform their obligations may be either prevented or redressed. . . . If it is competent for the state thus to administer justice according to its own laws for wrongs done and injuries suffered, when committed and inflicted by defendants while engaged in the business of interstate or foreign commerce, notwithstanding the power over those subjects conferred upon congress by the constitution, what is there to forbid the state, in the further exercise of the same jurisdiction, to prescribe the precautions and safeguards foreseen to be necessary and proper to prevent by anticipation those wrongs and injuries which, after they have been inflicted, it is admitted the state has power to redress and punish? If the state has power to secure to passengers conveyed by common carriers in their vehicles of transportation a right of action for the recovery of damages occasioned by the negligence of the carrier in not providing safe and suitable vehicles, or employes [*sic*] of sufficient skill and knowledge, or in not properly conducting and managing the act of transportation, why may not the state also impose, on behalf of the public, as additional means of prevention, penalties for the non-observance of these precautions? Why may it not define and declare what particular things shall be done and observed by such a carrier in order to insure the safety of the persons and things he carries, or of the persons and property of others liable to be affected by them? It is that law which defines who are or may be common carriers, and prescribes the means they shall adopt for the safety of that which is committed to their charge, and the rules according to which, under varying conditions, their conduct shall be measured and judged, which declares that the common carrier owes the duty of care, and what shall constitute that negligence for which he shall be responsible. But for the provisions on the subject found in the local law of each state, there would be no legal obligation on the part of the carrier, whether *ex contractu* or *ex delicto*, to those who employ him; or if the local law is held not to apply where the carrier is engaged in foreign or interstate commerce, then, in the absence of laws passed by congress or presumed to be adopted by it, there can be no rule of decision based upon rights and duties supposed to grow out of the relation of such carriers to the public or to individuals. In other words, if the law of the particular state does not govern that relation, and prescribe the rights and duties which it implies, then there is and can be no law that does, until congress expressly supplies it, or is held by implication to have supplied it, in cases within its jurisdiction over foreign and interstate commerce. The failure of congress to legislate can be construed only as an intention not to disturb what already exists, and is the mode by which it adopts, for cases within the scope of its power, the rule of the state law, which, until displaced, covers the subject.

There is no common law of the United States, in the sense of a national customary law, distinct from the common law of England, as adopted by the several states each for itself, applied as its local law, and subject to such alteration as may be provided by its own statutes. . . . A determination in a given case of what that law is may be different in a court of the United States from that which prevails in the judicial tribunals of a particular state. This arises from the circumstance that the courts of the United States, in cases within their jurisdiction, where they are called upon to administer the law of the state in which they sit or by which the transaction is governed, exercise an independent though concurrent jurisdiction, and are required to ascertain and declare the law according to their own judgment. . . .

There is, however, one clear exception to the statement that there is no national common law. The interpretation of the constitution of the United States is necessarily influenced by the fact that its provisions are framed in the language of the English common law, and are to be read in the light of its history. The code of constitutional and statutory construction which, therefore, is gradually formed by the judgments of this court, in the application of the constitution and the laws and treaties made in pursuance thereof, has for its basis so much of the common law as may be implied in the subject, and constitutes a common law resting on national authority. . . . The statute of Alabama, the validity of which is drawn in question in this case, does not fall within this exception. It would, indeed, be competent for congress to legislate upon its subject-matter, and to prescribe the qualifications of locomotive engineers for employment by carriers engaged in foreign or interstate commerce. It has legislated upon a similar subject by prescribing the qualifications for pilots and engineers of steam-vessels engaged in the coasting trade and navigating the inland waters of the United States while engaged in commerce among the states, . . . and such legislation undoubtedly is justified on the ground that it is incident to the power to regulate interstate commerce. In *Sinnot* v. *Davenport*, 22 How. 227, this court adjudged a law of the state of Alabama to be unconstitutional, so far as it applied to vessels engaged in interstate commerce, which prohibited any steam-boat from navigating any of the waters of the state without complying with certain prescribed conditions, inconsistent with the act of congress of February 17, 1793, in reference to the enrollment and licensing of vessels engaged in the coasting trade. In that case it was said, . . . "The whole commercial marine of the country is placed by the constitution under the regulation of congress, and all laws passed by that body in the regulation of navigation and trade, whether foreign or coastwise, is therefore but the exercise of an undisputed power. When, therefore, an act of the legislature of a state prescribes a regulation of the subject repugnant to and inconsistent with the regulation of congress, the state law must give way, and this without regard to the source of power whence the state legislature derived its enactment." The power might with equal authority be exercised in prescribing the qualifications for locomotive engineers employed by railroad companies engaged in the transportation of passengers and goods among the states, and in that case would supersede any conflicting provisions on the same subject made by local authority.

But the provisions on the subject contained in the statute of Alabama under consideration are not regulations of interstate commerce. It is a misnomer to call them such. Considered in themselves, they are parts of that body of the local law which, as we have already seen, properly governs the relation between carriers of passengers and merchandise, and the public who employ them, which are not displaced until they come in conflict with express enactments of congress in the exercise of its power over commerce, and which, until so displaced, according to the evident intention of congress, remain as the law governing carriers, in the discharge of their obligations, whether engaged in the purely internal commerce of the state or in commerce among the states. No objection to the statute, as an impediment to the free transaction of commerce among the states, can be found in any of its special provisions. It requires that every locomotive engineer shall have a license, but it does not limit the number of persons who may be licensed, nor prescribe any arbitrary conditions to the grant. . . . The applicant is required, before obtaining his license, to satisfy a board of examiners in reference to his knowledge of practical mechanics, his skill in operating a locomotive engine, and his general competency as an engineer, and the board, before issuing the license, is required to inquire into his character and habits, and to withhold the license if he be found to be reckless or intemperate. Certainly it is the duty of every carrier, whether engaged in the domestic commerce of the state or in interstate commerce, to provide and furnish itself with locomotive engineers of this precise description; competent and well qualified, skilled and sober; and if, by reason of carelessness in the selection of an engineer not so qualified, injury or loss are caused, the carrier, no matter in what business engaged, is responsible according to the local law admitted to govern in such cases, in the absence of congressional legislation.

The statute in question further provides that any engineer licensed under the act shall forfeit his license if at any time found guilty by the board of examiners of an act of recklessness, carelessness, or negligence while running an engine, by which damage to person or property is done, or who shall immediately preceding or during the time he is engaged in running an engine be in a state of intoxication; and the board are authorized to revoke and cancel the license whenever they shall be satisfied of the unfitness or incompetency of the engineer by reason of any act or habit unknown at the time of his examination, or acquired or formed subsequent to it. . . . If a locomotive engineer, running an engine, as was the petitioner in this case, in the business of transporting passengers and goods between Alabama and other states, should, while in that state, by mere negligence and recklessness in operating his engine, cause the death of one or more passengers carried, he might certainly be held to answer to the criminal laws of the state if they declare the offense in such a case to be manslaughter. The power to punish for the offense after it is committed certainly includes the power to provide penalties directed, as are those in the statute in question, against those acts of omission which, if performed, would prevent the commission of the larger offense. It is to be remembered that railroads are not natural highways of trade and commerce. They are artificial creations; they are constructed within the territorial limits of a state, and by the authority of its laws, and ordinarily by means of corporations exercising their franchises by limited grants from the state. The places where they may be located, and the plans according to which they must be constructed, are prescribed by the legislation of the state. Their operation requires the use of instruments and agencies attended with special risks and dangers, the proper management of which involves peculiar knowledge, training, skill, and care. The safety of the public in person and property demands the use of specific guards and precautions. The width of the gauge, the character of the grades, the mode of crossing streams by culverts and bridges, the kind of cuts and tunnels, the mode of crossing other highways, the placing of watchmen and signals at points of special danger, the rate of speed at stations and through villages, towns, and cities, are all matters naturally and peculiarly within the provisions of that law from the authority of which these modern highways of commerce derive their existence. The rules prescribed for their construction and for their management and operation, designed to protect persons and property, otherwise endangered by their use, are strictly within the limits of the local law. They are not *per se* regulations of commerce; it is only when they operate as such in the circumstances of their application, and conflict with the expressed or presumed will of congress exerted on the same subject, that they can be required to give way to the supreme authority of the constitution.

In conclusion, we find, therefore—*First*, that the statute of Alabama, the validity of which is under consideration, is not, considered in its own nature, a regulation of interstate commerce, even when applied as in the case under consideration; *secondly*, that it is properly an act of legislation within the scope of the admitted power reserved to the states to regulate the relative rights and duties of persons being and acting within its territorial jurisdiction, intended to operate so as to secure for the public safety of person and property; and, *thirdly*, that, so far as it affects transactions of commerce among the states, it does so only indirectly, incidentally, and remotely, and not so as to burden or impede them, and, in the particulars in which it touches those transactions at all, it is not in conflict with any express enactment of congress on the subject, nor contrary to any intention of congress to be presumed from its silence. For these reasons, we hold this statute, so far as it is alleged to contravene the constitution of the United States, to be a valid law. The judgment of the supreme court of Alabama is therefore affirmed.

BRADLEY, J., dissented.

SOUTHERN PACIFIC COMPANY v. ARIZONA

UNITED STATES SUPREME COURT

325 U.S. 761 (1945)

The Arizona Train Limit Law of 1912 made it unlawful to operate within the state a railroad train of more than fourteen passenger or seventy freight cars. The law also provided that the state could recover a money penalty for each violation. The State of Arizona brought suit against the Southern Pacific Co. for violating the law. Admitting that it had indeed violated the provisions of the law, the Company defended itself in part on the grounds that the state law contravened the commerce clause of the United States Constitution. The trial court decided for the Company but was reversed by the Arizona supreme court. Consequently, the Company brought the case to the Supreme Court of the United States on appeal.

Mr. Chief Justice STONE delivered the opinion of the Court.

. . . .

THE [*Arizona*] Supreme Court left undisturbed the findings of the trial court and made no new findings. It held that the power of the state to regulate the length of interstate trains had not been restricted by Congressional action. It sustained the Act as a safety measure to reduce the number of accidents attributed to the operation of trains of more than the statutory maximum length, enacted by the state legislature in the exercise of its "police power." This power the court held extended to the regulation of the operations of interstate commerce in the interests of local health, safety and well-being. It thought that a state statute, enacted in the exercise of the police power, and bearing some reasonable relation to the health, safety and well-being of the people of the state, of which the state legislature is the judge, was not to be judicially overturned, notwithstanding its admittedly adverse effect on the operation of interstate trains.

. . . .

Congress, in enacting legislation within its constitutional authority over interstate commerce, will not be deemed to have intended to strike down a state statute designed to protect the health and safety of the public unless its purpose to do so is clearly manifested . . . or unless the state law, in terms or in its practical administration, conflicts with the Act of Congress, or plainly and palpably infringes its policy. . . . Congress, although asked to do so, has declined to pass legislation specifically limiting trains to seventy cars. We are therefore brought to appellant's principal contention, that the state statute contravenes the commerce clause of the Federal Constitution.

Although the commerce clause conferred on the national government power to regulate commerce, its possession of the power does not exclude all state power of regulation. . . . [*For many years*], it has been recognized that, in the absence of conflicting legislation by Congress, there is a residuum of power in the state to make laws governing matters of local concern which nevertheless in some measure affect interstate commerce or even, to some extent, regulate it. . . . Thus the states may regulate matters which, because of their number and diversity, may never be adequately dealt with by Congress. . . . When the regulation of matters of local concern is local in character and effect, and its impact on the national commerce does not seriously interfere with its operation, and the consequent incentive to deal with them nationally is slight, such regulation has been generally held to be within state authority. . . .

But ever since Gibbons v. Ogden, 9 Wheat. 1, the states have not been deemed to have authority to impede substantially the free flow of commerce from state to state, or to regulate those phases of the national commerce which, because of the need of national uniformity, demand that their regulation, if any, be prescribed by a single authority. . . .

In the application of these principles some enactments may be found to be plainly within and others plainly without state power. But between these extremes lies the infinite variety of cases in which regulation of local matters may also operate as a regulation of commerce, in which reconciliation of the conflicting claims of state and national power is to be attained only by some appraisal and accommodation of the competing demands of the state and national interests involved. . . .

For a hundred years it has been accepted constitutional doctrine that the commerce clause, without the aid of Congressional legislation, thus affords some protection from state legislation inimical to the national commerce, and that in such cases, where Congress has not acted, this Court, and not the state legislature, is under the commerce clause the final arbiter of the competing demands of state and national interests. . . .

Congress has undoubted power to redefine the distribution of power over interstate commerce. It may either permit the states to regulate the commerce in a manner which would otherwise not be permissible, . . . or exclude state regulation even of matters of peculiarly local concern which nevertheless affect interstate commerce. . . .

But in general Congress has left it to the courts to formulate the rules thus interpreting the commerce clause in its application, doubtless because it has appreciated the destructive consequences to the commerce of the nation if their protection were withdrawn, . . . and has been aware that in their application state laws will not be invalidated without the support of relevant factual material which will "afford a sure basis" for an informed judgment. . . . Meanwhile, Congress has accommodated its legislation, as have the states, to these rules as an established feature of our constitutional system. There has thus been left to the states wide scope for the regulation of matters of local state concern, even though it in some measure affects the commerce, provided it does not materially restrict the free flow of commerce across state lines, or interfere with it in matters with respect to which uniformity of regulation is of predominant national concern.

Hence the matters for ultimate determination here are the nature and extent of the burden which the state regulation of interstate trains, adopted as a safety measure, imposes on interstate commerce, and whether the relative weights of the state and national interests involved are such as to make inapplicable the rule, generally observed, that the free flow of interstate commerce and its freedom from local restraints in matters requiring uniformity of regulation are interests safeguarded by the commerce clause from state interference.

While this Court is not bound by the findings of the state court, and may determine for itself the facts of a case upon which an asserted federal right depends, . . . the facts found by the state trial court showing the nature of the interstate commerce involved, and the effect upon it of the train limit law, are not seriously questioned. Its findings with respect to the need for and effect of the statute as a safety measure, although challenged in some particulars which we do not regard as material to our decision, are likewise supported by evidence. Taken together the findings supply an adequate basis for decision of the constitutional issue.

The findings show that the operation of long trains, that is trains of more than fourteen passenger and more than seventy freight cars, is standard practice over the main lines of the railroads of the United States, and that, if the length of trains is to be regulated at all, national uniformity in the regulation adopted, such as only Congress can prescribe, is practically indispensable to the operation of an efficient and economical national railway system. On many railroads passenger trains of more than fourteen cars and freight trains of more than seventy cars are operated, and on some systems freight trains are run ranging from one hundred and twenty-five to one hundred and sixty cars in length. Outside of Arizona, where the length of trains is not restricted, appellant runs a substantial proportion of long trains. In 1939 on its comparable route for through traffic through Utah and Nevada from 66 to 85% of its freight trains were over 70 cars in length and over 43% of its passenger trains included more than fourteen passenger cars.

In Arizona, approximately 93% of the freight traffic and 95% of the passenger traffic is interstate. Because of the Train Limit Law appellant is required to haul over 30% more trains in Arizona than would otherwise have been necessary. The record shows a definite relationship between operating costs and the length of trains, the increase in length resulting in a reduction of operating costs per car. The additional cost of operation of trains complying with the Train Limit Law in Arizona amounts for the two railroads traversing that state to about $1,000,000 a year. The reduction in train lengths also impedes efficient operation. More locomotives and more manpower are required; the necessary conversion and reconversion of train lengths at terminals and the delay caused by breaking up and remaking long trains upon entering and leaving the state in order to comply with the law, delays the traffic and diminishes its volume moved in a given time, especially when traffic is heavy.

. . . .

The unchallenged findings leave no doubt that the Arizona Train Limit Law imposes a serious burden on the interstate commerce conducted by appellant. It materially impedes the movement of appellant's interstate trains through that state and interposes a substantial obstruction to the national policy proclaimed by Congress, to promote adequate, economical and efficient railway transportation service. . . . Enforcement of the law in Arizona, while train lengths remain unregulated or are regulated by varying standards in other states, must inevitably result in an impairment of uniformity of efficient railroad operation because the railroads are subjected to regulation which is not uniform in its application. Compliance with a state statute limiting train lengths requires interstate trains of a length lawful in other states to be broken up and reconstituted as they enter each state according as it may impose varying limitations upon train lengths. The alternative is for the carrier to conform to the lowest train limit restriction of any of the states through which its trains pass, whose laws thus control the carriers' operations both within and without the regulating state.

Although the seventy car maximum for freight trains is the limitation which has been most commonly proposed, various bills introduced in the state legislatures provided for maximum freight train lengths of from fifty to one hundred and twenty-five cars, and maximum passenger train lengths of from ten to eighteen cars. With such laws in force in states which are interspersed with those having no limit on train lengths, the confusion and difficulty with which interstate operations would be burdened under the varied system of state regulation and the unsatisfied need for uniformity in such regulation, if any, are evident.

At present the seventy freight car laws are enforced only in Arizona and Oklahoma, with a fourteen car passenger car limit in Arizona. The record here shows that the enforcement of the Arizona statute results in freight trains being broken up and reformed at the California border and in New Mexico, some distance from the Arizona line. Frequently it is not feasible to operate a newly assembled train from the New Mexico yard nearest to Arizona, with the result that the Arizona limitation governs the flow of traffic as far east as El Paso, Texas. For similar reasons the Arizona law often controls the length of passenger trains all the way from Los Angeles to El Paso.

If one state may regulate train lengths, so may all the others, and they need not prescribe the same maximum limitation. The practical effect of such regulation is to control train operations beyond the boundaries of the state exacting it because of the necessity of breaking up and reassembling long trains at the nearest terminal points before entering and after leaving the regulating state. The serious impediment to the free flow of commerce by the local regulation of train lengths and the practical necessity that such regulation, if any, must be prescribed by a single body having a nationwide authority are apparent.

The trial court found that the Arizona law had no reasonable relation to safety, and made train operation more dangerous. Examination of the evidence and the detailed findings makes it clear that this conclusion was rested on facts found which indicate that such increased danger of accident and personal injury as may result from the greater length of trains is more than offset by the increase in the number of accidents resulting from the larger number of trains when train lengths are reduced. In considering the effect of the statute as a safety measure, therefore, the factor of controlling significance for present purposes is not whether there is basis for the conclusion of the Arizona Supreme Court that the increase in length of trains beyond the statutory maximum has an adverse effect upon safety of operation. The decisive question is whether in the circumstances the total effect of the law as a safety measure in reducing accidents and casualties is so slight or problematical as not to outweigh the national interest in keeping interstate commerce free from interferences which seriously impede it and subject it to local regulation which does not have a uniform effect on the interstate train journey which it interrupts.

The principal source of danger of accident from increased length of trains is the resulting increase of "slack action" of the train. Slack action is the amount of free movement of one car before it transmits its motion to an adjoining coupled car. This free movement results from the fact that in railroad practice cars are loosely coupled, and the coupling is often combined with a shock-absorbing device, a "draft gear," which, under stress, substantially increases the free movement as the train is started or stopped. Loose coupling is necessary to enable the train to proceed freely around curves and is an aid in starting heavy trains, since the application of the locomotive power to the train operates on each car in the train successively, and the power is thus utilized to start only one car at a time.

The slack action between cars due to loose couplings varies from seven-eighths of an inch to one and one-eighth inches and, with the added free movement due to the use of draft gears, may be as high as six or seven inches between cars. The length of the train increases the slack since the slack action of a train is the total of the free movement between its several cars. The amount of slack action has some effect on the severity of the shock of train movements, and on freight trains sometimes results in injuries to operatives, which most frequently occur to occupants of the caboose. The amount and severity of slack action, however, are not wholly dependent upon the length of train, as they may be affected by the mode and conditions of operation as to grades, speed, and load. And accidents due to slack action also occur in the operation of short trains. On comparison of the number of slack action accidents in Arizona with those in Nevada, where the length of trains is now unregulated, the trial court found that with substantially the same amount of traffic in each state the number of accidents was relatively the same in long as in short train operations. While accidents from slack action do occur in the operation of passenger trains, it does not appear that they are more frequent or the resulting shocks more severe on long than on short passenger trains. Nor does it appear that slack action accidents occurring on passenger trains, whatever their length, are of sufficient severity to cause serious injury or damage.

As the trial court found, reduction of the length of trains also tends to increase the number of accidents because of the increase in the number of trains. The application of the Arizona law compelled appellant to operate 30.08%, or 4,304, more freight trains in 1938 than would otherwise have been necessary. And the record amply supports the trial court's conclusion that the frequency of accidents is closely related to the number of trains run. The number of accidents due to grade crossing collisions between trains and motor vehicles and pedestrians, and to collisions between trains, which are usually far more serious than those due to slack action, and accidents due to locomotive failures, in general vary with the number of trains. Increase in the number of trains results in more starts and stops, more "meets" and "passes," and more switching movements, all tending to increase the number of accidents not only to train operatives and other railroad employees, but to passengers and members of the public exposed to danger by train operations.

Railroad statistics introduced into the record tend to show that this is the result of the application of the Arizona Train Limit Law to appellant, both with respect to all railroad casualties within the state and those affecting only trainmen whom the train limit law is supposed to protect. The accident rate in Arizona is much higher than on comparable lines elsewhere, where there is no regulation of length of trains. The record lends support to the trial court's conclusion that the train length limitation increased rather than diminished the number of accidents. This is shown by comparison of appellant's operations in Arizona with those in Nevada, and by comparison of operations of appellant and of the Santa Fe Railroad in Arizona with those of the same roads in New Mexico, and by like comparison between appellant's operations in Arizona and operations throughout the country.

Upon an examination of the whole case the trial court found that "if short-train operation may or should result in any decrease in the number or severity of the 'slack' or 'slack-surge' type of accidents or casualties, such decrease is substantially more than offset by the increased number of accidents and casualties from other causes that follow the arbitrary limitation of freight trains to 70 cars * * * and passenger trains to 14 cars."

We think, as the trial court found,

that the Arizona Train Limit Law, viewed as a safety measure, affords at most slight and dubious advantage, if any, over unregulated train lengths, because it results in an increase in the number of trains and train operations and the consequent increase in train accidents of a character generally more severe than those due to slack action. Its undoubted effect on the commerce is the regulation, without securing uniformity, of the length of trains operated in interstate commerce, which lack is itself a primary cause of preventing the free flow of commerce by delaying it and by substantially increasing its cost and impairing its efficiency. . . .

The principle that, without controlling Congressional action, a state may not regulate interstate commerce so as substantially to affect its flow or deprive it of needed uniformity in its regulation is not to be avoided by "simply invoking the convenient apologetics of the police power. . . ."

Similarly the commerce clause has been held to invalidate local "police power" enactments fixing the number of cars in an interstate train and the number of passengers to be carried in each car, . . . regulating the segregation of colored passengers in interstate trains, . . . requiring burdensome intrastate stops of interstate trains, . . . requiring an interstate railroad to detour its through passenger trains for the benefit of a small city, . . . interfering with interstate commerce by requiring interstate trains to leave on time, . . . regulating car distribution to interstate shippers, . . . or establishing venue provisions requiring railroads to defend accident suits at points distant from the place of injury and the residence and activities of the parties. . . .

More recently . . . we have pointed out that when a state goes beyond safety measures which are permissible because only local in their effect upon interstate commerce, and "attempts to impose particular standards as to structure, design, equipment, and operation [of vessels plying interstate], which in the judgment of its authorities may be desirable, but pass beyond what is plainly essential to safety and seaworthiness, the state will encounter the principle that such requirements, if imposed at all, must be through the action of Congress which can establish a uniform rule. Whether the state in a particular matter goes too far must be left to be determined when the precise question arises."

Here we conclude that the state does go too far. Its regulation of train lengths, admittedly obstructive to interstate train operation, and having a seriously adverse effect on transportation efficiency and economy, passes beyond what is plainly essential for safety since it does not appear that it will lessen rather than increase the danger of accident. Its attempted regulation of the operation of interstate trains cannot establish nationwide control such as is essential to the maintenance of an efficient transportation system, which Congress alone can prescribe. The state interest cannot be preserved at the expense of the national interest by an enactment which regulates interstate train lengths without securing such control, which is a matter of national concern. To this the interest of the state here asserted is subordinate.

Appellees especially rely on the full train crew cases, . . . as supporting the state's authority to regulate the length of interstate trains. While the full train crew laws undoubtedly placed an added financial burden on the railroads in order to serve a local interest, they did not obstruct interstate transportation or seriously impede it. They had no effects outside the state beyond those of picking up and setting down the extra employees at the state boundaries; they involved no wasted use of facilities or serious impairment of transportation efficiency, which are among the factors of controlling weight here. In sustaining those laws the Court considered the restriction a minimal burden on the commerce comparable to the law requiring the licensing of engineers as a safeguard against those of reckless and intemperate habits, sustained in Smith v. Alabama, . . . or those afflicted with color blindness. . . .

. . . .

The contrast between the present regulation and the full train crew laws in point of their effects on the commerce, and the like contrast with the highway safety regulations, in point of the nature of the subject of regulation and the state's interest in it, illustrate and emphasize the considerations which enter into a determination of the relative weights of state and national interests where state regulation affecting interstate commerce is attempted. Here examination of all the relevant factors makes it plain that the state interest is outweighed by the interest of the nation in an adequate, economical and efficient railway transportation service, which must prevail.

Reversed.

Mr. Justice RUTLEDGE concurs in the result.

Mr. Justice BLACK, dissenting.

. . . .

For more than a quarter of a century, railroads and their employees have engaged in controversies over the relative virtues and dangers of long trains. Railroads have argued that they could carry goods and passengers cheaper in long trains than in short trains. They have also argued that while the danger of personal injury to their employees might in some respects be greater on account of the operation of long trains, this danger was more than offset by an increased number of accidents from other causes brought about by the operation of a much larger number of short trains. These arguments have been, and are now, vigorously denied. While there are others, the chief causes assigned for the belief that long trains unnecessarily jeopardize the lives and limbs of railroad employees relate to "slack action." Cars coupled together retain a certain free play of movement, ranging between 1½ inches and 1 foot, and this is called "slack action." Train brakes do not ordinarily apply or release simultaneously on all cars. This frequently results in a severe shock or jar to cars, particularly those in the rear of a train. It has always been the position of the employees that the dangers from "slack action" correspond to and are proportionate with the length of the train. The argument that "slack movements" are more dangerous in long trains than in short trains seems never to have been denied. The railroads have answered it by what is in effect a plea of confession and avoidance. They say that the added cost of running long trains places an unconstitutional burden on interstate commerce. Their second answer is that the operation of short trains requires the use of more separate train units; that a certain number of accidents resulting in injury are inherent in the operation of each unit, injuries which may be inflicted either on employees or on the public; consequently, they have asserted that it is not in the public interest to prohibit the operation of long trains.

. . . .

This controversy between the railroads and their employees, which was nationwide, was carried to Congress. Extensive hearings took place. The employees' position was urged by members of the various Brotherhoods. The railroads' viewpoint was presented through representatives of their National Association. In 1937, the Senate Interstate

Commerce Committee after its own exhaustive hearings unanimously recommended that trains be limited to 70 cars as a safety measure. The Committee in its Report reviewed the evidence and specifically referred to the large and increasing number of injuries and deaths suffered by railroad employees; it concluded that the admitted danger from slack movement was greatly intensified by the operation of long trains; that short trains reduce this danger; that the added cost of short trains to the railroad was no justification for jeopardizing the safety of railroad employees; and that the legislation would provide a greater degree of safety for persons and property, increase protection for railway employees and the public, and improve transportation services for shippers and consumers. The Senate passed the bill but the House Committee failed to report it out.

During the hearings on that measure, frequent references were made to the Arizona statute. It is significant, however, that American railroads never once asked Congress to exercise its unquestioned power to enact uniform legislation on that subject, and thereby invalidate the Arizona law. That which for some unexplained reason they did not ask Congress to do when it had the very subject of train length limitations under consideration, they shortly thereafter asked an Arizona state court to do.

In the state court a rather extraordinary "trial" took place. Charged with violating the law, the railroad admitted the charge. It alleged that the law was unconstitutional, however, and sought a trial of facts on that issue. The essence of its charge of unconstitutionality rested on one of these two grounds: (1) The legislature and people of Arizona erred in 1912 in determining that the running of long cars was dangerous; or (2) railroad conditions had so improved since 1912 that previous dangers did not exist to the same extent, and that the statute should be stricken down either because it cast an undue burden on interstate commerce by reason of the added cost, or because the changed conditions had rendered the Act "arbitrary and unreasonable." Thus, the issue which the Court "tried" was not whether the railroad was guilty of violating the law, but whether the law was unconstitutional either because the legislature had been guilty of misjudging the facts concerning the degree of the danger of long trains, or because the 1912 conditions of danger no longer existed.

. . . .

Under those circumstances, the determination of whether it is in the interest of society for the length of trains to be governmentally regulated is a matter of public policy. Someone must fix that policy—either the Congress, or the state, or the courts. A century and a half of constitutional history and government admonishes this Court to leave that choice to the elected legislative representatives of the people themselves, where it properly belongs both on democratic principles and the requirements of efficient government.

. . . .

We are not left in doubt as to why, as against the potential peril of injuries to employees, the Court tips the scales on the side of "uniformity." For the evil it finds in a lack of uniformity is that it (1) delays interstate commerce, (2) increases its cost and (3) impairs its efficiency. All three of these boil down to the same thing, and that is that running shorter trains would increase the cost of railroad operations. The "burden" on commerce reduces itself to mere cost because there was no finding, and no evidence to support a finding, that by the expenditure of sufficient sums of money, the railroads could not enable themselves to carry goods and passengers just as quickly and efficiently with short trains as with long trains. Thus the conclusion that a requirement for long trains will "burden interstate commerce" is a mere euphemism for the statement that a requirement for long trains will increase the cost of railroad operations.

In the report of the Senate Committee, supra, attention was called to the fact that in 1935, 6,351 railroad employees were injured while on duty, with a resulting loss of more than 200,000 working days, and that injuries to trainmen and enginemen increased more than 29% in 1936. Nevertheless, the Court's action in requiring that money costs outweigh human values is sought to be buttressed by a reference to the express policy of Congress to promote an "economical national railroad system." I cannot believe that if Congress had defined what it meant by "economical," it would have required money to be saved at the expense of the personal safety of railway employees. Its whole history for the past 25 years belies such an interpretation of its language. Judicial opinions rather than legislative enactments have tended to emphasize costs. . . .

. . . Everyday knowledge as well as direct evidence presented at the various hearings, substantiates the report of the Senate Committee that the danger from slack movement is greater in long trains than in short trains. It may be that offsetting dangers are possible in the operation of short trains. The balancing of these probabilities, however, is not in my judgment a matter for judicial determination, but one which calls for legislative consideration. Representatives elected by the people to make their laws, rather than judges appointed to interpret those laws, can best determine the policies which govern the people. That at least is the basic principle on which our democratic society rests. I would affirm the judgment of the Supreme Court of Arizona.

Mr. Justice DOUGLAS, dissenting.

I have expressed my doubts whether the courts should intervene in situations like the present and strike down state legislation on the grounds that it burdens interstate commerce. . . . My view has been that the courts should intervene only where the state legislation discriminated against interstate commerce or was out of harmony with laws which Congress had enacted. . . . It seems to me particularly appropriate that that course be followed here. For Congress has given the Interstate Commerce Commission broad powers of regulation over interstate carriers. The Commission is the national agency which has been entrusted with the task of promoting a safe, adequate, efficient, and economical transportation service. It is the expert on this subject. It is in a position to police the field. And if its powers prove inadequate for the task, Congress, which has paramount authority in this field, can implement them.

. . . .

. . . Whether the question arises under the Commerce Clause or the Fourteenth Amendment, I think the legislation is entitled to a presumption of validity. If a State passed a law prohibiting the hauling of more than one freight car at a time, we would have a situation comparable in effect to a state law requiring all railroads within its borders to operate on narrow gauge tracks. The question is one of degree and calls for a close appraisal of the facts. I am not persuaded that the evidence adduced by the railroads overcomes the presumption of validity to which this train-limit law is entitled. For the reasons stated by Mr. Justice BLACK, Arizona's train-limit law should stand as an allowable regulation enacted to protect the lives and limbs of the men who operate the trains.

SOUTH CAROLINA STATE HIGHWAY DEPARTMENT v. BARNWELL BROS. INC.

UNITED STATES SUPREME COURT
303 U.S. 177 (1938)

The facts in the case are spelled out in the Court's opinion. Pay particular attention to the summary of the complex decision rendered by the Federal district court which held the original trial and the decision of which was appealed to the United States Supreme Court.

Mr. Justice Stone delivered the opinion of the Court.

. . . .

Act No. 259 of the General Assembly of South Carolina, of April 28, 1933, . . . prohibits use on the state highways of motor trucks and "semi-trailer motor trucks" whose width exceeds 90 inches, and whose weight including load exceeds 20,000 pounds. For purposes of the weight limitation, section 2 of the statute provides that a semitrailer motortruck, which is a motor propelled truck with a trailer whose front end is designed to be attached to and supported by the truck, shall be considered a single unit. The principal question for decision is whether these prohibitions impose an unconstitutional burden upon interstate commerce.

Appellees include the original plaintiffs below, who are truckers and interstate shippers; the Interstate Commerce Commission; and certain others who were permitted to intervene as parties plaintiff. The suit was brought in the District Court for Eastern South Carolina against various state officials, to enjoin them from enforcing sections 4 and 6 of the act among others, on the ground that they have been superseded by the Federal Motor Carrier Act of 1935, . . . that they infringe the due process clause of the Fourteenth Amendment; and that they impose an unconstitutional burden on interstate commerce. Certain railroads interested in restricting the competition of interstate motor carriers were permitted to intervene as parties defendant.

The District Court of three judges, after hearing evidence, ruled that the challenged provisions of the statute have not been superseded by the Federal Motor Carrier Act, . . . and adopted as its own the ruling of the state Supreme Court in State ex rel. Daniel v. John P. Nutt Co., 185 S.E. 25, that the challenged provisions, being an exercise of the state's power to regulate the use of its highways so as to protect them from injury and to insure their safe and economical use, do not violate the Fourteenth Amendment. But it held that the weight and width prohibitions place an unlawful burden on interstate motor traffic passing over specified highways of the state, which for the most part are of concrete or a concrete base surfaced with asphalt. It accordingly enjoined the enforcement of the weight provision against interstate motor carriers on the specified highways, and also the width limitation of 90 inches, except in the case of vehicles exceeding 96 inches in width. It exempted from the operation of the decree, bridges on those highways "not constructed with sufficient strength to support the heavy trucks of modern traffic or too narrow to accommodate such traffic safely," provided the state highway department should place at each end of the bridge proper notices warning that the use of the bridge is forbidden by trucks exceeding the weight or width limits and provided the proper authorities take the necessary steps to enforce the law against such use of the bridges. The case comes here on appeal. . . .

The trial court rested its decision that the statute unreasonably burdens interstate commerce, upon findings, not assailed here, that there is a large amount of motortruck traffic passing interstate in the southeastern part of the United States, which would normally pass over the highways of South Carolina, but which will be barred from the state by the challenged restrictions if enforced, and upon its conclusion that, when viewed in the light of their effect upon interstate commerce, these restrictions are unreasonable.

To reach this conclusion the court weighed conflicting evidence and made its own determinations as to the weight and width of motortrucks commonly used in interstate traffic and the capacity of the specified highways of the state to accommodate such traffic without injury to them or danger to their users. It found that interstate carriage by motortrucks has become a national industry; that from 85 to 90 per cent of the motortrucks used in interstate transportation are 96 inches wide and of a gross weight, when loaded, of more than 10 tons; that only four other states prescribe a gross load weight as low as 20,000 pounds; and that the American Association of State Highway Officials and the National Conference on Street and Highway Safety in the Department of Commerce have recommended for adoption weight and width limitations in which weight is limited to axle loads of 16,000 to 18,000 pounds and width is limited to 96 inches.

It found in detail that compliance with the weight and width limitations demanded by the South Carolina act would seriously impede motortruck traffic passing to and through the state and increase its cost; that 2,417 miles of state highways, including most of those affected by the injunction, are of the standard construction of concrete or concrete base with asphalt surface, 7½ or 8 inches thick at the edges and 6 or 6½ inches thick at the center; that they are capable of sustaining without injury a wheel load of 8,000 to 9,000 pounds or an axle load of double those amounts, depending on whether the wheels are equipped with high-pressure or low-pressure pneumatic tires; that all but 100 miles of the specified highways are from 18 to 20 feet in width; that they constitute a connected system of highways which have been improved with the aid of federal money grants, as a part of a national system of highways; and that they constitute one of the best highway systems in the southeastern part of the United States.

It also found that the gross weight of vehicles is not a factor to be considered in the preservation of concrete highways, but that the appropriate factor to be considered is wheel or axle weight; that vehicles engaged in interstate commerce are so designed and the pressure of their weight is so distributed by their wheels and axles that gross loads of more than 20,000 pounds can be carried over concrete roads without damage to the surface; that a gross weight limitation of that amount, especially as applied to semitrailer motortrucks, is unreasonable as a means of preserving the highways; that it has no reasonable relation to safety of the public using the highways; and that the width limitation of 90 inches is unreasonable when applied to standard concrete highways of the state, in view of the fact that all other states permit a width of 96 inches, which is the standard width of trucks engaged in interstate commerce.

In reaching these conclusions, and at the same time holding that the weight and width limitations do not infringe the Fourteenth Amendment, the court proceeded upon the assumption that the commerce clause, Const. art. 1, § 8, cl. 3, imposes upon state regulations to secure the safe and economical use of highways a standard of reasonableness which is more exacting when applied to the interstate traffic than that required by the Fourteenth Amendment as to all traffic; that a standard of weight and width of motor vehicles which is an appropriate state regulation when applied to intrastate traffic may be prohibited because of its effect on interstate commerce, although the conditions attending the two classes of traffic with respect to safety and protection of the highways are the same.

South Carolina has built its highways and owns and maintains them. It has received from the federal government, in aid of its highway improvements, money grants which have been expended upon the highways to which the injunction applies. But appellees do not challenge here the ruling of the District Court that Congress has not undertaken to regulate the weight and size of motor vehicles in interstate motor traffic, and has left undisturbed whatever authority in that regard the states have retained under the Constitution.

While the constitutional grant to Congress of power to regulate interstate commerce has been held to operate of its own force to curtail state power in some measure, it did not forestall all state action affecting interstate commerce. Ever since Willson v. Black Bird Creek Marsh Co., 2 Pet. 245, and Cooley v. Board of Port Wardens, 12 How. 299, it has been recognized that there are matters of local concern, the regulation of which unavoidably involves some regulation of interstate commerce but which, because of their local character and their number and diversity, may never be fully dealt with by Congress. Notwithstanding the commerce clause, such regulation in the absence of congressional action has for the most part been left to the states by the decisions of this Court, subject to the other applicable constitutional restraints.

The commerce clause by its own force, prohibits discrimination against interstate commerce, whatever its form or method, and the decisions of this Court have recognized that there is scope for its like operation when state legislation nominally of local concern is in point of fact aimed at interstate commerce, or by its necessary operation is a means of gaining a local benefit by throwing the attendant burdens on those without the state. . . . It was to end these practices that the commerce clause was adopted. . . . The commerce clause has also been thought to set its own limitation upon state control of interstate rail carriers so as to preclude the subordination of the efficiency and convenience of interstate traffic to local service requirements.

But the present case affords no occasion for saying that the bare possession of power by Congress to regulate the interstate traffic forces the states to conform to standards which Congress might, but has not adopted, or curtails their power to take measures to insure the safety and conservation of their highways which may be applied to like traffic moving intrastate. Few subjects of state regulation are so peculiarly of local concern as is the use of state highways. There are few, local regulation of which is so inseparable from a substantial effect on interstate commerce. Unlike the railroads, local highways are built, owned, and maintained by the state or its municipal subdivisions. The state has a primary and immediate concern in their safe and economical administration. The present regulations, or any others of like purpose, if they are to accomplish their end, must be applied alike to interstate and intrastate traffic both moving in large volume over the highways. The fact that they affect alike shippers in interstate and intrastate commerce in large number within as well as without the state is a safeguard against their abuse.

From the beginning it has been recognized that a state can, if it sees fit, build and maintain its own highways, canals, and railroads, and that in the absence of congressional action their regulation is peculiarly within its competence, even though interstate commerce is materially affected. . . . Congress not acting, state regulation of intrastate carriers has been upheld regardless of its effect upon interstate commerce. . . . With respect to the extent and nature of the local interests to be protected and the unavoidable effect upon interstate and intrastate commerce alike, regulations of the use of the highways are akin to local regulation of rivers, harbors, piers, and docks, quarantine regulations, and game laws, which, Congress not acting, have been sustained even though they materially interfere with interstate commerce.

The nature of the authority of the state over its own highways has often been pointed out by this Court. It may not, under the guise of regulation, discriminate against interstate commerce. But, "In the absence of national legislation especially covering the subject of interstate commerce, the state may rightly prescribe uniform regulations adapted to promote safety upon its highways and the conservation of their use, applicable alike to vehicles moving in interstate commerce and those of its own citizens." Morris v. Duby, 274 U.S. 135, 143. This formulation has been repeatedly affirmed, . . . and never disapproved. This Court has often sustained the exercise of that power, although it has burdened or impeded interstate commerce. It has upheld weight limitations lower than those presently imposed, applied alike to motor traffic moving interstate and intrastate. . . . Restrictions favoring passenger traffic over the carriage of interstate merchandise by truck have been similarly sustained, . . . as has the exaction of a reasonable fee for the use of the highways. . . .

In each of these cases regulation involves a burden on interstate commerce. But so long as the state action does not discriminate, the burden is one which the Constitution permits because it is an inseparable incident of the exercise of a legislative authority, which, under the Constitution, has been left to the states.

Congress, in the exercise of its plenary power to regulate interstate commerce, may determine whether the burdens imposed on it by state regulation, otherwise permissible, are too great, and may, by legislation designed to secure uniformity or in other respects to protect the national interest in the commerce, curtail to some extent the state's regulatory power. But that is a legislative, not a judicial, function, to be performed in the light of the congressional judgment of what is appropriate regulation of interstate commerce, and the extent to which, in that field, state power and local interests should be required to yield to the national authority and interest. In the absence of such legislation the judicial function, under the commerce clause, . . . as well as the Fourteenth Amendment, stops with the inquiry whether the state Legislature in adopting regulations such as the present has acted within its province, and whether the means of regulation chosen are reasonably adapted to the end sought. . . .

Here the first inquiry has already been resolved by our decisions that a state may impose nondiscriminatory restrictions with respect to the character of motor vehicles moving in interstate commerce as a safety measure and as a means of securing the economical use of its highways. In resolving the second, courts do not sit as Legislatures, either state or national. They cannot act as Congress does when, after weighing all the conflicting interests, state and national, it determines when and how much the state regulatory power shall yield to the larger interests of a national commerce. And in reviewing a state highway regulation where Congress has not acted, a court is not called upon, as are state Legislatures, to determine what, in its judgment, is the most suitable restriction to be applied of those that are possible, or to choose that one which in its opinion is best adapted to all the diverse interests affected. . . . When the action of a Legislature is within the scope of its power, fairly debatable questions as to its reasonableness, wisdom, and propriety are not for the determination of courts, but for the legislative body, on which rests the duty and responsibility of decision. . . . This is equally the case when the legislative power is one which may legitimately place an incidental burden on interstate commerce. It is not any the less a legislative power committed to the states because it affects interstate commerce, and courts are not any the more entitled, because interstate commerce is affected, to substitute their own for the legislative judgment. . . .

Since the adoption of one weight or width regulation, rather than another, is a legislative, not a judicial, choice, its constitutionality is not to be determined by weighing in the judicial scales the merits of the legislative choice and rejecting it if the weight of evidence presented in court appears to favor a different standard. . . . Being a legislative judgment it is presumed to be supported by facts known to the Legislature unless facts judicially known or proved preclude that possibility. Hence, in reviewing the present determination, we examine the record, not to see whether the findings of the court below are supported by evidence, but to ascertain upon the whole record whether it is possible to say that the legislative choice is without rational basis. . . . Not only does the record fail to exclude that possibility but it shows affirmatively that there is adequate support for the legislative judgment.

At the outset it should be noted that underlying much of the controversy is the relative merit of a gross weight limitation as against an axle or wheel weight limitation. While there is evidence that weight stresses on concrete roads are determined by wheel rather than gross load weights, other elements enter into choice of the type of weight limitation. There is testimony to show that the axle or wheel weight limitation is the more easily enforced through resort to weighing devices adapted to ascertaining readily the axle or wheel weight. But it appears that in practice the weight of truck loads is not evenly distributed over axles and wheels; that commonly the larger part of the load—sometimes as much as 70 to 80 per cent.—rests on the rear axle, and that it is much easier for those who load trucks to make certain that they have complied with a gross load weight limitation than with an axle or wheel weight limitation. While the report of the National Conference on State and Highway Safety, on which the court below relied, suggested a wheel weight limitation of 8,000 or 9,000 pounds, it also suggested that a gross weight limitation might be adopted and should be subject to the recommended wheel limitation. But the Conference declined to fix the amount of gross weight limitation, saying: "In view of the varying conditions of traffic, and lack of uniformity in highway construction in the several States, no uniform gross-weight limitations are here recommended for general adoption throughout the country." The choice of a weight limitation based on convenience of application and consequent lack of need for rigid supervisory enforcement is for the Legislature, and we cannot say that its preference for the one over the other is in any sense arbitrary or unreasonable. The choice is not to be condemned because the Legislature prefers a workable standard, less likely to be violated than another under which the violations will probably be increased but more easily detected. It is for the Legislature to say whether the one test or the other will in practical operation better protect the highways from the risk of excessive loads.

If gross load weight is adopted as the test, it is obvious that the permissible load must be somewhat lighter than if the axle or wheel weight test were applied. With the latter the gross weight of a loaded motortruck can never exceed twice the axle and four times the wheel limit. But the fact that the rear axle may and often does support as much as 70 or 80 per cent. of the gross load, with wheel weight in like proportion, requires that a gross load limit be fixed at considerably less than four times the permissible wheel limit.

There was testimony before the court to support its conclusion that the highways in question are capable of sustaining without injury a wheel load of 8,000 or 9,000 pounds, the difference depending upon the character of the tire in use, as against a wheel load of as much as 8,000 pounds, which would be possible under the statutory load limit of 20,000 pounds as applied to motortrucks, and approximates the axle limit in addition to the gross load limit recommended by the National Conference on Street and Highway Safety. Much of this testimony appears to have been based on theoretical strength of concrete highways laid under ideal conditions, and none of it was based on an actual study of the highways of South Carolina or of the subgrade and other road building conditions which prevail there and which have a material bearing on the strength and durability of such highways. There is uncontradicted testimony that approximately 60 per cent. of the South Carolina standard paved highways in question were built without a longitudinal center joint which has since become standard practice, the portion of the concrete surface adjacent to the joint being strengthened by reinforcement or by increasing its thickness; and that owing to the distribution of the stresses on concrete roads when in use, those without a center joint have a tendency to develop irregular longitudinal cracks. As the concrete in the center of such roads is thinner than that at the edges, the result is that the highway is split into two irregular segments, each with a weak inner edge which, according to the expert testimony, is not capable of supporting indefinitely wheel loads in excess of 4,200 pounds.

There is little in the record to mark any controlling distinction between the application of the gross load weight limitation to the motortruck and to the semitrailer motortruck. There is testimony which is applicable to both types of vehicle, that in case of accident the danger from the momentum of a colliding vehicle increases with gross load weight. The record is without convincing evidence of the actual distribution, in practice, of the gross load weight over the wheels and axles of the permissible types of semitrailer motortrucks, but this does not enable us to say that the Legislature was without substantial ground for concluding that the relative advantages of a gross load over a wheel weight limitation are substantially the same for the two types, or that it could not have concluded that they were so nearly alike for regulatory purposes as to justify the adoption of a single standard for both, as a matter of practical convenience. Even if the Legislature were to accept appellees' assumption that net load weights are, in practice, evenly distributed over the wheels supporting the load of a permissible semitrailer so that with the statutory gross load limit the load on the rear axle would be about 8,000 pounds it might, as we have seen, also conclude that the danger point would then have been reached in the case of some 1,200 miles of concrete state roads constructed without a center joint.

These considerations, with the presumption of constitutionality, afford adequate support for the weight limitation without reference to other items of the testimony tending to support it. Furthermore, South Carolina's own experience is not to be ignored. Before adoption of the limitation South Carolina had had experience with higher weight limits. In 1924 it had adopted a combined gross weight limit of 20,000 pounds for vehicles of four wheels or less, and an axle weight limit of 15,000 pounds. In 1930 it had adopted a combined gross weight limit of 12½ tons with a five-ton axle weight limit for vehicles having more than two axles. . . . In 1931 it appointed a commission to investigate motor transportation in the state, to recommend legislation, and to report in 1932. The present weight limitation was recommended by the commission after a full consideration of relevant data, including a report by the state engineer who had constructed the concrete highways of the state and who advised a somewhat lower limitation as necessary for their preservation. The fact that many states have adopted a different standard is not persuasive. The conditions under which highways must be built in the several states, their construction, and the demands made upon them, are not uniform. The road building art, as the record shows, is far from having attained a scientific certainty and precision, and scientific precision is not the criterion for the exercise of the constitutional regulatory power of the states. . . . The Legislature, being free to exercise its own judgment, is not bound by that of other Legislatures. It would hardly be contended that if all the states had adopted a single standard none, in the light of its own experience and in the exercise of its judgment upon all the complex elements which enter into the problem, could change it.

Only a word need be said as to the width limitation. While a large part of the highways in question are from 18 to 20 feet in width, approximately 100 miles are only 16 feet wide. On all the use of a 96-inch truck leaves but a narrow margin for passing. On the road 16 feet wide it leaves none. The 90-inch limitation has been in force in South Carolina since 1920, and the concrete highways which it has built appear to be adapted to vehicles of that width. The record shows without contradiction that the use of heavy loaded trucks on the highways tends to force other traffic off the concrete surface onto the shoulders of the road adjoining its edges, and to increase repair costs materially. It appears also that as the width of trucks is increased it obstructs the view of the highway, causing much inconvenience and increased hazard in its use. It plainly cannot be said that the width of trucks used on the highways in South Carolina is unrelated to their safety and cost of maintenance, or that a 90-inch width limitation, adopted to safeguard the highways of the state, is not within the range of the permissible legislative choice.

The regulatory measures taken by South Carolina are within its legislative power. They do not infringe the Fourteenth Amendment, and the resulting burden on interstate commerce is not forbidden.

Reversed.

Mr. Justice CARDOZO and Mr. Justice REED took no part in the consideration or decision of this case.

ALASKA v. ARCTIC MAID

UNITED STATES SUPREME COURT

366 U.S. 199 (1961)

The facts are spelled out in the opinion.

Mr. Justice DOUGLAS delivered the opinion of the Court.

WHILE ALASKA was a Territory, the Territorial Legislature amended . . . its taxing statutes, to read, in relevant part, as follows:

* * * * * *

> "(b) Freezer ships and other floating cold storages: An annual license tax equal to 4% of the value of the raw halibut, halibut livers and viscera, salmon and bottom fish, shellfish or other fishing resource bought or otherwise obtained for processing through freezing. . . ."

Respondents use freezer ships for the taking and preservation of salmon along Alaska's shores. These freezer ships use "catcher boats" which respondents own or have under contract and which catch salmon off Alaska. The freezer ships sometimes purchase salmon from independent fishermen.

Bristol Bay is a famous fishing ground for salmon. When operating in the Bristol Bay area, the freezer ships anchor more than three miles from the coast, because of the shallow waters in Bristol Bay. They serve as a base for their catcher boats that fish within the territorial waters. In other areas both the freezer ships and the catcher boats stay within the territorial waters.

When the catcher boats—which are shallow-draft and known as gillnetters—have a load or desire to discontinue fishing or when the open season ends, they return to the "mother" ship and unload. The salmon are usually dumped into quick-freezing brine tanks. At other times they are placed in freezing compartments and frozen by blasts of air. The freezer ships eventually return to Puget Sound in the State of Washington where the salmon are canned.

Alaska, when a Territory, brought these suits in the District Court of Alaska for taxes claimed to be due and owing under the foregoing Act. The District Court entered judgments for the plaintiff. . . . It held that the taking of the fish was the taxable event, not the freezing of the fish.

On appeal the Court of Appeals held that respondents were taxable for fish caught by their catcher boats within territorial waters, even though the freezer ships remained outside the three-mile limit. In its view the catcher boats "operated by the freezer ship itself are but an extension of that ship's operations." It held, however, that respondents were not responsible for taxes on fish taken "by independent catcher boats but purchased by the freezer ships" outside territorial waters. There was a rehearing *en banc* and on the rehearing the Court of Appeals held that the tax incident was not taking fish but "the freezing and cold storage of fish aboard freezer ships." It held that the tax could not be levied even if the freezer ships received the salmon in territorial waters. It rea soned that the freezing and storage of the fish was an inseparable part of interstate commerce and could not be taxed locally any more than the loading and unloading of interstate carriers. . . . Accordingly it reversed the District Court. . . . The case is here on a petition for certiorari which we granted because of the importance of the ruling to the new State of Alaska. . . .

A tax on an integral part of an interstate movement might be imposed by other States "with the net effect of prejudicing or unduly burdening commerce" as the Court said in Michigan-Wisconsin Pipe Line Co. v. Calvert. . . .

We have no such problem here. This tax is one imposed on those "prosecuting or attempting to prosecute * * * lines of business in connection with Alaska's commercial fisheries." . . . The taxable event is "prosecuting" the "business" of "Freezer ships and other floating cold storages." Part of the business is, of course, transporting frozen fish interstate. Yet it is plain that a freezer ship is more—much more—than an interstate carrier. Part of its business is freezing fish. Yet these ships do more than freeze fish and transport them interstate. Taking the fish directly through their own catcher boats or obtaining them from other fishermen is also a part of respondents' business. Without the taking or obtaining of the fish, the freezer ship would have no function to perform.

It is clear that Alaska has power to regulate and control activity within her territorial waters, at least in the absence of conflicting federal legislation. . . . Alaska's jurisdiction to tax respondents' operations within her territorial waters —whether those activities are taking fish or purchasing fish taken by others—is equally clear. . . .

If the fish were taken or purchased outside Alaska's territorial waters, all of respondents' business in the Bristol Bay area would be beyond Alaska's reach. But since some of the fish in all of the cases before us were taken in Alaska's waters or otherwise acquired there, respondents are engaged in business in Alaska when they operate their "freezer ships." For we know from this record that in this particular business taking and freezing are practically inseparable. Fish are highly perishable and cannot be kept fresh very long even in Alaska's latitude. The process of gathering fish either through the catcher boats that are part of respondents' fleet or through independent operators is a "local activity" . . . in a vivid sense of the term. We see no reason why our cases involving the taking of shrimp (Toomer v. Witsell [334 *U.S.* 385]) and the extraction of ore (Oliver Iron Mining Co. v. Lord, 262 U.S. 172) are not dispositive of this controversy. The Oliver Iron case is indeed a first cousin of the present case. Here, as there, the tax is an occupation tax. Here, as there, the market for the product obtained locally is interstate, the taking being a step in a process leading to an interstate market. In both the local product is promptly loaded for interstate shipment. But in each there is a preliminary local business being conducted—an occupation made up of a series of local activities which the State can constitutionally reach. Catching the fish or obtaining them in other ways from the local market is but an extension of the freezer ship's operations within Alaska's waters.

It is claimed that there was no tax on salmon caught and frozen in Alaska and destined for canning in Alaska and that therefore this law is discriminatory against freezer ships. Alaskan canneries, however, paid a six-percent tax on the value of salmon obtained for canning; and local fish processors, which sell to the fresh-frozen consumer market, paid a one-percent tax. The freezer ships do not compete with those who freeze fish for the retail market. The freezer ships take their catches south for canning. Their competitors are the Alaskan canners; and we know from the record that fish canned locally usually are not frozen. When we look at the tax laid on local canners and those laid on "freezer ships," there is no discrimination in favor of the former and against the latter. For no matter how the tax on "freezer ships" is computed, it did not exceed the six-percent tax on the local canners. . . . If there is a difference between the taxes imposed on these freezer ships and the taxes imposed on their competitors, they are not so "palpably disproportionate" . . . as to run afoul of the Commerce Clause. No "iron rule of equality" between taxes laid by a State on different types of business is necessary. . . .

The judgment is reversed. Since we do not know how many fish, if any, were obtained outside Alaska's territorial waters, we remand the cause to the Court of Appeals for proceedings in conformity with this opinion.

Reversed.

Mr. Justice HARLAN, dissenting.

It is with reluctance that I have reached the conclusion that this Alaska tax offends the Commerce Clause of the Federal Constitution. . . .

The Court of Appeals concluded that the taxable event under this statute is the process of freezing fish aboard ship, ... Accepting, as I do, this construction of the statute, I agree with the Court of Appeals that a *privilege* tax directed solely at shipboard freezing, preparatory to interstate shipment, exceeds the limitations the Commerce Clause imposes upon the States, for in its requirement of a license such a tax asserts a power to deny what is a necessary local incident of the right to make interstate purchases. . . .

As I understand the Court's opinion, it seeks to meet this objection by denying that the Alaskan tax is imposed on the privilege of freezing fish aboard ships. It says that the tax is rather upon the local taking or purchase of fish *by or for freezer boats*. But even on this view of the incidence of the tax, I could not agree that the present tax on obtaining fish by or for interstate freezer boats would be constitutional in the given circumstances, for I do not think that Alaska can place a higher tax on the obtaining and freezing of fish for interstate markets than it places on the obtaining and freezing of fish for local markets. . . . As shown in the Court's opinion, under the Alaska scheme of taxation freezer boats, which operate solely in interstate commerce, must pay a tax for taking and freezing Alaskan fish for later canning in Washington which is four times that imposed on a local freezer whose product is sold to consumers in Alaska. A shore-based freezer who sells his frozen product to Alaskan canners pays no tax at all.

For these reasons I would affirm the judgment of the Court of Appeals.

MICHIGAN-WISCONSIN PIPE LINE COMPANY v. CALVERT

UNITED STATES SUPREME COURT

347 U.S. 157 (1954)

A Texas statute imposed a tax on the occupation of gathering gas. The Michigan-Wisconsin Pipe Line Co. sued in a Texas court to recover the money it had paid to Texas in complying with the statute. The Company argued that, since it was an interstate natural gas pipeline company, application of the tax law to the Company on its interstate operation constituted a state infringement of the Commerce Clause. The trial court upheld the contention of the Company but was reversed by a Texas court of civil appeals. When the Texas supreme court refused to take the case on appeal, the Company brought the case to the Supreme Court of the United States.

Mr. Justice CLARK delivered the opinion of the Court.

. . . .

THE QUESTION presented is whether the Commerce Clause is infringed by a Texas tax on the occupation of "gathering gas," measured by the entire volume of gas "taken," as applied to an interstate natural gas pipeline company, where the taxable incidence is the taking of gas from the outlet of an independent gasoline plant within the State for the purpose of immediate interstate transmission. In relevant part the tax statute provides that "In addition to all other licenses and taxes levied and assessed in the State of Texas, there is hereby levied upon every person engaged in gathering gas produced in this State, an occupation tax for the privilege of engaging in such business, at the rate of $\frac{9}{20}$ of one cent per thousand (1,000) cubic feet of gas gathered." Using a beggared definition of the term "gathering gas," the Act further provides that "In the case of gas containing gasoline or liquid hydrocarbons that are removed or extracted at a plant within the State by scrubbing, absorption, compression or any other process, the term 'gathering gas' means the first taking or the first retaining of possession of such gas for other processing or transmission whether through a pipeline, either common carrier or private, or otherwise after such gas has passed through the outlet of such plant." It also prohibits the "gatherer" as therein defined from shifting the burden of the tax to the producer of the gas, and provides that the tax shall not be levied as to gas gathered for local consumption if declared unconstitutional as to that gathered for interstate transmission.

Michigan-Wisconsin Pipe Line Company and Panhandle Eastern Pipe Line Company, appellants, are Delaware corporations and are natural gas companies holding certificates of convenience and necessity under the Natural Gas Act of 1938, . . . for the transportation and sale in interstate commerce of natural gas. The nature of their activities has been stipulated.

Michigan-Wisconsin has constructed a pipeline extending from Texas to Michigan and Wisconsin. At points in these two States and in Missouri and Iowa it sells gas to distribution companies which serve markets in those areas. It sells no gas in Texas. The company produces no gas; it purchases its supply from Phillips Petroleum Company in Texas, under a long-term contract. Phillips collects the gas from the wells and pipes it to a gasoline plant, where certain liquefiable hydrocarbons, oxygen, sulphur, hydrogen sulphide, dust and foreign substances are removed preparatory to the transmission of the residue. As this residue gas leaves the absorbers it flows through pipes owned by Phillips for a distance of 300 yards to the outlet of its gasoline plant, at the boundary between property of Phillips and property of Michigan-Wisconsin. Phillips has installed gas meters in its pipes at this point. The gas emerging from the outlet flows directly into two 26-inch pipelines of Michigan-Wisconsin. It is this "taking" that is made the taxable incidence of the statute. After the gas has been taken into the Michigan-Wisconsin pipes it flows a distance of approximately 1,215 feet to a compressor station owned and operated by Michigan-Wisconsin at which station the pressure of the gas is raised from about 200 pounds to some 975 pounds to facilitate movement to distant markets. In the course of its flow through this station the gas is compressed, cooled, scrubbed and dehydrated and then passes into a 24-inch pipeline which carries it 1.74 miles to the Oklahoma border and thence to markets outside Texas. Additional motive power is furnished by 15 other compressor stations in other states through which the gas is transported.

The entire movement of the gas, from producing wells through the Phillips gasoline plant and into the Michigan-Wisconsin pipeline to consumers outside Texas, is a steady and continuous flow. All of Michigan-Wisconsin's gas is purchased from Phillips for transportation to points outside Texas, and is in fact so transported.

Exclusive of the tax in question, Michigan-Wisconsin pays an ad valorem tax on the value of all its facilities and leases within the State. The State also levies on producers a tax of 5.72% of the value at the well of all gas produced in the State and a special tax to cover expenses in enforcing the conservation and proration laws.

The appellees place much emphasis upon the fact that Texas through these conservation and proration measures has afforded great benefits and protection to pipeline companies. It is beyond question that the enforcement of these laws has been not only in the public interest but to the commercial advantage of the industry. But, though this be an appealing truth, these benefits are relevant here only to show that essential requirements of due process have been met sufficiently to justify the imposition of *any* tax on the interstate activity. No challenge is made of the validity of the tax under the Due Process Clause, the appellants basing their objections only on the Commerce Clause, and when we proceed to examine the tax under the latter its validity "depends upon other considerations of constitutional policy having reference to the substantial effects, actual or potential, of the particular tax in suppressing or burdening unduly the commerce." . . . We proceed, therefore, to discuss only those relevant factors involved in the testing of the tax under the Commerce Clause.

The tax here assailed applies equally to gas moving in intrastate and interstate commerce. It is levied in addition to all other licenses and taxes and is denominated an occupation tax for the privilege of engaging in the "gathering of gas." Obviously appellants are not engaged in "gathering gas" within the meaning of that term in its ordinary usage; but the tax statute gives the term a transcendent scope; as to appellants' operations it is defined as "the first taking * * * of possession of such gas for other processing or transmission * * * after such gas has passed through the outlet" of a gasoline plant. The State Appellate Court realistically found "the taxable event described by the statute" to be "the taking or retaining of the gas at the gasoline plant outlet * * *." It thought that since this local activity was not subject to repetition elsewhere, "the sole question is whether such local activities are so closely related to and such an integral part of the interstate business of [appellants] who transport gas in interstate commerce as to be within the scope of the Commerce Clause of the Constitution." The court concluded that such taking "is just as local in nature as the production itself is local," and held the tax valid principally on the authority of Utah Power & Light Co. v. Pfost, 1932, 286 U.S. 165, and Hope Natural Gas Co. v. Hall, 1927, 274 U.S. 284.

We accept the State court's determination of the operating incidence of the tax, and we think the court has correctly stated the essential question presented. But we are unable to agree with its answer thereto or with its conclusion of constitutionality.

Appellants' business is the interstate transportation and sale of natural gas. Under the Commerce Clause interstate commerce and its instrumentalities are not totally immune from state taxation, absent action by Congress. Frequently it has been said that interstate business must pay its way . . . ; and the Court has done more than pay lip service to this idea. Numerous cases have upheld state levies where it is thought that the tax does not operate to discriminate against commerce or unduly burden it either directly or by the possibility of multiple taxation resulting from other taxes of the same sort being imposed by other states. The recurring problem is to resolve a conflict between the Constitution's mandate that trade between the states be permitted to flow freely without unnecessary obstruction from any source, and the state's rightful desire to require that interstate business bear its proper share of the costs of local government in return for benefits received. Some have thought that the wisest course would be for this Court to uphold all state taxes not patently discriminatory, and wait for Congress to adjust conflicts when and as it wished. But this view has not prevailed, and the Court has therefore been forced to decide in many varied factual situations whether the application of a given state tax to a given aspect of interstate activity violates the Commerce Clause. It is now well settled that a tax imposed on a local activity related to interstate commerce is valid if, and only if, the local activity is not such an integral part of the interstate process, the flow of commerce, that it cannot realistically be separated from it. . . . And if a genuine separation of the taxed local activity from the interstate process is impossible, it is more likely that other states through which the commerce passes or into which it flows can with equal right impose a similar levy on the goods, with the net effect of prejudicing or unduly burdening commerce.

The problem in this case is not whether the State could tax the actual gathering of all gas whether transmitted in interstate commerce or not, . . . but whether here the State has delayed the incidence of the tax beyond the step where production and processing have ceased and transmission in interstate commerce has begun. . . . The incidence of the tax here at issue, as stated by the Texas appellate court, is appellants' "taking" of gas from Phillips' gasoline plant. This event, as stipulated, occurs after the gas has been produced, gathered and processed by others than appellants. The "taking" into appellants' pipelines is solely for interstate transmission and the gas at that time is not only actually committed to but is moving in interstate commerce. What Texas seeks to tax is, therefore, more than merely the loading of an interstate carrier which was condemned in Joseph v. Carter & Weekes Stevedoring Co., 1947, 330 U.S. 422, for the gas here simultaneously enters the pipeline carrier and moves on continuously to its outside market. "There is no break, no period of deliberation, but a steady flow ending as contemplated from the beginning beyond the state line." . . . As early as Gloucester Ferry Co. v. Commonwealth of Pennsylvania, 1885, 114 U.S. 196, this Court said, "Receiving and landing passengers and freight is incident to their transportation." But receipt of the gas in the pipeline is more than its "taking"; from a practical standpoint it is its "taking off" in appellants' carrier into commerce; in reality the tax is, therefore, on the exit of the gas from the State. This economic process is inherently unsusceptible of division into a distinct local activity capable of forming the basis for the tax here imposed, on the one hand, and a separate movement in commerce, on the other. It is difficult to conceive of a factual situation where the incidence of taking or loading for transmission is more closely related to the transmission itself. This Court has held that much less integrated activity is "so closely related to interstate transportation as to be practically a part of it." We are therefore of the opinion that the taking of the gas here is essentially a part of interstate commerce itself. . . .

. . . .

Here it is perhaps sufficient that the privilege taxed, namely the taking of the gas, is not so separate and distinct from interstate transportation as to support the tax. But additional objection is present if the tax be upheld. It would "permit a multiple burden upon that commerce," . . . for if Texas may impose this "first taking" tax measured by the total volume of gas so taken, then Michigan and the other recipient states have at least equal right to tax the first taking or "unloading" from the pipeline of the same gas when it arrives for distribution. Oklahoma might then seek to tax the first taking of the gas as it crossed into that State. The net effect would be substantially to resurrect the customs barriers which the Commerce Clause was designed to eliminate. "The very purpose of the Commerce Clause was to create an area of free trade among the several States. That clause vested the power of taxing a transaction forming an unbroken process of interstate commerce in the Congress, not in the States." . . .

Reversed.

WILLIAMS v. *NORTH CAROLINA*

UNITED STATES SUPREME COURT

325 U.S. 226 (1945)

The facts in the case are spelled out in the opinion. Note carefully that this case was before the Supreme Court of the United States twice. The opinion offered below is from the second Williams *case. The citation for the first case is 317 U.S. 287 (1942).*

Mr. Justice FRANKFURTER delivered the opinion of the Court.

THIS CASE is here to review judgments of the Supreme Court of North Carolina, affirming convictions for bigamous cohabitation, assailed on the ground that full faith and credit, as required by the Constitution of the United States, was not accorded divorces decreed by one of the courts of Nevada. Williams v. North Carolina, 317 U.S. 287 [*the first case*], decided an earlier aspect of the controversy. It was there held that a divorce granted by Nevada, on a finding that one spouse was domiciled in Nevada, must be respected in North Carolina, where Nevada's finding of domicil was not questioned though the other spouse had neither appeared nor been served with process in Nevada and though recognition of such a divorce offended the policy of North Carolina. The record then before us did not present the question whether North Carolina had the power "to refuse full faith and credit to Nevada divorce decrees because, contrary to the findings of the Nevada court, North Carolina finds that no bona fide domicil was acquired in Nevada." Williams v. North Carolina, supra, 317 U.S. at page 302. This is the precise issue which has emerged after retrial of the cause following our reversal. Its obvious importance brought the case here. . . .

The implications of the Full Faith and Credit Clause, Article IV, Section 1 of the Constitution, first received the sharp analysis of this Court in Thompson v. Whitman, 18 Wall. 457. . . . The essence of the matter was thus put in what Thompson v. Whitman adopted from Story: " 'The Constitution did not mean to confer (upon the States) a new power or jurisdiction, but simply to regulate the effect of the acknowledged jurisdiction over persons and things within their territory.' " . . . In short, the Full Faith and Credit Clause puts the Constitution behind a judgment instead of the too fluid, ill-defined concept of "comity."

But the Clause does not make a sister-State judgment a judgment in another State. The proposal to do so was rejected by the Philadelphia Convention. . . . "To give it the force of a judgment in another state, it must be made a judgment there." . . . It can be made a judgment there only if the court purporting to render the original judgment had power to render such a judgment. A judgment in one State is conclusive upon the merits in every other State, but only if the court of the first State had power to pass on the merits—had jurisdiction, that is, to render the judgment.

. . . .

Under our system of law, judicial power to grant a divorce—jurisdiction, strictly speaking—is founded on domicil. . . . The framers of the Constitution were familiar with this jurisdictional prerequisite, and since 1789 neither this Court nor any other court in the English-speaking world has questioned it. Domicil implies a nexus between person and place of such permanence as to control the creation of legal relations and responsibilities of the utmost significance. The domicil of one spouse within a State gives power to that State, we have held, to dissolve a marriage wheresoever contracted. In view of Williams v. North Carolina, supra, the jurisdictional requirement of domicil is freed from confusing refinements about "matrimonial domicil,". . . Divorce, like marriage, is of concern not merely to the immediate parties. It affects personal rights of the deepest significance. It also touches basic interests of society. Since divorce, like marriage, creates a new status, every consideration of policy makes it desirable that the effect should be the same wherever the question arises.

It is one thing to reopen an issue that has been settled after appropriate opportunity to present their contentions has been afforded to all who had an interest in its adjudication. This applies also to jurisdictional questions. After a contest these cannot be relitigated as between the parties. . . . But those not parties to a litigation ought not to be foreclosed by the interested actions of others; especially not a State which is concerned with the vindication of its own social policy and has no means, certainly no effective means, to protect that interest against the selfish action of those outside its borders. The State of domiciliary origin should not be bound by an unfounded, even if not collusive, recital in the record of a court of another State. As to the truth or existence of a fact, like that of domicil, upon which depends the power to exert judicial authority, a State not a party to the exertion of such judicial authority in another State but seriously affected by it has a right, when asserting its own unquestioned authority, to ascertain the truth or existence of that crucial fact.

These considerations of policy are equally applicable whether power was assumed by the court of the first State or claimed after inquiry. This may lead, no doubt, to conflicting determinations of what judicial power is founded upon. Such conflict is inherent in the practical application of the concept of domicil in the context of our federal system. . . . "Neither the Fourteenth Amendment nor the full faith and credit clause * * * requires uniformity in the decisions of the courts of different states as to the place of domicil, where the exertion of state power is dependent upon domicil within its boundaries." . . . * * * If a finding by the court of one State that domicil in another State has been abandoned were conclusive upon the old domiciliary State, the policy of each State in matters of most intimate concern could be subverted by the policy of every other State. This Court has long ago denied the existence of such destructive power. The issue has a far reach. For domicil is the foundation of probate jurisdiction precisely as it is that of divorce. . . .

. . . .

All the world is not party to a divorce proceeding. What is true is that all the world need not be present before a court granting the decree and yet it must be respected by the other forty-seven States provided—and it is a big proviso—the conditions for the exercise of power by the divorce-decreeing court are validly established whenever that judgment is elsewhere called into question. In short, the decree of divorce is a conclusive adjudication of everything except the jurisdictional facts upon which it is founded, and domicil is a jurisdictional fact. To permit the necessary finding of domicil by one State to foreclose all States in the protection of their social institutions would be intolerable.

But to endow each State with controlling authority to nullify the power of a sister State to grant a divorce based upon a finding that one spouse had acquired a new domicil within the divorcing State would, in the proper functioning of our federal system, be equally indefensible. No State court can assume comprehensive attention to the various and potentially conflicting interests that several States may have in the institutional aspects of marriage. The necessary accommodation between the right of one State to safeguard its interest in the family relation of its own people and the power of another State to grant divorces can be left to neither State.

The problem is to reconcile the reciprocal respect to be accorded by the members of the Union to their adjudications with due regard for another most important aspect of our federalism whereby "the domestic relations of husband and wife * * * were matters reserved to the States," . . . and do not belong to the United States. . . . The rights that belong to all the States and the obligations which membership in the Union imposes upon all, are made effective because this Court is open to consider claims, such as this case presents, that the courts of one State have not given the full faith and credit to the judgment of a sister State that is required by . . . the Constitution.

But the discharge of this duty does

not make of this Court a court of probate and divorce. Neither a rational system of law nor hard practicality calls for our independent determination, in reviewing the judgment of a State court, of that rather elusive relation between person and place which establishes domicil. "It is not for us to retry the facts," as was held in a case in which, like the present, the jurisdiction underlying a sister-State judgment was dependent on domicil. . . . The challenged judgment must, however, satisfy our scrutiny that the reciprocal duty of respect owed by the States to one another's adjudications has been fairly discharged, and has not been evaded under the guise of finding an absence of domicil and therefore a want of power in the court rendering the judgment.

What is immediately before us is the judgment of the Supreme Court of North Carolina. . . . We have authority to upset it only if there is want of foundation for the conclusion that that Court reached. The conclusion it reached turns on its finding that the spouses who obtained the Nevada decrees were not domiciled there. The fact that the Nevada court found that they were domiciled there is entitled to respect, and more. The burden of undermining the verity which the Nevada decrees import rests heavily upon the assailant. But simply because the Nevada court found that it had power to award a divorce decree cannot, we have seen, foreclose reexamination by another State. Otherwise, as was pointed out long ago, a court's record would establish its power and the power would be proved by the record. Such circular reasoning would give one State a control over all the other States which the Full Faith and Credit Clause certainly did not confer. . . . If this Court finds that proper weight was accorded to the claims of power by the court of one State in rendering a judgment the validity of which is pleaded in defense in another State, that the burden of overcoming such respect by disproof of the substratum of fact—here domicil—on which such power alone can rest was properly charged against the party challenging the legitimacy of the judgment, that such issue of fact was left for fair determination by appropriate procedure, and that a finding adverse to the necessary foundation for any valid sister-State judgment was amply supported in evidence, we can not upset the judgment before us. And we cannot do so even if we also found in the record of the court of original judgment warrant for its finding that it had jurisdiction. If it is a matter turning on local law, great deference is owed by the courts of one State to what a court of another State has done. . . . But when we are dealing as here with an historic notion common to all English-speaking courts, that of domicil, we should not find a want of deference to a sister State on the part of a court of another State which finds an absence of domicil where such a conclusion is warranted by the record.

When this case was first here, North Carolina did not challenge the finding of the Nevada court that petitioners had acquired domicils in Nevada. . . . Upon retrial, however, the existence of domicil in Nevada became the decisive issue. The judgments of conviction now under review bring before us a record which may be fairly summarized by saying that the petitioners left North Carolina for the purpose of getting divorces from their respective spouses in Nevada and as soon as each had done so and married one another they left Nevada and returned to North Carolina to live there together as man and wife. Against the charge of bigamous cohabitation under . . . the North Carolina General Statutes, petitioners stood on their Nevada divorces and offered exemplified copies of the Nevada proceedings. The trial judge charged that the State had the burden of proving beyond a reasonable doubt that (1) each petitioner was lawfully married to one person; (2) thereafter each petitioner contracted a second marriage with another person outside North Carolina; (3) the spouses of petitioners were living at the time of this second marriage; (4) petitioners cohabited with one another in North Carolina after the second marriage. The burden, it was charged, then devolved upon petitioners "to satisfy the trial jury, not beyond a reasonable doubt nor by the greater weight of the evidence, but simply to satisfy" the jury from all the evidence, that petitioners were domiciled in Nevada at the time they obtained their divorces. The court further charged that "the recitation" of bona fide domicil in the Nevada decree was "prima facie evidence" sufficient to warrant a finding of domicil in Nevada but not compelling "such an inference." If the jury found, as they were told, that petitioners had domicils in North Carolina and went to Nevada "simply and solely for the purpose of obtaining" divorces, intending to return to North Carolina on obtaining them, they never lost their North Carolina domicils nor acquired new domicils in Nevada. Domicil, the jury was instructed, was that place where a person "has voluntarily fixed his abode * * * not for a mere special or temporary purpose, but with a present intention of making it his home, either permanently or for an indefinite or unlimited length of time."

The scales of justice must not be unfairly weighted by a State when full faith and credit is claimed for a sister-State judgment. But North Carolina has not so dealt with the Nevada decrees. She has not raised unfair barriers to their recognition. North Carolina did not fail in appreciation or application of federal standards of full faith and credit. Appropriate weight was given to the finding of domicil in the Nevada decrees, and that finding was allowed to be overturned only by relevant standards of proof. There is nothing to suggest that the issue was not fairly submitted to the jury and that it was not fairly assessed on cogent evidence.

State courts cannot avoid review by this Court of their disposition of a constitutional claim by casting it in the form of an unreviewable finding of fact. . . . This record is barren of such attempted evasion. What it shows is that petitioners, long-time residents of North Carolina, came to Nevada, where they stayed in an auto-court for transients, filed suits for divorce as soon as the Nevada law permitted, married one another as soon as the divorces were obtained, and promptly returned to North Carolina to live. It cannot reasonably be claimed that one set of inferences rather than another regarding the acquisition by petitioners of new domicils in Nevada could not be drawn from the circumstances attending their Nevada divorces. It would be highly unreasonable to assert that a jury could not reasonably find that the evidence demonstrated that petitioners went to Nevada solely for the purpose of obtaining a divorce and intended all along to return to North Carolina. Such an intention, the trial court properly charged, would preclude acquisition of domicils in Nevada. . . . And so we can not say that North Carolina was not entitled to draw the inference that petitioners never abandoned their domicils in North Carolina, particularly since we could not conscientiously prefer, were it our business to do so, the contrary finding of the Nevada court.

If a State cannot foreclose, on review here, all the other States by its finding that one spouse is domiciled within its bounds, persons may, no doubt, place themselves in situations that create unhappy consequences for them. This is merely one of those untoward results inevitable in a federal system in which regulation of domestic relations has been left with the States and not given to the national authority. But the occasional disregard by any one State of the reciprocal obligations of the forty-eight States to respect the constitutional power of each to deal with domestic relations of those domiciled within its borders is hardly an argument for allowing one State to deprive the other forty-seven States of their constitutional rights. Relevant statistics happily do not justify lurid forebodings that parents without number will disregard the fate of their offspring by being unmindful of the status of dignity to which they are entitled. But, in any event, to the extent that some one State may, for considerations of its own, improperly intrude into domestic relations subject to the authority of the other States, it suffices to suggest that any such indifference by a State to the bond of the Union should be discouraged not encouraged.

In seeking a decree of divorce outside the State in which he has theretofore maintained his marriage, a person is necessarily involved in the legal situation created by our federal system whereby one State can grant a divorce of validity in other States only if the applicant has a bona fide domicil in the State of the court purporting to dissolve a prior legal marriage. The petitioners therefore assumed the risk that this Court would find that North Carolina justifiably concluded that they had not been domiciled in Nevada. Since the divorces which they sought and received in Nevada had no legal validity in North Carolina and their North Carolina spouses were still alive, they subjected themselves to prosecution for bigamous cohabitation under North Carolina law. The legitimate finding of the North Carolina Supreme Court that the petitioners were not in truth domiciled in Nevada was not a contingency against which the petitioners were protected by anything in the Constitution of the United States. A man's fate often depends, as for instance in the enforcement of the Sherman Law, . . . on far greater risks that he will estimate "rightly, that is, as the jury subsequently estimates it, some matter of degree. If his judgment is wrong, not only may he incur a fine or a short imprisonment, as here; he may incur the penalty of death." . . . The objection that punishment of a person for an act as a crime when ignorant of the facts making it so, involves a denial of due process of law has more than once been overruled. In vindicating its public policy and particularly one so important as that bearing upon the integrity of family life, a State in punishing particular acts may provide that "he who shall do them shall do them at his peril and will not be heard to plead in defense good faith or ignorance." . . . Mistaken notions about one's legal rights are not sufficient to bar prosecution for crime.

We conclude that North Carolina was not required to yield her State policy because a Nevada court found that petitioners were domiciled in Nevada when it granted them decrees of divorce. North Carolina was entitled to find, as she did, that they did not acquire domicils in Nevada and that the Nevada court was therefore without power to liberate the petitioners from amenability to the laws of North Carolina governing domestic relations. And, as was said in connection with another aspect of the Full Faith and Credit Clause, our conclusion "is not a matter to arouse the susceptibilities of the states, all of which are equally concerned in the question and equally on both sides." . . .

As for the suggestion that Williams v. North Carolina, supra, foreclosed the Supreme Court of North Carolina from ordering a second trial upon the issue of domicil, it suffices to refer to our opinion in the earlier case.

Affirmed.

Mr. Justice MURPHY, concurring.

While I join in the opinion of the Court, certain considerations compel me to state more fully my views on the important issues presented by this case.

The State of Nevada has unquestioned authority, consistent with procedural due process, to grant divorces on whatever basis it sees fit to all who meet its statutory requirements. It is entitled, moreover, to give to its divorce decrees absolute and binding finality within the confines of its borders.

But if Nevada's divorce decrees are to be accorded full faith and credit in the courts of her sister states it is essential that Nevada have proper jurisdiction over the divorce proceedings. This means that at least one of the parties to each ex parte proceeding must have a bona fide domicil within Nevada for whatever length of time Nevada may prescribe. This elementary principle has been reiterated by this Court many times. . . .

. . . .

The jury has here found that the petitioner's alleged domicil in Nevada was not a bona fide one, which in common and legal parlance means that it was acquired fraudulently, deceitfully or in bad faith. This means, in other words, that the jury found that the petitioners' residence in Nevada for six weeks was not accompanied by a bona fide intention to make Nevada their home and to remain there permanently or at least for an indefinite time, as required even by Nevada law. . . . This conclusion is supported by overwhelming evidence satisfying whatever standard of proof may be propounded. Under these circumstances there is no reason to doubt the efficacy of jury trials in relation to the question of domicil or to speculate as to whether another jury might have reached a different verdict on the same set of facts.

Thus the court below properly concluded that Nevada was without jurisdiction so as to give extraterritorial validity to the divorce decrees and that North Carolina was not compelled by the Constitution to give full faith and credit to the Nevada decrees. North Carolina was free to consider the original marriages still in effect, the Nevada divorces to be invalid, and the Nevada marriage to be bigamous, thus giving the Nevada marriage the same force and effect that Nevada presumably would have given it had Nevada considered the original marriages still outstanding. . . .

By being domiciled and living in North Carolina, petitioners secured all the benefits and advantages of its government and participated in its social and economic life. As long as petitioners and their respective spouses lived there and retained that domicil, North Carolina had the exclusive right to regulate the dissolution of their marriage relationships. However harsh and unjust North Carolina's divorce laws may be thought to be, petitioners were bound to obey them while retaining residential and domiciliary ties in that state.

No justifiable purpose is served by imparting constitutional sanctity to the efforts of petitioners to establish a false and fictitious domicil in Nevada. Such a result would only tend to promote wholesale disregard of North Carolina's divorce laws by its citizens, thus putting an end to "the existence of all efficacious power on the subject of divorce." . . . Certainly no policy of Nevada dictates lending the full faith and credit clause to protect actions grounded in deceit. Nevada has a recognizable interest in granting only two types of ex parte divorces: (a) Those effective solely within the borders of Nevada, and (b) those effective everywhere on the ground that at least one of the parties had a bona fide domicil in the state at the time the decree was granted. Neither type of divorce is involved here. And Nevada has no interest that we can respect in issuing divorce decrees with extraterritorial effect to those who are domiciled elsewhere and who secure sham domicils in Nevada solely for divorce purposes.

There are no startling or dangerous implications in the judgment reached by the Court in this case. All of the uncontested divorces that have ever been granted in the forty-eight states are as secure today as they were yesterday or as they were before our previous decision in this case. Those based upon fraudulent domicils are now and always have been subject to later reexamination with possible serious consequences.

Whatever embarrassment or inconvenience resulting to those who have made property settlements, contracted new marriages or otherwise acted in reliance upon divorce decrees obtained under conditions found to exist in this case is not insurmountable. The states have adequate power, if they desire to exercise it, to enact legislation providing for means of validating any such property settlements or marriages or of relieving persons from other unfortunate consequences.

Nor are any issues of civil liberties at stake here. It is unfortunate that the petitioners must be imprisoned for acts which they probably committed in reliance upon advice of counsel and without intent to violate the North Carolina statute. But there are many instances of punishment for acts whose criminality was unsuspected at the time of their occurrence. Indeed, for nearly three-quarters of a century or more individuals have been punished under bigamy statutes for doing exactly what petitioners have done. . . . Petitioners especially must be deemed to have been aware of the possible criminal consequences of their actions in view of the previously settled North Carolina law on the matter. . . . This case, then, adds no new uncertainty and comes as no surprise for those who act fraudulently in establishing a domicil and who disregard the laws of their true domiciliary states.

. . . .

The CHIEF JUSTICE and Mr. Justice JACKSON join in these views.

Mr. Justice RUTLEDGE, dissenting.

Once again the ghost of "unitary domicil" returns on its perpetual round, in the guise of "jurisdictional fact," to upset judgments, marriages, divorces, undermine the relations founded upon them, and make this Court the unwilling and uncertain arbiter between the concededly valid laws and decrees of sister states. . . .

Nevada's judgment has not been voided. It could not be, if the same test applies to sustain it as upholds the North Carolina conviction. It stands, with the marriages founded upon it, unimpeached. For all that has been determined or could be, unless another change is in the making, petitioners are lawful husband and wife in Nevada. . . . They may be such everywhere outside North Carolina. Lawfully wedded also, in North Carolina, are the divorced spouse of one and his wife, taken for all we know in reliance upon the Nevada decree. That is, unless another jury shall find they too are bigamists for their reliance. No such jury has been impanelled. But were one called, it could pronounce the Nevada decree valid upon the identical evidence from which the jury in this case drew the contrary conclusion. That jury or it and another, if petitioners had been tried separately, could have found one guilty, the other innocent, upon that evidence unvaried by a hair. And, by the Court's test, we could do nothing but sustain the contradictory findings in all these cases.

I do not believe the Constitution has thus confided to the caprice of juries the faith and credit due the laws and judgments of sister states. Nor has it thus made that question a local matter for the states themselves to decide. Were all judgments given the same infirmity, the full faith and credit clause would be only a dead constitutional letter.

I agree it is not the Court's business to determine policies of divorce. But precisely its function is to lay the jurisdictional foundations upon which the states' determinations can be made effective, within and without their borders. For in the one case due process, in the other full faith and credit, commands of equal compulsion upon the states and upon us, impose that duty.

I do not think we perform it, we rather abdicate, when we confide the ultimate decision to the states or to their juries. This we do when, for every case that matters, we make their judgment conclusive. It is so in effect when the crucial concept is as variable and amorphous as "domicil," is always a conclusion of "ultimate fact," and can be established only by proof from which, as experience shows, contradictory inferences may be made as strikes the local trier's fancy. The abdication only becomes more obviously explicit when we avowedly confess that the faith and credit due may be determined either way, wherever "it cannot reasonably be claimed that one set of inferences rather than another" could not be drawn concerning the very matter determined by the judgment; and the final choice upon such a balance is left with the local jury.

No more unstable foundation, for state policies or marital relations, could be formulated or applied. In no region of adjudication or legislation is stability more essential for jurisdictional foundations. Beyond abnegating our function, we make instability itself the constitutional policy when the crux is so conceived and pivoted.

. . . .

Mr. Justice BLACK, dissenting.

Anglo-American law has, until today, steadfastly maintained the principle that before an accused can be convicted of crime, he must be proven guilty beyond a reasonable doubt. These petitioners have been sentenced to prison because they were unable to prove their innocence to the satisfaction of the State of North Carolina. They have been convicted under a statute so uncertain in its application that not even the most learned member of the bar could have advised them in advance as to whether their conduct would violate the law. In reality the petitioners are being deprived of their freedom because the State of Nevada, through its legislature and courts, follows a liberal policy in granting divorces. They had Nevada divorce decrees which authorized them to remarry. Without charge or proof of fraud in obtaining these decrees, and without holding the decrees invalid under Nevada law, this Court affirms a conviction of petitioners, for living together as husband and wife. I cannot reconcile this with the Full Faith and Credit Clause and with congressional legislation passed pursuant to it.

It is my firm conviction that these convictions cannot be harmonized with vital constitutional safeguards designed to safeguard individual liberty and to unite all the states of this whole country into one nation. The fact that two people will be deprived of their constitutional rights impels me to protest as vigorously as I can against affirmance of these convictions. Even more, the Court's opinion today will cast a cloud over the lives of countless numbers of the multitude of divorced persons in the United States. The importance of the issues prompts me to set out my views in some detail.

Statistics indicate that approximately five million divorced persons are scattered throughout the forty-eight states. More than 85% of the divorces were granted in uncontested proceedings. Not one of this latter group can now retain any feeling of security in his divorce decree. Ever present will be the danger of criminal prosecution and harassment.

All these decrees were granted by state courts. . . . These judicial "laws" are represented by decrees, judgments and court opinions. Today's opinion, however, undermines and makes uncertain the validity of every uncontested divorce decree. It wipes out every semblance of their finality and decisiveness. It achieves what the Court terms the "desirable effect" of providing the "same" quality to *every* divorce decree, "wherever the question arises"—it endows them all alike with the "same" instability and precariousness. The result is to classify divorced persons in a distinctive and invidious category. . . .

The petitioners were married in Nevada. North Carolina has sentenced them to prison for living together as husband and wife in North Carolina. This Court today affirms those sentences without a determination that the Nevada marriage was invalid under that State's laws. This holding can be supported, if at all, only on one of two grounds: (1) North Carolina has extraterritorial power to regulate marriages within Nevada's territorial boundaries, or (2) North Carolina can punish people who live together in that state as husband and wife even though they have been validly married in Nevada. A holding based on either of these two grounds encroaches upon the general principle recognized by this Court that a marriage validly consummated under one state's laws is valid in every other state. If the Court is today abandoning that principle, it takes away from the states a large part of their hitherto plenary control over the institution of marriage. A further consequence is to subject people to criminal prosecutions for adultery and bigamy merely because they exercise their constitutional right to pass from a state in which they were validly married into another state which refuses to recognize their marriage. Such a consequence runs counter to the basic guarantees of our federal union. . . . It is true that persons validly married under the laws of one state have been convicted of crime for living together in other states. But those state convictions were not approved by this Court. And never before today has this Court decided a case upon the assumption that men and women validly married under the laws of one state could be sent to jail by another state for conduct which involved nothing more than living together as husband and wife.

. . . .

The Court permits North Carolina to disregard the decrees on the following line of reasoning. No state need give full faith and credit to a "void" decree. A decree rendered by a court without "jurisdiction" is "void." No state court has "jurisdiction" to grant a divorce unless one of the parties is "domiciled" in the state. The North Carolina court has decided that these petitioners had no "domicile" in Nevada. Therefore, the Nevada court had no "jurisdiction," the decrees are "void," and North Carolina need not give them faith or credit. The solution to all these problems depends in turn upon the question common to all of them—does State law or Federal law apply?

. . . .

This brings me to the Court's holding that Nevada decrees were "void." That conclusion rests on the premise that the Nevada court was without jurisdiction because the North Carolina Court found that the petitioners had no "domicile" in Nevada. The Nevada court had based its decree on a finding that "domicile" had been established by evidence before it. As I read that evidence, it would have been sufficient to support the findings, had the case been reviewed by us. Thus, this question of fact has now been adjudicated in two state courts with different results. . . . The Court today, however, seems to place its holding that the Nevada decrees are void on the basis that the Due Process Clause makes domicile an indispensable prerequisite to a state court's "jurisdiction" to grant divorce. It further holds that this newly created federal restriction of state courts projects fact issues which the state courts cannot finally determine for themselves. . . .

I cannot agree to this latest expansion of federal power and the consequent diminution of state power over marriage and marriage dissolution which the Court derives from adding a new content to the Due Process Clause. The elasticity of that clause necessary to justify this holding is found, I suppose, in the notion that it was intended to give this Court unlimited authority to supervise all assertions of state and federal power to see that they comport with our ideas of what are "civilized standards of law." . . . Certainly, there is no language in the Constitution which even remotely suggests that the Federal government can fix the limits of a state court's jurisdiction over divorces. In doing so, the Court today exalts "domicile," dependent upon a mental state, to a position of constitutional dignity. State jurisdiction in divorce cases now depends upon a state of mind as to future intent. Thus "a hair perhaps divides" the constitutional jurisdiction or lack of jurisdiction of state courts to grant divorces. . . . And this "hair-line" division involves a federal question, apparently open to repeated adjudications at the instance of as many different parties as can be found to raise it. Moreover, since it is a federal question, each new litigant has a statutory right to ask us to pass on it.

. . . .

Implicit in the majority of the opinions rendered by this and other courts, which, whether designedly or not, have set up obstacles to the procurement of divorces, is the assumption that divorces are an unmitigated evil, and that the law can and should force unwilling persons to live with each other. Others approach the problem as one which can best be met by moral, ethical and religious teachings. Which viewpoint is correct is not our concern. I am confident, however, that today's decision will no more aid in the solution of the problem than the Dred Scott decision aided in settling controversies over slavery. This decision, I think, takes the wrong road. Federal courts should have less, not more, to do with divorces. Only when one state refuses to give that faith and credit to a divorce decree which Congress and the Constitution command, should we enter this field.

. . . .

. . . While the doctrine that "Ignorance of the law excuses no man" has sometimes been applied with harsh consequences, American courts have not been in the habit of making ignorance of law the crucial and controlling element in a penitentiary offense. Men have from time to time been sent to prison for violating court commands which were later held invalid. It is quite a different thing, however, to send people to prison for lacking the clairvoyant gift of prophesying when one judge or jury will upset the findings of fact made by another.

In earlier times, some Rulers placed their criminal laws where the common man could not see them, in order that he might be entrapped into their violation. Others imposed standards of conduct impossible of achievement to the end that those obnoxious to the ruling powers might be convicted under the forms of law. No one of them ever provided a more certain entrapment, than a statute which prescribes a penitentiary punishment for nothing more than a layman's failure to prophesy what a judge or jury will do. This Court's decision of a federal question today does just that.

Mr. Justice DOUGLAS joins in this dissent.

ARMSTRONG v. ARMSTRONG

UNITED STATES SUPREME COURT

350 U.S. 568 (1956)

The facts are set forth in the opinion.

Mr. Justice MINTON delivered the opinion of the Court.

. . . .

THE PETITIONER, while residing in Dade County, Florida, filed a suit for divorce from his wife, who had separated from him and gone to Ohio, where she had established her residence. The wife was not personally served, nor did she appear in person or by attorney in the Florida suit. Service on her was constructive only. A divorce decree was granted petitioner by the Florida court, and he contends that that court also denied alimony to the respondent.

Later, the respondent wife instituted a suit in Ohio for divorce and for alimony. The petitioner appeared and set up the divorce obtained in Florida. The Ohio court found that the respondent had established grounds for divorce in Ohio but denied the divorce because Florida had already decreed a divorce to the petitioner. The Ohio court proceeded to pass on the question of alimony and granted the wife alimony, taking into account the total property owned by the petitioner. The petitioner appealed to the Court of Appeals, . . . and then to the Supreme Court of Ohio, which affirmed the judgments of the lower courts. . . . Petitioner argued and contends here that the Ohio courts have denied full faith and credit to the Florida decree. We granted certiorari. . . .

The sole question presented by the petition for certiorari was whether the Ohio courts were required to give full faith and credit to the *ex parte* Florida divorce decree, which petitioner alleges not only granted him a divorce but also decreed that the wife was not entitled to alimony. As we interpret the Florida decree, however, the Florida court did not purport to adjudicate the absent wife's right to alimony. The Ohio courts, therefore, in awarding alimony to the wife, did not in fact fail to give full faith and credit to the Florida decree. Accordingly, we do not reach the constitutional question sought to be presented. But even if there is doubt as to the meaning of the Florida decree, we should construe its action as a refusal to pass on the question of alimony and thus avoid the constitutional question as to its power to do so.

The Florida court found that Mrs. Armstrong "has not come into this court in good faith or made any claim to the equitable conscience of the court and has made no showing of any need on her part for alimony. It is, therefore, specifically decreed that no award of alimony be made to the defendant * * *." Taken literally, that language means only that, for the reasons it gave, the court would refrain from making an affirmative award of alimony to the wife, not that it adjudicated in favor of the husband that his wife was not entitled to alimony. The husband's bill of complaint did not ask for greater relief. It offered to show that Mrs. Armstrong's interest in jointly held property was "ample to support the defendant and that she has no further need of alimony." The purpose of this offer, however, was revealed by the next sentence of the complaint: "Nevertheless the plaintiff hereby offers to do equity and to abide by such orders or decrees, with reference to the settlement of the property affairs, as to this court may be deemed equitable." Thus the husband did not seek a decree holding the wife not entitled to alimony but rather merely submitted to the court's jurisdiction to condition its grant of divorce to him upon an award of alimony to his wife. The prayer for relief was fully satisfied by the decision that protection of the absent wife did not require the court to fix alimony before granting the divorce.

The Florida master's report is confirmatory of the limited scope of the decree. The master stated that "the question of the wife's alimony, if any, cannot be determined at this stage of the proceeding," pointing out that most of the marital property was in the wife's possession in Ohio and was the subject matter of litigation pending there. He accordingly found that "the defendant is not entitled to receive alimony * * * under the facts and circumstances presented in this case" and recommended "that no award of alimony be made." The master's recommendation meant no more than that the question of alimony should not be decided because the wife had in her possession property adequate to meet her immediate needs, and the unresolved litigation made it impossible to determine her future needs. Presumably, the court's decree meant no more when it adopted in terms the master's recommendation that "no award of alimony be made." Like the master's report, the decree expressly recognized that the parties' property rights depended upon the outcome of the pending litigation in Ohio and that the wife had not shown any need for alimony.

When the Florida court said, "it is, therefore, specifically decreed that no award of alimony be made to the defendant," it recognized that no issue of alimony should be decided by it. The court simply said that no award of alimony be made—a purely negative assertion that it would not pass on the question.

It is true that the decree "that no award of alimony be made" was followed in the same sentence by a declaration, based on the court's and master's view of Florida property law, quieting title in the husband to certain Florida real property. At most, however, the fact that both matters were dealt with in a single sentence suggests only that the court might have reserved alimony out of that specific property had it concluded that such action was necessary to protect the wife's interest. That it did not do so is consistent with our conclusion that the Florida court did no more than refrain from awarding alimony at that time.

There was a valid decree in Florida dissolving the bonds of matrimony. There was no decree as to alimony. Ohio had personal service on both parties in a suit for divorce and alimony brought there by Mrs. Armstrong. The court denied her a decree of divorce because Florida had already dissolved the bonds of matrimony. The Ohio court found that, but for the decree in Florida, Mrs. Armstrong had established grounds for divorce in the Ohio suit. It considered that the matter before it was not a division of property, but an application for alimony, and it proceeded to hear evidence on that basis and finally entered a personal judgment against the defendant husband for alimony. The Ohio court, which had complete jurisdiction of both parties and the cause of action, entered a decree as to alimony only, which decree seems clearly authorized by the Ohio cases. . . . The Florida judgment was given full faith and credit by Ohio as far as the judgment in Florida went, and no other questions are presented here.

The judgment is affirmed.

Affirmed.

. . . .

[*Mr. Justice FRANKFURTER argued in a concurring opinion that the case should have been dismissed "for want of jurisdiction."*]

Mr. Justice BLACK, with whom The CHIEF JUSTICE, Mr. Justice DOUGLAS, and Mr. Justice CLARK join, concurring.

The opinion of the Court takes the position that the Florida court did not adjudicate Mrs. Armstrong's right to alimony. We cannot agree. In the husband's Florida complaint he alleged that his wife's property was "ample to support the defendant and that she has no further need of alimony or property settlement." The Florida court expressly held that it had jurisdiction over both parties and over the subject matter of the complaint. It then proceeded to find that the wife was at fault in leaving her husband and the "matrimonial domicile." The court even suggested that Mrs. Armstrong was guilty of a criminal act in taking some of her husband's money and securities to Ohio. The decree continued: "This court, *therefore*, finds the defendant has not come into this court in good faith or made any claim to the equitable conscience of the court and has made no showing of any need on her part for alimony. It is, *therefore, specifically decreed* that no award of alimony be made to the defendant * * *." (Emphasis added.) This was plainly a denial of alimony, not on the ground that the court was leaving the matter open but because the judge thought the wife should not have alimony.

We agree with the majority that the Ohio decree was an alimony judgment and not a division of property. Thus in our view there is a direct conflict between that decree and the decree of the Florida court denying alimony to the wife. We therefore reach the constitutional question whether the Ohio court was justified in denying full faith and credit to the Florida decree.

We believe that Ohio was not compelled to give full faith and credit to the Florida decree denying alimony to Mrs. Armstrong. Our view is based on the absence of power in the Florida court to render a personal judgment against Mrs. Armstrong depriving her of all right to alimony although she was a nonresident of Florida, had not been personally served with process in that State, and had not appeared as a party. It has been the constitutional rule in this country at least since Pennoyer v. Neff, 95 U.S. 714, decided in 1878, that nonresidents cannot be subjected to personal judgments without such service or appearance. We held in Estin v. Estin, 334 U.S. 541, that an alimony judgment was this kind of "personal judgment." . . . The Estin case was much like this one. There, after the wife had obtained a separation and permanent alimony decree in New York, the husband went to Nevada and obtained a divorce. In accord with our previous holding in Williams v. State of North Carolina, 317 U.S. 287, . . . we held that the Nevada divorce was valid and must be given full faith and credit by New York even though rendered without personal service on the wife. It was argued that New York also had to recognize Nevada's rule of law that the dissolution of a marriage put an end to a support order. We held, however, that Nevada could not adjudicate rights of the wife under the New

York judgment because she had not been personally served with process and did not appear in the Nevada proceedings. 334 U.S. at 547–549. The considerations supporting that holding are applicable here. The fact that Mrs. Estin's claim to support had been reduced to judgment prior to divorce while Mrs. Armstrong's had not is not a meaningful distinction. Mrs. Armstrong's right to support before judgment like Mrs. Estin's right to support after judgment, is the kind of personal right which cannot be adjudicated without personal service. . . .

The husband here seeks to distinguish the Estin case on the ground that there the husband left the "matrimonial domicile" and established a residence elsewhere, while here the husband kept his domicile in Florida and the wife fled from him. He argues, as the Florida court held, that it was impossible as a matter of law for Mrs. Armstrong to obtain a new domicile separate and apart from that of her husband. He bases this argument on the Florida court's finding on *ex parte* evidence that Florida, where the couple had resided during a considerable part of their marriage, was the "matrimonial domicile," and that the wife had left her home in Florida without cause. On this premise, the Florida court held that she "did not have the right to separate and claim a separate legal domicile and in truth and in fact, her domicile was that of her husband." The fiction that a woman cannot have a separate "domicile" from that of her husband is a relic of the old discredited idea that women must always play a subordinate role in society; it does not justify a departure from settled constitutional principles. The concept of "matrimonial domicile" was expressly repudiated in both the Williams cases. Yet the Court is asked to say here that a State's power over an alimony case is to depend on which spouse is to blame in leaving the other. We adhere to what was said in the first Williams case: "the question as to where the fault lies has no relevancy to the existence of state power in such circumstances." . . .

Relying on Milliken v. Meyer, 311 U.S. 457, the husband further contends that regardless of "matrimonial domicile" personal service was unnecessary because Mrs. Armstrong was actually domiciled in Florida at the time the Florida action was brought. The Florida court did find she was domiciled there, but that was in an uncontested proceeding. This finding was open to challenge in Ohio. . . . The issue was tried in Ohio with both parties present, and the trial court expressly found that Mrs. Armstrong had returned to Ohio and was a "resident" there within the meaning of the Ohio divorce statute at the time the Florida divorce proceedings were instituted. . . . This statute has been uniformly interpreted by the Ohio courts to require residence accompanied by an intention to make the State of Ohio a permanent home. . . . We would accept the Ohio court's finding that Mrs. Armstrong was such a resident of Ohio when the Florida suit was brought as amply supported by evidence in the record. Consequently the husband's reliance on Milliken v. Meyer is misplaced.

There was nothing novel in our holding in Estin v. Estin that a State where one of the parties to a marriage is domiciled can dissolve the marriage without personal service but that it cannot render a personal decree granting or denying alimony. The distinction between a decree which grants a divorce and one which grants a personal money judgment was recognized and the reasons for the distinction were stated by this Court in Pennoyer v. Neff. . . . The state courts have long recognized the rule that a court lacking personal jurisdiction over a husband cannot render a valid alimony judgment against him. We see no reason why a court lacking personal jurisdiction over a wife should be allowed to render a valid judgment denying alimony to her. Personal jurisdiction is as necessary to protect a wife's interests as it is to protect a husband's. . . .

. . . .

For the foregoing reasons we concur with the Court in affirming the judgment of the Supreme Court of Ohio.

HUGHES v. *FETTER*

UNITED STATES SUPREME COURT
341 U.S. 609 (1951)

Harold Hughes was fatally injured in an automobile accident in Illinois. *Corbin D. Hughes, the administrator of his estate, brought suit against Fetter and an insurance company in a* Wisconsin *court alleging that Fetter's negligent driving had been the cause of Harold Hughes' death. The fact that both Corbin D. Hughes and Fetter were residents of* Wisconsin *(as the deceased had been at the time of the accident) explains the logic of filing suit in a* Wisconsin *court. Unfortunately,* Wisconsin *law creates a right of action for wrongful death only when the death has been caused within the state. Hughes, therefore, sought to have the* Wisconsin *court decide the case on the basis of the* Illinois *wrongful death statute. The trial court dismissed the case, holding that the* Wisconsin *law in effect established a state public policy against entertaining suits under the wrongful death statutes of other states. Hughes appealed the decision to the* Wisconsin *supreme court on the grounds that the trial court's interpretation of* Wisconsin *law constituted a violation of the full faith and credit clause of the United States Constitution. The* Wisconsin *supreme court was not persuaded by that contention. Consequently, it affirmed the decision of the trial court. Corbin D. Hughes then brought the case to the United States Supreme Court on appeal.*

Mr. Justice BLACK delivered the opinion of the Court.

. . . .

WE ARE called upon to decide the narrow question whether Wisconsin, over the objection raised, can close the doors of its courts to the cause of action created by the Illinois wrongful death act. Prior decisions have established that the Illinois statute is a "public act" within the provision of Art. IV, § 1 that "Full Faith and Credit shall be given in each State to the public Acts * * * of every other State." It is also settled that Wisconsin cannot escape this constitutional obligation to enforce the rights and duties validly created under the laws of other states by the simple device of removing jurisdiction from courts otherwise competent. We have recognized, however, that full faith and credit does not automatically compel a forum state to subordinate its own statutory policy to a conflicting public act of another state; rather, it is for this Court to choose in each case between the competing public policies involved. The clash of interests in cases of this type has usually been described as a conflict between the public policies of two or more states. The more basic conflict involved in the present appeal, however, is as follows: On the one hand is the strong unifying principle embodied in the Full Faith and Credit Clause looking toward maximum enforcement in each state of the obligations or rights created or recognized by the statutes of sister states, on the other hand is the policy of Wisconsin, as interpreted by its highest court, against permitting Wisconsin courts to entertain this wrongful death action.

We hold that Wisconsin's policy must give way. That state has no real feeling of antagonism against wrongful death suits in general. To the contrary, a forum is regularly provided for cases of this nature, the exclusionary rule extending only so far as to bar actions for death not caused locally. The Wisconsin policy, moreover, cannot be considered as an application of the *forum non conveniens* doctrine, whatever effect that doctrine might be given if its use resulted in denying enforcement to public acts of other states. Even if we assume that Wisconsin could refuse, by reason of particular circumstances, to hear foreign controversies to which nonresidents were parties, the present case is not one lacking a close relationship with the state. For not only were appellant, the decedent and the individual defendant all residents of Wisconsin, but also appellant was appointed administrator and the corporate defendant was created under Wisconsin laws. We also think it relevant, although not crucial here, that Wisconsin may well be the only jurisdiction in which service could be had as an original matter on the insurance company defendant. And while in the present case jurisdiction over the individual defendant apparently could be had in Illinois by substituted service, in other cases Wisconsin's exclusionary statute might amount to a deprivation of all opportunity to enforce valid death claims created by another state.

Under these circumstances, we conclude that Wisconsin's statutory policy which excludes this Illinois cause of action is forbidden by the national policy of the Full Faith and Credit Clause. The judgment is reversed and the cause is remanded to the Supreme Court of Wisconsin for proceedings not inconsistent with this opinion.

Reversed and remanded.

Mr. Justice FRANKFURTER, whom Mr. Justice REED, Mr. Justice JACKSON, and Mr. Justice MINTON join, dissenting.

. . . The Wisconsin courts, obeying the command of the Wisconsin statute, dismissed the action. I cannot agree that the Wisconsin statute, so applied, is contrary to Art. IV, § 1 of the United States Constitution: "Full Faith and Credit shall be given in each State to the public Acts, Records, and judicial Proceedings of every other State."

The Full Faith and Credit Clause was derived from a similar provision in the Articles of Confederation. Art. IV, par. 3. The only clue to its meaning in the available records of the Constitutional Convention is a notation in Madison's Debates that "Mr. Wilson & Docr. Johnson [who became members of the committee to which the provision was referred] supposed the meaning to be that Judgments in one State should be the ground of actions in other States, & that acts of the Legislatures should be included, for the sake of Acts of insolvency etc—." . . . This Court has, with good reason, gone far in requiring that the courts of a State respect judgments entered by courts of other States. . . . But the extent to which a State must recognize and enforce the rights of action created by other States is not so clear.

1. In the field of commercial law—where certainty is of high importance—we have often imposed a rather rigid rule that a State must defer to the law of the State of incorporation, or to the law of the place of contract. . . .

. . . .

2. In cases involving workmen's compensation, there is also a pre-existing re-

lationship between the employer and employee that makes certainty of result desirable. The possible interest of the forum in protecting the workman, however, has made this Court reluctant to impose rigid rules. . . .

In Alaska Packers Ass'n v. Industrial Acc. Commission, 294 U.S. 532, we held that California—where the contract of employment was entered into—was free to apply the terms of its own workmen's compensation statute to an employee injured in Alaska, although an Alaska statute purported to give an exclusive remedy to persons injured there. . . .

. . . .

3. In the tort action before us, there is little reason to impose a "state of vassalage" on the forum. The liability here imposed does not rest on a pre-existing relationship between the plaintiff and defendant. There is consequently no need for fixed rules which would enable parties, at the time they enter into a transaction, to predict its consequences.

. . . .

This Court should certainly not require that the forum deny its own law and follow the tort law of another State where there is a reasonable basis for the forum to close its courts to the foreign cause of action. The decision of Wisconsin to open its courts to actions for wrongful deaths within the State but close them to actions for deaths outside the State may not satisfy everyone's notion of wise policy. . . . But it is neither novel nor without reason. Compare the similar Illinois statute which was before this Court in Kenney v. Supreme Lodge [252 *U.S.* 411]. Wisconsin may be willing to grant a right of action where witnesses will be available in Wisconsin and the courts are acquainted with a detailed local statute and cases construing it. It may not wish to subject residents to suit where out-of-state witnesses will be difficult to bring before the court, and where the court will be faced with the alternative of applying a complex foreign statute—perhaps inconsistent with that of Wisconsin on important issues—or fitting the statute to the Wisconsin pattern. The legislature may well feel that it is better to allow the courts of the State where the accident occurred to construe and apply its own statute, and that the exceptional case where the defendant cannot be served in the State where the accident occurred does not warrant a general statute allowing suit in the Wisconsin courts. The various wrongful death statutes are inconsistent on such issues as beneficiaries, the party who may bring suit, limitations on liability, comparative negligence, and the measure of damages. . . . The measure of damages and the relation of wrongful death actions to actions for injury surviving death have raised extremely complicated problems, even for a court applying the familiar statute of its own State. . . .

No claim is made that Wisconsin has discriminated against the citizens of other States and thus violated Art. IV, § 2 of the Constitution. . . . Nor is a claim made that the lack of a forum in Wisconsin deprives the plaintiff of due process. . . . Nor is it argued that Wisconsin is flouting a federal statute. . . . The only question before us is how far the Full Faith and Credit Clause undercuts the purpose of the Constitution, made explicit by the Tenth Amendment, to leave the conduct of domestic affairs to the States. Few interests are of more dominant local concern than matters governing the administration of law. This vital interest of the States should not be sacrificed in the interest of a merely literal reading of the Full Faith and Credit Clause.

There is no support, either in reason or in the cases, for holding that this Court is to make a *de novo* choice between the policies underlying the laws of Wisconsin and Illinois. I cannot believe that the Full Faith and Credit Clause provided a "writer's inkhorn" so that this Court might separate right from wrong. "*Prima facie* every state is entitled to enforce in its own courts its own statutes, lawfully enacted. One who challenges that right, because of the force given to a conflicting statute of another state by the full faith and credit clause, assumes the burden of showing, upon some rational basis, that of the conflicting interests involved those of the foreign state are superior to those of the forum." . . . In the present case, the decedent, the plaintiff, and the individual defendant were residents of Wisconsin. The corporate defendant was created under Wisconsin law. The suit was brought in the Wisconsin courts. No reason is apparent—and none is vouchsafed in the opinion of the Court—why the interest of Illinois is so great that it can force the courts of Wisconsin to grant relief in defiance of their own law.

Finally, it may be noted that there is no conflict here in the policies underlying the statute of Wisconsin and that of Illinois. The Illinois wrongful death statute has a proviso that "no action shall be brought or prosecuted in this State to recover damages for a death occurring outside of this State where a right of action for such death exists under the laws of the place where such death occurred and service of process in such suit may be had upon the defendant in such place." . . . The opinion of the Court concedes that "jurisdiction over the individual defendant apparently could be had in Illinois by substituted service." . . . Thus, in the converse of the case at bar—if Hughes had been killed in Wisconsin and suit had been brought in Illinois—the Illinois courts would apparently have dismissed the suit. There is no need to be "more Roman than the Romans."

TRENTON v. *NEW JERSEY*

UNITED STATES SUPREME COURT
262 U.S. 182 (1923)

A New Jersey statute of 1907 provided among other things that municipalities "now diverting water of streams or lakes for the purpose of a public water-supply shall make annual payments . . . for all water diverted in excess of the amount now being legally diverted." The city of Trenton refused to pay the state for water "in excess . . ." on the grounds that the state, many years before, had granted a private water company a perpetual right to take all the water required for the use of the city of Trenton and its inhabitants without charge and that, when the city bought out the water company, it had acquired all the rights granted to the company. The state brought action in the New Jersey supreme court to recover judgment against the city and won the case. On appeal within the state judicial system, the decision was upheld. Subsequently, the city brought its case to the United States Supreme Court alleging that if the state law required Trenton to pay for any water, it violated two provisions of the United States Constitution. First, the city argued that the state, by changing the terms of the original grant, had in effect passed a law impairing the obligation of contracts and this a state is expressly forbidden to do by the Constitution. Second, the city maintained that the state act as applied to Trenton contravened the Fourteenth Amendment because it constituted a taking of property without due process of law.

Mr. Justice BUTLER delivered the opinion of the Court.

. . . .

THE STATE undoubtedly has power, and it is its duty, to control and conserve the use of its water resources for the benefit of all its inhabitants, and the Act of 1907 was passed pursuant to the policy of the State to prevent waste and to economize its water resources. . . . The only way the City could acquire the right to take the water of the Delaware River was by grant from the State or by authorized purchase or condemnation from one to whom the right had been granted by the State. . . . The power to determine the conditions upon which waters may be so diverted is a legislative function. The State may grant or withhold the privilege as it sees fit. Assuming in favor of the City, that its grantor received a perpetual right, unburdened by license fee or other charge, to divert all the water required for the use of the City and its inhabitants, does it follow that the State as against the City is bound by contract and is without power to impose a license fee as provided in the act?

The relations existing between the State and the water company were not the same as those between the State and the City. The company was organized and carried on its business for pecuniary profit. Its rights and property were privately owned and therefore safeguarded by the constitutional provisions here sought to be invoked by the City against the legislation of the State. The City is a political subdivision of the State, created as a convenient agency for the exercise of such of the governmental powers of the State as may be entrusted to it. The diversion of waters from the sources of supply for the use of the inhabitants of the State is a proper and legitimate function of the State. This function may be left to private enterprise, subject to regulation by the State; it may be performed directly; or it may be delegated to bodies politic created for that purpose, or to the municipalities of the State. Power to own, maintain and operate public utilities, such as waterworks, gas and electric plants, street railway systems, public markets, and the like is frequently conferred by the States upon their cities and other political subdivisions. For the purpose of carrying on such activities, they are given power to hold and manage personal and real property.

As said by this Court, speaking through Mr. Justice Moody, in *Hunter* v. *Pittsburgh*, 207 U.S. 161, 178, 179:

"The number, nature and duration of the powers conferred upon these corporations and the territory over which they shall be exercised rests in the absolute discretion of the State. Neither their charters, nor any law conferring governmental powers, or vesting in them property to be used for governmental purposes, or authorizing them to hold or manage such property, or exempting them from taxation upon it, constitutes a contract with the State within the meaning of the Federal Constitution. The State, therefore, at its pleasure may modify or withdraw all such powers, may take without compensation such property, hold it itself, or vest it in other agencies, expand or contract the territorial area, unite the whole or a part of it with another municipality, repeal the charter and destroy the corporation. All this may be done, conditionally or unconditionally, with or without the consent of the citizens, or even against their protest. In all these respects the State is supreme, and its legislative body, conforming its action to the state constitution, may do as it will, unrestrained by any provision of the Constitution of the United States. . . . The power is in the State and those who legislate for the State are alone responsible for any unjust or oppressive exercise of it."

In New Jersey it has been held that within the limits prescribed by the state constitution, the legislature may delegate to municipalities such portion of political power as they may deem expedient, withholding other powers, and may withdraw any part of that which has been delegated. *Van Cleve* v. *Passaic Valley Sewerage Commissioners*, 71 N. J. L. 183, 198.

In the absence of state constitutional provisions safeguarding it to them, municipalities have no inherent right of self government which is beyond the legislative control of the State. A municipality is merely a department of the State, and the State may withhold, grant or withdraw powers and privileges as it sees fit. However great or small its sphere of action, it remains the creature of the State exercising and holding powers and privileges subject to the sovereign will. . . .

In *Mount Pleasant* v. *Beckwith*, 100 U.S. 514, it was held that where a municipal corporation is legislated out of existence and its territory annexed to other corporations, the latter, unless the legislature otherwise provides, become entitled to all its property and immunities. In the opinion it is said . . . :

"Institutions of the kind, whether called cities, towns, or counties, are the auxiliaries of the State in the important business of municipal rule; but they cannot have the least pretension to sustain their privileges or their existence upon anything like a contract between themselves and the legislature of the State, because there is not and cannot be any reciprocity of stipulation between the parties, and for the further reason that their objects and duties are utterly incompatible with everything partaking of the nature of compact."

The power of the State, unrestrained by the contract clause or the Fourteenth Amendment, over the rights and property of cities held and used for "governmental purposes" cannot be questioned. In *Hunter* v. *Pittsburgh*, reference is made to the distinction between property owned by municipal corporations in their public and governmental capacity and that owned by them in their private or proprietary capacity, and decisions of this Court which mention that distinction are referred to. In none of these cases was any power, right or property of a city or other political subdivision held to be protected by the contract clause or the Fourteenth Amendment. This Court has never held that these subdivisions may invoke such restraints upon the power of the State.

In *East Hartford* v. *Hartford Bridge Co.*, 10 How. 511, it appeared that for many years a franchise to operate a ferry over the Connecticut River belonged to the town of Hartford; that upon the incorporation of East Hartford, the legislature granted to it one-half of the ferry during the pleasure of the General Assembly, and that subsequently, after the building of a bridge across the river, the legislature discontinued the ferry. It was held that this was not inconsistent with the contract clause of the Federal Constitution. The reasons given in the opinion . . . support the contention of the State here made that the City cannot possess a contract with the State which may not be changed or regulated by state legislation.

. . . .

The distinction between the municipality as an agent of the State for governmental purposes and as an organization to care for local needs in a private or proprietary capacity has been applied in various branches of the law of municipal corporations. The most numerous illustrations are found in cases involving the question of liability for negligent acts or omissions of its officers and agents. . . . It has been held that municipalities are not liable for such acts and omissions in the exercise of the police power, or in the performance of such municipal faculties as the erection and maintenance of a city hall and courthouse, the protection of the city's inhabitants against disease and unsanitary conditions, the care of the sick, the operation of fire departments, the inspection of steam boilers, the promotion of education and the administration of public charities. On the other hand, they have been held liable when such acts or omissions occur in the exercise of the power to build and maintain bridges, streets and highways, and waterworks, construct sewers, collect refuse and care for the dump where it is deposited. Recovery is denied where the act or omission occurs in the exercise of what are deemed to be governmental powers, and is permitted if it occurs in a proprietary capacity. The basis of the distinction is difficult to state, and there is no established rule for the determination of what belongs to the one or the other class. It originated with the courts. Generally it is applied to escape difficulties, in order that injustice may not result from the recognition of technical defenses based upon the governmental character of such corporations. But such distinction furnishes no ground for the application of constitutional restraints here sought to be invoked by the City of Trenton against the State of New Jersey. They do not apply as against the State in favor of its own municipalities. We hold that the City cannot invoke these provisions of the Federal Constitution against the imposition of the license fee or charge for diversion of water specified in the state law here in question. In view of former opinions of this Court, no substantial federal question is presented. . . .

The writ of error is dismissed.

CITY OF TACOMA v. TAXPAYERS OF TACOMA

UNITED STATES SUPREME COURT

357 U.S. 320 (1958)

The city of Tacoma applied for a license from the Federal Power Commission to construct a power project including two dams on the Cowlitz River. The Commission held a public hearing at which the state attorney general appeared on the state's behalf to oppose the granting of the license to the city because the proposed project would among other things: (1) destroy fishery resources of the state; (2) violate a state law which limited the size of dams built on certain tributaries of the Columbia River; and (3) flood a valuable state-owned hatchery, which the city would have to take by eminent domain, a power it does not have with respect to state property. Despite the state's position in the matter, the Commission granted the license to the city. The state petitioned for a review of the Commission's order in the appropriate Federal court of appeals, which it was entitled to do under Federal law. The state based its case primarily on the grounds that the city "as a creature of the State of Washington, cannot act in opposition to the policy of the State or in derogation of its laws." The court of appeals held, however, that "state laws cannot prevent the Federal Power Commission from issuing a license or bar the licensee from acting under the license to build a dam on a navigable stream since the stream (as are all navigable streams) is under the dominion of the United States." The state then petitioned the Supreme Court of the United States for a writ of certiorari; *the petition was denied. While the case was pending before the court of appeals, the city endeavored to issue and sell revenue bonds to finance the project as well as to award contracts for the construction of one of the dams. These efforts led to a series of suits and countersuits in state courts. The litigation was too intricate to describe briefly and, for our purposes here, not important enough to describe at length. Suffice it to say that eventually the city was forced to take its case to the United States Supreme Court to determine whether or not it could go ahead with its power project in the face of opposition from the state on the grounds first articulated by the state in the Federal Power Commission hearings.*

You may be wondering how the taxpayers of Tacoma came to be included among the defendants in the case. In the original state case, the city had come to court seeking a judgment declaring the city's right to issue and sell revenue bonds to finance the power project. In such actions, Washington law requires the court to name representative taxpayers as defendants and this the court did. Consequently, through the complex litigation the taxpayers of Tacoma remained a party to the controversy.

Mr. Justice WHITTAKER delivered the opinion of the Court.

. . . .

WE COME now to the core of the controversy between the parties, namely, whether the license issued by the Commission under the Federal Power Act to the City of Tacoma gave it capacity to act under that federal license in constructing the project and delegated to it federal eminent domain power to take, upon the payment of just compensation, the State's fish hatchery—essential to the construction of the project—in the absence of state legislation specifically conferring such authority.

At the threshold of this controversy petitioner, the City, asserts that, under the express terms . . . of the Act, . . . this question has been finally determined by the decision of the Court of Appeals (State of Washington, Dept. of Game v. Federal Power Comm., 9 Cir., 207 F.2d 391) and this Court's denial of certiorari (347 U.S. 936); and that respondents' cross-complaints, and proceedings thereon, in the subsequent bond validation suit in the Washington courts have been only impermissible collateral attacks upon the final judgment of the Court of Appeals. If this assertion is correct, the judgment of the Supreme Court of Washington now before us would necessarily have to be reversed, for obviously that court, like this one, may not, in such a case, reexamine and decide a question which has been finally determined by a court of competent jurisdiction in earlier litigation between the parties. We must turn then to an examination of petitioner's contention.

It is no longer open to question that the Federal Government under the Commerce Clause of the Constitution . . . has dominion, to the exclusion of the States, over navigable waters of the United States. . . . Congress has elected to exercise this power under the detailed and comprehensive plan for development of the Nation's water resources, which it prescribed in the Federal Power Act, to be administered by the Federal Power Commission. . . .

Section 313(b) of that Act, upon which petitioner's claim of finality depends, provides, in pertinent part:

> "(b) Any party to a proceeding under this chapter aggrieved by an order issued by the Commission in such proceeding may obtain a review of such order in the United States court of appeals for any circuit wherein the licensee or public utility to which the order relates is located * * * by filing in such court, within 60 days after the order of the Commission upon the application for rehearing, a written petition praying that the order of the Commission be modified or set aside in whole or in part. A copy of such petition shall forthwith be served upon any member of the Commission and thereupon the Commission shall certify and file with the court a transcript of the record upon which the order complained of was entered. Upon the filing of such transcript such court *shall have exclusive jurisdiction to affirm, modify, or set aside such order in whole or in part.* No objection to the order of the Commission shall be considered by the court unless such objection shall have been urged before the Commission in the application for rehearing unless there is reasonable ground for failure so to do. The finding of the Commission as to the facts, if supported by substantial evidence, shall be conclusive. * * * *The judgment and decree of the court, affirming, modifying, or setting aside, in whole or in part, any such order of the Commission, shall be final, subject to review by the Supreme Court of the United States upon certiorari or certification as provided in sections 346 and 347 of Title 28.*" 16 U.S.C. § 825*l*(b), 16 U.S.C.A. § 825*l*(b). (Emphasis added.)

This statute is written in simple words of plain meaning and leaves no room to doubt the congressional purpose and intent. It can hardly be doubted that Congress, acting within its constitutional powers, may prescribe the procedures and conditions under which, and the courts in which, judicial review of administrative orders may be had. . . . So acting, Congress in § 313(b) prescribed the specific, complete and exclusive mode for judicial review of the Commission's orders. . . . It there provided that any party aggrieved by the Commission's order may have judicial review, upon all issues raised before the

Commission in the motion for rehearing, by the Court of Appeals which "shall have exclusive jurisdiction to affirm, modify, or set aside such order in whole or in part," and that "[t]he judgment and decree of the court, affirming, modifying, or setting aside, in whole or in part, any such order of the Commission, *shall be final,* subject to review by the Supreme Court of the United States upon certiorari or certification * * *." (Emphasis added.) It thereby necessarily precluded *de novo* litigation between the parties of all issues inhering in the controversy, and all other modes of judicial review. Hence, upon judicial review of the Commission's order, all objections to the order, to the license it directs to be issued, and to the legal competence of the licensee to execute its terms, must be made in the Court of Appeals or not at all. For Congress, acting within its powers, has declared that the Court of Appeals shall have "exclusive jurisdiction" to review such orders, and that its judgment "shall be final," subject to review by this Court upon certiorari or certification. . . .

The State participated in the hearing before the Commission. It there vigorously objected to the issuance of the license upon the grounds, among others, "[t]hat the reservoirs which would be created by the proposed dams would inundate a valuable and irreplaceable fish hatchery owned by the State" and, hence, necessarily require the taking of it by the City under the license sought; that the City had not complied with the applicable laws of the State respecting construction of the project and performance of the acts necessarily incident thereto . . . ; and that the City was not authorized by the laws of the State to engage in such business. The Commission rejected these contentions of the State and made all the findings required by the Act to support its order granting the license . . . including the finding that:

> "The applicant * * * has submitted satisfactory evidence of compliance with the requirements of all applicable State laws insofar as necessary to effect the purposes of a license for the project; and it is a municipality within the meaning of § 3(7) of the Act."

The State then petitioned the Commission for a rehearing, reviving the foregoing contentions and raising others. The petition was denied.

Thereafter, the State, following the procedures prescribed by § 313(b), petitioned the proper Court of Appeals for review of the Commission's findings and order. After full hearing, that court rejected all contentions there raised by the State, did not disturb any of the Commission's findings, and affirmed its order without modification. . . . It made particular mention of, and approved, the Commission's finding, as rephrased by the court, that the City had submitted "such evidence of compliance with state law as, in the Commission's judgment, would be 'appropriate to effect the purposes of a Federal license on the navigable waters of the United States.' " . . .

Moreover, in its briefs in the Court of Appeals, the State urged reversal of the Commission's order on the grounds that the City "has not shown, nor could it show, that [it] has availed itself of * * * *any right to take or destroy the property of the State* of Washington [and that] Tacoma, as a creature of the State of Washington, *cannot act* [under the license] in opposition to the policy of the State or in derogation of its laws." (Emphasis added.) In rejecting these contentions—that the City does not have "any right to take or destroy property of the State" and "cannot act" in accordance with the terms of its federal license—the Court of Appeals said:

> ". . . we conclude that the state laws cannot prevent the Federal Power Commission from issuing a license *or bar the*

licensee from acting under the license to build a dam on a navigable stream since the stream is under the dominion of the United States." . . . (Emphasis added.)

We think these recitals show that the very issue upon which respondents stand here was raised and litigated in the Court of Appeals and decided by its judgment. But even if it might be thought that this issue was not raised in the Court of Appeals, it cannot be doubted that it could and should have been, for that was the court to which Congress had given "exclusive jurisdiction to affirm, modify, or set aside" the Commission's order. And the State may not reserve the point, for another round of piecemeal litigation, by remaining silent on the issue while its action to review and reverse the Commission's order was pending in that court—which had "exclusive jurisdiction" of the proceeding and whose judgment therein as declared by Congress "shall be final," subject to review by this Court upon certiorari or certification. After the Court of Appeals' judgment was rendered, the State petitioned this Court for a writ of certiorari which was denied. . . .

These were precisely the proceedings prescribed by Congress in § 313(b) of the Act for judicial review of the Commission's findings and order. They resulted in affirmance. That result, Congress has declared, "shall be final."

But respondents say that the Court of Appeals did not decide the question of legal capacity of the City to act under the license and, therefore, its decision is not final on that question, but left it open to further litigation. They rely upon the following language of the opinion:

> "However, we do not touch the question as to the legal capacity of the City of Tacoma to initiate and act under the license once it is granted. There may be limitations in the City Charter, for instance, as to indebtedness limitations. Questions of this nature may be inquired into by the Commission as relevant to the practicability of the plan, but the Commission has no power to adjudicate them." . . .

We believe that respondents' construction of this language is in error. The questioned language expressly refers to possible "indebtedness limitations" in the City's Charter and "questions of this nature," not to the right of the City to receive and perform, as licensee of the Federal Government under the Federal Power Act, the federal rights determined by the Commission and delegated to the City as specified in the license. That this was the meaning of the court, if its meaning might otherwise be doubtful, is made certain by the facts that the court did not disturb a single one of the Commission's findings; affirmed its order without modification; and said, in the sentence immediately preceding the questioned language: ". . . we conclude that the state laws cannot prevent the Federal Power Commission from issuing a license *or bar the licensee from acting under the license* to build a dam on a navigable stream since the stream is under the dominion of the United States." . . . (Emphasis added.)

The final judgment of the Court of Appeals was effective, not only against the State, but also against its citizens, including the taxpayers of Tacoma, for they, in their common public rights as citizens of the State, were represented by the State in those proceedings, and, like it, were bound by the judgment. . . .

We conclude that the judgment of the Court of Appeals, upon this Court's denial of the State's petition for certiorari, became final under § 313(b) of the Act, and is binding upon the State of Washington, its Directors of Fisheries and of Game, and its citizens, including the taxpayers of Tacoma; and that the objections and claims to the contrary asserted in the cross-complaints of the State, its Directors of Fisheries and of Game, and the Taxpayers of Tacoma, in this bond validation suit, were impermissible collateral attacks upon, and *de novo* litigation between the same parties of issues determined by, the final judgment of the Court of Appeals. Therefore, the judgment of the Supreme Court of Washington is reversed and the cause is remanded for further proceedings not inconsistent with this opinion.

Reversed and remanded.

Mr. Justice HARLAN, concurring.

I join the Court's opinion, but deem it appropriate to state my understanding of what the Court has held. The Court of Appeals in the earlier proceeding had jurisdiction to determine whether state or federal law governed Tacoma's power to condemn the State's hatchery, and that issue itself was a federal question. Section 313(b) of the Federal Power Act therefore foreclosed relitigation of this issue in the present case. I do not understand the Court to suggest that the Federal Power Act endowed the Commission and the Court of Appeals with authority to decide any issues of state law if such law were deemed controlling, or that had the Court of Appeals undertaken to do so, such a determination would have foreclosed re-examination of such a decision in other proceedings.

CHAPTER TWO

Constitutions

By what right and rules do particular people obtain control of the government? Those who are committed to the democratic form of government have traditionally regarded government as the product of a twofold contract (1) a contract entered into by all the people in the society with each other and (2) a contract between the governed and the governors. The contract theory is founded on the idea that all people in the society are of inherent equal value even if not endowed with equal talents. Consequently, everyone has an equal stake in the society and in its government.

In a very real sense, a written constitution in a democratic state is the executed contract. It contains the fundamental terms to which the people have agreed and, at the same time, it stipulates the basis on which the governors may govern. But even without the contract theory, the need for establishing the basic rules for an enterprise hardly needs explaining to Americans. Watch a group of students falling out on the campus for a touch football game. Almost certainly they will spend the first few minutes establishing boundaries, goals, and basic rules. Similarly, it is necessary in establishing a new government to give every participant some idea of what the basic mode of operation will be.

In the course of history, we have learned much about constitution-making. It is generally acknowledged, the British experience notwithstanding, that constitutions should be written so that the fundamental rules on which the government will operate will be better understood and disseminated. Although some of our state constitutions seem to indicate otherwise, we have learned that a constitution as differentiated from any other code of law ought to be brief and deal only with the basic rules such as the relation of the government to the people, the powers and functions of the various branches of the government, and the manner in which the constitution may be changed. As Chief Justice John Marshall stated many years ago in *McCulloch* v. *Maryland*, 4 Wheaton 316 (1819), a constitution which contains "an accurate detail of all the subdivisions of which its great powers will admit, and of all the means by which they may be carried into execution, would partake of the prolixity of a legal code, and could scarcely be embraced by the human mind. It would, probably, never be understood by the public. Its nature, therefore, requires, that only its great outlines should be marked, its important objects designated, and the minor ingredients which compose those objects, deduced from the nature of the objects themselves."

Despite our knowledge of constitution-making and constitutional interpretation, questions constantly arise about the meaning and force of constitutional provisions of our state and national constitutions. Less frequently, important questions are raised about the manner in which constitutions may legitimately be amended. We would like to demonstrate to you in a series of state court cases just how some of these questions actually have arisen, the nature of the problems involved, and how they have been resolved by various courts. We want to emphasize that we are presenting only some of the myriad of questions which have come up.

A. The Problem of Constitutional Interpretation

Words being what they are, it is sometimes an easy matter for different persons reading a provision of a constitution to interpret the meaning differently. In framing a law, legislators may find themselves at odds as to whether or not the proposed legislation is constitutional. Administrators may assume that the constitution grants them certain powers which others will argue are constitutionally beyond them. Ultimately, when government acts or fails to act and there are those who feel they have been injured by what they regard as unconstitutional action or inaction, someone may have standing to take a case to the appropriate court. In our system, when a case comes to court involving the meaning of a constitutional provision, the judiciary has the last word. At the same time it should be remembered that the constitution may be amended to overrule the judiciary, for amendment literally changes the provision itself. Needless to say, our courts have frequent opportunities to interpret constitutional provisions. In the course of doing so, the courts have suggested ways and means for divining meaning. Unfortunately, some of the ways and means conflict with each other. For example, in *Adams* v. *Bolin* (p. 81) the supreme court of Arizona was called upon to interpret a constitutional provision which read:

> The veto power of the governor, or the power of the legislature, to repeal or amend shall not extend to initiative or referendum measures approved by a *majority vote of the qualified electors.* [Italics supplied—*Eds.*]

Did the provision mean a majority of all the registered voters or only a majority of those voting in the election? The Arizona court found that the meaning of the words was "plain and leaves no room for construction." They went on to say, "But if rules of construction should be availed of, one of the many rules pertaining to constitutional provisions is that some meaning must be given to each phrase of the Constitution unless in giving the words their grammatical and common meaning will create some impossibility or unworkable situation, or lead to an absurdity." But compare the decision in that case with the decision in *Gaines* v. *O'Connell* (p. 88), where the court of appeals of Kentucky stated:

> It has often been said that all of the provisions of the Constitution are mandatory. But this broad statement is subject to the qualification, just as often declared, that they are not to be so regarded if by express language or necessary implication a different intention is manifest. It is a cardinal rule of construction that no part of the Constitution should be construed so as to defeat its substantial purpose or the reasonable intent of the people in adopting it. What is implied is as much a part of the instrument as what is expressed. Wherever the language admits a doubt, it is presumed that it was intended to be in accordance with generally recognized rules and principles of public policy. Still another familiar concomitant rule, no less binding on the courts, is that all reasonable doubts are to be resolved in favor of constitutionality of any act of the General Assembly.

As you read these two cases, see if you can determine whether or not the two courts are in agreement. How do you think one court would have resolved the case which the other had to decide?

In *Yelle* v. *Bishop* (p. 94) the supreme court of the State of Washington points up another "well-established rule of constitutional construction. . . . The express mention of one thing implies the exclusion of the other." It goes on to add, "This rule must yield when the surrounding facts and circumstances satisfactorily demonstrate the converse to be true." Does the Maryland court of appeals apply this rule and its corollary in *City of Frostberg* v. *Jenkins* (p. 99)? Read Judge Prescott's dissent with care. Would you agree with him or the majority on the merits of the case? If you agree with him are you rejecting the rule of construction described in *Yelle* v. *Bishop?*

A second problem involving constitutional interpretation arises out of the fact that no body of constitutional framers, however clairvoyant can foresee all the technological, political, and social changes which will take place in the society over a period of one hundred years or more. Did the framers of our national Constitution foresee the railroad and airplane? When they granted Congress power to regulate interstate commerce, did they have specifically in mind that this would include the power to regulate the railroads and the airlines? If they did, Madison must have thought the discussion unworthy of reporting in his notes.

In *City of Shawnee* v. *Williamson* (p. 106) the Oklahoma supreme court had to decide among other things whether or not a public parking lot was a public utility and as such covered by the constitutional provision dealing with public utilities. In deciding the case, the Court wrote:

> The ever increasing complications of modern civilization from time to time have compelled a new examination and application of the constitutional provision as to "public utilities." This is not to change the meaning of the Constitution to meet changing times as that would be an amending of the Consti-

tution by judicial decree. We merely re-examine the Constitution as written, and make judicial application thereof to the new situation presented.

As you read the case, try to determine whether or not the court is amending the constitution despite their disclaimer. At the same time consider the Minnesota supreme court in *Visina* v. *Freeman* (p. 109). In that case the court stated:

> While this case may illustrate the need for some constitutional revision, the fact remains that the right to amend the constitution rests with the people and should not be usurped by the courts in the guise of judicial interpretation. At the same time, when it becomes necessary to interpret the provisions of the constitution in the light of conditions which exist today that could not be contemplated at the time our constitution was adopted, we should attempt to give to it a reasonable meaning as applied to present conditions if that can be done without doing violence to the expressed language used in the constitution itself. If the language of the constitution permits, we should give it that meaning *which would have been expressed when adopted if the present conditions that are involved had then existed or had been within the contemplation of those who drafted the instrument.* [Italics supplied—*Eds.*]

Is it reasonable for a court to base a decision on what the framers might have done had conditions now prevailing existed at the time of framing? Is to do so an act of interpreting, or is it an act of amending the constitution?

B. The Problem of Consent of the Governed and the Amending Process

It has been said that people live by a host of fictions. To a very large degree one of the fictions we live by is that our governments in the United States are based upon consent of the governed. We live for the most part under constitutions drawn up generations ago. True, these constitutions reflect the consensus of the generations which drew them up. But do they reflect the consensus of the present generations? Certainly, we can amend our constitutions, but note that it requires far more than a simple majority to do so. Therefore, in a practical sense, a minority can prevent the majority from forming a new consensus as to what our constitutions should contain. Thomas Jefferson had views on this subject so interesting and instructive as to warrant lengthy quotation:

> Some men look at constitutions with sanctimonious reverence, and deem them like the arc of the covenant, too sacred to be touched. They ascribe to the men of the preceding age a wisdom more than human, and suppose what they did to be beyond amendment. I knew that age well; I belonged to it, and labored with it. It deserved well of its country. It was very like the present, but without the experience of the present; and forty years of experience in government is worth a century of bookreading; and this they would say themselves, were they to rise from the dead. I am certainly not an advocate for frequent and untried changes in laws and constitutions. I think moderate imperfections had better

be borne with; because, when once known, we accommodate ourselves to them, and find practical means of correcting their ill effects. But I know also, that laws and institutions must go hand in hand with the progress of the human mind. As that becomes more developed, more enlightened, as new discoveries are made, new truths disclosed, and manners and opinions change with the change of circumstances, institutions must advance also, and keep pace with the times. We might as well require a man to wear still the coat which fitted him when a boy, as civilized society to remain ever under the regimen of their barbarous ancestors. It is this preposterous idea which has lately deluged Europe in blood. Their monarchs, instead of wisely yielding to the gradual change of circumstances, of favoring progressive accommodation to progressive improvement, have clung to old abuses, entrenched themselves behind steady habits, and obliged their subjects to seek through blood and violence rash and ruinous innovations, which, had they been referred to the peaceful deliberations and collected wisdom of the nation, would have been put into acceptable and salutary forms. Let us follow no such examples, nor weakly believe that one generation is not as capable as another of taking care of itself, and of ordering its own affairs. Let us, as our sister States have done, avail ourselves of our reason and experience, to correct the crude essays of our first and unexperienced, although wise, virtuous, and well-meaning councils. And lastly, let us provide in our constitution for its revision at stated periods. What these periods should be, nature herself indicates. By the European tables of mortality, of the adults living at any one moment of time, a majority will be dead in about nineteen years. At the end of that period, then, a new majority is come into place; or, in other words, a new generation. Each generation is as independent as the one preceding, as that was of all which had gone before. It has then, like them, a right to choose for itself the form of government it believes most promotive of its own happiness; consequently, to accommodate to the circumstances in which it finds itself, that received from its predecessors; and it is for the peace and good of mankind, that a solemn opportunity of doing this every nineteen or twenty years, should be provided by the constitution; so that it may be handed on, with periodical repairs, from generation to generation, to the end of time, if anything human can so long endure. It is now forty years since the constitution of Virginia was formed. The same tables inform us, that, within that period, two-thirds of the adults then living are now dead. Have then the remaining third, even if they had the wish, the right to hold in obedience to their will, and to laws heretofore made by them, the other two-thirds, who, with themselves, compose the present mass of adults? If they have not, who has? The dead? But the dead have no rights. They are nothing; and nothing cannot own something. Where there is no substance, there can be no accident. This corporeal globe, and everything upon it, belong to its present corporeal inhabitants, during their generation. They alone have a right to direct what is the concern of themselves alone, and to declare the law of that direction; and this declaration can only be made by their majority. That majority, then, has a right to depute representatives to a convention, and to make the constitution what they think will be the best for themselves. But how collect their voice? This is the real difficulty. If invited by private authority, or county or district meetings, these divisions are so large that few will attend; and their voice will be imperfectly, or falsely pronounced. Here, then, would be one of the advantages of the ward divisions I have proposed. The mayor of every ward, on a

> question like the present, would call his ward together, take the simple yea or nay of its members, convey these to the county court, who would hand on those of all its wards to the proper general authority; and the voice of the whole people would be thus fairly, fully, and peaceably expressed, discussed, and decided by the common reason of the society. If this avenue be shut to the call of sufferance, it will make itself heard through that of force, and we shall go on, as other nations are doing, in the endless circle of oppression, rebellion, reformation; and oppression, rebellion, reformation, again; and so on forever. . . .[1]

Jefferson's views, obviously, have not prevailed. Perhaps, the chief reason is the general belief that it would be dangerous to have periodic constitutional conventions, for they would serve only to encourage change even when there was no real need and would make the fundamental law more easily subject to change based on the passions of a particular time. All the constitutions in the United States provide opportunity for amendment, but the provisions for it require a rather extraordinary effort to achieve amendments. This may explain in large part why the courts have been willing to "amend" constitutions by interpretation. Or conversely, the courts willingness to do so, may have made it possible for our constitutions to endure without much formal amending. For, certainly, there would be great impetus for people to seek to change inflexible constitutions strictly interpreted when and if they became hopelessly outdated.

You might wonder what advantage Jefferson could see in having a constitution at all, if it were to be changed every generation. To those of Jeffersonian persuasion, a constitution drawn up in convention each generation would provide the society with an opportunity to think out and set down the fundamental principles of government in a sober moment, principles to guide and bind society through the periods when sobriety yields to passions of the moment arising out of contention over particular partisan issues. With this view in mind, it is better to decide in principle what to do about church and state before it is necessary to deal with a specific issue like Federal aid to parochial schools. But such a view presupposes that a constitutional convention would be above the passions of the moment. Would this be the case? Suppose we were to have a constitutional convention today. Would a provision regarding religion be debated without reference to the current school aid issue?

We are constantly witnessing efforts to amend our constitutions. Frequently, the efforts raise questions about the consent necessary to achieve an amendment. Some seventy years ago, the Mississippi supreme court had to decide whether or not a new constitution had to be ratified by popular vote when the legislature calling the convention did not require that it be ratified. Undoubtedly, on the basis of contract theory, it was argued that, "A constitutional convention has power only to prepare or frame the body of a constitution, and that when prepared or framed the instrument is of no force or effect until ratified by a popular vote of the people. . . ." The

[1] Letter to Samuel Kercheval, July 12, 1816, *The Writings of Thomas Jefferson*, ed. P. L. Ford (New York: G. P. Putnam's Sons, 1896), X, 37–45.

court rejected this contention asserting that a constitutional convention "is the highest legislative body known to free men in a representative government. It is supreme in its sphere. It wields the powers of sovereignty, specially delegated to it, for the purpose and the occasion, by the whole electoral body for the good of the whole commonwealth." As you read the case, *Sproule* v. *Fredericks* (p. 118), you might ponder these questions: (1) Would other state courts be likely to decide such a case the same way? (2) Was there anything special about the situation in Mississippi that would have made it difficult for the court to decide any other way? In attempting to answer these questions compare the Mississippi decision with the decision in *Staples* v. *Gilmer* (p. 120) and *Gaines* v. *O'Connell* (p. 88) where a Virginia and Kentucky court respectively seem to see differently the relationship of a constitutional convention to the people. On the basis of your political theory, which court(s) would you agree with?

C. *The Problem of Forcing Legislatures to Comply with the Constitution*

Occasionally, executives or legislatures will in effect defy the Constitution and remain unscathed in their defiance. This always causes consternation among students who feel that there should be a remedy for every wrong. But, alas, our system does not provide a feasible remedy for every wrong. One of the best cases in point was the time, before our entry into World War II, when Franklin D. Roosevelt traded American destroyers to England in return for leases to some bases. The United States Constitution specifically provides that only Congress can dispose of the property of the United States. How could President Roosevelt do this without legal consequence? First, there was no way of challenging his action in court. There was no one in the United States who had a sufficient personal interest, by Federal court standards, to have standing in a Federal court.[2] Congress could have endeavored to impeach the President, but bear in mind all the other factors congressmen had to weigh before deciding to do so. It just was not politically feasible for them to do so. Just as there was no *practical* way of reversing President Roosevelt's patently unconstitutional action, often there is no practical way for courts to do anything about a state legislature's unconstitutional acts of commission or omission. For example, in Minnesota, despite a clear constitutional debt limit, the legislature issued certificates of indebtedness for amounts far in excess of the limit. For years the courts permitted the legislature to do so. Finally in 1960 in *Naftalin* v. *King* (p. 128), the state supreme court decided to call a halt to the practice. But

[2] Many Americans have the mistaken notion that any one at any time can go to an appropriate court with an action and have the court hear him out and make a decision on the merits of his case. As a matter of fact, it is necessary for a litigant to demonstrate to the court, if it is not obvious, that he has "standing" to sue, *i.e.* that he has a legal right to appear before the court and has a legal cause of action. The law on standing is complex and sometimes conflicting. For a brief and excellent discussion, see C. Herman Pritchett, *The American Constitution* (New York: McGraw-Hill Book Co., Inc., 1959), p. 145–149; note also the discussion of standing in *Baker* v. *Carr*, p. 155.

notice how they delayed the impact of their decision. Was this a wise decision? Does the fact that the decision ultimately resulted in a constitutional amendment (1962) removing the debt limit affect your answer?

Courts are reluctant to tell legislatures what they cannot do, but they are even more reluctant to tell legislatures what they must do, in the face of a clear constitutional mandate. Again we can turn to Minnesota for a good example. The Minnesota Constitution specifies that "the representation in both houses [of its legislature] shall be apportioned equally throughout the different sections of the State, in proportion to the population thereof. . . ." Constitutionally, it is the legislature's duty to reapportion after each census. Yet for years the legislature refused to do so. When the issue came to the state supreme court in *Smith* v. *Holm* (p. 135), the court recognized that the legislature had the constitutional duty to reapportion but could see no way out save to rely on the "political conscience of the legislature, where lies the burden of the constitutional mandate." Since that time, the Federal courts have taken action in the field of apportionment, so the Minnesota case no longer is important for enlightenment on the law regarding apportionment, which incidently will be dealt with in Chapter III, but it is important as an indication of the general reluctance of courts to tell legislatures what they must do. Should courts be so deferential to legislatures?

ADAMS v. *BOLIN*

ARIZONA SUPREME COURT

247 P. 2D 617 (1952)

The Arizona legislature passed a resolution to submit to a referendum of the voters a measure which upon ratification would repeal a public employee retirement statute which had been enacted through the initiative process, in the course of which it had been approved by a majority of the voters voting on the question but not by a majority of voters participating in the election in which it was on the ballot. Adams and others sought a restraining order preventing Bolin, who was secretary of state, from placing the referendum on the ballot on the grounds that the legislature was without power to call for a referendum on a measure which had been enacted through the initiative process. The lower court dismissed the complaint of Adams et al. They then appealed the decision to the Arizona supreme court.

Mr. Justice LA PRADE delivered the opinion of the court.

. . . .

THE PUBLIC Employees' Retirement Act was initiated by petition and was adopted at the 1948 general election: 240,998 electors had qualified for this election by registering; at the election 184,323 ballots were cast; 86,989 electors voted for the retirement measure and 38,111 voted against it. Of the electors actually voting at the polls 59,223 did not vote on this measure; and, 56,675 registered electors failed to vote at all. All figures re registrations and votes cast were verified from records in the office of Secretary of State, of which we take judicial notice.

"A majority of the votes cast thereon" was 62,551 votes, and became a law upon proclamation of the Governor. Const. Art. 4, pt. 1, sec. 1(5).

"A majority vote of the qualified electors" was 120,500. Const. Art. 4, pt. 1, sec. 1(6).

It did not, however, receive the approval of "a majority vote of the qualified electors" so as to make it immune from repeal or amendment by the Legislature, . . . unless the phrase "approved by a majority vote of the qualified electors" is interpreted to be synonymous with the phrase "approved by a majority of the votes cast thereon."

The motion to dismiss the complaint was upon the ground that it failed to state a claim upon which relief could be granted. It was argued (1) that the court was without jurisdiction to restrain the submission of the referendum proposed by the Legislature, and (2) that the Legislature has constitutional authority to submit to the voters a referendum repealing an initiated law. The judgment ordered the complaint "dismissed for the reason and upon the ground that the Legislature of the State of Arizona does have the right to submit to the voters a referendum to repeal an initiative law, as a legislative measure."

It is the contention of appellants that an initiated measure, once adopted, can only be repealed in the same manner in which it was adopted, i.e., by an initiated repeal, and that the Legislature does not have the constitutional authority to order a referendum repealing an initiated law.

It is appellee's contention that not having received a majority vote of the qualified electors it is subject to repeal or amendment by the Legislature, and if subject to repeal by the Legislature, a fortiori the Legislature must have the power to refer a resolution of repeal. . . .

. . . .

A part of the controversy here stems from a difference of interpretation of the language of Art. 4, pt. 1, sec. 1(6) of the Constitution. This section reads as follows:

> "The veto power of the governor, or the power of the legislature, to repeal or amend shall not extend to initiative or referendum measures approved by a majority vote of the qualified electors."

This section as it now reads was amended by an initiated act approved at the general election on November 3, 1914, and effective December 14, 1914.

The original section read as follows:

> " '(6) The veto power of the governor shall not extend to initiative or referendum measures approved by a majority of the qualified electors.' "

It is thus seen that as originally adopted the governor alone was precluded from vetoing initiative or referendum measures approved by a majority of the qualified electors. By the amendment the Legislature was included in the prohibition and it was deprived of the power to repeal or amend initiative or referendum measures "approved by a majority vote of the qualified electors." Both before and after the amendment the prohibition extended to initiative and referendum measures "approved by a majority vote of the qualified electors."

It is also suggested that if the words "approved by a majority vote of the qualified electors" were not to mean what they say but were intended to mean "approved by majority of the qualified electors voting thereon," that the words "voting thereon" could easily have been added to the sentence, as was done in Art. 21, sec. 1 of the Constitution wherein it is provided that amendments to the Constitution shall become a part thereof "if a majority of the qualified electors *voting thereon* shall approve and ratify * * *." (Emp. Sup.) We believe there is merit in this contention.

On examination of the journal of proceedings of the constitutional convention, wherein the provisions of Art. 4, pt. 1 of the Constitution, relating to initiative and referendum were under discussion, we find that it was repeatedly stated that the Oregon constitution furnished the model for consideration. The sentence in the Oregon section comparable to our Subsection (6) reads: "The veto power of the governor shall not extend to measures referred to the people." Art. 4, § 1. Our Subsection (6) extended the prohibition not only to referred measures but to initiative measures. But it is to be noted that the prohibition in the Oregon section was to "[referendum] measures referred to the people" and then provided that "any measure referred to the people shall take effect and become the law when it is approved by a majority of the votes cast thereon, and not otherwise." It is thus seen that our constitution makers intentionally deviated from the Oregon model and provided that the veto power of the Governor and the Legislature should not extend to initiative or referendum measures *approved by a majority vote of the qualified electors.* It is most patent that the words "approved by a majority vote of the qualified electors" were intentionally and meticulously selected.

Nothing is more firmly settled than under ordinary circumstances, where there is involved no ambiguity or absurdity, a statutory or constitutional provision requires no interpretation. . . . We are not aware of any absurdity or inconsistency that will arise by construing this constitutional provision to mean what it says.

. . . .

There is a marked distinction between a law approved by a majority of the qualified electors and a law approved by a majority of the electors voting thereon. It is a matter of common knowledge, as disclosed by the records in the office of the Secretary of State, that even in presidential election years it is the rare exception when more than 75% of the qualified electors actually vote. It is all too clear that the constitution makers knew the difference between a majority of the votes cast thereon and a majority of the vote of the qualified electors. This is made clearer by reference to Art. 4, pt. 1, sec. 1(2), Constitution, where it was provided that "ten per centum of the qualified electors shall have the right to propose any measure * * *." In Subsection (3) it is provided that "five per centum of the qualified electors" might order a referendum. These two subsections taken together indicate that the required per centum in one instance is ten per centum of the qualified electors and in the other five per centum of the qualified electors. However, these required percentages are modified or reduced by Section 1(7) of Art. 4, pt. 1. This section provides that "The whole number of votes cast for all candidates for governor at the general election last preceding the filing of any initiative or referendum petition on a state or county measure shall be the basis on which the number of qualified electors required to sign such petition shall be computed."

So, Subsection (2) and (3) referring to the percentages required of the qualified electors, do not have to be literally complied with because of Subsection (7), which modifies Subsections (2) and (3) and makes definitely clear that for an initiative measure ten per centum of the qualified electors is not required but rather only ten per centum of the votes cast for all the candidates for governor at the general election last preceding.

. . . .

We have pointed out that the words "approved by a majority vote of the qualified electors" are plain and leave no room for construction. But if rules of construction should be availed of, one of the many rules pertaining to constitutional provisions is that some meaning must be given to each phrase of the Constitution unless in giving the words their grammatical and common meaning will create some impossibility or unworkable situation, or lead to an absurdity. . . . In the interpretation of a statute, city ordinance or city charter the cardinal principle is to give full effect to the intent of the lawmaker, and each word, phrase, clause and sentence must be given meaning so that no part will be void, inert, redundant or trivial. . . .

Some assistance can be had in this case by reference to our holding in Maxwell v. Fleming, 166 P.2d 831, wherein it was held that the phrase "majority of all votes cast at such election" in the Phoenix City Charter means exactly what it says—a majority of the total vote cast at the election, as opposed to a majority of the votes cast for one of the offices voted upon. By analogy, there can be no question that the phrase "majority of the votes cast thereon" appearing in Constitution of Arizona, Art. 4, pt. 1, sec. 1(5) means exactly what it says—a majority of the votes cast upon the initiative or referendum measure, as opposed to a majority of the votes cast at the election.

. . . we have held that strict rules of technical grammar will not be resorted to to defeat the plain purpose of the statute. . . . What was the plain purpose for which this limitation was put upon the power of the Legislature to amend or repeal initiative or referred measures? Was it to extend to all initiative or referred measures enacted and approved? The constitutional provision suggests that the answer is no. If attention is given to the constitutional provision the limitation on the legislature runs only to those measures that are approved by a majority vote of the qualified electors. If this latter phrase, "approved by a majority vote of the qualified electors," is not susceptible of more than one meaning, then this court must enforce it according to its terms. . . .

To interpret and enforce this constitutional provision according to its terms will not create an impossible or unworkable situation, nor will it result in an absurdity. To enforce it according to its terms will mean that only those initiated and referred measures which receive the majority vote of the qualified electors will be immune from legislative amendment or repeal. We are fully aware of the stated reasons actuating the constitution makers to reserve to the people the right to enact laws and refer measures enacted by the Legislature. We are also cognizant of the mischief it was felt the reservation of these powers would reach and the objects and remedy that was contemplated. But with the advent of the initiative and referendum there was no general concept that initiated and referred measures were sacrosanct. At the time of the adoption of our constitutional provisions and the amendment of Section 1(6), it was felt that Oregon had best conceived and expressed the ideas inherent in the reservations. But Oregon only withheld the veto power from the governor alone, and his veto power extended only to referred measures. In California the veto power was withheld from the governor on measures initiated or adopted by the people and the Legislature was precluded from amending or repealing any act, law or amendment to the Constitution adopted by the people at the polls under the initiative provisions. Calif.Const., Article 4, section 1.

According to the journal of the proceedings before the convention, this California provision was before our constitution makers and it would appear that the California provision furnished the idea for the Arizona constitution makers to enlarge the prohibition to include the Legislature as to initiative and referred acts. But in this respect the California constitution was exact and concise in withholding the veto power of the Legislature to measures initiated or "adopted by the people at the polls." Id.

The Washington constitutional provision was also before our constitution makers. The comparable provision from the Constitution of the state of Washington reads as follows: "No act, law, or bill approved by a majority of the electors *voting thereon* shall be amended or repealed by the legislature within a period of two years following such enactment." (Emp. Sup.) . . . It would appear from the reported cases many constitutions and municipal charters contain express inhibitions, absolutely or for a specified time against repeal, abrogation or amendment by the Legislature or municipal councils, of initiative or referendum measures. The examination of these constitutional provisions and the reported cases referring to constitutional and charter prohibitions plainly depict that there was no universal or general concept of the inviolability of initiated or referred measures. Reference in each instance must be had to the particular constitutional or charter provision. We have been referred to no case, and our own industry has furnished none, in which the exact language under consideration has been considered. In this respect we are on our own in attempting to construe the words "approved by a majority vote of the qualified electors." Regardless of the fact that they are simple and explicit we have nevertheless tried to make a thorough examination of them, taking into consideration the sections in pari materia, the circumstances under which they were adopted, the purposes to be accomplished by their use, and the evils to which they were addressed. All this search and contemplation leads us to the conclusion that the words mean simply what they say.

The Wyoming case of State ex rel. Blair v. Brooks, 99 P. 874, furnishes some excellent reasoning which by way of analogy fortifies the conclusion that we have reached in this case. In this Wyoming case the voters, by a vote of 12 to 1, approved a constitutional amendment. The Constitution, art. 20, § 1, required that ratification had to be by "majority of the electors." At the election 37,561 votes were cast. Of these, 12,160 voted in favor of the adoption of the amendment and 1363 voted against it. The question was, did it receive the approval of "a majority of the electors"? The court said no. In an explanation thereof and in expounding its reason for its conclusion, it said:

> "The provision of the Constitution is explicit in its terms. Such proposed amendment can only be ratified by a majority of the electors. It would be anomalous to say, in view of the section taken as a whole, that it was intended to mean only those who actually voted upon the amendment, or in other words, a majority of some of the electors, excluding others. It requires the proposed amendment to be submitted to the electors of the state, those who are entitled to vote, and it is by a majority of the electors—that is, electors of the state—and not a majority of those actually voting upon the question, that such a proposed amendment is ratified. Any other construction would authorize the counting of all who did not vote on the question as in favor of the adoption, a construction which is not borne out by the language, nor is it in harmony with the spirit of the Constitution. While it is true that a majority or a plurality of the votes cast elects a candidate for an office, yet when a voter fails to cast his vote for any candidate for a particular office, the preference of the elector has not been legally expressed, and there is nothing to record in favor of or against any such candidate. The word 'elector' is defined in the Constitution (section 2, art. 6) as follows: (definition omitted). There is no room for doubt as to what the constitutional convention meant when it used the word 'electors' in section 1, art. 20. The word, according to the definition given it by those who framed the Constitution, means those who are entitled to vote; and, when the Constitution says a majority of the electors, it means, in the absence of any qualifying phrase, a majority of those who are entitled to vote. This is made more evident from the fact that the phrase 'if ratified by a majority of the electors' follows the provision that the proposed amendment shall be submitted to the electors of the state; and the words 'the electors,' without other qualification, a majority of whom is required to ratify the amendment, clearly means the electors of the state. The language is broader in meaning than a mere majority of the electors who actually vote upon the proposition. Neither residence of the elector nor failure to vote can militate against this proposition. The word 'elector' is generic. It includes, not only those who vote, but those who are qualified, yet fail to exercise the right of franchise. To hold otherwise would, in effect, give to the word 'electors' a narrower and more restricted meaning than that given to it in the Constitution."

. . . .

Counsel for appellants suggest that to make a distinction between initiative and referendum measures approved by a majority of the qualified electors and those approved by a majority vote of the votes cast thereon would throw out of harmony the various provisions of our Constitution on the subject of initiated and referred laws and would create a seriously confused condition that would take years of litigation to straighten out. If we thought that this dire consequence were in store we would most earnestly seek a way, if possible, to adopt appellants' interpretation. We are of the opinion that to permit the legislature to make needed amendments to ill-considered initiated laws or referred measures that, through the passage of time, have become obsolete, will be a step forward and relieve the people of shackling legislation. Although it is true that many worthwhile general ideas are incorporated in initiative measures, it is also true that they do not have the advantage of open debate and analysis, and oftentimes incorporate provisions that are out of harmony with and contradict the general scheme of legislation. If the people think that any legislative repeal or amendment of initiated law is not desirable, five per centum of the qualified electors can force a referendum against it and the people will again have an opportunity to express their opinion thereon.

There are on the books a total of sixteen initiated measures, one of which became a law by 13,941 votes, another by 16,754 votes and another by 18,936 votes. We now have fourteen laws that were referred by petition, two of them receiving less than 11,000 votes, two more receiving less than 12,000 votes, four of them receiving less than 14,000 votes and two of them receiving less than 15,000 votes; three were referred by the Legislature. The total number of votes cast for all the candidates for governor in the 1950 general election was 195,227. In order to initiate a repeal or amendment to any of these 33 initiated and referred laws would require an initiative petition, to bear valid signatures of 19,523 qualified electors. In order to propose an amendment or repeal of an initiated or referred law at the present time, for the most part, requires one and one-half times as many signatures as the measure received when it was enacted or approved, a most expensive and laborious undertaking; so much so, in fact, that many of them die a-borning. To give to the Legislature the outright power to amend or repeal, both subject to the referendum, can only result in good; not "good" that we, as members of the court view it, but the opportunity for "good" as envisioned and authorized by the Constitution.

. . . .

We therefore hold:

1. That the Legislature has constitutional power to repeal or amend an initiated measure approved by less than a majority of the qualified electors;

2. That the Legislature has the constitutional power to refer to the electors an act repealing an initiated law. . . .

. . . .

The judgment is affirmed.

UDALL, C. J., and PHELPS and DE CONCINI, JJ., concurring.

STANFORD, Justice (dissenting).

The Legislature is empowered, but limited under the referendum provisions of the Constitution, to refer laws enacted by it. Concurrent Resolution No. 4 now refers to a vote of the people, not a law "enacted by the Legislature" but a proposal only to become law when approved by the voters. The Legislature is thus attempting to submit to the voters, as an initiative measure, a proposal to repeal the Employees' Retirement Act.

The Employees' Retirement Act, having been initiated, is not subject to repeal or amendment by the Legislature. The majority opinion, however, is of the opinion that not having been adopted by a majority of the electors as appears on the roll of registered voters, the power still exists in the Legislature to repeal or amend notwithstanding the measure was adopted as an initiative measure. The answer, of course, to that proposition is that Concurrent Resolution No. 4 was neither a "repeal nor amendment."

Not having repealed the Retirement Act by concurrent resolution, the only question therefore before the court is whether the Legislature has been given the power to initiate, and to submit to the voters a measure under the initiative provisions of the Constitution.

While the Legislature has power to enact legislation, not prohibited by the State or Federal constitutions, it is not an inherent legislative power to delegate the law-making power to the people, either by initiative or referendum. . . .

The authority to initiate, or refer laws, springs from the Constitution itself, as a power delegated, not as power inherent in the Legislature. Therefore, such power may be exercised only in the manner as delegated. . . .

The referendum powers give the Legislature, or 5% of the voters, authority to have placed upon the ballot any measure enacted by the Legislature, for approval or veto, while under the Initiative no authority to submit laws proposed by the Legislature is delegated to the Legislature, but is limited to a petition signed by 10% of the qualified electors. The Legislature therefore has no power to initiate a law by concurrent resolution, and Resolution No. 4 under consideration is unauthorized and is an unconstitutional exercise of the legislative powers.

Art. 4, pt. 1, sec. 1(5), of our Constitution provides that any measure submitted to the qualified electors shall become law when approved by a majority of the votes cast thereon, and section 1(6) of the same Article follows and denies the Governor the right to veto, and the Legislature the right to repeal or amend, any measure approved by a majority *vote* of the qualified electors. The majority opinion reads into the Constitution as though "qualified electors" had the words following "as appears on the registration roll of voters," although and notwithstanding that Art. 4, pt. 1, sec. 1(5) defines the necessary qualified voters to enact the measure as being the majority of votes cast thereon.

No initiated or referred measure since statehood has been adopted by a majority of the qualified electors. To accept the interpretation now given the Initiative and Referendum measures means that the Governor could have vetoed any measure that has ever been adopted, and the Legislature may now repeal or amend any initiated or referred measure enacted since statehood.

When only 50% of the voters exercise their right to vote it will be seen how impossible it becomes to hereafter place beyond the power of the Legislature to immediately repeal any law enacted by the people.

It has been the accepted construction of the language of the Constitution, by all Governors, the Legislature, and the courts, that initiated and referred measures were beyond the power of the Legislature to disturb. The majority opinion has completely nullified the interpretation of that provision of the Constitution prohibiting the Governor from vetoing, or the Legislature from repealing, initiative and referred measures. Hereafter only an amendment of the Constitution itself by the people can restore and preserve the laws enacted through the Initiative and Referendum.

GAINES v. O'CONNELL

KENTUCKY COURT OF APPEALS

204 S.W. 2D 425 (1947)

Gaines and others filed suit against O'Connell, secretary of state, to enjoin him from proceeding with preparations for an election on the question of calling a constitutional convention. They contended that the acts of the state legislature providing for the election violated the state constitution in two respects (1) they did not specifically allow for a proper period of notice; and (2) they required the convention, if held, to submit its production to the people for ratification. The lower court held that the acts were valid. Consequently, Gaines et al. *appealed the decision to the Kentucky court of appeals.*

Commissioner STANLEY delivered the opinion of the court.

. . . .

SECTION 263 of the Constitution reads as follows: "Before a vote is taken upon the question of calling a Convention, the Secretary of State shall cause notice of the election to be published in such manner as may be provided by the act directing said vote to be taken."

But the General Assembly made no provision for publishing notice of the election. Therein lies the difficulty.

Notwithstanding the absence of such explicit provision, on the day the petition in this case was filed, on the advice of the Attorney General, the Secretary of State caused publication of notices to begin in Louisville and Lexington newspapers of general circulation throughout the State. This was 78 days before the election. . . .

The primary contention of the appellants is that since the Legislature failed to prescribe the manner of publication of notice, the Secretary of State was without authority to do so, hence his action is abortive. The real question is not the constitutionality of the Acts of the Legislature but whether they are operative.

The argument of the appellants is that all of Section 263 is mandatory; that the Secretary of State is required to cause notice to be published in a manner prescribed by the Legislature and in no other way; hence it is also mandatory on the Legislature so to prescribe, and it failed. The argument is no ingenious refinement, or one without merit. It seems to be sustainable by a strict construction of the Constitution.

The contention of the appellees is that the word "shall," used in Section 263 in relation to the duties of the Secretary of State, makes the provision mandatory as to him, but the word "may," used in relation to the manner of publication to be prescribed by the General Assembly, being a word of permission or discretion, leaves it open for that body to prescribe the manner or not to do so; hence, its omission cannot cancel the obligatory duty of the Secretary of State. It is submitted that the Legislature having failed to exercise the power, the official was nevertheless required to perform his duty under the self-executing provision applying to him, and in doing so he has properly exercised a prudent and reasonable judgment as to what was adequate.

It has often been said that all the provisions of the Constitution are mandatory. . . . But this broad statement is subject to the qualification, just as often declared, that they are not to be so regarded if by express language or necessary implication a different intention is manifest. It is a cardinal rule of construction that no part of the Constitution should be construed so as to defeat its substantial purpose or the reasonable intent of the people in adopting it. . . . What is implied is as much a part of the instrument as what is expressed. . . . Wherever the language admits a doubt, it is presumed that it was intended to be in accordance with generally recognized rules and principles of public policy. Still another familiar concomitant rule, no less binding on the courts, is that all presumptions and all reasonable doubts are to be resolved in favor of constitutionality of any act of the General Assembly. . . .

The foregoing are canons of construction applicable to legislation of the usual character. A fortiori, are they applicable to the present inquiry. We are not dealing with pure legislation affecting commercial or personal affairs, nor with legislation with which the people in their capacity of electors have nothing to do. We are dealing with machinery and procedure under the Constitution. The actions of the Legislature and the Secretary of State are but steps toward the end. The great mass of the electors of the Commonwealth constitutes the body which considers and determines the question of whether there shall be a constitutional convention. Their vote is the paramount act. The framers of the Constitution well appreciated that this is a government by the people and that a revision of the organic law must be made by them. They well knew that substance is supreme and more potent than method and form. Method and form may not be disregarded, to be sure, for by them the essentials are secured. But they are not themselves the essentials. We are dealing with a matter in which the sovereign people are vitally concerned—with the inherent right of the people to express themselves with respect to revising their charter of government. It is sound and proper to hold that a case of this character requires an extremely liberal construction, just as would an Act which might violate the Bill of Rights require a rigid construction in order to protect the people.

We are not without precedent. In Green v. Weller, 32 Miss. 650, it was said in reference to the adoption of an amendment to a constitution: "The means provided for the exercise of their sovereign right of changing their Constitution should receive such a construction as not to trammel the exercise of the right."

In Baker v. Moorhead, 174 N.W. 430, it was held in reference to a statute defining the manner of electing delegates to a constitutional convention (as stated in the syllabi prepared by the court):

"The general rule that the provisions of a Constitution will be construed as mandatory, rather than directory, does not apply with the same strictness to provisions of the Constitution providing for future constitutional conventions, as it applies to other parts of the Constitution"; and

"A construction of a provision of the Constitution which would make difficult or impossible any fair and just method of revising it will not be adopted by the courts."

. . . .

Our own case of Denton v. Pulaski County, 185 S.W. 481, involved the construction of that part of Section 256 of the Constitution which provides that where a majority of votes were cast for an amendment it shall become a part of the Constitution "and shall be so proclaimed by the Governor, and published in such manner as the General Assembly may direct." The Legislature had provided for publishing the result of the election but not as to how an adoption should be proclaimed or published. The result had been so published and the Governor had recommended appropriate action by the Legislature to effectuate the amendment, but there was no formal proclamation. We said: "In the absence of legislative action prescribing the particular manner in which an amendment shall be proclaimed and published, we conclude that the foregoing steps constituted a substantial compliance with the Constitution." The decision was influenced by the relative unimportance of the official post-election procedure. The people well knew the effect of a majority vote.

The Constitution clothes the General Assembly with the power to initiate the proceedings for a convention. It assumes that the legislature will appropriate the entire machinery of the general election law, changed only by explicit provisions in order to make it workable for the unusual purpose. Publication of notice of the election is not an act of finality but of procedural detail. It has been done in this instance in a manner sanctioned many times in many circumstances by statute and by custom. With the exception of the time element, it has been in strict accordance with the statute relating to notice of elections on adopting amendments to the Constitution. . . . Moreover, the Court has judicial knowledge that the members of both Houses at both sessions of the General Assembly have with practical unanimity concurred in the submission to the people of the question of the expediency of calling the Convention. We cannot feign ignorance of the fact that in addition to the official publication the issue has been and is being given widespread publicity in the press and public forums of the State; a greater and better publication than has been or could be given in formal official notice, which, as a matter of fact, is always quite inconspicuous. The object of Section 263 of the Constitution is clear. It is that the people shall know about the referendum which their Legislature has authorized. It has been and is being accomplished.

With this broad prospective and sensible view, the court ought not nullify this vast political operation, stop the machinery and thereby prevent an expression of the popular will unless a sure sensibility of constitutional duty demands it. To do so would be by a rigid construction of the Constitutional processes and, as we feel, by ignoring the underlying aim and object of the instrument as expressed in Section 263. It would be to surrender reality for technicality, substance for form, and common sense for pure legalism.

We are of opinion that the action taken by the Secretary of State in the absence of specific statutory direction, and the legal effect of that action, can be consistently and reasonably sustained. The conclusion rests not only upon the considerations already recited, but more particularly the analysis of the six sections of the Constitution relating to a Convention.

Section 258 is addressed to the General Assembly and also to the Secretary of State in prescribing his duties after an election has been held. It is meticulous. Sections 259, 260 and 261 are addressed to the members of the Convention. Section 262 deals with contests of election of delegates and is addressed to the Convention and the General Assembly. The series concludes with Section 263, which we have quoted. It is addressed to the Secretary of State—not to the General Assembly. It is significant, we think, that the framers of the Constitution in the same sentence used the mandatory word "shall" in relation to the official upon whom they placed the duty, and used the word "may" in relation to the General Assembly. They well knew the distinction. The word "may" generally carries the meaning of permission or option; but that was not necessary here, for the Legislature has all power except where restricted by federal or state constitutions. . . . It is seldom used in the sense of permission except to qualify or exclude from a mandatory provision. . . . The word often imports contingency, and the clause "may be" is the equivalent of possibly or perhaps. Webster's New International Dictionary. That, we think, is the sense in which the clause was used here. It is also of significance that in the several sections relating to the duties of the General Assembly the word "shall" is used exclusively. Therefore, it is only by implication that it can be said that Section 263 places the exclusive duty upon the General Assembly to prescribe the manner of notice—how, when and what—to be followed by the Secretary of State. It is only assumed that the General Assembly will provide the manner.

It may be noted as a matter of interest, if not of significance, that Section 263 is the last in the category, though it would seem a logical arrangment would place it next to Section 258 as a part of the machinery for holding the election rather than with the post-election sections. It may possibly have been an afterthought in the preparation of the title "Mode of Revision," though there is nothing in the Constitutional Debates that sheds any light on the unusual arrangement, or, indeed, on the whole problem as to the proper construction of the section.

The Legislature may have construed Section 263 as not requiring that it should provide the manner of publication, and believed the usual and generally recognized practices would not only be observed but be sufficient. The doctrine of presumption of constitutional validity stems from the fact that the members of the General Assembly take an oath to support the Constitution and frame their legislation according to their interpretation of it. . . .

All enactments of this general character are carried into execution by officers elected or appointed for the purpose, and these are often clothed with authority which necessarily involve a large degree of discretion. The Constitution, as do the statutes, seldom defines with precision the scope of official duties. True it is, as the appellants say, and as we have recognized above, where a power is conferred by the Constitution it must be exercised in the way directed by law. But many incidents are based on what may be necessarily implied from duties or powers expressly conferred. . . .

We cannot accede to appellants' alternative argument, that, in any event, the publication of notice commencing 78 days before the election is not due and timely. It rests upon the application of Section 257 of the Constitution, which requires that such notices as to an election on the adoption of an amendment must be begun not less than 90 days before. . . . This is an explicit provision in that section only, and is exclusive in its application. There is reason why a more extended official notice should be given in such a case, for the result of the election itself makes the change in the fundamental law. In the calling a Convention, the result has no finality. It is a step, and a very important one, but it is not the ultimate end.

We conclude by again recognizing that the substantial execution of the clear intent and the accomplishment of the object of the constitutional provision is the essential and dominant thing. It is that which governs our decision to affirm the judgment on this issue.

We come to consider the legal effect of the following direction to the proposed Constitutional Convention contained both in the Act of 1944 (Chapter

4) and the Act of 1946 (Chapter 145) concurring and making provision for the referendum: "Before any Constitution agreed upon by a convention that may be called pursuant to this Act and to Section 258 of the present Constitution shall take effect and become operative, the same shall be submitted to the qualified voters of this Commonwealth, after at least ninety days' notice, and ratified by a majority of those voting."

The challenge of this limitation upon the Convention, if one should be held, is that the constitutional provisions with respect to this mode of revision deal with every phase of the calling, organization and duties of a convention, and contain no authority for the General Assembly to bind the members to submit their work to a vote of the people. Hence, it is argued, the framers of the present constitution did not intend to confer upon the Legislature the power to restrict or limit the action of the convention.

The Act of the Legislature initiating the call for the convention which framed our present constitution contained a similar provision. The constitution of the time, that of 1851, had no provision giving the Legislature the power to require a submission of the work of the convention to a vote of the people. The instrument was submitted to the people and approved by a large majority. Thereafter the delegates reassembled and made numerous changes in the instrument. As thus altered, it was proclaimed as the Constitution of Kentucky. In a notable opinion, this court, then composed of four judges, held that since the Constitution had been promulgated according to law and its validity had been recognized by both the executive and legislative branches of the government, it was not within the power of the judiciary to declare the instrument not to be the Constitution. The question was regarded as a political and not a judicial one. Miller v. Johnson, 18 S.W. 522. The majority opinion recognized the divergent views of the courts and constitutional authorities on the subject of the power of a legislature to bind a constitutional convention, but expressed no opinion concerning either view. In an able dissenting opinion, Judge Bennett contended that all material changes which had been made by the Convention after it reassembled were void. He reasoned that there was no authority in the members to alter the instrument (except to make grammatical corrections) because "the delegates to the convention of 1890–91 were expressly limited in their authority. The people refused to give them absolute power, but reserved to themselves the right to approve or reject the work of their agents, which they, however, disregarded." Therefore, the question is an open one in this jurisdiction.

It has been held by some courts that a constitutional convention derives its powers from the action of the people and not from that of the Legislature which may have issued the call; that it exercises sovereign, plenary power, subject only to the limitations on the powers of the State contained in the Constitution of the United States. Hence, that an act of a legislature expressly providing that no constitution or amendments framed by a convention should go into effect until submitted to the vote of the people and approved by them is not binding and need not be observed if the convention so wills. This conception or doctrine, that a constitutional convention inherently possesses unlimited sovereign power, seems to have had its origin in what are generally termed "Revolutionary Conventions." . . . The reason for the view, therefore, fails under our firm and stable "government of law." . . . "No argument for the implied power of absolute sovereignty in a convention can be drawn from revolutionary times, when necessity begets a new government. Governments thus accepted and ratified by silent submission afford no precedents for the power of a convention in a time of profound tranquility, and for a people living under self-established, safe institutions."

However, under the terms peculiar to the constitutions of some states that extreme power seems to exist and the legislatures may not impose any condition upon the constitutional conventions.

It is not surprising to find in "Constitutional Conventions" by Roger Sherman Hoar, at page 71, the generally accepted rule, namely: "The theory with the greatest weight of authority behind it is based upon the fact that there would be no convention unless the people voted affirmatively, that an affirmative vote would result in holding exactly the sort of convention in every detail provided in the act, and that the people are presumed to know the terms of the act under which they vote. The conclusion drawn from this is that the convention act in its every detail is enacted by the people voting under it."

. . . .

A clear statement, fully sustained by the weight of authority, is made in Re Opinion to the Governor, 55 R.I. 56 . . . : "In the second instance, the Legislature summons the convention only after the people have expressed their will to this effect. If, at the time the question of calling the convention is submitted to them, the people are informed of the scope of the convention and the manner in which it is to conduct its deliberations, and report its results by virtue of the act of the General Assembly specifying such matters, then a convention called in this manner will be limited as therein set forth and the convention will then be bound to confine itself within the stated limits of the act of the Assembly. The reason for this is that it is the people, under such circumstances, who prescribe the conditions in the legislative act by approving the call for the convention in accordance with the provisions of such act. The Legislature merely proposes the conditions. It is the vote of the people for the convention that ratifies them and makes them binding upon the delegates."

This view was recently accepted by our sister state of Virginia, in Staples v. Gilmer, 33 S.E.2d 49. In that case the General Assembly, as a means of obtaining quicker amendment of the constitution to liberalize voting rights of members of the armed forces than could be had through the submission of separate amendments, provided for a vote of the people on calling a convention to accomplish the purpose. The act limited the convention to the consideration of two changes only and authorized it to proclaim and ordain the revisions adopted within the scope of the powers conferred upon it by the act without submitting the same to the electors for approval. Reviewing the principle and the authorities, the court held the limitations valid and binding. In a concurring opinion by Judge Holt, it is well said: "It is good to know that they (the conclusions of the court) find ample support in ancient precedents and modern instances. * * * [And] it is interesting to note that nowhere are provisions made for an unrestricted convention. Such a convention would be a revolutionary convention, but provisions are made for a convention to revise the Constitution and amend the same. The extent of this revision or of these amendments is nowhere defined."

Since the constitution of Kentucky likewise contains no inhibition or restriction upon the General Assembly in this matter of initiating a call for a Constitutional Convention, it was at liberty to exercise its plenary power in attaching the condition to the submission of the question of calling a convention. When they vote upon it, they will do so with the assurance that the result of the deliberations of the Convention, if called, will be submitted to them for ratification or rejection. By this course, the people keep a firm hold upon their liberties and may obtain a charter of government wanted by the majority. This is sustained by the customs and traditions of the Commonwealth, as well as principles of constitutional government. If the instrument be approved, then the people of the Commonwealth will literally "ordain and establish" the new Constitution.

We are of opinion, therefore, that the judgment to that effect is correct.

The judgment is affirmed.

YELLE v. BISHOP

STATE OF WASHINGTON SUPREME COURT

347 P. 2D. 1081 (1959)

For the purpose of improving over-all fiscal management, the Washington legislature enacted a state budgeting and accounting act which transferred certain functions, including that of pre-audit, from the state auditor to the state budget director (a new position created by the act). Yelle, the state auditor went to court seeking to test the constitutionality of the act by instituting an action for a declaratory judgment. He felt that the most appropriate defendants in such a suit were Bishop, the state budget director, who under the law would be taking over some of Yelle's functions, and Martin, the state treasurer. Yelle's principal contention was that the law would deprive the auditor of some of his constitutional powers and prerogatives. The trial court decided against him. Yelle, thereupon, appealed to the state supreme court.

Judge HUNTER delivered the opinion of the court.

. . . .

THE TRIAL court held that the transferring of functions from the state auditor under the act was valid and constitutional; that the other constitutional issues raised in the complaint were not properly before the court, and entered judgment accordingly. The state auditor appeals.

It is not disputed that the budget and accounting act takes from the state auditor all of his pre-auditing functions, which are presently the auditing of claims against the state treasury and the issuing of warrants to the state treasurer for payment of claims thus approved. Nor is it disputed that the post-auditing functions of the auditor are not in any way disturbed by the questioned enactment.

The office of state auditor is established in the executive department by Art. III, § 1, of the state constitution as follows:

> "The executive department shall consist of a governor, lieutenant governor, secretary of state, treasurer, auditor, attorney general, superintendent of public instruction, and a commissioner of public lands, who shall be severally chosen by the qualified electors of the state at the same time and place of voting as for the members of the legislature."

The powers and duties of the office thus established are set forth in Art. III, § 20:

"The auditor shall be auditor of public accounts, and shall have such powers and perform such duties *in connection therewith* as may be prescribed by law. * * *" (Italics ours.)

To infer from the above language the existence of implied constitutional powers raises the question of what the framers of the constitution intended. The appellant argues that the traditional and inherent powers of the office were fully understood by the framers of our constitution, they therefore intended that such powers attach to the constitutional office of auditor. The respondent, on the other hand, contends the express language of § 20 places all of the powers and duties of the state auditor exclusively in the hands of the lawmaking body.

In determining the meaning of a constitutional provision, the intent of the framers, and the history of events and proceedings contemporaneous with its adoption may properly be considered. . . .

In considering these contentions as to what was intended by the language of § 20, it is proper to examine the deliberations of the delegates at the constitutional convention, when the establishment of the office was under consideration. The official minutes of proceedings of the constitutional convention in some respects are incomplete; however, the proceedings of July 25, 1889, were reported in the Tacoma Daily Ledger on July 26, 1889. This report, a first-hand account of a contemporaneous event, may properly be considered under the rule stated above. It reads as follows:

"Executive Department Article Considered in Committee of the Whole.

* * * * * *

"Section 1 of the executive department article was read:

"Sec. 1. The executive department shall consist of governor, lieutenant governor, secretary of state, treasurer, auditor, attorney general, superintendent of public instruction, and a commissioner of public lands, who shall be severally chosen by the qualified electors of the state at the same time and place of voting for the members of the legislative assembly.

"Moved To Strike Out.

"Mr. Sharpstein moved to amend the section by striking out lieutenant governor and commissioner of public lands.

"Mr. Dickey called for a division of the question. Mr. Sharpstein had no objection. He merely did not want useless officers, and did not think that either officer was required.

"The question was considered separately.

"Mr. Weir said the impression seems to be that the lieutenant governor would be only a presiding officer of the senate. The committee believed that there would be many state institutions and such an officer as supervisor was necessary.

"Mr. Dunbar, as a politician, would be in favor of the office of lieutenant governor, but as a member of the convention he thought such an officer would be a superfluity just at this time.

"Thought It Necessary.

"Mr. Browne regarded the office of lieutenant governor as a necessary office.

"Mr. Godman thought a lieutenant governor was not usually selected for his ability but for his peculiar ability as a political manipulator.

"Mr. Dyer said a lieutenant governor would be necessary to serve as chairman of the boards it will be found advisable to constitute.

"Mr. Buchanan opposed the amendment, and stated that as the president of the senate succeeded the governor, it would take a man off the floor as a representative of his constituency.

"Mr. McElroy was opposed to any unnecessary officers.

"Mr. Gowey spoke in favo· of the report of the committee.

. . . .

"The motion to strike out lieutenant governor was defeated by a vote of 38 to 31.

. . . .

On July 26, 1889, at the time of the adoption of Art. III, § 25 (which was then § 27), in the Minutes of Proceedings of Constitutional Convention, the following appears:

"Mr. Godman moved to amend by adding to section 27,

" 'The legislature may in its discretion abolish the offices of lieutenant governor, auditor and commissioner of public lands.' * * * And the following thirty-seven members voted aye. * * * the following thirty-two members voted no. * * *"

From these intriguing deliberations by the fathers of our constitution, it appears clear there was disagreement as to the necessity of including these three offices in the executive department as constitutional offices; and their establishment was with the qualification that their continued existence be at the will and pleasure of the legislature, as provided by its authority for their abolishment in § 25.

The attitude of the framers in regard to the necessity of designating the office of auditor as a constitutional office is again exemplified in Art. XI, § 5, where they provided for certain county offices, but the office of county auditor was not among those enumerated; the framers again chose to leave the existence or nonexistence of such office within the legislative discretion.

With this attitude of the framers of our constitution toward these offices, we do not believe it reasonable to conclude they intended any powers for the office of state auditor, except as they specifically provided by the express language of Art. III, § 20:

" * * * The auditor *shall be auditor of public accounts,* and shall have such powers and perform such duties *in connection therewith* as may be prescribed by law. * * *" (Italics ours.)

We believe the words *"in connection therewith"* relate directly to his duty as *auditor of public accounts* to be fixed by the lawmaking body; that his powers and duties as auditor, by this language, are within the exclusive discretion of the legislature, which may be fixed, enlarged, or diminished by that body at any time.

This conclusion is further supported by the well-established rule of constitutional construction, *"expressio unius est exclusio alterius."* The express mention of one thing implies the exclusion of the other. . . . By the application of this principle, it is only when the constitution is silent as to these duties that constitutional duties may be implied. This rule must yield when the surrounding facts and circumstances satisfactorily demonstrate the converse to be true. However, the facts and circumstances surrounding the adoption of Art. III, §§ 1, 20 and 25, necessitate the application of the rule in this case. The principle of *expressio unius* was properly applied in the case of Lockwood v. Jordan, 1951, 231 P.2d 428. In that case the constitutionality of an enactment was being challenged which created the office of post auditor. Under the Arizona constitution, the state auditor was named as an officer of the executive department, whose duties were to be as prescribed by law. The court said:

"Section 9 of article 5 provides: 'The powers and duties of secretary of state, state treasurer, state auditor, attorney-general, and superintendent of public instruction shall be as prescribed by law.'

. . . .

"This court . . . observed that if the constitution had created the office of attorney general without referring to its powers and duties it might have been true under the authorities cited that the term 'attorney general' had been used in its common law acceptation since Arizona is a state in which the common law prevails; but that when the constitution provided in the same article in which it created the office of attorney general that he should perform such duties as were prescribed by the constitution and as may be provided by law and that his duties 'shall be "as prescribed by law"' it could not be said that the constitution was silent as to his powers and duties; that while it was true the constitution did not enumerate his duties but in stating that they shall be as 'prescribed by law' it referred to them and clearly made it the duty of the legislature to say what they should be. The court asserted that the expressions, 'as provided by law' and 'as prescribed by law' are susceptible of no other construction. It then concluded that the attorney general was not a common law officer, upon whom 'the duties and powers of the attorney general as the same was known at common law' had been engrafted but was one whose powers and duties could be ascertained only by resort to the statutes. The court further said:

"'Notwithstanding the holding in these cases, (cases cited by respondent) we are clearly of the view that the mere naming of the attorney general in the constitution of this state does not amount to an implied restriction on the authority of the legislature in prescribing his duties. It is true in this state, as in others, that the office of attorney general, together with the other executive offices created by the constitution, is imbedded in that instrument, but it is equally true that the authority of the legislature to prescribe what the duties and powers of those occupying these offices shall be is imbedded there also, and, this being true, no common-law powers or duties can attach to that office but only those prescribed by statute.' * * *"

In the instant case the Washington constitution is not silent as to the powers and duties of the office of auditor and the common-law duties or implied powers cannot attach to the office, but only those *as may be prescribed by law*. Moreover, the Washington constitution is a limitation upon the powers of the legislature, instead of a grant of powers, and so far as the power of the legislature is not limited by the constitution it is unrestrained. . . . This being so, in view of the affirmative direction that the powers and duties of the state auditor shall be as prescribed by law, it cannot be reasonably concluded that Art. III, §§ 1 and 20, was intended as a limitation upon the powers of the legislature.

The appellant relies heavily upon . . . cases . . . which hold that the legislature cannot denude a constitutional office of all its powers in the absence of authority from the constitution to do so, as this would amount to an abolishment of the office for which their constitutions did not provide. In the instant case the office was not denuded of all its powers and, contrary to the constitutions of those states, our constitution expressly provides for the abolishment of the office by the legislature.

We do not find it necessary to further discuss the cases cited from other jurisdictions since Washington is the only state in the Union which has the constitutional provision providing for the abolishment of the office of state auditor. This unique provision is singularly significant in view of the fact that the framers of our constitution questioned the necessity of establishing such an office. We are satisfied that Art. III, § 20, considered in the light of the state of mind of our convention delegates at the time of the adoption of this section, nullifies any inference that this office was to have any powers other than statutory powers, as they specifically provided.

. . . .

We are satisfied the legislature acted within the constitutional mandate of

Art. III, § 20, when by Laws of 1959, chapter 328, it removed all of the pre-auditing functions from the office of state auditor, previously given to that office by this same law-making body. These duties are statutory only, and the trial court did not err in so holding.

. . . .

. . . the judgment of the trial court establishing its validity is affirmed.

WEAVER, C. J., and FINLEY, ROSELLINI, and OTT, JJ., concur.

DONWORTH, J., concurs in the result.

HILL, Judge (dissenting).

I dissent. The constitution of the state of Washington says "The auditor shall be the auditor of public accounts." Art. III, § 20.

The majority see in the additional words "and shall have such powers and perform such duties in connection therewith as may be prescribed by law," the authority of the legislature to strip the office of its authority over public accounts.

In my view, those words are not intended to authorize the subtraction by the legislature of anything from the primary duty indicated, *i. e.*, "The auditor shall be the auditor of public accounts," but rather to enable the legislature to amplify his powers and duties in connection with that primary duty.

Historically, the purpose of an independent auditor was to be able to challenge the legality of the expenditure of funds by the various agencies, branches, and divisions of state government before the public funds had gone down the drain.

The state auditor has, through the years, refused to issue vouchers where he questioned the propriety of the use being made of public funds.

Sometimes we have held that he was mistaken and directed the issuance of certain vouchers . . . and, sometimes, we have held that he was right and that the expenditure could not lawfully be made. . . .

I concede, of course, that the legislature can, if it so desires, abolish the office of state auditor; but until it does, or until the constitutional statement of his duties is amended, "The auditor should remain the 'auditor of public accounts.'"

By the provisions of Laws of 1959, chapter 328, the state auditor ceases to be the "auditor of public accounts," and to that extent I would hold the act to be unconstitutional.

MALLERY and FOSTER, JJ., concur.

CITY OF FROSTBURG v. JENKINS

MARYLAND COURT OF APPEALS
136 A. 2D 852 (1957)

Under a Maryland enabling act, the city of Frostburg passed an ordinance authorizing a special bond election for the purpose of obtaining voter approval for a proposal to purchase an industrial site for a privately owned manufacturing company. Jenkins and other taxpayers and voters filed suit for a declaratory judgment. They contended that the enabling act and the city ordinance were unconstitutional because they authorized the use of public funds for a private purpose. This contention was upheld by the trial court which issued a decree restraining city officials from holding the election. The city appealed the case to the Maryland court of appeals.

Judge HENDERSON delivered the opinion of the court.

. . . .

IT IS the general rule that the public funds of municipalities cannot properly be devoted to private use, even when expressly authorized by the legislature. . . . The exact constitutional source of the prohibition is somewhat obscure. It was once supposed to reside in the Fourteenth Amendment to the Federal Constitution, because of the broad language of Loan Association v. City of Topeka, 87 U.S. 655. In that case the court affirmed a judgment in favor of the city, in a suit on its bonds, which had been donated to a manufacturer to induce it to locate in the city, pursuant to statutory authorization. But Mr. Justice Holmes, in his dissent in Madisonville Traction Company v. Saint Bernard Mining Co., 196 U.S. 239, observed that the decision in the Loan Association case was not, and could not have been, rested on the Fourteenth Amendment. . . . Another decision holding that the Fourteenth Amendment is not applicable in a situation like that in the instant case, is Miller v. Police Jury of Washington Parish, 74 So.2d 394. There a similar scheme for financing new industry was put into effect after an amendment to the state constitution had removed a prohibition against lending credit.

We have noted that the phrase "Law of the Land" in Article 23 of our Declaration of Rights expresses the same concept as "due process of law" in the Fourteenth Amendment, and that decisions of the Supreme Court in this field are "practically direct authorities." . . .

Although Sections 34 and 54 of Article III of the Maryland Constitution were not relied upon below or in this Court, it was suggested in argument that they might bar the extension of credit in the instant case. The prohibition in Section 34, in terms, runs only against the State, and this construction would seem to be supported by the qualified prohibition in Section 54 in the case of the counties. See also Article XI, Section 7, applicable to Baltimore City. . . .

The leading Maryland case that laid down the proposition that public funds cannot properly be devoted to a private purpose is Baltimore & E. S. R. Co v. Spring, 1895, 31 A. 208. In that case a legislative act authorized Talbot County to issue bonds and apply the proceeds to the payment of claims against an insolvent railroad for the benefit of local creditors. It was held that this was a private purpose, and a violation of Article 15 of the Declaration of Rights. The Article as it then stood was revised by Chapter 390, Acts of 1914, ratified November 2, 1915, but although it did not and does not now, in terms limit the taxing power we think it is settled, particularly since the decision in Finan v. Mayor & City Council of Cumberland, supra [*141 A. 269*], that taxes, by whomsoever laid or authorized, can only be imposed to raise money for public purposes. It is also recognized that, with due regard to the legislative prerogative, the courts have a duty to determine whether the particular use is within the scope of the constitutional power. . . . But in the application of the principle, it is agreed that "What is a public purpose for which public funds may be expended is not a matter of exact definition; it is almost entirely a matter of general acceptation." Finan v. Mayor & City Council of Cumberland, supra. We may add that the line of demarcation is not immutable or incapable of adjustment to changing social and economic conditions that are properly of public and governmental concern. . . . Perhaps the best illustration of change is to be found in the field of social security, until recently not considered a governmental responsibility.

The only declaration of public policy in the enabling act before us is the statement that the power is granted "in order to encourage industrial development." The legislative purpose, however, is somewhat amplified in the allegations of the answer, which are admitted for the purpose of this case, and we might, indeed, take judicial notice of the fact that the location of new industry in a municipality furnishes employment and measurably increases the resources of the community and its financial wellbeing. As the Supreme Court recognized in the Carmichael case, supra, the relief of unemployment is a legitimate public purpose. The fact that incidental benefits are passed on to the locating corporation is not fatal, if there are substantial public benefits to support the action taken. . . .

In the instant case there are obvious benefits passing to the private corporation, and enuring to the benefit of its stockholders. One benefit is the financing of its building program at a favorable interest rate. It is common knowledge that municipal bonds can usually be floated at a lower yield than industrial bonds, because of the tax immunities, and because they are supported by tax revenues instead of earnings. Although interest rates are not fixed in the Ordinance, we assume that the scheme contemplates that the saving be passed on to the corporation under its contract to purchase the land and building in installments in twenty-five years. Another benefit may arise from the fact that title will remain in the City during that period. We assume that the property so held would not be subject to property taxes. But whether these private benefits outweigh the public benefits accruing from the location of the plant within the municipality seems to us to be primarily a legislative rather than a judicial problem.

The attraction of new industries to this State, by means of tax exemptions, has been recognized as within the legislative power over a long period of years. . . . We see no real difference between the tax exemptions there created, and that in the instant case. True, those exemptions were made applicable to all manufacturers as a class, whereas in the instant case it only applies at this time, as a practical matter, to one. Yet this is due solely to the limitation upon the funds available. The only novel feature of the present scheme is the extension of municipal credit as an aid to the financing of the building program. Such aid is not without precedent in Baltimore, in respect to port development. . . .

Schemes for the attraction and financing of new industry have been adopted in other states, and have generally been sustained by the courts. In Faulconer v. City of Danville, 232 S.W.2d 80, a city was authorized to acquire a site and erect a factory thereon, to be leased to a private corporation under a long term lease. The legislation was sustained. In that case, the city did not pledge its credit, but the bonds were to be payable out of the rents. But in Dyche v. City of London, Ky., 288 S.W.2d 648, a plan calling for the issuance of municipal bonds was sustained. A similar plan was sustained in Mississippi in Albritton v. City of Winona, supra [178 So. 799]. A similar plan involving revenue bonds was sustained in Tennessee. . . .

On the other hand, in New Hampshire, a scheme to provide industrial parks and other facilities to attract industry was disapproved on the narrow ground that the legislation did not contain sufficient guides or standards. In re Opinion of the Justices, 114 A.2d 514. In Florida, a scheme to finance an industrial enterprise through revenue bonds was disapproved in sweeping terms. State v. Town of North Miami, Fla., 59 So.2d 779. The court said: "The financing of private enterprises by means of public funds is entirely foreign to a proper concept of our constitutional system. Experience has shown that such encroachments will lead inevitably to the ultimate destruction of the private enterprise system. * * * Every new business, manufacturing plant, or industrial plant which may be established in a municipality will be of some benefit to the municipality. A new super market, a new department store, a new meat market, a steel mill, a crate manufacturing plant, a pulp mill, or other establishments which could be named without end, may be of material benefit to the growth, progress, development and prosperity of a municipality. But these considerations do not make the acquisition of land and the erection of buildings, for such purposes, a municipal purpose." This decision was followed in State ex rel. Beck v. City of York, 82 N.W.2d 269. We can not accept the reasoning of these cases. The Constitution does not guarantee a static condition of society, or write into our basic law the economic doctrine of laissez-faire. So long as the legislation has a substantial relation to the public welfare and can fairly be said to serve a public purpose, it is not the courts' function to strike it down, merely because we fear it may lead to unwise or unfortunate results. We think the legislation in the instant case is not beyond the bounds of legislative power.

Decree reversed, with costs, and case remanded for the passage of a decree in accordance with the views expressed in this opinion.

PRESCOTT, Judge (dissenting).

It is regrettable, when one member of the Court is unable to concur with the majority upon such an important and far reaching question as is here involved, that time will not permit a careful and comprehensive statement of the reasons why that member cannot yield his full concurrence. As sufficient time is not available, the following is freely acknowledged to be a hurriedly put together statement of some of those reasons.

The majority opinion holds that under the provisions of section 103 of Chapter 662 of the Acts of 1953, the City of Frostburg, if authorized by a referendum, may constitutionally issue bonds or certificates of indebtedness for the purpose of buying land and erecting thereon buildings to be used by *private* manufacturing companies for *private* profit. The statute recites no public distress or urgent public need, as do similar acts elsewhere, but states its simple purpose is, "in order to encourage industrial development." It likewise fails to state how the bonds or certificates are to be redeemed, but it is axiomatic that this must be done by taxation.

This Court, many years ago, held that taxes can not be imposed for a private purpose; that by Art. 15 of the Declaration of Rights and the fundamental maxims of free government taxes can only be imposed to raise money for *public* purposes; that counties (the same certainly also applies to municipalities) have no inherent power of taxation; what power of taxation they exercise must be delegated to them by the legislature; the legislature, however, cannot delegate a power prohibited by the constitution; therefore, the taxing power, when exercised by the counties, "is but the exercise of the taxing power of the legislature delegated to them, and is *subject to every constitutional limitation* to which the taxing power of the legislature is subject." (Emphasis supplied.) . . .

Art. III, sec. 34, of our Constitution, in part, reads as follows: "The credit of the State shall not in any manner be given, or loaned to, or in aid of any individual, association or corporation * * *." Art. III, sec. 54, and Art. XI, sec. 7, permit the counties and Baltimore City to do so under certain conditions, but there is no provision in the Constitution with reference to municipalities.

Thus, the questions are presented: (1), Will the taxes to raise the funds for the payment of the bonds be imposed for a public purpose? and, (2), When the bonds are issued, will the credit of the State "in any manner be given, or loaned to, or in aid of any individual, association or corporation"?

The Supreme Court of the United States and several of our sister States have made rulings on these points; and as they express reasons that are, to me, persuasive, I shall quote at some length from them.

The recent case of State ex rel. Beck v. City of York, 1957, 82 N.W.2d 269, seems to be on all fours with the case at bar. The City of York entered into an agreement with the York Cold Storage Company and the York Packing Company, that upon the completion of certain industrial buildings to be constructed by the first named company, the City would purchase the same by issuing revenue bonds, pursuant to legislative authority; and upon the purchase of said industrial buildings, the City proposed to lease them to the York Packing Company as a packing plant. The constitutional provision involved was practically identical with ours. It read: "The credit of the state shall never be given or loaned in aid of any individual, association, or corporation." The unanimous Court, with much of its cogent reasoning omitted, said:

"It is here contended that the prohibition contained in the foregoing constitutional provision applies only to the State as an entity and has no application to political subdivisions thereof. We do not concur in this view. Political subdivisons of the State exist at the will of the State exercised through the Legislature. For us to say that the State may not loan its credit to an individual, association, or corporation, but that it might create a political subdivision and authorize it to do that which the State itself is prohibited from doing would be, to say the least, a very anomalous situation. It would permit the State to do by indirection the very thing it could not directly do, a theory which has been consistently condemned by this court.

* * * * * *

"The defendants cite cases from other states upholding the constitutionality of similar acts . . . (cases cited and relied upon in our majority opinion). These cases are based on what we deem fundamental fallacies of reasoning. The first is that a revenue bond for which a city is not generally liable is not within the prohibition against the State giving or loaning its credit. The second is that the issuance of such revenue bonds for the construction of industrial plants for private users is a valid exercise of the proprietary powers of a municipality. The third is that the issuance of revenue bonds for the construction of industrial buildings for private use is for a public purpose.

* * * * * *

"We summarize as follows: The constitutional prohibition against the State as to giving or loaning its credit to an individual association, or corporation is applicable to all subdvisions of the State. * * * The money realized from revenue bonds is public money and it may not be appropriated for a private purpose or used for the purpose of acquiring property for the benefit of a private concern. It is not material what such undertakings may be called, or what forms are devised to conceal their main purpose, or how worthwhile they may appear to be, when the question of constitutionality is presented, their substance will be examined. The financing of private enterprises with public funds is foreign to the fundamental concepts of our constitutional system. To permit such encroachments upon the prohibitions of the Constitution would bring about, as experience and history have demonstrated, the ultimate destruction of the private enterprise system. We have not overlooked the fact that the Legislature determined that the Act was for a public purpose. While such a legislative declaration is entitled to great weight, it is not conclusive. There are limits beyond which the Legislature cannot go. It cannot authorize a city to spend public money, or lend or give away, directly or indirectly, its credit or property for a purpose which is not a public one.

"The purpose of the Statute, and the contract in the present case springing therefrom, is to assist a private corporation that is engaged in an enterprise for profit. It is true, of course, that the city may be benefited by the location of the company in the city. It may produce employment for citizens of the community. It may tend to balance a locally restricted economy. But general benefit to the economy of a community does not justify the use of public funds of the city unless it be for a public as distinguished from a private purpose. This is simply a case where the city is attempting to use the powers, credits, and public moneys of the city to purchase land and erect industrial buildings thereon for the use of a private corporation for private profit and private gain. It serves no public or municipal purpose. The Act purports to grant powers to cities which are beyond the authority of the Legislature to confer.

* * * * * *

"To permit legislation of this character to stand in the face of constitutional prohibitions would constitute a death blow to the private enterprise system and reduce the Constitution to a shambles in so far as its protection of private enterprise is concerned. The contract pleaded in the petition is void and the act upon which it is based is a plain violation of the letter and spirit of Article XIII, section 3, of the Constitution of this State."

. . . .

Some years ago, there was a devastating fire in the City of Boston which destroyed an important part of that great city. The governor of the state convened the legislative body of Massachusetts, called the General Court, for the express purpose of dealing with the distressing situation. An act was passed which authorized the city to issue $20,000,000 worth of bonds. The proceeds of the bonds were to be loaned to the owners of the land, the buildings upon which had been burned, and the loans were to be secured by first mortgages, etc. The Supreme Judicial Court, unanimously, held the act unconstitutional, and during the course of their opinion stated:

"The power to levy taxes is founded on the right, duty and responsibility to maintain and administer all the governmental functions of the State, and to provide for the public welfare. To justify any exercise of the power requires that the expenditure which it is intended to meet shall be for some public service, or some object which concerns the public welfare. The promotion of the interests of individuals, either in respect of property or business, although it may result incidentally in the advancement of the public welfare, is, in its essential character, a private and not a public object. However certain and great the resulting good to the general public, it does not, by reason of its comparative importance, cease to be incidental. The incidental advantage to the public, or to the State, which results from the promotion of private interests, and the prosperity of private enterprises or business, does not justify their aid by the use of public money raised by taxation, or for which taxation may become necessary. It is the essential character of the direct object of the expenditure which must determine its validity, as justifying a tax, and not the magnitude of the interests to be affected, nor the degree to which the general advantage of the community, and thus the public welfare, may be ultimately benefited by their promotion." Lowell v. City of Boston, 111 Mass. 454.

The Supreme Court of the United States has also had occasion to pass upon the question. The legislature of Kansas attempted to authorize municipalities to issue bonds to aid and encourage the building of bridges, etc. The City of Topeka issued its bonds to aid and encourage a certain company in establishing bridge shops within the city. The Court held the act unconstitutional upon the ground that the taxes required for the redemption of the bonds would not be imposed for a *public* purpose. During the course of its opinion, the Court stated:

"To lay with one hand the power of the government on the property of the citizen, and with the other to bestow it upon favored individuals to aid private enterprises and build up private fortunes, is none the less a robbery because it is done under the forms of law and is called taxation. This is not legislation. It is a decree under legislative forms.

* * * * * *

"It is undoubtedly the duty of the legislature which imposes or authorizes municipalities to impose a tax to see that it is not to be used for purposes of private interest instead of a public use, and the courts can only be justified in interposing when a violation of this principle is clear and the reason for interference cogent. And in deciding whether, in the given case, the object for which the taxes are assessed falls upon the one side or the other of this line, they must be governed mainly by the course and usage of the government, the objects for which taxes have been customarily and by long course of legislation levied, what objects or purposes have been considered necessary to the support and for the proper use of the government, whether State or municipal. Whatever lawfully pertains to this and is sanctioned by time and the acquiescence of the people may well be held to belong to the public use, and proper for the maintenance of good government, though this may not be the only criterion of rightful taxation.

"But in the case before us, *in which the towns are authorized to contribute aid by way of taxation to any class of manufacturers, there is no difficulty in holding that this is not such a public purpose as we have been considering.* If it be said that a benefit results to the local public of a town by establishing manufactures, the same may be said of any other business or pursuit which employs capital or labor. The merchant, the mechanic, the innkeeper, the banker, the builder, the steamboat owner are equally promoters of the public good, and equally deserving the aid of the citizens by forced contributions. No line can be drawn in favor of the manufacturer which would not open the coffers of the public treasury to the importunities of two-thirds of the business men of the city or town." (Emphasis supplied.) Loan Association v. City of Topeka, 87 U.S. 655.

. . . The Supreme Court has adopted a policy of attempting to permit the highest Courts of the States [*to*] determine what is, and what is not, a public purpose. It may be assumed they would disagree in case of a flagrant misinterpretation.

Art. III, sec. 34, above, first placed in our Constitution in 1851, was not original with the framers of that Constitution. It is practically, if not, identical with a provision of the New York Constitution, this provision being added in 1846. Its purpose, as stated by Judge Cardozo, was "to put an end to the use of the credit of the state in *fostering the growth of private enterprise and business*." (Emphasis supplied.) Should not this statement alone make us reexamine the statute we are presently considering? The Court of Appeals of New York, in the case of People v. Westchester County National Bank, 132 N.E. 241, 248, held that a soldiers' and sailors' bonus bill was in violation of that State's constitutional provision (the one that is the same as ours), although the taxes that would be required to redeem the bonds would be imposed for a public purpose; that no matter how worthy the cause, or how useful the objects designed by the legislature, the bonus bill proposed to give the credit of the state to the veterans, which was prohibited by the above named section of the constitution. . . .

I shall not attempt to analyse all of the Maryland decisions that relate to the points being considered. There is no previous Maryland case that controls the decision here. The majority decision is new law in Maryland. This Court has held, rightfully in my opinion, that the legislature may authorize expenditures for public highways, education, hospitals, wharves, etc., where public services were rendered, and there was no *private profit*. I have found, and been referred to, no Maryland case, before the majority opinion herein, where public funds were used to establish private enterprise for private profit. The port development project in Baltimore anticipated, as incidental to its over-all object of opening the harbor of Baltimore to the markets of the world, leasing at least some of the wharves to private concerns. Merchant v. City of Baltimore, 126 A. 884.

In Finan v. Mayor & City Council of Cumberland, 141 A. 269, this Court sanctioned, as a public purpose, the expenditure of public funds for the purposes of a hospital conducted by the Allegany Hospital of Sisters of Charity, although a private eleemosynary corporation. It will be noted that this was an eleemosynary institution and no private profit was involved. It would seem that this liberal construction of section 34 and of what is a public purpose should certainly be the borderline; to go further, as permitted by the majority opinion, will be, in my opinion, the utilization of taxation for private purposes, and will contravene the explicit inhibition of section 34 that, "the credit of the State shall not *in any manner* be given, or loaned to, or in aid of any individual, association, or corporation."

Before concluding, let us consider one simple illustration. Suppose A owns a parcel of land in Frostburg and desires to erect thereon a manufactory to make shoes. B is interested in conducting a shirt manufactory, and the desirable location therefore is A's parcel of ground. Are there many persons who would consider that B's undertaking is such a "public purpose" as would entitle the City of Frostburg to condemn A's property in order to erect an establishment for B, paying both for the property and the erection of the building from the proceeds of the bonds issued in pursuance of the act being considered? I think not; yet the majority opinion holds that the bonds to be issued are for a "public purpose."

With due deference to, and respect for, my colleagues, I think the act is unconstitutional and void; that, as stated by the Nebraska, Florida and other Courts, the ruling will strike a terrific blow to private enterprise, a system under which this country has thrived and prospered; and with the government of Maryland and all of its municipalities in business, it is difficult to visualize the boundaries to which the principle may extend.

CITY OF SHAWNEE v. *WILLIAMSON*

OKLAHOMA SUPREME COURT

338 P. 2D 355 (1959)

The city of Shawnee issued some parking lot bonds. State law required the city to submit the bonds to the attorney general of the state for approval before selling them. In accordance with the law, Shawnee submitted the parking lot bonds to Williamson, the attorney general. He refused to approve them on the grounds that to him in his official capacity there was a question as to the legality of the purpose of the bonds. The city then sought a writ of mandamus *in the Oklahoma supreme court to compel Williamson to approve the bonds.*

Justice WELCH delivered the opinion of the court.

. . . .

THIS ACTION then presents the question whether a public parking lot is a "public utility" within the purview and meaning of Section 27, Article 10 of the Constitution of the State of Oklahoma; and whether the bonded indebtedness proposed to be incurred by the City of Shawnee as to the "parking lots," constitutes an unlawful and unauthorized attempt to impose a tax for a purpose not sanctioned by law.

Section 27, Article 10 of the Constitution of Oklahoma reads as follows:

> "Any incorporated city or town in this State may, by a majority of the qualified property tax paying voters of such city or town, voting at an election to be held for that purpose, be allowed to become indebted in a larger amount than that specified in section twenty-six, for the purpose of purchasing or constructing public utilities, or for repairing the same, to be owned exclusively by such city: Provided, That any such city or town incurring any such indebtedness requiring the assent of the voters as aforesaid, shall have the power to provide for, and, before or at the time of incurring such indebtedness, shall provide for the collection of an annual tax in addition to the other taxes provided for by this Constitution, sufficient to pay the interest on such indebtedness as it falls due, and also to constitute a sinking fund for the payment of the principal thereof within twenty-five years from the time of contracting the same."

The defendant in support of the contention that a parking lot is not a public utility has cited . . . [*a number of cases*]. We have examined these authorities and find that they all have held that street improvements do not constitute public utilities, since the streets are not exclusively owned and controlled by the municipality. We must agree with these authorities, however, we cannot agree that they are applicable to the question here presented, since the parking lots are to be exclusively owned by the municipality and they are not to be managed or used in the same manner as streets.

Defendant next contends that the provisions of Title 11 O.S. 1951 §§ 1352 to 1359, inclusive, as amended by the 1953 Legislature, were designed to alleviate the existing problems of automotive congestion in cities, and indicate a legislative intent to relieve the taxpaying voters from any burden incident to the purchase, construction or maintenance of public parking lots. It is argued that by providing a specific method of financing a parking lot project, the Legislature apparently intended to bar and exclude every other method. We cannot agree that the suggested intent is apparent, nor that the Legislature intended to bar or could bar any method authorized by provision of the Constitution. Furthermore, in the case of Application of the City Council of City of Tahlequah, Okl., 285 P.2d 418, it was held:

> "All portions of 11 O.S. Supp. 1953, Sec. 449.1 to 449.20 (Title 11, Chapter 8, 1953 Session Laws of Oklahoma) purporting to authorize certain cities and towns to become indebted in excess of the amount fixed in Oklahoma Constitution, Art. X, sec. 26, without complying with all provisions of section 27 thereof are unconstitutional and void."

Neither our Constitution nor statutes have defined a public utility, nor has our court heretofore had the question of whether a parking lot owned by a municipality would constitute a public utility. However, this court, in a long line of decisions, has uniformly held that the term "public utilities" as used in Section 27, Article 10 of the State Constitution, is synonymous with the term "public use." . . .

We have held that public parks, sidewalks and paving of the streets through parks, convention halls, sewers, public fire stations, electric light plants, municipal owned airports, public waterworks, cemeteries, public libraries, museums, all are public utilities within the meaning of that term as used in Section 27, Article 10 of the Constitution. . . .

The ever increasing complications of modern civilization from time to time have compelled a new examination and application of the constitutional provision as to "public utilities." This is not to change the meaning of the Constitution to meet changing times as that would be an amending of the Constitution by judicial decree. We merely reexamine the Constitution as written, and make judicial application thereof to the new situation presented. In order to cover new applications the term "public utility" has become somewhat synonymous with the term "public good or public use." The courts in other jurisdictions have consistently defined "public use" to mean public utility, advantage, or what is productive of public benefit.

The evident object and purpose of Section 27, supra, is primarily to empower the incorporated cities and towns of this state by a majority of the qualified taxpaying voters voting at an election held for such purpose to become indebted in a larger amount than that specified in Section 26, for the purpose of purchasing or constructing public utilities or for repairing the same, to be owed exclusively by such municipalities, and it is the duty of the court to so construe the provisions as to carry out its purpose. The construction of a constitutional provision must not be so strict or technical as to defeat the evident object and purpose of its adoption.

Where a constitutional provision is complete in itself it needs no further legislation to put it into force. And where it asserts a certain right, or lays down a certain principle of law or procedure, it speaks for the entire people as their supreme law, and is full authority for all that is done in pursuance of its provision. In short, if complete in itself, it executes itself. . . .

We are irresistibly led to the conclusion that Section 27, Article 10, supra, is a grant of power to the people of the municipalities of the state, and not a limitation.

Section 1 of Art. 2 of our Constitution provides that:

> "All political power is inherent in the people; and government is instituted for their protection, security, and benefit, and to promote their general welfare."

This general underlying idea that the people themselves have the power by direct vote to control their own affairs is very persuasive that it was the intention of the Constitution to give to municipal corporations directly the right to become indebted by vote of the taxpayers for the construction of public utilities. Therefore since it has been held that public utility and public use are synonymous, and that usually or generally whatever is beneficially employed for the community is of public use, we are of the opinion that the taxpaying voters of a municipality have some qualification to determine whether a parking lot would be a public use and benefit, and when they have so determined by their vote, the court should give a fair and just construction and decision as to what constitutes a public utility under Section 27, Article 10, supra.

It is obvious from the authorities hereinabove cited and referred to, that from time to time as our population has increased and modern civilization has progressed, both a demand and the necessity for various public services have increased. The increased use of motor vehicles has created a serious parking problem in all municipalities to the extent that a municipally owned parking lot is not only a convenience such as public libraries, museums, public parks, etc., which have heretofore been held to be public utilities, but is a necessary service to the public for the control of congested traffic on the streets, and for the protection of pedestrians and property owners within the municipality.

For the reasons above stated, we are of the opinion, and so hold, that parking lots exclusively owned and operated by municipalities are public utilities within the meaning of that term as used in Section 27, Article 10 of our Constitution.

Writ granted.

VISINA v. FREEMAN

MINNESOTA SUPREME COURT
89 N.W. 2D 635 (1958)

Visina, a resident and taxpayer of Duluth, Minnesota, brought action in a Minnesota court for a judgment declaring that laws which established the Seaway Port Authority were unconstitutional. Freeman was governor of Minnesota at the time. Both parties to the suit moved for a summary judgment after stipulating (agreeing without argument) as to the facts. Thereupon, the trial court decided that the acts in question were constitutional. Visina appealed to the Minnesota supreme court.

Justice KNUTSON delivered the opinion of the court.

. . . .

THE VALIDITY of some or all of these acts is attacked upon numerous constitutional grounds. In some cases it is claimed that all three acts violate certain constitutional provisions, and in other cases it is claimed that some of the acts are in contravention of our constitution. The nature of the claimed illegality will be stated in connection with the discussion of each of the constitutional provisions involved in these attacks.

Plaintiff contends that all three acts violate that portion of Minn. Const. art. 4, § 33, M.S.A., which as far as material here reads:

> "* * * The legislature shall pass no local or special law * * * authorizing public taxation for a private purpose";

that part of art. 9, § 1, which reads:

> "* * * Taxes shall be uniform upon the same class of subjects, and shall be levied and collected for public purposes";

and art. 10, § 2, which reads:

> "No corporations shall be formed under special acts, except for municipal purposes."

Initially, in order to determine whether there is any merit to plaintiff's contentions that these acts are in contravention of the above constitutional provisions, it is necessary to determine whether the establishment and operation of a port having for its purpose the improvement of a harbor and the furnishing of port terminal facilities is or may involve the performance of a governmental or public function as distinguished from one private in nature. In the determination of this question some related rules should be kept in mind.

1. It is well settled in this state that the state or its municipal subdivisions or agencies may expend public money only for a public purpose. What is a "public purpose" that will justify the expenditure of public money is not capable of a precise definition, but the courts generally construe it to mean such an activity as will serve as a benefit to the community as a body and which, at the same time, is directly related to the functions of government.

2. In determining whether an act of the state constitutes a performance of a governmental function or a public purpose which will justify the expenditure of public money, a legislative declaration of public purpose is not always control-

ling. The determination of what is and what is not a public purpose, or the performance of a governmental function, initially is for the legislature, but in the final analysis it must rest with the courts.

3. The mere fact that some private interest may derive an incidental benefit from the activity does not deprive the activity of its public nature if its primary purpose is public. The rule is clearly stated in Burns v. Essling, 194 N.W. 404, 405, as follows:

> "* * * if the primary object of an expenditure of municipal funds is to subserve a public purpose, the expenditure is legal, although it may also involve as an incident an expenditure which, standing alone, would not be lawful. It is equally well settled that, if the primary object is to promote some private end, the expenditure is illegal, although it may incidentally serve some public purpose also."

4. Essentially, it is the contention of plaintiff that the Port of Duluth has already been built up extensively by private capital and industry and that no necessity exists for action on the part of the state, county, or city to enter this field. Quite apart from the question of what has been done in the past (and the evidence warrants a finding that up to now the port has deteriorated considerably) is the question generally as to whether the function of operating a port such as the one contemplated for the harbor at Duluth, with the prospect in the immediate future of greatly increased shipping as a result of the development and opening of the Great Lakes–St. Lawrence Seaway project, can be considered the performance of a governmental function.

Historically, the establishment and maintenance of ports, at least on the sea, intended to provide terminal facilities for shipping open to all who wish to use them, has been considered universally to be a function of government. Various forms of commissions have been set up to supervise and control port facilities, but whenever they have been engaged principally in establishing and operating an open port furnishing terminal facilities and docking privileges to all who wish to use it, subject to uniform and reasonable rules and regulations, the function has been considered to be a governmental one. The establishment and maintenance of ports in many parts of the old world are related in Commissioner of Internal Revenue v. Ten Eyck, 76 F.2d 515, a case in which the court held that the Albany (New York) Port District Commission was engaged in the performance of an essential governmental function. In an exhaustive opinion reviewing this entire matter, the court said (76 F.2d 518):

> "* * * it is clear that ownership, control, and operation of port facilities are essentially and usually prerogatives of sovereignty; especially of the sovereignty of the constituent state governments of the United States. In England and in Scotland, the right to erect a port was part of the royal prerogative. No port could exist except under the authority of the sovereign."

In State of California v. Anglim, D.C. N.D.Cal., 37 F.Supp. 663, 664, the court . . . said:

> "The establishment by government of ports and harbors, wherever conditions exist which render harbor development advantageous, is designed to afford a medium for the attraction and flow of commerce into and through the seaport area for the benefit and prosperity of the numerous persons necessarily affected by the resulting stimulation of industrial and trade activity in such area. In its scope and effect, port and harbor development, designed to facilitate the flow of commerce, cannot properly be classified as commerce itself, normally conducted by private industry.

> The importance to the general welfare, the public at large, of adequate ports and harbors for the stimulation of navigation and commerce; the fact that the development of ports and harbors has not occurred at the hands of private industry, but has remained in the reigns of government as a recognized sovereign right and duty, these considerations, in the opinion of this court, have rightfully marked the operation of ports and harbors a proper function of government."

In Cook v. Port of Portland, 27 P. 263, 266, the Oregon court said:

> "* * * that anything that will cheapen the handling of what the country exports and imports will be a benefit to all is a self-evident fact, and leaves no doubt of the public interest in this improvement."

In Port of New York Authority v. J. E. Linde Paper Co., 127 N.Y.S.2d 155, the court said:

> "The Port Authority is an arm and agency of the States of New York and New Jersey, and in all of its activities, is engaged in the performance of essential governmental functions."

. . . .

In two prior cases before this court we referred to port authorities as a "municipal commission," but it must be admitted that in neither of those cases was the constitutional question now before us presented or considered. . . .

The question of whether the operation of a port constitutes the performance of a public or governmental function has arisen most frequently in connection with the rights of a state, or a municipal subdivision or agency thereof, to take private property for use for docks or wharves or the improvement of a harbor under its power of eminent domain. While it has been said that no good reason is apparent why a public purpose for which property may be taken by a municipality, including the state, under the power of eminent domain should not be considered a public purpose for which a municipality may spend its money or incur an indebtedness, that statement, taken generally, is too broad. "Public use," as required for the exercise of the power of eminent domain, is not necessarily synonymous with "public purpose" required for the expenditure of public money. It may be safe to assume that, if the activity constitutes a public purpose which will justify the expenditure of public money, it also constitutes a public use which will permit the exercise of the power of eminent domain, but it does not necessarily follow that, if the use to be made of the property is a public use within the meaning of our eminent domain statutes and laws, it also constitutes a public purpose for which public money may be spent. We have, for instance, frequently granted railroads and other public utilities, and even private persons, the right to condemn private property for a use declared to be public, but it does not follow that public money may be spent to assist such condemnors in carrying out the purpose for which the condemnation is permitted. However, the cases relied on here, involving the right of ports or port authorities of one kind or another to condemn property, are of such a nature that the use of the term "public use" or "public purpose" authorizing condemnation is broad enough to encompass a public purpose permitting the expenditure of public money, not because it is a public use which will justify an exercise of the power of public eminent domain but, in a broader sense, because it is such a public purpose as includes, as well, the right to spend public money. To that extent the cases are helpful. The following are illustrative thereof.

In Marchant v. City of Baltimore, 126 A. 884, 887, the court had the following to say about the public nature of a port commission:

> "* * * The development of the harbor of Baltimore, according to a comprehensive plan by which the commerce of the port will be most advantageously served, and its future growth encouraged, is a project of distinctively public interest and purpose. It is concerned with the improvement and extension of a harbor service which constitutes an essential part of a system of water transportation connecting the port of Baltimore with the markets of the world. The public character of the use to which the harbor structures are devoted is not affected by the fact that they may not all be made available for the indiscriminate use of the public. By the allocation or lease of certain docks for the separate use of persons or corporations having a regular or continuous need of such conveniences, the city does not convert into a private use the public port service which is thus in part provided. The municipal ownership is not thereby surrendered, and the use remains consistent with the public purpose for which the port accommodations as a whole are maintained."

In Moore v. Sanford, 24 N.E. 323, the court was considering the validity of the taking of certain flats for the purpose of improving the harbor of Boston, and, with respect to the public nature of the improvement, said:

> "* * * That the improvement of Boston Harbor is an object of a public nature, and thus that lands taken for this purpose are taken for a public use, can hardly be controverted. It is not necessary that the entire community should directly enjoy or participate in an improvement or enterprise in order to constitute a public use, and a benefit to the principal harbor of the commonwealth is much more than a local advantage."

The whole matter is well summarized in 1 Dillon, Municipal Corporations (5 ed.) § 269, as follows:

> "The *construction of docks and wharves by a municipality for general public use is a public purpose* which justifies the exercise of the power of eminent domain. . . ."

In the final analysis, the right of a state to establish and maintain terminal port facilities is but an incident of its power to control its navigable waters. The mere fact that up until the present time private interests have developed harbor facilities at Duluth suitable and sufficient to take care of their own specialized shipping requirements does not detract from the fact that furnishing such facility for the use of all who may wish to enter the port constitutes the performance of an essential governmental function. Up until the present time, ships on the Great Lakes have been limited in size and the area in which they travel. They have not been oceangoing vessels. The evidence in this case shows that with the opening of the Great Lakes–St. Lawrence Seaway about 75 percent of all oceangoing vessels will be able to reach Duluth. The possibility of greatly increased shipping to and from all ports of the world requires little imagination. This state as a whole is vitally interested in cheaper transportation costs for those products which it is prepared to export as well as those which it wishes to import. With the opening of this waterway, Duluth will virtually become the farthest inland seaport in this country. The area useful for harbor facilities is limited, and the regulation of shipping and the proper and efficient use of terminal facilities so that they will be readily available to all who wish to use them is essential if this new traffic is to be attracted to our newly available "seaport."

. . . .

It seems clear to us . . . that the purposes for which the port authority is established involve the establishment of an agency of the state for the administration of a purely governmental function. As such, the argument that the acts of the legislature involved herein contravene the above constitutional provisions must fail.

5. That L.1957, c. 849, violates Minn. Const. art. 9, § 5, which reads:

> "* * * The state shall never contract any debts for works of internal improvements, or be a party in carrying on such works, * * *."

Plaintiff concedes that this provision of our constitution applies only to the state so that the acts of the legislature dealing with the expenditure of money by the county and city for development of the port are not involved. In Davidson v. County Com'rs of Ramsey County, 18 Minn. 482, we so held, where we said:

> "* * * the prohibition is in terms expressly confined to the state, and does not extend to cities, counties, and towns."

That interpretation of the constitution has never been altered.

Plaintiff relies for the most part on Rippe v. Becker, 57 N.W. 331. That case involved the constitutionality of L.1893, c. 30, under which the legislature attempted to establish a terminal elevator at the Port of Duluth. We held that the act was violative of Minn.Const. art. 9, § 5. In so doing we held that the term "internal improvements" included any "public improvements." However, we recognized an exception to the constitutional proscription when dealing with activities pertaining to proper governmental functions. In that respect we said (57 N.W. 334):

> "* * * it was not supposed that it was proper or competent for the state to embark in any public improvements, *except such as strictly pertained to its proper governmental functions.*" (Italics supplied.)

That interpretation of this constitutional provision has been followed consistently since that time. . . .

. . . .

Our former decisions holding that this provision of our constitution does not apply to works of the state used in the performance of a governmental function are sufficient to dispose of this question in view of our determination that the port authority involved here is engaged in the performance of a governmental function, but there are other reasons why the act should not be held in contravention of this constitutional provision. Where one construction of a statute will make it void for conflicting with our constitution and another will render it valid, the latter, if not a forced and unreasonable one, will be adopted.

While the plain meaning of language used in our fundamental law may not be tampered with to accomplish a desired result no matter how archaic it has become by virtue of social and economic changes which have occurred since its adoption, neither should the proper interpretation of constitutional provisions ignore such changes. In determining whether an act of the legislature contravenes a constitutional provision we should endeavor to interpret the provision in the light of existing conditions, particularly when those conditions could not have been foreseen at the time the constitution was adopted. If the Great Lakes–St. Lawrence Seaway had been a reality instead of a dream when our constitution was adopted, it can hardly be supposed that the framers of our constitution, and the people who adopted it, would have proscribed the expenditure of public money to improve harbor and dock facilities to enable our state to have contact by water transportation with all other ports of the world. The limitation on spending public money for internal improvements obviously was not intended to circumscribe such activity. In a true sense, the development of a seaport to facilitate water transportation between our state and other ports of the world is not an internal improvement at all. . . .

While this case may illustrate the need for some constitutional revision, the fact remains that the right to amend the constitution rests with the people and should not be usurped by the courts in the guise of judicial interpretation. At the same time, when it becomes necessary to interpret the provisions of the constitution in the light of conditions which exist today that could not be contemplated at the time our constitution was adopted, we should attempt to give to it a reasonable meaning as applied to present conditions if that can be done without doing violence to the expressed language used in the constitution itself. If the language of the constitution permits, we should give to it that meaning which would have been expressed when adopted if the present conditions that are involved had then existed or had been within the contemplation of those who drafted the instrument.

For these reasons, we conclude that c. 849 does not violate Minn.Const. art. 9, § 5.

6. That the act in question contravenes Minn.Const. art. 9, § 10, which reads:

> "The credit of the State shall never be given or loaned in aid of any individual, association or corporation, * * *."

We have heretofore held that this provision applies only to the state. Davidson v. County Com'rs of Ramsey County, 18 Gil. 432, 18 Minn. 482.

It is the contention of plaintiff that the Port of Duluth will be improved at the expense of the public for the benefit and convenience of shipping companies, railroads, truckers, importers, exporters, and other shippers. It can hardly be denied that those who use the port will derive some incidental benefit from it. However, the fact that some private interests may derive some incidental benefit from the development and operation of the port does not deprive the port authority of its public character. As we have stated above, it is the primary purpose which controls. If it is engaged in a governmental function or public purpose, it does not matter that some private interests may derive some incidental benefit from the operation of the authority. Here, the primary purpose is to facilitate and encourage the development of shipping to and from the port and to control the orderly use of the port and its facilities so that it will be open and available to all who wish to use the port. The incidental benefit which may come to shippers has never been held to deprive such port of its public nature, and neither does it come within the prohibition of the above constitutional provision.

7. That they violate Minn.Const. art. 9, § 1, which reads:

> "The power of taxation shall never be surrendered, suspended or contracted away. Taxes shall be uniform upon the same class of subjects, and shall be levied and collected for public purposes, * * *."

The portion of this constitutional provision which plaintiff contends is violated is that which reads: "Taxes shall be uniform upon the same class of subjects." The argument here is that the state is imposing a tax on portions of its people which derive no benefit from the improvement financed by such tax.

Absolute equality of taxation is never attained. In all segments of the population there are those who must pay taxes for a purpose from which, it might be argued, they derive no direct benefit. But absolute equality has never been required. If there is a reasonable relationship to the apportionment of the taxes and the benefit to be derived by that segment of our population required to bear the financial burden, it lies within the province of the legislature to make such apportionment. Here it has been determined that Duluth will benefit to the greatest extent. Its per capita burden is the greatest. It is reasonable to suppose that the residents of St. Louis County will next benefit the most from the improvement. Its per capita burden is next highest; and last, it is reasonable to believe that the state as a whole will benefit to some extent from the increased traffic and availability of cheaper transportation for the products which it exports and imports. We think that the financial apportionment provided by the legislature bears a reasonable relationship to the benefits which can be anticipated. Having further determined that the activities of the port authority constitute a public purpose and the performance of a governmental function, we find no violation of this constitutional provision.

8. That these acts contravene that portion of Minn.Const. art. 4, § 33, which reads:

> "In all cases when a general law can be made applicable, no special law shall be enacted; and whether a general law could have been made applicable in any case is hereby declared a judicial question, and as such shall be judicially determined without regard to any legislative assertion on that subject."

This provision of our constitution has been the source of much litigation. It is fruitless to try to harmonize or reconcile the numerous decisions involving the application of this question to varying factual situations.

. . . .

The best that can be done is to ascertain if the facts in the case before us come within the general requirements of the provision of our constitution as construed by our decisions.

[*The rules we have established to determine if a statute violated the above constitutional provision*] . . . were summarized in Hamlin v. Ladd, 14 N.W. 2d 396, as follows:

(1) A law is general when it is uniform in its operation even though it divides the subjects of its operation into classes and applies different rules to different classes. It need not operate alike upon all the inhabitants of the state, or all the cities, or all the villages in the state.

(2) A law is general in the constitutional sense which applies to and operates uniformly upon all members of any class of persons, places, or things requiring legislation peculiar to itself in matters covered by the law.

(3) A special law is one which relates and applies to particular members of a class, either particularized by the express terms of the act or separated by any method of selection from the whole class to which the law might, but for such limitation, be applicable.

(4) The classification must be based upon "substantial distinctions"—those which make one class really different from another. The distinction must be based "upon some natural reason,—some reason suggested by necessity, by some difference in the situation and circumstances of the subjects placed in the different classes, suggesting the necessity of different legislation with respect to them."

(5) The classification must be germane to the purpose of the law; that is, there must be an evident connection between the distinctive features to be regulated and the regulations adopted.

(6) To whatever class the law ap-

plies, it must apply to every member of that class; that is to say, it must treat all alike who are similarly situated; "all who are brought within its influence, but in its classification it must bring within its influence all who are under the same conditions."

(7) One alone may constitute a class as well as many, but the fewer there are in a class the more closely will courts scrutinize an act to see if its classification constitutes an evasion of the constitution.

From State ex rel. Board of Courthouse & City Hall Com'rs, etc. v. Cooley, supra [58 *N.W.* 150], have come certain rules adopted as guides to construction in determining whether a statute contravenes this constitutional provision that are particularly applicable here. In the first place, it is recognized that the legislature has the power to classify subjects for legislation, and the courts will not interfere with such classification unless it is so manifestly arbitrary as to evince a legislative purpose of evading the constitution. The fact that there is now only one subject in the class is not decisive. If the statute is so framed as to apply to other municipalities as they acquire characteristics of the class designated, it usually is held to be general rather than special.

. . . .

We think that there is a reasonable relationship between the classification and the subject matter of the legislation. It follows that the classification was within the legislative discretion; hence that it is not special legislation within the meaning of Minn.Const. art. 4, § 33.

9. That c. 849 is in violation of that part of Minn.Const. art. 9, § 5, which reads:

> "For the purpose of defraying extraordinary expenditures, the state may contract public debts, but such debts shall never, in the aggregate, exceed two hundred and fifty thousand dollars; * * *."

. . . .

It is well settled that, while the legislature may not delegate legislative power, it may delegate legislative functions which are merely administrative or executive in carrying out the mandate of the legislature as provided by law. The legislature has a large discretion in determining by what agency its laws are to be administered. A public corporation engaged in performing a sovereign legislative function acts as an arm of the state. There is no essential difference between the functions to be performed by the port authority involved in the acts of the legislature now before us and those to be performed by the Metropolitan Airports Commission, the constitutionality of which has heretofore been upheld.

. . . .

We find no unconstitutional delegation of power here.

11. Finally, plaintiff contends that cc. 648 and 831 do not meet the constitutional requirements of Minn.Const. art. 4, § 27, which reads:

> "No law shall embrace more than one subject, which shall be expressed in its title."

The title of c. 648 reads:

> "An act relating to port authorities, authorizing county tax levies and bonds in aid of seaway port development and amending Minnesota Statutes 1953, Section 458.14, as amended."

The title of c. 831 reads:

> "An act relating to port authority commissions, amending Minnesota Statutes 1953, Sections 458.09, 458.11 and 458.15."

We have frequently held that this provision of our constitution should be given a liberal construction.

In Johnson v. Harrison, 50 N.W. 923, we established the applicable rule, since followed in construing this constitutional provision, where we said:

> "* * * All that is necessary is that the act should embrace some one general subject; and by this is meant, merely, that all matters treated of should fall under some one general idea, be so connected with or related to each other, either logically or in popular understanding, as to be parts of, or germane to, one general subject."

In State ex rel. Pearson v. Probate Court, 287 N.W. 297, we said:

> "The objects of the constitutional provision have been often expressed in the decisions of this court. They are, first, to prevent 'log-rolling legislation' or 'omnibus bills,' by which a large number of different and disconnected subjects are united in one bill and then carried through by a combination of interests; and, secondly, to prevent surprise and fraud upon the people and the legislature by including provisions in a bill whose title gives no intimation of the proposed legislation, or of the interests affected."

. . . .

We have frequently held that the title of a bill is not intended to be an index of the bill. In C. Thomas Stores Sales System, Inc. v. Spaeth, 297 N.W. 9, we said:

> "The subject of a statute is the matter to which it relates and with which it deals. A subject embraces all provisions which are germane to it; they may be parts of it, incident to it, or means auxiliary to the end in view. The subject must be single; the provisions by which the object is accomplished may be multifarious. The constitutional provision ought to be practically and liberally construed."

Tested by these rules, we think that the titles are sufficient. Chapters 648 and 831 are mainly amendments of existing laws. While the three acts were passed as separate bills, they were enacted more or less as a single package. It is hard to believe that any member of the legislature was misled by the title of any one of these acts. Tested by the above rules, we think that the titles sufficiently meet the constitutional requirements.

We find no objection to any of the three acts involved on any constitutional ground raised by plaintiff.

Affirmed.

SPROULE v. FREDERICKS

MISSISSIPPI SUPREME COURT

11 SO. 472 (1892)

When Fredericks defeated Sproule for election to the office of county assessor, Sproule alleged that he had been "robbed." In the course of litigation over the contested election, the case reached the Mississippi supreme court. One of the issues raised there was whether or not the Mississippi constitution of 1890, under whose provisions the election had been conducted, was valid. It is the court's opinion with reference to that issue which is reproduced herewith.

Judge WOODS delivered the opinion of the court.

. . . .

THE VALIDITY of the constitution of 1890 is called in question by counsel for appellee, in a supplemental brief filed recently, by consent of the court, and, as the challenge meets us on the threshold of the case, we proceed at once to its consideration, briefly. In support of this view of the invalidity of the constitution, two propositions are asserted: (1) A constitutional convention has power only to prepare or frame the body of a constitution, and that when prepared or framed the instrument is of no force or effect until ratified by a popular vote of the people, and the constitution of 1890, having never been submitted to or ratified by the people, is invalid; and (2) the changes made by the constitution in the basis of suffrage are violative of the act of congress readmitting the state of Mississippi into the Union in the year 1870, and invalidate that instrument.

With confidence, we reject both propositions as unsound. It will be remembered that the case at bar is free from the difficulties which are supposed by some writers to arise out of a failure or refusal of a constitutional convention to yield to the direction of the legislature which summoned it that the constitution framed shall be submitted to the people for ratification. The act of the legislature which provided for the assembling of the constitutional convention of 1890 declared that the end sought to be attained, the work to be done, was the revision and amendment of the constitution of 1869, or the enactment of a new constitution; and it did not attempt to limit the powers of the convention by imposing, or seeking to impose, upon that sovereign tribunal the mere legislative will that the constitution enacted should be submitted to the people for ratification. We have simply the case of a constitutional convention enacting a new constitution, and putting it into effect without an appeal to the people, in strict conformity to the legislative call which assembled it. We have spoken of the constitutional convention as a sovereign body, and that characterization perfectly defines the correct view, in our opinion, of the real nature of that august assembly. It is the highest legislative body known to freemen in a representative government. It is supreme in its sphere. It wields the powers of sovereignty, specially delegated to it, for the purpose and the occasion, by the whole electoral body, for the good of the whole commonwealth. The sole limitation upon its powers is that no change in the form of government shall be done or attempted. The spirit of republicanism must breathe through every part of the framework, but the particular fashioning of the parts of this framework is confided to the wisdom, the faithfulness, and the patriotism of this great convocation, representing the people in their sovereignty. The theorizing of the political essayist and the legal *doctrinaire*, by which it is sought to be established that the expression of the will of the legislature shall fetter and control the constitution-making body, or, in the absence of such attempted legislative direction, which seeks to teach that the constitutional convention can only prepare the frame of a constitution and recommend it to the people for adoption, will be found to degrade this sovereign body below the level of the lowest tribunal clothed with ordinary legislative powers. This theorizing will reduce that great body, which in our state, at least, since the beginning of its existence, except for a single brief interval, in an exceptional period, by custom and the universal consent of the people, has been regarded as the repository and executor of the powers of sovereignty, to a mere commission, stripped of all power and authorized only to make a recommendation.

Whatever may be the safer and wiser course, as to putting into operation the completed work of the constitutional convention, the opinions of the political theorists, which we are considering, will be found to rest upon grounds largely imaginary and fanciful. The constitutional convention itself, according to this theory, is looked upon with suspicion and distrust, as being the introduction into our governmental system of a revolutionary device; the chosen representatives of the sovereign people are dreaded, as likely to prove unfaithful to their mighty trust; and the liberties of the people are in danger of subversion. This succinct statement of the grounds of these political theorists will demonstrate the unreal foundation upon which their teachings rest. The general judgment of the people of our own state has practically and strikingly repudiated the theory, from the foundation of the government. The usage in Mississippi, with a solitary exception in an extraordinary conjuncture of public affairs, gives it no support. That the government has lived from its birth to this hour with no valid fundamental law on which to rest, except for a brief interval, cannot be true.

2. There is as little ground for the second branch of the contention. The regulation of the right of suffrage belongs to the state, and the only limitation thereon to be found in the constitution of the United States, or the latest amendments thereto, will be found to be the prohibition of discrimination against persons on account of race or color. It is idle consumption of time to talk of this as at all doubtful. The supreme court of the United States has more than once affirmed it. Despite the act of congress referred to, when the state was readmitted to her place in the federal Union, she was restored to all her rights, dignities, and powers. She was admitted as the equal of any other state, with the same power to regulate the right of suffrage in her borders enjoyed by the other states. But the contention is so manifestly untenable, and has been so effectually disposed of by the utterances of the supreme court of the United States, that we decline to say more.

. . . .

[*The court then went on to the question of fraud in the election. It said nothing further on the constitutional issue.*]

STAPLES v. GILMER

VIRGINIA SUPREME COURT OF APPEALS
33 S.E. 2D 49 (1945)

*In 1944, while the war was on, the Virginia legislature passed a law which required that the question of whether or not there should be a constitutional convention to amend the constitution to make it easier for members of the armed services to vote be submitted to the voters. The law provided an appropriation of $25,000 to cover some of the expenses of the election, particularly the printing of the ballots. According to the law, the money was to be paid out by warrants drawn on the treasury by the comptroller. Gilmer, the comptroller, informed the attorney general, Staples, that he doubted the constitutionality of the act and that he would not draw warrants until the constitutionality of the act was tested. Under the circumstances, Staples had no choice but to go to the Virginia supreme court of appeals seeking a writ of manda-*mus *to compel Gilmer to draw the warrants.*

To understand the following opinion, it is essential first to familiarize yourself with these two provisions of the Virginia constitution:

Section 197

"Constitutional convention; how called. At such time as the general assembly may provide, a majority of the members elected to each house being recorded in the affirmative, the question 'shall there be a convention to revise the Constitution and amend the same?' shall be submitted to the electors qualified to vote for members of the general assembly; and in case a majority of the electors so qualified, voting thereon, shall vote in favor of a convention for such purpose, the general assembly, at its next session, shall provide for the election of delegates to such convention; and no convention for such purpose shall be otherwise called."

Section 196

"Amendments.—Any amendment or amendments to the Constitution may be proposed in the senate or house of delegates, and if the same shall be agreed to by a majority of the members elected to each of the two houses, such proposed amendment or amendments shall be entered on their journals, with the ayes and noes taken thereon, and referred to the general assembly at its first regular session held after the next general election of members of the house of delegates, and shall be published for three months previous to the time of such election. If, at such regular session or any subsequent extra session of that general assembly the proposed amendment or amendments shall be agreed to by a majority of all the members elected to each house, then it shall be the duty of the general assembly to submit such proposed amendment or amendments to the people, in such manner and at such times as it shall prescribe; and if the people shall approve and ratify such amendment or amendments by a majority of the electors, qualified to vote for members of the general assembly, voting thereon, such amendment or amendments shall become part of the Constitution."

This was a *per curiam* opinion, that is, an opinion written by the whole court as distinguished from an opinion written by one judge.

. . . .

We are not concerned with the wisdom or expediency of the challenged Act. We are interested only in whether it is in conflict with and forbidden by . . . the Constitution. . . . Of course, we must presume that this Act of the legislature is valid, and unless it is clearly prohibited by . . . the Constitution it must stand. That section does not expressly or impliedly forbid the legislation here questioned. It does not provide that the question of whether there shall be a convention to revise the whole Constitution shall be submitted to the electors. The affirmative vote of the electors on the question as to whether the Constitution shall be revised and amended in any of its particular parts is not prohibited. For instance it might be necessary and expedient that a convention be called to revise and amend the tax laws of the Constitution or the suffrage laws without amending and revising the rest of the Constitution. There is no language . . . [*in the Constitution*] which would prohibit such a partial revision.

A bare reading of the Act will clearly disclose that it simply submits to the people the question whether they wish to have a convention possessing the limited powers which are defined in the Act. If they vote in favor of such a convention, they and not the legislature will limit the work of the convention and its scope, and the convention to be held will be limited in its authority to effecting the amendments submitted to and approved by the electors. The distinguished counsel for respondent concedes that this is so if the Act be valid.

The authorities generally sustain the petitioner's contention. In re Opinion to the Governor, 178 A. 433, the principle was stated in this clear language:

"In the second instance, the Legislature summons the convention only after the people have expressed their will to this effect. If, at the time the question of calling the convention is submitted to them, the people are informed of the scope of the convention and the manner in which it is to conduct its deliberations, and report its results by virtue of the act of the General Assembly specifying such matters, then a convention called in this manner will be limited as therein set forth and the convention will then be bound to confine itself within the stated limits of the act of the Assembly. The reason for this is that it is the people, under such circumstances, who prescribe the conditions in the legislative act by approving the call for the convention in accordance with the provisions of such act. The Legislature merely proposes the conditions. It is the vote of the people for the convention that ratifies them and makes them binding upon the delegates. . . . For this reason, in order that the delegates be so bound, it is necessary for the General Assembly to propose the conditions before the election is held, and to take all necessary steps to bring them to the attention of the people seasonably before the time of voting at the election."

. . . .

The power to amend or revise in whole or in part the Virginia Constitution resides in the people, not in the State legislature. The people are possessed with ultimate sovereignty and are the source of all State authority. See section 2, Virginia Constitution. The people have the unlimited power to control and alter their Constitution, subject only to such limitations and restraints as may be imposed by the Constitution of the United States. Cooley's Constitutional Limitations, 8th Ed. Vol. 1, p. 84. The people of Virginia have placed sections 196 and 197 in the Constitution to define the means by which it may be revised and amended. They must be followed if a valid revision or amendment is to result. 11 Am.Jur., Constitutional Law, sec. 22.

The respondent argues that the legislature, in restricting the question submitted by the Act, thereby limits the scope of the convention. With this we cannot agree, for the people themselves limit the work of the convention, if they vote for it under the terms of the Act. . . . As previously indicated, . . . the Constitution does not prohibit the revision and amendment of a part of the Constitution by the convention method. The purpose of the procedure initiated here is to revise the Constitution and amend the same—not the entire Constitution, but a part thereof.

An amendment of a Constitution and a revision of a Constitution are defined in this language in 16 C.J.S., Constitutional Law, § 7, p. 31: "Every proposition which effects a change in a constitution, or adds or takes away from it, is an amendment * * *, while a revision implies a re-examination and restatement of the constitution, or some part of it, in a corrected or improved form * *." . . .

In submitting the question to the electors whether there shall be a convention, the legislature is performing an exclusive function for the people delegated to it . . . [*by the Constitution*]. In no other way may a convention be initiated in Virginia. If the legislature refused to submit the question to the electors whether there shall be a convention, nothing can be done about it except for the electors to replace its membership by others who will submit the question.

The sovereign power being in the people, it can be exercised only through an agency of the people. . . . The constitutional convention is an agency of the people to formulate or amend and revise a Constitution. The convention does not possess all of the powers of the people but it can exercise only such powers as may be conferred upon it by the people. The people may confer upon it limited powers.

Undoubtedly the people have a right to "reform, alter or abolish," within democratic principles, a part or parts of their fundamental law without reforming, altering or abolishing all of it. The first binding declaration of this fundamental principle was made on the 6th of May, 1776, since which time it has been retained in the Constitution without substantial change as sections 2 and 3 of the Bill of Rights. The pertinent part, as originally approved, reads: "* * *, whenever any government shall be found inadequate or contrary to these purposes, a majority of the community hath an indubitable, inalienable, and indefeasible right to reform, alter or abolish it, in such manner as shall be judged most conducive to the public weal."

The people did not destroy their right to reform or alter a part or parts of the Constitution by means of a convention when they approved the provisions of section 197 of the present Constitution. If by section 197 the entire Constitution may be revised and amended, certainly the people, the source of all power, could exercise the lesser power and revise and amend only a part of it "in such manner as shall be judged (by the people) most conducive to the public weal."

Prior to the so-called Underwood Constitution which was assembled by an Act of Congress of the United States, 14 Stat. 428, on December 3, 1867, there was no constitutional provision for making future changes in the Constitution. Then the authority to call a constitutional convention resided in the legislature. Under article 12 of the Underwood Constitution provision was made for amendments, and at the general election to be held in 1888 and each twentieth year thereafter, the question of calling a convention was to be submitted to the people, and also at such time as the General Assembly might by law provide, the question "shall there be a convention to revise the Constitution and amend the same?" was to be decided by the electors. It will be noted that the words used in the question are identical with those in our present [*constitution*]. It is further noted that in addition to the mandatory duty of submitting the question every twentieth year after 1888, the legislature, of its own motion, was given the power to submit to the electors the question whether to call a convention at any time.

The constitutional conventions of 1829 and of 1850–51, were called by the legislature, and their powers were limited, even though there was no constitutional provision for making future changes in the Constitution at the time.

. . . .

. . . in Virginia, since the Underwood Constitution of 1869, and later, by virtue of the convention of 1902, *the people,* . . . may authorize a convention. They, by their vote, determine whether to call a convention or not. Section 197 [*of the present Constitution*] expressly provides: "At such time as the general assembly may provide * * * the question 'shall there be a convention to revise the Constitution and amend the same?' shall be submitted to the electors * * *." Certainly since the enactment of section 197 in 1902 the electors have possessed the exclusive power and right to call a convention. The legislature, as we have seen, is purely an agent of the people to ascertain their wishes.

Counsel for the respondent freely admits that section 197 permits a convention for the purpose of *amending* the Constitution. In his brief he says: "* * * We again remind the Court that *provision for amendment by convention* exists in the Constitution." The power to amend, as well as the power to revise, by a convention is expressly incorporated in section 197, for it says in the question to the electors, "Shall there be a convention to revise the Constitution and *amend* the same?" If the electors vote in favor of a convention, it may amend the Constitution as well as revise it, and where the legislature, in the performance of its representative function, asks the electors if they desire a convention to amend or revise a certain part of the Constitution but not the whole Constitution, an affirmative vote of the people on such question would have the binding effect of the people themselves limiting the scope of the convention to the very portion of the Constitution suggested to them by the legislature. The wishes of the people are supreme. Some agency must ascertain the desire of the people, and the legislature, by section 197, has been selected by them to do so.

In the convention of 1901–02 section 197 was debated at length by Mr. Barbour, Mr. Braxton, and others. . . . It was stated that unless the legislature submitted to the people the question as to whether there should be a convention, it could call a convention with unlimited powers at any time. It is there shown that the main purpose of section 197 is to prohibit the legislature calling a convention of its own motion whenever it might want to do so without first ascertaining the wishes of the people. A reading of the debates will justify this conclusion.

Sections 196 and 197 were placed in the Constitution to facilitate the making of future changes in the Constitution, not to obstruct them. By section 196 the legislature *proposes* amendments which the people adopt or reject. By section 197 the legislature *propounds* the question to the people, who by their vote answer whether they do or do not want a convention. Prior to the Underwood Constitution the legislature not only called the convention but actually set out its work, prescribing the changes to be made. The legislatures convening just prior to the conventions of 1829, 1851, and the secession convention of

1861, limited the scope of those conventions. Congress limited the scope of the convention of 1869. The manifest purpose and effect of section 197 is not to curtail the right to limit the work of a convention but rather to take that right from the legislature and place it in the people. So now the people have the right to limit the work of a convention in any respect they choose, section 197 providing the machinery for that purpose.

The constitutional changes that will be necessary to carry out the purposes of the Act of the legislature, if the people vote for a convention, will not be limited to the adoption of a single amendment to a single section. In fact a large part of article 2 embracing many sections of the Constitution will be affected. Some of those sections may have to be substantially revised and rewritten. It may be necessary to amend others. The convention method, in addition to being more expeditious under the conditions obtaining, likely will more readily lend itself to effectuating these changes than the amendment process under section 196.

We are satisfied that the convention of 1901–02 and the revision of 1928 did not intend, by section 197, to take away from the people the right to vote to call a convention to revise and amend a portion of the Constitution. Our conclusion is that the legislative Act brought in question by this proceeding does not run counter to that section.

The respondent contends that sections 196 and 197 occupy separate fields, and that each within its respective field is exclusive of the other. It is stated that amending the Constitution by convention, as provided in section 197, is available to the people only in cases where a general revision of the entire Constitution is proposed, whereas section 196 can be used only when a few specific amendments are to be submitted to the people for approval or rejection. It is contended that the amendment sought to be made by the challenged Act should have been made under section 196 rather than by the convention method under section 197.

In our opinion sections 196 and 197 are not mutually exclusive. Amendments under section 196 are those which come in due course, but the procedure therein provided for requires a considerable period of time. On the other hand, in an emergency, when time is of the essence, it might be better to proceed under section 197. Whether the one course rather than the other should be followed is a matter delegated to the discretion of the General Assembly.

In 1928 we had a general revision of the Constitution without a convention. This revision was effected not by following the provisions of section 197, but by following those of section 196. The General Assembly in 1926 . . . created a commission of seven members to be appointed by the Governor, to "study the Constitution of Virginia and propose in detail such revision of the same as it may be of opinion will be for the best interest of the Commonwealth." The commission reported to the Extra Session of 1927. . . . In this report it was proposed to strike out from the Constitution all of the articles and sections thereof except five, and insert in lieu thereof the articles and sections appearing on pages 47 to 103, inclusive, of said Acts. The next regular session of the General Assembly in 1928 acted upon the 1927 joint resolutions proposing said amendments and revisions by enacting chapter 205, page 636, of the Acts of 1928, entitled "An Act to provide for the submission to the people for ratification or rejection the proposed revision and/or amendments." Then follow all of the articles and sections in the Constitution except section 170. Included in the revision were both sections 196 and 197, the former with a slight, immaterial change, the latter with no change. Provision was made for the vote to be taken on the *general revision.* It was framed in this language: "For the general revision of the Constitution of Virginia, except sections * * *." The vote was favorable, and Virginia had a new Constitution. In fact, every section was re-examined. The Governor, the legislature, and the people all approved and ratified the revised Constitution. No one challenged its validity on the ground that it had been revised and amended in its entirety under the provisions of section 196 instead of by a convention under the provisions of section 197. In this revised Constitution, as we have already stated, sections 196 and 197 were readopted.

Section 196 was in effect construed to be broad enough to authorize a general revision of the Constitution without a convention. That construction makes available that section (196) for a revision and amendment of the entire Constitution. Its meaning is identical with the meaning of the words used in section 197, "revise the Constitution and amend the same." This would seem to be conclusive of the interchangeability of the two sections, and that now the people are permitted to use either section which better fits the occasion to amend or revise the Constitution. That construction is made conclusive by the readoption of the two sections, 196 and 197 in the revision of 1928.

On the whole we are of opinion that the Act in question, Acts 1944, Ex.Sess., ch. 1, does not contravene any provision in the Constitution and is therefore valid; that in the event a majority of the electors vote in favor of the convention, the powers of the convention to consider, adopt or propose revisions or amendments to the Constitution will be legally restricted or limited, as defined in the Act, and in the informatory statement printed on the ballot to be used in the proposed referendum election; and that the mandamus prayed for in the petition in this cause should issue.

Writ awarded.

CAMPBELL, C. J., dissenting.

HOLT, J., concurring.

HOLT, Justice (concurring).

I am in complete accord with the conclusions which our court has reached. It is good to know that they find ample support in ancient precedents and modern instances. But we do not have to rely upon extraneous authorities, nor to look beyond the very letter of our Constitution. Section 196 provides for amendments in due course. Before they can become effective, they must have been approved by two Legislatures. Relief under these conditions in the instant case is manifestly inadequate.

Emergencies can and do arise in which time may be of the essence. The power to meet them rests in the people. It is a substantive and continuing right. Procedural and complete relief is pointed out in section 197. It is interesting to note that nowhere are provisions made for an unrestricted convention. Such a convention would be a revolutionary convention, but provisions are made for a convention to revise the Constitution and amend the same. The extent of this revision or of these amendments is nowhere defined. That there are such limitations is conceded. No one would contend that in order to proceed at all every section of our present Constitution should be revised or amended or that the Bill of Rights should be tinkered with.

Suggestions for amendments and revision come from the Legislature. Plainly John Doe cannot call a constitutional convention unless he proposes to start a revolution. In due course they are submitted to the qualified electors. If not approved, there can be no convention, and that is that. If the electors do approve, a convention is called that they may be adopted.

The Legislature, of course, cannot change the Constitution; the people can. That is an inalienable right guaranteed to them, and if not guaranteed it would still be inalienable. In the event of approval, there is delegated to the convention the power to make suggested changes, and no other power is delegated to it. Those made beyond this delegated power would be void. The Legislature makes suggestions, but the mandate to the convention comes from the people. They may make any changes which meet with their approval, provided they do not undertake to override the Federal Constitution. They may change one section of their own constitution or two, at their election.

CAMPBELL, Chief Justice (dissenting).

I am unable to concur in the conclusion reached by a majority of the court, that the act in question—"to provide for the submitting to the qualified electors the question whether there shall be a convention to revise and amend certain provisions of the Constitution of Virginia and providing an appropriation therefor"—is constitutional.

In the oral argument, it was suggested by the Attorney General that only certain elements were opposed to the act.

I have no intention of entering upon a political discussion of the question involved. I feel impelled, however, to state that as a father of three sons who volunteered for foreign service shortly after Pearl Harbor, two of whom are now serving their country in the Pacific area, and the eldest of whom, while discharging his duties as a bombardier on a B-24, was killed in action in the European area on May 23, 1944, I have no fear whatever that I will be charged with disloyalty to our service men and women.

As one of two State officers who for fifty years has been affiliated with what is known in Virginia as "the Organization," I have no apprehension of being charged with being an "organization baiter."

As the youngest member of the Constitutional Convention of 1901–02, I voted for the poll tax provision of the Constitution.

Hence, I approach this vital and important question without bias or prejudice. It is because of my conscientious conviction that the act in question is subversive of my every concept of democratic principles that I feel constrained to dissent. Though it be admitted that the act has its Genesis in the beneficent purpose of furnishing the service man a medium for the exercise of the right of suffrage without the payment of a poll tax, its Revelation is to deny him the right of democratic action in selecting his public servants to serve in a Constitutional Convention unhampered by legislative restriction.

The fundamental question involved in the case at bar is: Which shall prevail, expediency or legality? If expediency is to prevail, then our boys who have died in order that liberty and democracy (as established by their forefathers) should continue, have died in vain.

The legal question involved is this: Has the General Assembly the power to restrict the action of a Constitutional convention called into being under the provisions of section 197 of the Constitution?

In discussing the question, I wish to acknowledge my indebtedness to Honorable Albert V. Bryan, the attorney appointed by this court to represent the comptroller, for the learned and illuminating brief filed by him.

It is stated and re-stated in the majority opinion that the electors, and not the legislature, impose the restraint provided for in the act. This argument is but "a sticking in the bark."

Under the provisions of the act, the electors, when they exercise their right of suffrage, have only one of two choices—either to vote "no," or to vote for a convention in which their representatives have no volition save that prescribed by the legislature in the act. If, as contended, the power rests in the electors to call a limited convention, then the friendly office of the legislature was unnecessary. Except in the performance of a revolutionary act, the people and the legislature are controlled by constitutional limitations. How can a legislature restrict a constitutional right?

The compass which determines the constitutional course is section 197 of our Constitution. That section reads:

"At such time as the general assembly may provide, a majority of the members elected to each house being recorded in the affirmative, the question 'shall there be a convention to revise the Constitution and amend the same?' shall be submitted to the electors qualified to vote for members of the general assembly; * * *."

In the majority opinion, this is said: "That section does not expressly or impliedly forbid the legislation here questioned."

If the mandatory language, "To revise *the Constitution* and *amend the same*," is not a prohibition to merely *revise and amend only a part* of the Constitution, then the English language has lost its potency.

. . . .

As I comprehend the full import of section 197 of the Constitution, it provides for the calling of a convention without limitation to *revise and amend* the Constitution. If it means otherwise, then there is no reason for the existence of section 196 of the Constitution which provides merely for amendments to the Constitution.

It cannot be denied that the General Assembly is the creature of the Constitution. That being true, then it is a paradox to say that the creature, by legislative fiat, can become greater than its creator.

The historical sketch in the opinion regarding constitutional conventions in Virginia, while illuminating, throws no light on the dominant issue, to-wit, a construction of section 197 of the Constitution. In none of the conventions mentioned was there an attempt made to restrict the operation of the convention. Whatever action has heretofore been taken, was taken without reference to a provision similar to section 197. That section offers the only medium to "amend and revise the constitution." It is inescapable that when the Constitution embodies such a provision, the Constitution then dominates the field of amendment and revision to the exclusion of every other governmental body; that the purpose there expressed cannot be modified; that the ways and means for the submission of the question and call of the convention are likewise exclusive; and that strict adherence is requisite.

I challenge the applicability of the authorities cited in the opinion and relied upon to sustain the power of restriction. In the cases cited there is not found a single expression which indicates that the case involved a question similar to the one here involved. Wherever provision is found in the Constitution for a convention to amend and revise, no case and no text-writer allows the legislature to restrict the purpose of the convention.

. . . .

Great reliance is placed upon the view expressed by Mr. Braxton in the quotation from his article in 7 Va.Law Register. I have no quarrel with the individual view of Mr. Braxton for whom I had a deep affection and a high regard, but it appears from the "Debates Constitutional Convention" that his views were not accepted by a majority of his brethren, as will hereafter be shown. In the opinion we read this language:

"In the convention of 1901–02 section 197 was debated at length by Mr. Barbour, Mr. Braxton, and others. These debates are found on pages 2752 to 2759, inclusive, in Vol. 2 of the debates. It was stated that unless the legislature submitted to the people the question as to whether there should be a convention, it could call a convention with unlimited powers at any time. It is there shown that the main purpose of section 197 is to prohibit the legislature calling a convention of its own motion whenever it might want to so so without first ascertaining the wishes of the people. A reading of the debates will justify this conclusion."

I am unable to agree with the construction placed upon the debate in regard to section 197. . . .

. . . .

In my opinion the petitioner has failed to carry the burden of showing the power of the legislature to restrict the proposed convention and, therefore, the writ should be denied.

NAFTALIN v. KING

MINNESOTA SUPREME COURT

102 N.W. 2D 301 (1960)

The legislature of the state of Minnesota was specifically prohibited by the state constitution from incurring public debts in excess of $250,000 except in time of war or invasion. To evade the severely restrictive debt limit, the legislature had, from time to time, issued "certificates of indebtedness" against which were pledged future tax collections. The state supreme court as early as 1909 had decided that such certificates did not constitute a "public debt" and the court had reaffirmed that decision as late as 1958. However, there were many in the state including some political leaders who were unhappy with the court's position. Some felt that it was imperative to hold back state spending and, toward that end, felt that the constitutional debt limit should be interpreted strictly. Even some who thought that it was necessary for the state to be able to exceed the debt limit were uneasy about the fact that it appeared that the constitution was being circumvented by a fiction. They preferred a more direct approach to the problem, a constitutional amendment revising the debt limit. Therefore, when in 1959 the legislature provided for the issuance and sale of up to some 52 million dollars worth of "state building certificates of 1959–1978" indicating what tax levies would be used to pay off the indebtedness, the stage was set for a challenge to the legislature's action. Democrat Naftalin, commissioner of administration, certified to Republican King, the state auditor, that the funds appropriated to Naftalin's department were needed and requested King to issue and sell building certificates. In response, King informed Naftalin that he believed it would violate the constitution for him (King) to do so. Thereupon, Naftalin went to court seeking a declaratory judgment to determine the constitutionality of the legislature's action.

As an important consequence of the decision in this case, a proposal for a constitutional amendment changing the debt limit was placed on the ballot, and passed, in the election of 1962.

Justice GALLAGHER delivered the opinion of the court.

. . . .

. . . THIS COURT was confronted with the precise issue now before us in Naftalin v. King, [*a previous case*] 90 N.W.2d 185. There we decided that a state indebtedness is not created within the meaning of Minn.Const. art. 9, §§ 5, 6, and 7, where certificates of indebtedness are authorized and issued pursuant to a legislative act which makes them exclusively payable from a special fund, the proceeds of which are derived from the levy and collection of a tax authorized for that particular purpose. It is our opinion that the same rule should be used in the instant case.

In State ex rel. Foster v. Naftalin, 74 N.W.2d 249, with respect to the rule of stare decisis we stated:

> "* * * It is true that stare decisis does not apply with the same strictness in some fields of law as in others. In the field of real estate or property law, for instance, it is applied with the greatest force for the reason that in those fields property rights may have become vested in reliance upon our decision. However, it is not inapplicable in any field. Before decisions of this court should be overruled or ignored in subsequent cases, there should be some good reason for doing so. That is particularly true of decisions construing our constitution. Where such decisions have stood unchallenged for many years they should not be lightly overruled."

In that case the doctrine of stare decisis was applied even in view of the fact that no business or property rights were involved which would be impaired by the application of the rule. We stated . . . :

> "* * * Government by law instead of by man, which is the main bulwark to our democratic form of government, demands a decent respect for the rule of stare decisis in order that citizens of this state will be assured that decisions of the court are good for more than 'one trip and one day only.' "

The rule of stare decisis is not an inflexible rule of law. It is a guiding policy of the law when all factors involved in following or not following the rule are taken into consideration. . . . Whether or not the rule of stare decisis should be followed is a question entirely within the discretion of the court which is again called upon to consider a question once decided. . . .

In view of the fact that the applicability of the doctrine of stare decisis is discretionary with the court, we must consider the factors here involved. In the present case the appropriations, including reappropriations, from the Minnesota State Building Fund involved a total of $52,994,612. This amount is for the construction, alteration, repair, and rehabilitation of various state hospitals. . . . In addition the appropriation includes funds to be used in connection with the state reformatories for men and women, state prison, training schools for boys and girls, various youth camps, and the Minnesota Youth Treatment Center. Also funds for use at the five state colleges; the University of Minnesota; and other appropriations for the Capitol group of buildings, land acquisitions, parks, and contingencies.

It might appear at first glance that no vested rights would be impaired by reversing our former decision of Naftalin v. King, supra, and holding c. 90 unconstitutional. However, the complaint in this action indicates that the State Board of Investment has agreed to purchase $3,300,000 of the certificates of indebtedness issued pursuant to c. 90. Assuming that this allegation is correct inasmuch as there is no denial, then it would appear that vested rights would be impaired by holding c. 90 unconstitutional. Also, although not involving vested rights, certainly the reliance upon our former decision as reflected by the legislature in passing c. 90 would be impaired.

If we failed to follow Naftalin v. King, supra, in connection with c. 90 at this time, the construction, alterations, repairs, and rehabilitation of the various state buildings referred to above would be curtailed and chaos, delay, hardship, and confusion might well result. To tie up the state building program by declaring that the $52,994,612 cannot be made available will create a problem which in our opinion would be far more serious than is now recognized by the public. It can produce hardship in our mental institutions which are already crying for relief; it can retard educational development and progress and cause unnecessary delay in meeting a situation which must be faced before a constitutional amendment can be submitted and approved. After all, a majority of both houses of the 1959 legislature passed c. 90, now under consideration, even though the house and senate did not get together on the matter of submitting the constitutional amendment. The final vote on c. 90, after being submitted to a Conference Committee, was 57 yeas and 5 nays in the senate (Journal of the Senate, 1959, p. 2535), and 71 yeas and 50 nays in the house (Journal of the House, 1959, Ex.Sess., p. 774).

We are not disregarding the fact that a close examination of the decisions upon which the previous Naftalin v. King case was decided indicates that they were decided upon fallacious reasoning. . . .

The Naftalin case, although relying on the Brown case, established a proposition relative to certificates of indebtedness which are to be retired from a state building fund, to which fund is appropriated moneys derived from a levy upon all the taxable property in the state. It established that such certificates when once issued are irrevocable obligations of the state and, until paid, pledge the credit of the state toward their repayment out of general ad valorem taxes levied against all the property of the state.

It follows logically from this that the issuance of such certificates creates a debt within the meaning of Minn.Const. art. 9, § 5, and to the extent that such amount exceeds $250,000, it is a violation of that provision.

Nevertheless, the Brown case was followed in Naftalin v. King, supra, which was decided largely because of the prior decisions of long standing.

As previously stated, the application of the doctrine of stare decisis is within the discretion of the court. It should be just as discretionary for the court to follow stare decisis as not to follow the doctrine. It therefore appears that stare decisis, in a given case, should be followed where less injustice will result from the continuation as under the circumstances here, of an erroneous theory, than will follow from its correction. Also, that the exercise of our discretion in applying the doctrine of stare decisis should not necessarily be restricted to cases where vested contract rights pursuant to contract are involved. . . . In the exercise of discretion to invoke the doctrine of stare decisis, we base our opinion primarily on the reliance that has been placed upon the holding in our former Naftalin v. King decision, and on the delay and confusion which could result by the curtailment of that part of the building program provided for in Ex.Sess. L.1959, c. 90, in the event our former decision were not followed in this case.

We do not believe that our decision could declare c. 90 constitutional and at the same time prospectively declare unconstitutional—with binding effect—similar laws which might be passed in the future pledging the credit of the state as security. However, considered dicta can be expressed which would in the future eliminate the primary reason for now adhering to stare decisis and holding Ex.Sess. L.1959, c. 90, constitutional. It is true that obiter dicta cannot bind future decisions of courts. However, where dicta are found in an opinion which are *considered* dicta and not merely in the nature of passing comment, they should not be ignored and are even entitled to great weight. . . .

. . . .

In a footnote in our 1958 decision of Naftalin v. King, supra, we said that largely because of our prior decisions of long standing we were holding that the building certificates of indebtedness authorized by the 1955 and 1957 acts did not contravene Minn.Const. art 9, §§ 5, 6, and 7, however, that it was the opinion of all the members of the court at that time that a word of caution as to future state finances was in order.

To the extent that dicta may be binding, and to the extent to which others may rely on the instant decision in passing laws similar to . . . c. 90, it is our opinion now that if this court is again presented with the issue in connection with future laws pledging the credit of the state as security such laws should be declared in violation of Minn.Const. . . . [Italics supplied—*Eds.*]

Affirmed.

NELSON, Justice (concurring specially).

I concur in the majority opinion on the basis of the rule of stare decisis.

KNUTSON, Justice (dissenting).

I dissent.

The majority admits that the act under consideration contravenes Minn. Const. art. 9, § 5, but refuses to declare the act unconstitutional. They say, after considering some of the facts involved in the case and the decisions upon which they rest their opinion:

> "It follows logically from this that the issuance of such certificates creates a debt within the meaning of Minn. Const. art. 9, § 5, and to the extent that such amount exceeds $250,000, it is a violation of that provision."

I refuse to join in the type of reasoning that permits an admitted unconstitutional act to be called constitutional by the simple process of ignoring what we know to be right. In effect, what the majority say is that we know that the act under consideration is unconstitutional but we will not say so now, and by way of dicta they say that we hope this court in the future will have the courage to declare similar acts unconstitutional. I think that we should have the courage to declare our convictions now, no matter how unpopular it may be to do so.

. . . .

While courts are and should be reluctant to overrule former decisions except in cases where they are clearly wrong, the doctrine of stare decisis, under our law, is intended to serve as a guide in future decisions in order that there might be stability to law, rather than an inexorable rule which must be followed regardless of error in prior decisions. It is not intended as a rule under which former decisions of this court are forever to be perpetuated without reexamination, whether right or wrong. In other words, *the rule is not intended to perpetuate judicial error*. . . .

. . . .

In effect, the majority holds that we now again uphold the constitutionality of the act before us, even though contrary to our constitution, and by dicta attempts to bind the court in the future to do just the opposite and to indicate that future acts of the same kind will not be upheld. Except on the basis of stare decisis, which furnished the prop on which we have heretofore rested decision in these cases without reexamination of the correctness of prior decisions, there is no legal basis for application of such rule. If we are to decide the constitutionality of a legislative act without regard to former decisions, it is imperative that we apply the constitution as it is, divorced from the fiction that by some legal ingenuity we can arrive at a desired result first and then construe the constitution as we see fit so as to sustain that result.

. . . .

In view of the juristic philosophy which we have adopted as set forth in this case, it is difficult to see how we can now hold that the act before us is constitutional today and will be unconstitutional in the future. If, when overruling former decisions, we are to adhere to the rule that former decisions are to be regarded as never having been the law, except as to contracts made or rights acquired thereunder, how can we hold that an act is constitutional now and that in the future the same act will be unconstitutional with any degree of consistency.

The correct rule, I think, has been expressed by this court on a number of occasions. In Bowe v. City of St. Paul, 73 N.W. 184, we said:

> "* * * The act cannot be constitutional to-day and unconstitutional to-morrow. If it may in the future become unconstitutional, it is so when passed."

. . . .

Nor can it be said that expediency justifies the action now taken. The legislature was fully cognizant of the doubtful constitutionality of this type of financing.

. . . .

With these observations in mind, I proceed to a reexamination of the question of whether the type of financing here involved does or does not constitute an indebtedness of the state so as to contravene Minn.Const. art. 9, §§ 5, 6, and 7.

Minn.Const. art. 9, § 5, as far as here material, reads:

> "For the purpose of defraying extraordinary expenditures, the state may contract public debts, but such debts shall never, in the aggregate, exceed two hundred and fifty thousand dollars; . . . ."

. . . .

It must be admitted, I believe, that, if the certificates of indebtedness authorized by Ex.Sess. L.1959, c. 90, . . . create a debt within the meaning of these constitutional provisions, they cannot be upheld. I think that the majority in this decision are the only ones who would quarrel with that proposition. The constitution does not define what is a debt. Webster's New International Dictionary (2d ed.) (1947) p. 678, says that a debt is that which is due from another. It is universally held, I think, that, as applied to a state or municipal obligation, any obligation payable out of general or ad valorem taxes is a debt. . . .

It is obvious that the correctness of our prior decisions rests upon a determination of whether Brown v. Ringdal, 109 Minn. 6, 122 N.W. 469, is legally sound. All subsequent decisions construing the type of financing here involved are based on the assumption that the legality thereof was finally determined in the Brown case. Each subsequent decision has been used to bolster the Brown case, but if that case is legally untenable the whole fabric of our prior decisions is destroyed. . . .

. . . .

The fallacy of the reasoning in the Brown case, we think, is found in this statement (122 N.W. 470):

> "The certificates in and of themselves create no indebtedness against the state. On the contrary, they are mere evidence of the holder's right to demand and receive 'from the State Treasurer the proceeds of the tax authorized by the act to be levied and collected, and known and classified as the "Prison Building Fund."' Fairly construed, the act contemplates their payment from this fund exclusively, and *they are not general obligations of the state.*" (Italics supplied.)

. . . .

It is now apparent that Brown v. Ringdal, supra, as construed . . . establishes the proposition that these certificates of indebtedness, when once issued, are irrevocable obligations of the state and, until paid, pledge the credit of the state toward their repayment out of general ad valorem taxes levied against all the property of the state. It is difficult to see how we can longer hold that such obligation does not create a debt within the meaning of our constitution.

It is probably unfortunate that we have not heretofore undertaken a reexamination of the correctness of Brown v. Ringdal, supra. It has been argued, among other things, that we should adhere to that decision, whether right or wrong, in order that the planned building program now under way might proceed. That the debt limitation in our constitution may now be unrealistic in view of present conditions furnishes no excuse for ignoring it. If the constitution needs amendment, the right to bring that about rests exclusively with the people. Neither this court nor the legislature has a right to ignore clear provisions of the constitution. We are bound by our oath of office to support and uphold it as it is. In the hope that the legislature would propose an amendment to be submitted to the people of this state, we did issue a warning in Naftalin v. King, that future issues of such certificates of indebtedness might not be approved. The action taken by the legislature is set forth above. I think that we are now compelled to face the issue squarely.

. . . .

. . . This type of financing began innocently enough but has now reached such proportions that each succeeding issue of so-called certificates of indebtedness exceeds the other, now running into millions of dollars, *all of which apparently must be approved by this court before any buyer dares purchase them.* We, in turn, are asked to place our stamp of approval on each issue, solely because we have made the mistake of approving a prior issue, knowing full well that what we do is contrary to the language of our constitution. Thus, we are asked to proceed on the theory that each wrong decision adds support to prior error and that what was wrong to begin with has now become right by repetition. Apparently the idea is that if we have enough erroneous decisions the constitution may in that manner become so completely eroded that we need pay no further attention to it. . . .

We have on frequent occasions been called upon to consider the question of whether obligations of municipalities or public corporations constitute a debt where they are actually payable out of a special fund. A true special fund is distinguished from the so-called special fund that we now have before us in that the obligations are payable solely out of the proceeds of something other than ad valorem taxes. While recognizing that such obligations do not constitute a debt of the municipality, it must be apparent that, where the credit of the state stands behind such obligations and they are payable out of general ad valorem taxes levied against all the property of the state, they are no less a debt of the state simply because the proceeds of the taxes are placed in a so-called special fund for the payment of the obligations. The distinction relates rather to the source of the funds from which the obligations are to be paid than the manner in which the payment is to be made.

. . . .

Where certificates of indebtedness such as we have here bind the credit of the state and are payable out of general ad valorem taxes levied against property in the future, they do constitute a debt of the state and, except to the limited extent provided in Minn.Const. art. 9, § 5, contravene our constitution. Apparently the majority agree. The type of financing that we have here does not constitute a special-fund type of financing at all. It is a special fund in name only. Putting it bluntly, these certificates of indebtedness constitute an irrevocable obligation of the state, payable out of ad valorem taxes levied generally against all the property of the state, and, as such, it can be nothing but a state debt. If such obligations do not constitute a debt within the meaning of our constitution, there is no such thing.

It will furnish little comfort for a taxpayer to know that we say that the obligation to pay these certificates of indebtedness, for the payment of which his property stands as security, is not a debt of the state when he knows that the taxes from which payment is to come in the future encumber his property for the full term of the bond issue.

It is simply senseless to continue to hold that these obligations of the state for the payment of which the credit of the state is pledged, and which are to be paid out of ad valorem taxes levied generally against all the property in the state, do not constitute an indebtedness of the state for the reason that they are paid out of a fund which, in name only, is designated as a special fund. It would be equally valid to say that a mortgage on a taxpayer's property does not constitute a debt simply because part of it is to be paid in the future in installments. In determining the net worth of an individual or corporation, no financial institution would be impressed with such argument. Courts should not close their eyes to that which is generally known to everyone else.

. . . .

Thus, while the easy way out is to hold that what we have done before we must do again even though we are now of the opinion that we have heretofore been wrong, I am now convinced that certificates of indebtedness authorized by Ex.Sess. L.1959, c. 90, § 14, if issued, will constitute evidence of a state indebtedness; that the law under consideration authorizes issuance of such certificates in amounts that contravene the limit of state debt permitted by our constitution; and that as a result, consistent with our oath of office to uphold the constitution, we are compelled to hold that § 14 is unconstitutional. We need not pass upon other provisions of c. 90 in this case since the only thing involved is whether such certificates may be issued and sold.

DELL, Chief Justice (dissenting).

I concur in the dissent of Mr. Justice KNUTSON.

The late Mr. Justice MATSON having taken part in the hearing of this case died prior to the determination thereof and took no part in the decision.

LOEVINGER, J., having been appointed as the successor to Mr. Justice MATSON, not having qualified or taken part in the hearing of the case, took no part in the consideration or determination thereof.

SMITH v. HOLM

MINNESOTA SUPREME COURT

19 N.W. 2D 914 (1945)

Minnesota's constitution provides that "The representation in both houses of the legislature shall be apportioned equally throughout the different sections of the State, in proportion to the population thereof. . . ." The legislature, however, had not up to 1945 redistricted since 1913. Smith brought suit against Holm, the secretary of state, seeking a declaratory judgment to the effect that the legislative redistricting act of 1913 had become unconstitutional since representation in the legislature was no longer equal. The case came to the state supreme court on appeal from a lower court.

Chief Justice LORING delivered the opinion of the court.

. . . .

ON THE merits, the sole question presented is whether such changes in equality of representation have operated to vitiate the constitutionality of the act and leave the state without a valid law creating legislative districts. . . .

. . . .

[*The Act*] soon after its passage was challenged as to its conformance with the [*constitution*] and was held to be constitutional against the very charges of inequality now made against it. State ex rel. Meighen v. Weatherill, 147 N.W. 105. In that case this court, in announcing the rule under which it would test the validity of the act here under consideration, quoted with approval the rule stated in State ex rel. Atty Gen. v. Cunningham, 51 N.W. 724, as follows:

"* * * perfect exactness in the apportionment according to the number of inhabitants is neither required nor possible. But there should be as close an approximation to exactness as possible, and this is the utmost limit for the exercise of legislative discretion. If * * * there is such a wide and bold departure from this constitutional rule that it cannot possibly be justified by the exercise of any judgment or discretion, and that evinces an intention on the part of the legislature to utterly ignore and disregard the rule of the constitution in order to promote some other object than a constitutional apportionment, then the conclusion is inevitable that the legislature did not use any judgment or discretion whatever."

In short, if the legislature exercises its judgment and discretion in enacting an apportionment law, the result is not vulnerable to attack in the courts.

Does the subsequent change in relative representation annul its provisions adjudged valid when enacted?

Counsel for plaintiff and the trial court seem to have assumed that the question must be answered in the affirmative. No case has been cited to us, nor have we found any, supporting the contention that it should be so answered, although a similar situation has developed in many states. The plaintiff in his brief does no more than state an assumption. In support of its position, the trial court has cited some cases in which laws activating the police power have been held to have become unconstitutional as discriminatory or confiscatory when sought to be applied to circumstances radically changed since their enactment. The act here involved is not an exercise of the police power, but of a political, administrative power involving the exercise of judgment and discretion, and is a governmental function in the sense that it is commanded by the constitution in furtherance of the structure of the state government. . . . This clearly distinguishes it from the police power cases.

The division of powers is the fundamental principle upon which American constitutional government is based, and the success of our form of government depends, in large measure, upon the respect paid to that principle by each of the three divisions in its relations with the others. Under art. 3 of our state constitution, the initiative in legislation lies entirely in the legislature, and by art. 4 the redistricting power is placed wholly in that body, Fergus v. Marks, 152 N.E. 557, 559. In that case the court said: "Neither one of these departments [of government] can arrogate to itself any control over either one of the other departments in matters which have been solely confided by the Constitution to such other department." In State ex rel. Holm v. District Court, 194 N.W. 630, this court, in commenting on the division of governmental powers into three independent branches, quoted with approval its previous language . . . as follows: "Neither is responsible to the other for the manner in which it exercises its discretion in the performance of duties which are governmental or political in their character." In . . . [*an earlier case*] this court, speaking through Mr. Justice Holt, in discussing the division of powers, said: "* * * the judicial has not the power to control, coerce, or restrain the action of the other two within the sphere allotted them by the Constitution wherein to exercise judgment and discretion," and he speaks of such action as "unthinkable." The judicial branch may not, therefore, directly or indirectly interfere with this legislative power in any other way than by passing upon the constitutionality, as of the time of their enactment, of such laws as the one before us for failure to comply with the rule hereinbefore stated. The responsibility to heed the constitutional mandate to redistrict is laid upon the legislature, and it is, at most, only when as of the time of enactment there appears a clear and palpable violation of the fundamental law that the courts would have the power to upset the law. . . .

Absent a violation of the announced rule in the enactment, the mere change in relative population and consequent inequality of representation subsequent to enactment does not render the act void. The plaintiff concedes that the courts have no power to compel the legislature to act. It follows from that lack of power that an apportionment act, constitutionally enacted, remains in force until superseded by a valid act. The division of powers leaves the legislature free from compulsion. Its judgment and discretion are its own to exercise or not, as its conscience permits. In State ex rel. Warson v. Howell, 159 P. 777, a situation almost identical with that now prevailing in Minnesota was before that court in 1916. The last apportionment in that state had been enacted in 1901, and the constitutional requirement that after each state and federal census the legislature "shall apportion and district anew the members" of the legislature had been entirely ignored, notwithstanding changes which rendered the inequalities in population "exceedingly gross." The court said . . . :

"* * * It may be remarked here, however, that this latter fact furnishes no ground for declaring the legislative apportionment unconstitutional. While it argues strongly against the failure of the

Legislature to perform its duty, *it states no ground for setting aside a legislative apportionment valid when enacted.* It is held by all of the courts that the Legislature cannot be compelled to redistrict the state as directed by the Constitution, and as a corollary thereto, it must follow that *an apportionment act, lawfully enacted, will continue in force until superseded by a subsequent valid act.*" (Italics supplied.)

This seems sound doctrine to us. It is our opinion that a reapportionment act, valid when enacted, may not be held unconstitutional by reason of subsequent changes in the relative population of the districts, and that it continues in force until superseded by a valid act. . . . The cases cited by the trial court involving the police power are not in point. The remedy lies in the political conscience of the legislature, where lies the burden of the constitutional mandate. It is not within the province of this court to prompt the action of that conscience. It is usually sensitive enough to promptings from the electorate.

. . . .

[*Although there may be some doubt as to what the court actually decided, the effect of the decision was to uphold the constitutionality of the Act of 1913.*]

CHAPTER THREE

Legislative Power

One of the current phenomena of democratic governments everywhere is the disenchantment with legislatures. Despite professed and deeply held convictions that democratic ideals are best, democrats everywhere have become impatient with their legislatures. In part, the impatience has been an outgrowth of the failure of legislatures to perform well in our troubled, complex times.

Over the years, the initiative in lawmaking has passed from the legislative to the executive branch of government. In modern society, the complexities of government virtually require that the executive branch, which is daily working with the problems of government, take a leading role in lawmaking. Specifically, the daily operation of government gives the executive branch an unusual insight into the needs for legislative changes. Not only that, but the executives by constant association with particular areas of government acquire an *expertise* in these areas that legislators dealing simultaneously in all areas can hardly hope to acquire. This is not to imply that the executive branch makes law by fiat. We are only trying to point out the obvious fact that in all democracies the executive branch plays a larger and larger role in proposing and drafting legislation which the legislatures act upon, in contrast to past centuries where the legislature largely did its own proposing and drafting.

This heavier reliance upon executive leadership was, of course, inevitable as government grew more complex. However, this does not mean that the legislature in a democratic society no longer has an important role to play. It means only that it must play a different role. The legislature can and should retain for itself the power of determining the broad general direction of public policy; it can and should study and act on the most important issues. At the same time, in behalf of the people it can and should maintain a sharp eye on the way the executive branch performs its tasks. Of course, all legislatures now do these things to some extent, some better than others.

But at the same time and in one way or another, they attempt to reassert themselves by becoming involved in all the minute details of proposed legislation, important and otherwise. When they do so, they appear inept, because they are ill-equipped to perform this task efficiently. Furthermore, legislatures in recent years have tended to move into areas which are normally considered to be the province of the executive and judicial branches of government. The classic example of this tendency is the legislative investigation. Properly conceived, legislative investigations should be employed judiciously and sparingly for well-defined legislative objectives. But for the confused and frustrated legislator an investigation is a definable task in which he can deeply involve himself and thereby justify his existence. Consequently, we are afforded the spectacle of legislative investigations which attempt to perform the functions of courts and administrative agencies. As a result of this changing role of the legislature, the public and some chief executives as well, have been confused as to what they should and do expect of the legislatures.

Paradoxically, democrats are ambivalent about democratic ideals and authoritarian leadership. We have a great deal of admiration for the "strong man." To give evidence, when students have been asked to indicate quickly whether their immediate reaction was favorable or unfavorable to leaders such as Caesar, Napoleon, and Bismarck, the overwhelming majority, who believe they are devoted to democratic ideals, have consistently responded with a favorable reaction to each of these men. Yet it is obvious that each of these men in large measure represented the antithesis of democratic ideals. Remember the question was not whether these men were great or not, but rather whether the students had a favorable or unfavorable disposition to them. At first thought this reaction appears to be a consequence of our practice of teaching history in terms of the "great men" without corresponding emphasis on democratic values. Would you agree? If not, how do you account for the fact that in any test of strength between the chief executive and the legislature, the chief executive more often than not will receive the support of public opinion, even when the executive has acted in an authoritarian fashion? When Abraham Lincoln suspended the writ of *habeas corpus* and when Franklin D. Roosevelt "traded" American destroyers, both patently exceeding their constitutional powers, the public generally approved their actions.

Another evidence of ambivalence is found in the relative prestige accorded the respective branches of government. To a people devoted to democratic ideals, the legislature should have great prestige. Yet it is commonplace to ridicule legislators. Satirists in newspapers and other mass media constantly poke fun at legislators. Al Capp for years has made this kind of satire a feature of his cartoon strip. Certainly, we should have a sense of humor about these things, and good institutions are not endangered by being satirized. This is not to say that Presidents have not been and are not the subjects of political satire. However, it is important to note that satire of the chief executive is more often directed toward the personal characteristics of the particular man in office, and not toward the office itself.

To further illustrate the ambivalence we have been discussing, we would like to relate what happened when one of the editors invited the Governor of Minnesota to speak to his class. In the course of his presentation the Governor indicated his concern that the people have come to rely too heavily upon the executive branch for legislative leadership. The student editors of *The Minnesota Daily*, who throughout the year had truly manifested a devotion to democratic ideals, responded with the following editorial:

LEADER RESPONSIBILITIES

On the contrary Gov. Andersen, strong leadership is your responsibility.

The Governor, speaking to a political science class Wednesday, intimated that, when all branches of government are "functioning properly," there is no need for strong executive leadership.

He said: "if they (the various branches of government) don't" function properly, "people want strong leadership, and that is dangerous."

What then does Andersen consider his role as Governor? Certainly it can't be just titular. The Governor must exert strong leadership not only over administrative departments, but also in dealing with the Legislature.

It is evident from his statements, however, the Governor does not think so. "Americans," he said, "must avoid looking to an executive to lead them through troubled times, but must instead rely on the separation-of-powers system that has built this country to what it is today."

But such thinking is folly. The separation-of-powers system is a safeguard against political tyranny, not a substitute for executive leadership.

People look to the chief executive not only to formulate a favorable legislative program, but to work indefatigably for Legislative approval. And during "troubled times," certainly a Legislature riddled with factions and special-interest groups can't provide firm leadership. This must come from the Governor. . . .[1]

Professor Chase thinking to set the record straight responded to the editorial in the following manner.

To the editor:

I was distressed by your editorial of February 2 in which you took the Governor to task. You suggest that the Governor, lecturing to a political science class, eschewed executive leadership. That was not my understanding of the sum of what he said.

The Governor made it very clear, it seemed to me, that each branch of our government should do its job and that a governor must be a leader. He did inveigh, however, against excessive reliance upon executive leadership. He pointed out that the legislature has its responsibilities, too, in our system of government and that we should not want the executive branch to take over completely the legislative functions. To argue that the Governor is wrong on this point, it seems to me, is to argue that democracy is no longer a viable concept

[1] John Shaver, *The Minnesota Daily*, February 2, 1962. Reprinted with permission.

and that some form of authoritarian government is the best hope for the future. I know *The Minnesota Daily* would not take such a position. . . .[2]

On the substantive issue of the proper relationship between the Governor and the legislature, with whom do you agree, the student editors or Professor Chase?

The disenchantment with legislatures, whatever the reasons, is not healthy. Disenchantment with legislatures can very well become the first step to disenchantment with all democratic institutions, ideas, and ideals. The remedy lies in the ultimate realization by legislators, executives, and the public that the functions of legislatures have changed. Legislatures must, if they are to win back the respect they need in healthy democratic societies, become great deliberative assemblies which debate wisely and well the major issues of the society and which oversee the operation of the executive branch maturely and wisely.

A. *The Problem of Reapportionment*

On first learning that urban and suburban residents have for years been systematically underrepresented in state legislatures, students from those areas tend to be outraged and want to know why something has not been done sooner to remedy what appears to be an injustice. The nature of the problem has been such as to make an easy solution impossible.

In the early days of our national history, there was no attempt systematically or otherwise to underrepresent the urban and suburban dwellers. As a matter of fact, what cities there were in 1790 were exceedingly small by current standards. Philadelphia, the largest city, had a population of 42,000; New York, 33,000; and Boston, 18,000. To determine the representation in the legislature, the existing subdivisions, counties, and townships were usually used as election districts. Frequently, the most sparsely settled subdivisions were combined with others in order to make election districts roughly equal in population at the time. In some states no special conscious effort was made to equalize population; the state was simply divided into a set of smaller areas of about the same size. But when the population was largely rural, districts so drawn were not as a matter of fact so disparate in population as to make for gross inequities in representation. Remember in 1790, 5.1% of the people lived in urban areas as against 94.9% in rural areas. As late as 1840, only 10.8% of the population lived in urban areas. Surprisingly enough, in 1850, only six cities had a population of over 100,000 (New York, 515,547; Baltimore, 169,054; Boston, 136,881; Philadelphia, 121,376; New Orleans, 116,376; Cincinnati, 115,435). But for good or evil a dramatic change in population patterns was wrought by the enormous industrial growth of the United States in the latter half of the nineteenth century. After 1840, the urban areas came to hold an ever-increasing percentage of the population. By 1927, a majority of the population was centered in urban areas (51.2%). Today that percentage is pressing 75%.

[2] Harold W. Chase, *ibid.* Reprinted with permission.

What this change means in terms of representation can be seen from the following diagram. The shaded area represents a concentration of population in a metropolitan area. As certain districts grew in population, they were still entitled (constitutionally or by law) only to the number of legislative representatives they had had in an earlier day.

5 Reps.	5 Reps.	5 Reps.	5 Reps.
5 Reps.	5 Reps.	5 Reps.	5 Reps.
5 Reps.	5 Reps.	5 Reps.	5 Reps.

Thus, even if the shaded area represented half the state's population, it had, unless reapportionment was accomplished, one-twelfth of the seats in the state legislature. And whose responsibility is it to reapportion legislative seats? In all but a few states, the state constitution gives that responsibility to the legislature! Since the majority in most state legislatures at any given time consisted of representatives of rural areas, to give urban areas more representation required that the rural representatives give up political power willingly. It is virtually axiomatic that no group gives up political power willingly and gracefully. It should, therefore, be no surprise that rural legislators have been unwilling to undertake reapportionment schemes which would give a majority of legislative seats to the cities. True, from time to time modifications and concessions have been made, short of giving up control. But there have also been times when the party in control of a legislature has changed district lines in order to insure continued majorities; this, of course, is the gerrymandering process with which you are already familiar. By and large, rural legislators have maintained control of our state legislatures, even when the legislatures represented far less than a majority of the voters of the state. Thus, *The New York Times* could lament editorially in early 1962 that "in only six states does it require 40 per cent or more of the population to elect a majority of the legislature. In the state of New York 36.9 per cent of the population can elect a majority of the State Senate and 38.2 per cent of the population a majority of the Assembly. In thirteen states one-third of the population or less can elect a majority of both houses of the State Legislature." [3]

Human nature being what it is, it became necessary to rationalize what appeared to be an injustice. Rural legislators long ago developed a political theory which argued that the farmers who were close to the land and who were landowners had a more enduring interest in the state than city dwellers who tended to be transients. Along Jeffersonian lines, they sang the praises of the virtuous farmers as compared to the turbulent and radical workers in the factories. To some extent, they argued that the farmers needed the control of the legislature as protection from the whims of a hostile majority in

[3] *The New York Times*, March 27, 1962.

the cities and that the minority has rights which may need more protection than those of the majority.

Rationalizations aside, what can be done if the legislature refuses to reapportion on an equitable basis when it has the responsibility to do so? When a state constitution provided for or permitted the use of the initiative (which a little less than half the states do), it was possible for a group to endeavor to capitalize on the voting power of the urbanites in any *statewide* election and thereby bring about a change in representation. But this was and is not as easy as it sounds. For one thing, if it is decided to use the initiative, it takes an unusual effort to organize a drive to change the status quo. To achieve a successful conclusion requires a great deal of money and in the context of American politics the real zeal of some of our more potent pressure groups. Most of the special interest groups who have been traditionally effective in our politics have not been interested in promoting reapportionment. For many of them, the status quo which gives a preponderance of legislative power to the rural legislators is better in their self-interest than a change. For example, business interests in the city may justifiably prefer rural domination of the legislature because in general the agrarians tend to be for the same things they are, such as lower taxes and less welfare legislation. Consequently, there are important elements in every city which are not partial to greater representation for the city. This factor makes it difficult but not impossible, then, to muster the kind of support and interest necessary to make the initiative an effective remedy. Actually, people in three states, Washington, Oregon, and Colorado achieved some success through the use of the initiative. Nor is it a simple matter to change the state constitution to place responsibility for reapportionment elsewhere, particularly when that same constitution gives the legislature a key role in the amendment process as our state constitutions do.

Until very recently, the judiciary at both the state and Federal levels seemed powerless, or at least unwilling, to remedy the inequities in representation. State courts have traditionally been reluctant to attempt to force state legislatures to reapportion on the grounds that to do so would be a violation of the separation of powers principle. Recall the Minnesota supreme court's decision in *Smith* v. *Holm* (p. 135) which you read earlier.

Despite the discouragements and frustrations, proponents of reapportionment have persisted in their efforts. Eventually, they turned to the *Federal* courts. They felt and did so argue before these courts that unequal representation constituted a violation of that part of the Fourteenth Amendment of the *Federal* Constitution which reads: "nor shall any State . . . deny to any person within its jurisdiction the equal protection of the laws." Initially, the Federal courts took the position that there was nothing they could do to bring about reapportionment. In a landmark case, *Colegrove* v. *Green*, 328 U.S. 549 (1946), the Supreme Court of the United States in dealing with the question of reapportioning state *congressional* districts decided that the issue was "of a peculiarly political nature and therefore not meet for judicial determination." The fact that *Colegrove* dealt with state *congressional* districts meant that it was a better case to bring before a *Federal* court than one involving districting for a state legislature, for it was easier to argue that there was a Federal question involved. So, when the Supreme Court decided that, even as to congressional districting, the Court should not try to resolve the reapportionment problem, it was a foregone conclusion that the same Court would take the same posture as to reapportionment for the state legislatures. By way of explanation, the Supreme Court did not write a novel doctrine in *Colegrove*. The Court has traditionally taken the position that there are some constitutional questions that can be better resolved by the political branches (legislative and executive) than by the judiciary. Unfortunately, the Court has never provided precise criteria for what makes a question "political." Note carefully Justice Frankfurter's discussion of "political questions" in his dissent in *Baker* v. *Carr* (p. 166).

One striking aspect of the decisions of the Court in *Colegrove*, in which interestingly enough Justice Frankfurter wrote the *majority* opinion, is this dictum (an observation made by a judge which is not essential to the determination of the case): "Courts ought not to enter this political thicket. *The remedy for unfairness in districting is to secure State legislatures that will apportion properly*, or to invoke the ample powers of Congress." [Italics supplied—*Eds.*] Well, as to state legislatures, the use of Congress' power is questionable on constitutional grounds, and as for securing state legislatures that will apportion properly, how can it be done practically? As we pointed out earlier, there is really no practical way short of judicial intervention "to secure state legislatures that will apportion properly."

The continued disproportionate representation has had a marked effect on our state politics. In some states, it has frequently meant divided government. In states like New Jersey and New York, when there has been a Democratic governor, he has almost always been faced by a legislature controlled by the Republican Party. In a state-wide election, city votes count as much as rural votes, so that a Democrat could be elected governor by getting a majority of *all* votes cast, while the legislature composed of representatives of districts would have a majority of Republicans. Another consequence of the underrepresentation of the cities has been the belief of the cities that, rightly or wrongly, they cannot get a fair deal from their state legislatures. This belief has intensified efforts to try and obtain Home Rule charters for the cities in order to make them more independent of the state legislatures. Although a certain amount of independence is desirable, it is preferable to have it grow out of a spirit of cooperation rather than hostility. Also, it is understandable why our large cities have come to view the national government, when the Democrats are in power, as being more responsive to the needs of the cities than the state legislatures. For, as a matter of fact, our large cities tend to vote for Democratic leadership locally as well as nationally. Such reliance by the cities on the national government constitutes a countervailing force to those on the state level who try to recapture for the states functions and powers which have drifted to the national government. In that connection, failure to reapportion has rendered ineffective one of the stoutest arguments for returning functions and responsibilities to the states, i.e. that it is more democratic to have political issues resolved by that government closest to the people. Is it, indeed, more democratic to rely on a legislature which systematically discriminates against urban and suburban voters? This is not to imply that Congress is a strictly representative body, for it is not. But it is certainly understandable why city Democrats will look upon a Democratic President as the institution best able to perceive their problems and aspirations.

In the past decade, an interesting constitutional development took place which made a reconsideration of the reapportionment problem by the judiciary inevitable. As the courts began to decide cases involving state discriminations against Negroes as violations of the "equal protection" clause, it became natural to raise the question as to what the courts would do, when a state systematically discriminated against a Negro and made his vote worth less than a white person's. Later, when it became apparent from judicial decisions that such a discrimination against the Negro violated "equal protection," some people began to ask why the same logic should not apply to city voters who were underrepresented. Consequently, a number of cases have been brought to Federal courts in the last few years seeking reapportionment. Ultimately, the problem came again to the Supreme Court. In 1962, the Supreme Court decided in *Baker* v. *Carr* (p. 153) that "the allegations of a denial of equal protection present a justifiable constitutional cause of action upon which appellants are entitled to a trial and decision. The right asserted is within reach of judicial protection under the Fourteenth Amendment." In essence, what the Court decided was that reapportionment was not a political question, reversing the Court's earlier position. But it is extremely important to understand that the Supreme Court did not try to determine how and in what fashion the states must reapportion. Rather, the cause was remanded to the appropriate district court "for further proceedings consistent with this opinion." This means that Federal district courts must hear cases alleging unfair representation and decide them on their particular merits. Also, at this point, the Court left the initial matter of choosing remedies, when there is a violation of "equal protection," to those district courts. As a result of the decision in *Baker* v. *Carr*, a host of cases involving thirty or more states have been brought to district courts throughout the nation. It will be interesting to see how the courts determine whether or not reapportioning is necessary in particular cases and the kind of remedies invoked to bring about reapportionment when the courts deem them necessary. One question which is fascinating to speculate upon is: Will Federal courts permit one house of the state legislature to be based on geography rather than population as is the United States Senate? Can the same reasons for basing representation in the United States Senate on area justify doing the same on the state level? Review the reasons provided in *Federalist 62* for basing the United States Senate representation on area:

> The equality of representation in the Senate is another point, which, being evidently the result of compromise between the opposite pretensions of the large and small States, does not call for much discussion. If indeed it be right, that among a people thoroughly incorporated into one nation, every district ought to have a *proportional* share in the government, and that among independent and sovereign States, bound together by a simple league, the parties, however unequal in size, ought to have an *equal* share in the common councils, it does not appear to be without some reason that in a compound republic, partaking both of the national and federal character, the government ought to be founded on a mixture of the principles of proportional and equal representation. But it is superfluous to try, by the standard of theory, a part of the Constitution which is allowed on all hands to be the result, not of theory, but "of a spirit of amity, and that mutual deference and concession which the peculiarity of our political situation rendered indispensable." A common government, with powers equal to its objects, is called for by the voice, and still more loudly by the political situation, of America. A government founded on principles more consonant to the wishes of the larger States, is not likely to be obtained from the smaller States. The only option, then, for the former, lies between the proposed government and a government still more objectionable. Under this alternative, the advice of prudence must be to embrace the lesser evil; and instead of indulging a fruitless anticipation of the possible mischiefs which may ensue, to contemplate rather the advantageous consequences which may qualify the sacrifice. . . .

Does this logic apply to the question of whether or not one house in the state legislature should be based on area as has been the case in most states prior to *Baker* v. *Carr?* Bear in mind, too, that there is no Constitutional provision which requires Congress to afford "equal protection of the laws" as there is requiring the states to do so. The Supreme Court dealt with this difference in the legal positions of the national and state governments as it applies to school segregation in *Bolling* v. *Sharpe,* 347 U.S. 497 (1954). There, the Court felt that racial segregation in the public schools of the District of Columbia, for which Congress does the legislating, was a denial of "due process" protection guaranteed against the national government by the Fifth Amendment. But the Court did indicate in its decision that "equal protection" and "due process" were not the same.

A Maryland state judge has already ruled that the Maryland senate "can be constitutionally based upon area and geographical location regardless of population" comparing the Maryland legislature in that respect to Congress. But will Federal courts do likewise? The Michigan supreme court and the Federal district court in Virginia have ruled that representation in both houses must be proportioned to population. We have also had a very recent case in which a Federal court has undertaken to indicate what remedy it would invoke if the state legislature cannot or does not reapportion according to the court's conception of equity. That court appointed a former Wisconsin state supreme court justice to serve as a Master (i.e., an officer of a court who makes an inquiry into matters referred to him by the court and reports his findings in such form that a decree may be made) and draw up a proposed solution to Wisconsin's reapportionment problem. Interestingly enough, the Master ruled that the existing districts did not deny voters constitutional rights and recommended that the Federal court dismiss the suit.

In June of 1963, the Supreme Court decided that it would hear argument in eight districting cases in its next term, 1963–64. Perhaps, the Court has already heard the cases and rendered its decisions. If so, seek them out and see whether or not you agree with them. If the Court has not yet decided these cases, you might want to read the Court's recent decision with respect to the county-unit system of elections used in Georgia to see if it has application to the questions raised earlier. The citation for that case is *Gray* v. *Saunders*, 373 U.S. 368 (1963).

B. *The Problem of Legislative Investigations*

Americans in the 1960's need hardly be reminded of the importance of the investigative function of legislatures. All of us by now have witnessed parts of significant and/or colorful congressional investigations on television. Because legislative investigations vary tremendously in kind, a precise definition to fit them all is difficult to find. Professors Carr and Bernstein, in *American Democracy in Theory and Practice*, have provided a good one for congressional investigations which is applicable to state legislative investigations as well:

> A congressional investigation is to be contrasted with the normal, routine consideration of bills by the standing committees of Congress. An investigation is an inquiry into a *subject* or a *problem* rather than a specific legislative proposal. At its most formal, an investigation occurs where Congress specifically authorizes an inquiry into a particular subject, designating a committee to make this study, votes an appropriation to cover the costs of the inquiry, and grants the committee power to subpoena witnesses. . . .[4]

Although there has been a great deal of criticism of how particular investigations have been conducted and controversy over the *extent* of a legislature's power to investigate, there are few who would hold that legislatures should not have the power at all. First, a legislature must at times investigate in order to legislate wisely. As the Supreme Court reasoned many years ago, "a legislative body, cannot legislate wisely or effectively in the absence of information respecting the conditions which the legislature is intended to affect or change; and where the legislative body does not itself possess the requisite information—which not infrequently is true—recourse must be had to others who do possess it." Second, as pointed out earlier a legislature must oversee the activities of the executive branch of the government. In some instances, this can best be done by an investigation. A good example was the recent congressional inquiry to determine among other things, the Department of Agriculture's involvement in the Billy Estes' manipulations.

[4] Robert K. Carr, Marver H. Bernstein *et al., American Democracy in Theory and Practice*, 3rd ed. (New York: Holt, Rinehart and Winston, 1959), pp. 339–340. Reprinted with the permission of Holt, Rinehart and Winston.

Third, a legislature in a democratic society has an obligation to educate the public as to the need for legislation or to point up abuses by the executive branch. Generally, this can be best accomplished by debate in the legislature. But, sometimes, an investigation can better serve to dramatize the issues and capture the public's attention. The best rationale for investigating in order to inform the public was provided by Professor Woodrow Wilson long before he became President:

> It is the proper duty of a representative body to look diligently into every affair of government and to talk much about what it sees. It is meant to be the eyes and the voice, and to embody the wisdom and will of its constituents. Unless Congress have and use every means of acquainting itself with the acts and disposition of the administrative agents of the government, the country must remain in embarrassing crippling ignorance of the very affairs which it is most important that it should understand and direct. The informing function of Congress should be preferred even to its legislative function.[5]

What Wilson wrote as to Congress is logically applicable to state legislatures.

As indicated earlier, there has been controversy over the *scope* of the legislative power to inquire. There are those who argue that no legislature has the power to investigate matters which it cannot handle through legislation. It is suggested that, since no American legislature has the constitutional power to abridge First Amendment freedoms, it has no power to investigate in these areas nor the power to investigate any matter where the investigating will have the impact of abridging these freedoms. (It must be borne in mind that although the First Amendment forbids only Congress from abridging the First Amendment freedoms, our courts have read into the word "liberty" in the Fourteenth Amendment these freedoms, thus establishing a prohibition in the national Constitution against state legislative action abridging First Amendment freedoms.) Another potent criticism leveled at legislative investigations is that they have too frequently been used to *punish* people rather than to develop the facts pertaining to a particular problem. When legislative committees have intentionally tried to mete out punishment by investigation they have been doing what the Founding Fathers sought to prevent by inserting in the Constitution the specific prohibition against Bills of Attainder. According to the Supreme Court in 1866, "A bill of attainder is a legislative Act which inflicts punishment without judicial trial." Although an investigation is not a legislative "Act" in a strict legal sense, surely, the framers' abhorrence would logically extend to legislative actions of all types, except in those rare instances when the legislature sits constitutionally as a court as in impeachment proceedings.

The great difficulty our courts have encountered in trying to determine whether or not specific investigations have exceeded constitutional limitations is in determining what the intent of the legislative committee or its agent was in carrying on a particular investigation. Was it to limit a First Amend-

[5] Woodrow Wilson, *Congressional Government* (Boston: Houghton, Mifflin & Co., 1885), pp. 297, 303.

ment freedom or truly to safeguard against subversive activities? Was it to punish or to learn facts? So much depends upon the intent, yet courts quite wisely endeavor to refrain from psychoanalyzing legislators.

In the light of what we have been saying, the cases offered for your study here are intriguing. Justice Warren, writing the Court's opinion in *Sweezy* v. *New Hampshire* (p. 171), talked about but did not decide the constitutional issues which are posed by the case. Rather, the case was decided on a "technicality": "The lack of any indications that the legislature wanted the information the attorney general [who had been empowered to carry on the investigation for the New Hampshire legislature] attempted to elicit from petitioner must be treated as absence of authority." Justices Frankfurter and Harlan in concurring do deal with the question of whether or not the investigative power in this case does unconstitutionally abridge a First Amendment freedom, as do the dissenters Clark and Burton. On the constitutional issue, do you agree with Frankfurter or Clark? In view of the decision in *Sweezy*, how do you account for the Court's decision in *Uphaus* v. *Wyman* (p. 181)? The key to the difference probably lies in the Frankfurter opinion in *Sweezy*, for he and Harlan who agreed with him in *Sweezy* help make the new majority. Notice in *Uphaus* the discussion of whether or not the investigation is in fact legislative punishment. Also, note the discussion in the majority opinion concerning the question of whether or not state action has been precluded by congressional action—a question we explored earlier in connection with *Pennsylvania* v. *Nelson* (p. 11).

C. The Problem of the Constitutional Limits of the State Legislatures' Police Power

It has become commonplace for Americans to bemoan the "fact" that all governmental power has drifted to the national government. Nothing could be further from the truth. What has happened is that governments at all levels have increased the scope of their activities. In the American system, the state legislatures have enormous power which they do employ and which affects our daily lives profoundly. Whereas Congress is limited to the specific grants of power contained in the national Constitution, the state legislatures are not so constrained. And assertions to the contrary, Congress cannot act unless it can reasonably show that it is acting under one of its constitutional powers. In contrast to Congress which is limited to the enumerated powers as well as by constitutional prohibitions, state legislatures are only limited by the specific prohibitions in the national and their own state constitutions. The classic definition of the state legislatures' "police power" is cited in *Prentiss* v. *National Airlines* (p. 189): "The police power of a state may 'prescribe regulations to promote the health, peace, morals, education, and good order of the people, and to legislate so as to increase the industries of the state, develop its resources, and to add to its wealth and prosperity.'" As already indicated, this vast legislative power is limited only by national and state constitutional prohibitions. For example, a state legislature which passed a law markedly abridging free speech or denying someone equal protection of the laws would be exceeding its constitutional power, since the national Constitution forbids it to do so. But the determination of what is constitutionally permissible in all cases is not as easy to make as these examples suggest. The Fourteenth Amendment provides among other things that no state shall "deprive any person of life, liberty or property, without due process of law." Although the framers of the Constitution may well have had in mind, when they used the term in the Fifth Amendment, that "due process" only meant fair procedures, by judicial interpretation "due process" has come to have additional meaning. Our courts have determined that when the substantive content of legislation is *unreasonable* or *arbitrary*, that legislation is rendered invalid by virtue of the due process clause. Such use of the due process clause has come to be called substantive due process to distinguish it from the use of due process as a guarantee that government agencies will use fair procedures. You may well feel that substantive due process is a strained construction of the clause, but even if it is, it has become so well-accepted in our jurisprudence as to make it important for students to endeavor to understand it rather than to reject it out of hand.

For a time in our history, from about 1890 to 1937, substantive due process was in fact a considerable limitation on the state legislatures' police powers. Conservative judges employed the concept to strike down a host of state statutes regulating business activities. In recent years, courts have been reluctant to find state legislatures unreasonable or arbitrary in economic matters. A good example is the decision in *Prentiss* v. *National Airlines* (p. 189). However, in cases involving civil liberties, the courts, particularly the Supreme Court, have made ample use of the concept of substantive due process to strike down or limit the application of state and local legislation. *Lambert* v. *California* (p. 193) is a good example of such a case. As you read these cases consider this question, Are the courts justified in making wider use of substantive due process when legislation affects civil liberties than they do when legislation deals with the regulation of the economy?

D. The Problem of Delegation

However major a part a particular legislature retains in legislating on the larger issues, it invariably finds that it is impossible in modern times to participate directly in lawmaking of all kinds. There are a vast number of rules and "laws" which government must make on a day-to-day basis which for all practical purposes constitute lawmaking. When the government controls rates such as electricity rates and bus fares, should the legislature try to set these rates? Could the legislature set them wisely even if its members wanted to? Legislatures perforce delegate some legislative power thereby giving to other officials the responsibility for prescribing detailed rules in certain fields. Unfortunately, the delegation of power has not been as easy to do legally as it may appear. In the face of practical necessity for delegation, we have long revered an ancient maxim of Roman law, *potestas delegata non potest delegari.* Translated, this means that a delegated power must not be redelegated. Where our political theory regards the lawmaking power of the legislature as a delegation of power to it by the people, it follows that delegation by the legislature is redelegation. John Locke, for example, categorically asserted that "The Legislative neither must nor can transfer the power of making laws to anybody else, or place it anywhere but where the people have." Such concern over delegating power may seem much ado about nothing. Yet the principle of not delegating delegated power has a solid basis in practicality. Suppose the school board delegates authority and responsibility to the principal of a school to maintain order during recess and he in turn redelegates to a janitor who redelegates to an older student. Who is responsible if a student is injured during recess because of inadequate supervision? At what point should the transfer of delegation have stopped?

Political theory to the contrary, it has become impractical for legislatures not to delegate at least some of their powers. In the United States this has meant that the theory against delegation clashes constantly with the necessity for delegation. On the national level, the Supreme Court has virtually resolved the issue. In the early New Deal days, the Court found in two important cases, *Panama Refining Co.* v. *Ryan*, 293 U.S. 388 (1935) and *Schechter Poultry Corp.* v. *U.S.*, 295 U.S. 837 (1935), that Congress had gone too far in delegating lawmaking power. But out of these decisions emerged the principle that Congress could constitutionally delegate lawmaking power, provided Congress set the standards. As the Court said in *Schechter*, "We have repeatedly recognized the necessity of adapting legislation to complex conditions involving a host of details with which the national legislature cannot deal directly. We pointed out in the *Panama Company* case that the Constitution has never been regarded as denying Congress the necessary resources of flexibility and practicality, which will enable it to perform its function in laying down policies and establishing standards, while leaving to selected instrumentalities the making of subordinate rules within prescribed limits and the determination of facts to which the policy as declared by the legislature is to apply." Since 1935, Congress has been certain to prescribe some kind of standard for the delegates to follow. But even when these standards have been very vague like "rates shall be fair and reasonable," the courts have not once since 1935 struck down as unconstitutional a congressional act delegating power. This has led some eminent legal authorities to conclude that the decisions in the *Panama* and *Schecter* cases are no longer good law and that Congress can as a matter of fact delegate as it pleases.

However, whereas courts are now reluctant to restrain Congress in the matter of delegation they are not so restrained when it comes to state legislatures. The reasons for the different approach have been summed up by two outstanding legal authorities: "Statutes [state] often are not drafted with an eye to the nondelegation doctrine; the delegate may be a minor political official or representatives of the regulated activity; and procedural safeguards in the exercise of the delegated power may be lacking." [6] Expanding on these

[6] Walter Gellhorn and Clark Byse, *Cases and Materials on Administrative Law* (New York: The Foundation Press, 1954), p. 115. Reprinted with the permission of The Foundation Press.

points at a later time, they added another possible reason: "To some extent the state [court] holdings invalidating delegations may reflect judicial lack of sympathy with the substantive regulation at issue." [7]

To help you understand the problem of delegation at the state level we have edited four cases for you to read, *In re Opinion of the Judges* (p. 196), *State* v. *Traffic Telephone Workers' Federation of New Jersey* (p. 198), *Commonwealth* v. *Diaz* (p. 200), and *South Carolina State Highway Department* v. *Harbin* (p. 203). Although these cases deal with other problems as well, focus your attention on how the courts handle the delegation issue. You should bear in mind as you read these cases that they do not provide you with a simple answer as to when courts will or will not find delegations to be excessive. Unfortunately, court decisions on the state level are conflicting and confusing, and there are no meaningful guide lines as to when a state legislature has gone too far. These cases are offered only to give you insight into the problem.

As you read these cases, reflect on the following observations made by our foremost authority on administrative law, Professor Kenneth Culp Davis:

> The typical opinion of a state court on a delegation problem is quite unfortunate both in what it says and what it fails to say. It says that (1) legislative power may not be delegated, (2) that "filling up the details" is not an exercise of legislative power, (3) that legislative power is not delegated if the Legislature has laid down a standard to guide the exercise of the power, and (4) that presence or absence of vague verbalisms like "public interest" or "just and reasonable" make all the difference between valid legislation and unlawful delegation.
>
> The typical state court opinion on delegation fails to say anything about (1) the reasons for the legislative choice to make the particular delegation, (2) the practical consequences of allowing the Legislature to do what it is trying to do, (3) the usual lack of practical advantage in compelling the Legislature to dress up the statute with vague verbiage that the judges call standards, (4) the question whether in the circumstances good government calls for a headlong choice of policy by case-to-case adjudication conducted by those who have the advantage of knowing the facts of particular cases, (5) the need for protection against unfairness, arbitrariness, and favoritism, (6) the importance of procedural safeguards, of opportunity for a judicial check, and in some circumstances of a proper legislative or even administrative supervision or check, or (7) the need for providing help to the Legislature in its search for practical and efficient ways of accomplishing legislative objectives.[8]

Do we, as Professor Davis suggests, need a "new set of doctrines"?

[7] Gellhorn and Byse, *ibid.*, 1960 edition; see pp. 114–120 at p. 115.

[8] Kenneth C. Davis, *Administrative Law Text* (St. Paul: West Publishing Company, 1959), p. 49. Reprinted with the permission of West Publishing Company.

BAKER v. CARR

UNITED STATES SUPREME COURT
369 U.S. 186 (1962)

Despite major population increases and shifts over a sixty-year period and despite the state constitutional requirement that the number of representatives should be based proportionately on the number of qualified voters in districts or counties, the Tennessee legislature had not, since 1901, reapportioned the seats in the state legislature. Baker et al. *(a group of voters) brought suit in the appropriate Federal court against Carr the secretary of state, the attorney general, and various election officials seeking declaratory and injunctive relief on the grounds that the 1901 law was unconstitutional because it deprived Baker* et al. *of equal protection of the laws. The Federal district court dismissed the complaint, whereupon Baker* et al. *appealed to the United States Supreme Court.*

Mr. Justice BRENNAN delivered the opinion of the Court.

. . . .

WE TREAT the first ground of dismissal as "lack of jurisdiction of the subject matter." The second we consider to result in a failure to state a justiciable cause of action.

The District Court's dismissal order recited that it was issued in conformity with the court's *per curiam* opinion. The opinion reveals that the court rested its dismissal upon lack of subject-matter jurisdiction and lack of a justiciable cause of action without attempting to distinguish between these grounds. After noting that the plaintiffs challenged the existing legislative apportionment in Tennessee under the Due Process and Equal Protection Clauses, and summarizing the supporting allegations and the relief requested, the court stated that

> "the action is presently before the Court upon the defendants' motion to dismiss predicated upon three grounds: first, that the Court lacks jurisdiction of the subject matter; second, that the complaints fail to state a claim upon which relief can be granted; and third, that indispensable party defendants are not before the Court." 179 F.Supp., at 826.

The court proceeded to explain its action as turning on the case's presenting a "question of the distribution of political strength for legislative purposes." For,

> "from a review of [numerous Supreme Court] * * * decisions there can be no doubt that the federal rule, as enunciated and applied by the Supreme Court, is that the federal courts, whether from a lack of jurisdiction or from the inappropriateness of the subject matter for judicial consideration, will not intervene in cases of this type to compel legislative reapportionment." 179 F. Supp., at 826.

The court went on to express doubts as to the feasibility of the various possible remedies sought by the plaintiffs. 179 F.Supp., at 827–828. Then it made clear that its dismissal reflected a view not of doubt that violation of constitutional rights was alleged, but of a court's impotence to correct that violation:

> "With the plaintiffs' argument that the legislature of Tennessee is guilty of a clear violation of the state constitution and of the rights of the plaintiffs the Court entirely agrees. It also agrees that the evil is a serious one which should be corrected without further delay. But even so the remedy in this situation clearly does not lie with the courts. It has long been recognized and is accepted doctrine that there are indeed some rights guaranteed by the Constitution for the violation of which the courts cannot give redress." 179 F.Supp., at 828.

In light of the District Court's treatment of the case, we hold today only (a) that the court possessed jurisdiction of the subject matter; (b) that a justiciable cause of action is stated upon which appellants would be entitled to appropriate relief; and (c) because appellees raise the issue before this Court, that the appellants have standing to challenge the Tennessee apportionment statutes. Beyond noting that we have no cause at this stage to doubt the District Court will be able to fashion relief if violations of constitutional rights are found, it is improper now to consider what remedy would be most appropriate if appellants prevail at the trial.

. . . .

Article III, § 2 of the Federal Constitution provides that "the judicial Power shall extend to all Cases, in Law and Equity, arising under this Constitution, the Laws of the United States, and Treaties made, or which shall be made, under their Authority; * * *." It is clear that the cause of action is one which "arises under" the Federal Constitution. The complaint alleges that the 1901 statute effects an apportionment that deprives the appellants of the equal protection of the laws in violation of the Fourteenth Amendment. Dismissal of the complaint upon the ground of lack of jurisdiction of the subject matter would, therefore, be justified only if that claim were "so attenuated and unsubstantial as to be absolutely devoid of merit." . . . That the claim is unsubstantial must be "very plain." . . . Since the District Court obviously and correctly did not deem the asserted federal constitutional claim unsubstantial and frivolous, it should not have dismissed the complaint for want of jurisdiction of the subject matter. And of course no further consideration of the merits of the claim is relevant to a determination of the court's jurisdiction of the subject matter. . . .

. . . .

Since the complaint plainly sets forth a case arising under the Constitution, the subject matter is within the federal judicial power defined in Art. III, § 2, and so within the power of Congress to assign to the jurisdiction of the District Courts. Congress has exercised that power in . . . [*law*]:

> "The district courts shall have original jurisdiction of any civil action authorized by law to be commenced by any person * * * to redress the deprivation, under color of any State law, statute, ordinance, regulation, custom or usage, of any right, privilege or immunity secured by the Constitution of the United States * * *."

An unbroken line of our precedents sustains the federal courts' jurisdiction of the subject matter of federal constitutional claims of this nature. . . .

. . . .

The appellees refer to Colegrove v. Green, 328 U.S. 549, as authority that the District Court lacked jurisdiction of the subject matter. Appellees misconceive the holding of that case. The holding was precisely contrary to their reading of it. Seven members of the Court participated in the decision. Unlike many other cases in this field which have assumed without discussion that there was jurisdiction, all three opinions filed in Colegrove discussed the question. Two of the opinions expressing the views of four of the Justices, a majority, flatly held that there was jurisdiction of that subject matter. Mr. Justice Black joined by Mr. Justice Douglas and Mr. Justice Murphy stated: "It is my judgment that the District Court had jurisdiction * * *," . . . . Mr. Justice Rutledge, writing separately, expressed agreement with this conclusion. . . . Indeed, it is even questionable that the opinion of Mr. Justice Frankfurter, joined by Justices Reed and Burton, doubted jurisdiction of the subject matter. . . .

Several subsequent cases similar to Colegrove have been decided by the Court in summary *per curiam* statements. None was dismissed for want of jurisdiction of the subject matter. . . .

. . . .

We hold that the District Court has jurisdiction of the subject matter of the federal constitutional claim asserted in the complaint.

STANDING.

A federal court cannot "pronounce any statute, either of a state or of the United States, void, because irreconcilable with the constitution, except as it is called upon to adjudge the legal rights of litigants in actual controversies." . . .

Have the appellants alleged such a personal stake in the outcome of the controversy as to assure that concrete adverseness which sharpens the presentation of issues upon which the court so largely depends for illumination of difficult constitutional questions? This is the gist of the question of standing. It is, of course, a question of federal law.

The complaint was filed by residents of Davidson, Hamilton, Knox, Montgomery, and Shelby Counties. Each is a person allegedly qualified to vote for members of the General Assembly representing his county. These appellants sued "on their own behalf and on behalf of all qualified voters of their respective counties, and further, on behalf of all voters of the State of Tennessee who are similarly situated * * *." The appellees are the Tennessee Secretary of State, Attorney General, Coordinator of Elections, and members of the State Board of Elections; the members of the State Board are sued in their own right and also as representatives of the County Election Commissioners whom they appoint.

We hold that the appellants do have standing to maintain this suit. Our decisions plainly support this conclusion. Many of the cases have assumed rather than articulated the premise in deciding the merits of similar claims. And Colegrove v. Green, supra, squarely held that voters who allege facts showing disadvantage to themselves as individuals have standing to sue. A number of cases decided after Colegrove recognized the standing of the voters there involved to bring those actions.

These appellants seek relief in order to protect or vindicate an interest of their own, and of those similarly situated. Their constitutional claim is, in substance, that the 1901 statute constitutes arbitrary and capricious state action, offensive to the Fourteenth Amendment in its irrational disregard of the standard of apportionment prescribed by the State's Constitution or of any standard, effecting a gross disproportion of representation to voting population. The injury which appellants assert is that this classification disfavors the voters in the counties in which they reside, placing them in a position of constitutionally unjustifiable inequality *vis-à-vis* voters in irrationally favored counties. A citizen's right to a vote free of arbitrary impairment by state action has been judicially recognized as a right secured by the Constitution, when such impairment resulted from dilution by a false tally, . . . or by a refusal to count votes from arbitrarily selected precincts, . . . or by a stuffing of the ballot box. . . .

It would not be necessary to decide whether appellants' allegations of impairment of their votes by the 1901 apportionment will, ultimately, entitle them to any relief, in order to hold that they have standing to seek it. If such impairment does produce a legally cognizable injury, they are among those who have sustained it. They are asserting "a plain, direct and adequate interest in maintaining the effectiveness of their votes," . . . not merely a claim of "the right possessed by every citizen 'to require that the government be administered according to law * * *.' " . . . They are entitled to a hearing and to the District Court's decision on their claims. "The very essence of civil liberty certainly consists in the right of every individual to claim the protection of the laws, whenever he receives an injury." . . .

JUSTICIABILITY.

In holding that the subject matter of this suit was not justiciable, the District Court relied on Colegrove v. Green, supra, and subsequent *per curiam* cases. The court stated: "From a review of these decisions there can be no doubt that the federal rule * * * is that the federal courts * * * will not intervene in cases of this type to compel legislative reapportionment." . . . We understand the District Court to have read the cited cases as compelling the conclusion that since the appellants sought to have a legislative apportionment held unconstitutional, their suit presented a "political question" and was therefore nonjusticiable. We hold that this challenge to an apportionment presents no nonjusticiable "political question." The cited cases do not hold the contrary.

Of course the mere fact that the suit seeks protection of a political right does not mean it presents a political question. Such an objection "is little more than a play upon words." . . . Rather, it is argued that apportionment cases, whatever the actual wording of the complaint, can involve no federal constitutional right except one resting on the guaranty of a republican form of government, and that complaints based on that clause have been held to present political questions which are nonjusticiable.

We hold that the claim pleaded here neither rests upon nor implicates the Guaranty Clause and that its justiciability is therefore not foreclosed by our decisions of cases involving that clause. The District Court misinterpreted Colegrove v. Green and other decisions of this Court on which it relied. Appellants' claim that they are being denied equal protection is justiciable, and if "discrimination is sufficiently shown, the right to relief under the equal protection clause is not diminished by the fact that the discrimination relates to political rights." . . . To show why we reject the argument based on the Guaranty Clause, we must examine the authorities under it. But because there appears to be some uncertainty as to why those cases did present political questions, and specifically as to whether this apportionment case is like those cases, we deem it necessary first to consider the contours of the "political question" doctrine.

Our discussion, even at the price of extending this opinion, requires review of a number of political question cases, in order to expose the attributes of the doctrine—attributes which, in various settings, diverge, combine, appear, and disappear in seeming disorderliness. Since that review is undertaken solely to demonstrate that neither singly nor collectively do these cases support a conclusion that this apportionment case is nonjusticiable, we of course do not explore their implications in other contexts. That review reveals that in the Guaranty Clause cases and in the other "political question" cases, it is the relationship between the judiciary and the coordinate branches of the Federal Government, and not the federal judiciary's relationship to the States, which gives rise to the "political question."

We have said that "in determining whether a question falls within [the political question] category, the appropriateness under our system of government of attributing finality to the action of the political departments and also the lack of satisfactory criteria for a judicial determination are dominant considerations." . . . The nonjusticiability of a political question is primarily a function of the separation of powers. Much confusion results from the capacity of the "political question" label to obscure the need for case-by-case inquiry. Deciding whether a matter has in any measure been committed by the Constitution to another branch of government, or whether the action of that branch exceeds whatever authority has been committed, is itself a delicate exercise in constitutional interpretation, and is a responsibility of this Court as ultimate interpreter of the Constitution. . . .

. . . .

We come, finally to the ultimate inquiry whether our precedents as to what constitutes a nonjusticiable "political question" bring the case before us under the umbrella of that doctrine. A natural beginning is to note whether any of the common characteristics which we have been able to identify and label descriptively are present. We find none: The question here is the consistency of state action with the Federal Constitution. We have no question decided, or to be decided, by a political branch of government coequal with this Court. Nor do we risk embarrassment of our government abroad, or grave disturbance at home if we take issue with Tennessee as to the constitutionality of her action here challenged. Nor need the appellants, in order to succeed in this action, ask the Court to enter upon policy determinations for which judicially manageable standards are lacking. Judicial standards under the Equal Protection Clause are well developed and familiar, and it has been open to courts since the enactment of the Fourteenth Amendment to determine, if on the particular facts they must, that a discrimination reflects *no* policy, but simply arbitrary and capricious action.

This case does, in one sense, involve the allocation of political power within a State, and the appellants might conceivably have added a claim under the Guaranty Clause. Of course, as we have seen, any reliance on that clause would be futile. But because any reliance on the Guaranty Clause could not have succeeded it does not follow that appellants may not be heard on the equal protection claim which in fact they tender. True, it must be clear that the Fourteenth Amendment claim is not so enmeshed with those political question elements which render Guaranty Clause claims nonjusticiable as actually to present a political question itself. But we have found that not to be the case here.

. . . .

We conclude then that the nonjusticiability of claims resting on the Guaranty Clause which arises from their embodiment of questions that were thought "political," can have no bearing upon the justiciability of the equal protection claim presented in this case. Finally, we emphasize that it is the involvement in Guaranty Clause claims of the elements thought to define "political questions," and no other feature, which could render them nonjusticiable. Specifically, we have said that such claims are not held nonjusticiable because they touch matters of state governmental organization. Brief examination of a few cases demonstrates this.

When challenges to state action respecting matters of "the administration of the affairs of the State and the officers through whom they are conducted" have rested on claims of constitutional deprivation which are amenable to judicial correction, this Court has acted upon its view of the merits of the claim. For example, in Boyd v. Nebraska ex rel. Thayer, 143 U.S. 135, we reversed the Nebraska Supreme Court's decision that Nebraska's Governor was not a citizen of the United States or of the State and therefore could not continue in office. In Kennard v. Louisiana ex rel. Morgan, 92 U.S. 480, and Foster v. Kansas ex rel. Johnston, 112 U.S. 201, we considered whether persons had been removed from public office by procedures consistent with the Fourteenth Amendment's due process guaranty, and held on the merits that they had. And only last Term, in Gomillion v. Lightfoot, 364 U.S. 339, we applied the Fifteenth Amendment to strike down a redrafting of municipal boundaries which effected a discriminatory impairment of voting rights, in the face of what a majority of the Court of Appeals thought to be a sweeping commitment to state legislatures of the power to draw and redraw such boundaries.

Gomillion was brought by a Negro who had been a resident of the City of Tuskegee, Alabama, until the municipal boundaries were so recast by the State Legislature as to exclude practically all Negroes. The plaintiff claimed deprivation of the right to vote in municipal elections. The District Court's, 167 F. Supp. 405, dismissal for want of jurisdiction and failure to state a claim upon which relief could be granted was affirmed by the Court of Appeals, 5 Cir., 270 F.2d 594. This Court unanimously reversed. This Court's answer to the argument that States enjoyed unrestricted control over municipal boundaries was:

> "Legislative control of municipalities, no less than other state power, lies within the scope of relevant limitations imposed by the United States Constitution. * * * The opposite conclusion, urged upon us by respondents, would sanction the achievement by a State of any impairment of voting rights whatever so long as it was cloaked in the garb of the realignment of political subdivisions. 'It is inconceivable that guaranties embedded in the Constitution of the United States may thus be manipulated out of existence.' " . . .

To a second argument, that Colegrove v. Green, supra, was a barrier to hearing the merits of the case, the Court responded that Gomillion was lifted "out of the so-called 'political' arena and into the conventional sphere of constitutional litigation" because here was discriminatory treatment of a racial minority violating the Fifteenth Amendment.

> "A statute which is alleged to have worked unconstitutional deprivations of petitioners' rights is not immune to attack simply because the mechanism employed by the legislature is a redefinition of municipal boundaries. * * * While in form this is merely an act redefining metes and bounds, if the allegations are established, the inescapable human effect of this essay in geometry and geography is to despoil colored citizens, and only colored citizens, of their theretofore enjoyed voting rights. That was not Colegrove v. Green.
>
> "When a State exercises power wholly within the domain of state interest, it is insulated from federal judicial review. But such insulation is not carried over when state power is used as an instrument for circumventing a federally protected right.". . .

. . . .

We conclude that the complaint's allegations of a denial of equal protection present a justiciable constitutional cause of action upon which appellants are entitled to a trial and a decision. The right asserted is within the reach of judicial protection under the Fourteenth Amendment.

The judgment of the District Court is reversed and the cause is remanded for further proceedings consistent with this opinion.

Reversed and remanded.

Mr. Justice WHITTAKER did not participate in the decision of this case.

. . . .

Mr. Justice DOUGLAS, concurring.

While I join the opinion of the Court and, like the Court, do not reach the merits, a word of explanation is necessary. I put to one side the problems of "political" questions involving the distribution of power between this Court, the Congress, and the Chief Executive. We have here a phase of the recurring problem of the relation of the federal courts to state agencies. More particularly, the question is the extent to which a State may weight one person's vote more heavily than it does another's.

So far as voting rights are concerned, there are large gaps in the Constitution. Yet the right to vote is inherent in the republican form of government envisaged by Article IV, Section 4 of the Constitution. The House—and now the Senate—are chosen by the people. The time, manner, and place of elections of Senators and Representatives are left to the States (Article I, Section 4, Clause 1; Amendment XVII) subject to the regulatory power of Congress. A "republican form" of government is guaranteed each State by Article IV, Section 4, and each is likewise promised protection against invasion. . . . That the States may specify the qualifications for voters is implicit in Article I, Section 2, Clause 1, which provides that the House of Representatives shall be chosen by the people and that "the Electors (voters) in each state shall have the qualifications requisite for electors (voters) of the most numerous branch of the state legislature." The same provision, contained in the Seventeenth Amendment, governs the election of Senators. Within limits those qualifications may be fixed by state law. . . . Yet, . . . those who vote for members of Congress do not "owe their right to vote to the state law, in any sense which makes the exercise of the right to depend exclusively upon the law of the state." The power of Congress to prescribe the qualifications for voters and thus override state law is not in issue here. It is, however, clear that by reason of the commands of the Constitution there are several qualifications that a State may not require.

Race, color, or previous condition of servitude are impermissible standards by reason of the Fifteenth Amendment, and that alone is sufficient to explain Gomillion v. Lightfoot. . . .

Sex is another impermissible standard by reason of the Nineteenth Amendment.

There is a third barrier to a State's freedom in prescribing qualifications of voters and that is the Equal Protection Clause of the Fourteenth Amendment, the provision invoked here. And so the question is, may a State weight the vote of one county or one district more heavily than it weights the vote in another?

The traditional test under the Equal Protection Clause has been whether a State has made "an invidious discrimination," as it does when it selects "a particular race or nationality for oppressive treatment." . . . Universal equality is not the test; there is room for weighting. . . . "The prohibition of the Equal Protection Clause goes no further than the invidious discrimination."

I agree with my Brother CLARK that if the allegations in the complaint can be sustained a case for relief is established. We are told that a single vote in Moore County, Tennessee, is worth 19 votes in Hamilton County, that one vote in Stewart or in Chester County is worth nearly eight times a single vote in Shelby or Knox County. The opportunity to prove that an "invidious discrimination" exists should therefore be given the appellants.

It is said that any decision in cases of this kind is beyond the competence of courts. Some make the same point as regards the problem of equal protection in cases involving racial segregation. Yet the legality of claims and conduct is a traditional subject for judicial determination. Adjudication is often perplexing and complicated. An example of the extreme complexity of the task can be seen in a decree apportioning water among the several States. . . . The constitutional guide is often vague, as the decisions under the Due Process and Commerce Clauses show. The problem under the Equal Protection Clause is no more intricate. . . .

. . . .

Where the Constitution assigns a particular function wholly and indivisibly to another department, the federal judiciary does not intervene. . . .

There is no doubt that the federal courts have jurisdiction of controversies concerning voting rights. The Civil Rights Act gives them authority to redress the deprivation "under color of any state law" of any "right, privilege or immunity secured by the Constitution of the United States or by any Act of Congress providing for equal rights of citizens * * *." . . . [*Also, federal law*] gives the federal courts authority to award damages or issue an injunction to redress the violation of "any Act of Congress providing for the protection of civil rights, including the *right to vote*." (Italics added.) The element of state action covers a wide range. For as stated in United States v. Classic, 313 U.S. 299.

> "Misuse of power, possessed by virtue of state law and made possible only because the wrongdoer is clothed with the authority of state law, is action taken 'under color of' state law." And see Monroe v. Pape, 365 U.S. 167.

The right to vote in both federal and state elections was protected by the judiciary long before that right received the explicit protection it is now accorded by . . . [*law*]. Discrimination against a voter on account of race has been penalized . . . or struck down. . . . Fraudulent acts that dilute the votes of some have long been held to be within judicial cognizance. . . . The "right to have one's vote counted" whatever his race or nationality or creed was held in United States v. Mosley, 238 U.S. 383, to be "as open to protection by Congress as the right to put a ballot in a box." . . .

. . . .

Intrusion of the Federal Government into the election machinery of the States has taken numerous forms—investigations . . . ; criminal proceedings . . . ; collection of penalties . . . ; suits for declaratory relief and for an injunction . . . ; suits by the United States under the Civil Rights Act to enjoin discriminatory practices. . . .

As stated by Judge McLaughlin in Dyer v. Kazuhisa Abe, D.C., 138 F. Supp. 220 (an apportionment case in Hawaii which was reversed and dismissed as moot, 256 F.2d 728):

> "The whole thrust of today's legal climate is to end unconstitutional discrimination. It is ludicrous to preclude judicial relief when a mainspring of representative government is impaired. Legislators have no immunity from the

Constitution. The legislatures of our land should be made as responsive to the Constitution of the United States as are the citizens who elect the legislators."

With the exceptions of Colegrove v. Green, 328 U.S. 549, MacDougall v. Green, 335 U.S. 281, South v. Peters, 339 U.S. 276, and the decisions they spawned, the Court has never thought that protection of voting rights was beyond judicial cognizance. Today's treatment of those cases removes the only impediment to judicial cognizance of the claims stated in the present complaint.

The justiciability of the present claims being established, any relief accorded can be fashioned in the light of well-known principles of equity.

Mr. Justice CLARK, concurring.

One emerging from the rash of opinions with their accompanying clashing of views may well find himself suffering a mental blindness. The Court holds that the appellants have alleged a cause of action. However, it refuses to award relief here—although the facts are undisputed—and fails to give the District Court any guidance whatever. One dissenting opinion, bursting with words that go through so much and conclude with so little, contemns the majority action as "a massive repudiation of the experience of our whole past." Another describes the complaint as merely asserting conclusory allegations that Tennessee's apportionment is "incorrect," "arbitrary," "obsolete," and "unconstitutional." I believe it can be shown that this case is distinguishable from earlier cases dealing with the distribution of political power by a State, that a patent violation of the Equal Protection Clause of the United States Constitution has been shown, and that an appropriate remedy may be formulated.

. . . .

The controlling facts cannot be disputed. It appears from the record that 37% of the voters of Tennessee elect 20 of the 33 Senators while 40% of the voters elect 63 of the 99 members of the House. . . .

It is true that the apportionment policy incorporated in Tennessee's Constitution, *i. e.*, state-wide numerical equality of representation with certain minor qualifications is a rational one. On a county-by-county comparison a districting plan based thereon naturally will have disparities in representation due to the qualifications. But this to my mind does not raise constitutional problems, for the overall policy is reasonable. However, the root of the trouble is not in Tennessee's Constitution, for admittedly its policy has not been followed. The discrimination lies in the action of Tennessee's Assembly in allocating legislative seats to counties or districts created by it. Try as one may, Tennessee's apportionment just cannot be made to fit the pattern cut by its Constitution. This was the finding of the District Court. The policy of the Constitution referred to by the dissenters, therefore, is of no relevance here. . . .

. . . .

The truth is that—although this case has been here for two years and has had over six hours' argument (three times the ordinary case) and has been most carefully considered over and over again by us in Conference and individually—no one, not even the State nor the dissenters, has come up with any rational basis for Tennessee's apportionment statute.

No one—except the dissenters advocating the HARLAN "adjusted 'total representation' " formula—contends that mathematical equality among voters is required by the Equal Protection Clause.

But certainly there must be some rational design to a State's districting. The discrimination here does not fit any pattern—as I have said, it is but a crazy quilt. My Brother HARLAN contends that other proposed apportionment plans contain disparities. Instead of chasing those rabbits he should first pause long enough to meet appellants' proof of discrimination by showing that in fact the present plan follows a rational policy. Not being able to do this, he merely counters with such generalities as "classic legislative judgment," no "significant discrepancy," and "de minimis departures." I submit that even a casual glance at the present apportionment picture shows these conclusions to be entirely fanciful. If present representation has a policy at all, it is to maintain the *status quo* of invidious discrimination at any cost. Like the District Court, I conclude that appellants have met the burden of showing "Tennessee is guilty of a clear violation of the state constitution and of the [federal] rights of the plaintiffs. * * *"

Although I find the Tennessee apportionment statute offends the Equal Protection Clause, I would not consider intervention by this Court into so delicate a field if there were any other relief available to the people of Tennesee. But the majority of the people of Tennessee have no "practical opportunities for exerting their political weight at the polls" to correct the existing "invidious discrimination." Tennessee has no initiative and referendum. I have searched diligently for other "practical opportunities" present under the law. I find none other than through the federal courts. The majority of the voters have been caught up in a legislative strait jacket. Tennessee has an "informed, civically militant electorate" and "an aroused popular conscience," but it does not sear "the conscience of the people's representatives." This is because the legislative policy has riveted the present seats in the Assembly to their respective constituencies, and by the votes of their incumbents a reapportionment of any kind is prevented. The people have been rebuffed at the hands of the Assembly; they have tried the constitutional convention route, but since the call must originate in the Assembly it, too, has been fruitless. They have tried Tennessee courts with the same result, and Governors have fought the tide only to flounder. It is said that there is recourse in Congress and perhaps that may be, but from a practical standpoint this is without substance. To date Congress has never undertaken such a task in any State. We therefore must conclude that the people of Tennessee are stymied and without judicial intervention will be saddled with the present discrimination in the affairs of their state government.

Finally, we must consider if there are any appropriate modes of effective judicial relief. The federal courts are, of course, not forums for political debate, nor should they resolve themselves into state constitutional conventions or legislative assemblies. Nor should their jurisdiction be exercised in the hope that such a declaration, as is made today, may have the direct effect of bringing on legislative action and relieving the courts of the problem of fashioning relief. To my mind this would be nothing less than blackjacking the Assembly into reapportioning the State. If judicial competence were lacking to fashion an effective decree, I would dismiss this appeal. However, like the Solicitor General of the United States, I see no such difficulty in the position of this case. One plan might be to start with the existing assembly districts, consolidate some of them, and award the seats thus released to those counties suffering the most egregious discrimination. Other possibilities are present and might be more effective. But the plan here suggested would at least release the stranglehold now on the Assembly and permit it to redistrict itself.

In this regard the appellants have proposed a plan based on the rationale of state-wide equal representation. Not believing that numerical equality of representation throughout a State is constitutionally required, I would not apply such a standard albeit a permissive one. Nevertheless, the dissenters attack it by the application of the HARLAN "adjusted 'total representation'" formula. The result is that some isolated inequalities are shown, but this in itself does not make the proposed plan irrational or place it in the "crazy quilt" category. Such inequalities, as the dissenters point out in attempting to support the present apportionment as rational, are explainable. Moreover, there is no requirement that any plan have mathematical exactness in its application. Only where, as here, the total picture reveals incommensurables of both magnitude and frequency can it be said that there is present an invidious discrimination.

In view of the detailed study that the Court has given this problem, it is unfortunate that a decision is not reached on the merits. The majority appears to hold, at least *sub silentio*, that an invidious discrimination is present, but it remands to the three-judge court for it to make what is certain to be that formal determination. It is true that Tennessee has not filed a formal answer. However, it has filed voluminous papers and made extended arguments supporting its position. At no time has it been able to contradict the appellants' factual claims; it has offered no rational explanation for the present apportionment; indeed, it has indicated that there are none known to it. As I have emphasized, the case proceeded to the point before the three-judge court that it was able to find an invidious discrimination factually present, and the State has not contested that holding here. In view of all this background I doubt if anything more can be offered or will be gained by the State on remand, other than time. Nevertheless, not being able to muster a court to dispose of the case on the merits, I concur in the opinion of the majority and acquiesce in the decision to remand. However, in fairness I do think that Tennessee is entitled to have my idea of what it faces on the record before us and the trial court some light as to how it might proceed.

As John Rutledge (later Chief Justice) said 175 years ago in the course of the Constitutional Convention, a chief function of the Court is to secure the national rights. Its decision today supports the proposition for which our forebears fought and many died, namely that "to be fully conformable to the principle of right, the form of government must be representative." That is the keystone upon which our government was founded and lacking which no republic can survive. It is well for this Court to practice self-restraint and discipline in constitutional adjudication, but never in its history have those principles received sanction where the national rights of so many have been so clearly infringed for so long a time. National respect for the courts is more enhanced through the forthright enforcement of those rights rather than by rendering them nugatory through the interposition of subterfuges. In my view the ultimate decision today is in the greatest tradition of this Court.

. . . .

Mr. Justice STEWART, concurring.

[*Stewart's opinion is omitted.*]

. . . .

Mr. Justice FRANKFURTER, whom Mr. Justice HARLAN joins, dissenting.

The Court today reverses a uniform course of decision established by a dozen cases, including one by which the very claim now sustained was unanimously rejected only five years ago. The impressive body of rulings thus cast aside reflected the equally uniform course of our political history regarding the relationship between population and legislative representation—a wholly different matter from denial of the franchise to individuals because of race, color, religion or sex. Such a massive repudiation of the experience of our whole past in asserting destructively novel judicial power demands a detailed analysis of the role of this Court in our constitutional scheme. Disregard of inherent limits in the effective exercise of the Court's "judicial Power" not only presages the futility of judicial intervention in the essentially political conflict of forces by which the relation between population and representation has time out of mind been and now is determined. It may well impair the Court's position as the ultimate organ of "the supreme Law of the Land" in that vast range of legal problems, often strongly entangled in popular feeling, on which this Court must pronounce. The Court's authority—possessed neither of the purse nor the sword—ultimately rests on sustained public confidence in its moral sanction. Such feeling must be nourished by the Court's complete detachment, in fact and in appearance, from political entanglements and by abstention from injecting itself into the clash of political forces in political settlements.

A hypothetical claim resting on abstract assumptions is now for the first time made the basis for affording illusory relief for a particular evil even though it foreshadows deeper and more pervasive difficulties in consequence. The claim is hypothetical and the assumptions are abstract because the Court does not vouchsafe the lower courts—state and federal—guide-lines for formulating specific, definite, wholly unprecedented remedies for the inevitable litigations that today's umbrageous disposition is bound to stimulate in connection with politically motivated reapportionments in so many States. In such a setting, to promulgate jurisdiction in the abstract is meaningless. It is devoid of reality as "a brooding omnipresence in the sky" for it conveys no intimation what relief, if any, a District Court is capable of affording that would not invite legislatures to play ducks and drakes with the judiciary. For this Court to direct the District Court to enforce a claim to which the Court has over the years consistently found itself required to deny legal enforcement and at the same time to find it necessary to withhold any guidance to the lower court how to enforce this turnabout, new legal claim, manifests an odd—indeed an esoteric—conception of judicial propriety. One of the Court's supporting opinions, as elucidated by commentary, unwittingly affords a disheartening preview of the mathematical quagmire (apart from divers judicially inappropriate and elusive determinants), into which this Court today catapults the lower courts of the country without so much as adumbrating the basis for a legal calculus as a means of extrication. Even assuming the indispensable intellectual disinterestedness on the part of judges in such matters, they do not have accepted legal standards or criteria or even reliable analogies to draw upon for making judicial judgments. To charge courts with the task of accommodating the incommensurable factors of policy that underlie these mathematical puzzles is to attribute, however flatteringly, omnicompetence to judges. The Framers of the Constitution persistently rejected a proposal that embodied this assumption and Thomas Jefferson never entertained it.

Recent legislation, creating a district appropriately described as "an atrocity of ingenuity," is not unique. Considering the gross inequality among legislative electoral units within almost every State, the Court naturally shrinks from asserting that in districting at least substantial equality is a constitutional requirement enforceable by courts. Room continues to be allowed for weighting. This of course implies that geography, economics, urban-rural conflict, and all the other non-legal factors which have throughout our history entered into political districting are to some extent not to be ruled out in the undefined vista now opened up by review in the federal courts of state reapportionments. To some extent—aye, there's the rub. In effect, today's decision empowers the courts of the country to devise what should constitute the proper composition of the legislatures of the fifty States. If state courts should for one reason or another find themselves unable to discharge this task, the duty of doing so is put on the federal courts or on this Court, if State views do not satisfy this Court's notion of what is proper districting.

We were soothingly told at the bar of this Court that we need not worry about the kind of remedy a court could effectively fashion once the abstract constitutional right to have courts pass on a state-wide system of electoral districting is recognized as a matter of judicial rhetoric, because legislatures would heed the Court's admonition. This is not only an euphoric hope. It implies a sorry confession of judicial impotence in place of a frank acknowledgment that there is not under our Constitution a judicial remedy for every political mischief, for every undesirable exercise of legislative power. The Framers carefully and with deliberate forethought refused so to enthrone the judiciary. In this situation, as in others of like nature, appeal for relief does not belong here. Appeal must be to an informed, civically militant electorate. In a democratic society like ours, relief must come through an aroused popular conscience that sears the conscience of the people's representatives. In any event there is nothing judicially more unseemly nor more self-defeating than for this Court to make *in terrorem* pronouncements, to indulge in merely empty rhetoric, sounding a word of promise to the ear, sure to be disappointing to the hope.

This is the latest in the series of cases in which the Equal Protection and Due Process Clauses of the Fourteenth Amendment have been invoked in federal courts as restrictions upon the power of the States to allocate electoral weight among the voting populations of their various geographical subdivisions. . . .

. . . .

In sustaining appellants' claim, based on the Fourteenth Amendment, that the District Court may entertain this suit, this Court's uniform course of decision over the years are overruled or disregarded. Explicitly it begins with Colegrove v. Green, supra, decided in 1946, but its roots run deep in the Court's historic adjudicatory process.

Colegrove held that a federal court should not entertain an action for declaratory and injunctive relief to adjudicate the constitutionality, under the Equal Protection Clause and other federal constitutional and statutory provisions, of a state statute establishing the respective districts for the State's election of Representatives to the Congress. Two opinions were written by the four Justices who composed the majority of the seven sitting members of the Court. Both opinions joining in the result in Colegrove v. Green agreed that considerations were controlling which dictated denial of jurisdiction though not in the strict sense of want of power. While the two opinions show a divergence of view regarding some of these considerations, there are important points of concurrence. Both opinions demonstrate a predominant concern, first, with avoiding federal judicial involvement in matters traditionally left to legislative policymaking; second, with respect to the difficulty—in view of the nature of the problems of apportionment and its history in this country—of drawing on or devising judicial standards for judgment, as opposed to legislative determinations, of the part which mere numerical equality among voters should play as a criterion for the allocation of political power; and, third, with problems of finding appropriate modes of relief—particularly, the problem of resolving the essentially political issue of the relative merits of at-large elections and elections held in districts of unequal population.

The broad applicability of these considerations—summarized in the loose shorthand phrase, "political question" —in cases involving a State's apportionment of voting power among its numerous localities has led the Court, since 1946, to recognize their controlling effect in a variety of situations. (In all these cases decision was by a full Court.) The "political question" principle as applied in Colegrove has found wide application commensurate with its function as "one of the rules basic to the federal system and this Court's appropriate place within that structure." . . .

. . . .

The Colegrove doctrine, in the form in which repeated decisions have settled it, was not an innovation. It represents long judicial thought and experience. From its earliest opinions this Court has consistently recognized a class of controversies which do not lend themselves to judicial standards and judicial remedies. To classify the various instances as "political questions" is rather a form of stating this conclusion than revealing of analysis. . . .

. . . .

The Court has been particularly unwilling to intervene in matters concerning the structure and organization of the political institutions of the States. The abstention from judicial entry into such areas has been greater even than that which marks the Court's ordinary approach to issues of state power challenged under broad federal guarantees.

. . . .

At first blush, this charge of discrimination based on legislative underrepresentation is given the appearance of a more private, less impersonal claim, than the assertion that the frame of government is askew. Appellants appear as representatives of a class that is prejudiced as a class, in contradistinction to the polity in its entirety. However, the discrimination relied on is the deprivation of what appellants conceive to be their proportionate share of political influence. This, of course, is the practical effect of any allocation of power within the institutions of government. Hardly any distribution of political authority that could be assailed as rendering government nonrepublican would fail similarly to operate to the prejudice of some groups, and to the advantage of others, within the body politic. It would be ingenuous not to see, or consciously blind to deny, that the real battle over the initiative and referendum, or over a delegation of power to local rather than state-wide authority, is the battle between forces whose influence is disparate among the various organs of government to whom power may be given. No shift of power but works a corresponding shift in political influence among the groups composing a society.

What, then, is this question of legislative apportionment? Appellants invoke the right to vote and to have their votes counted. But they are permitted to vote and their votes are counted. They go to the polls, they cast their ballots, they send their representatives to the state councils. Their complaint is simply that the representatives are not sufficiently numerous or powerful—in short, that Tennessee has adopted a basis of representation with which they are dissatisfied. Talk of "debasement" or "dilution" is circular talk. One cannot speak of "debasement" or "dilution" of the value of a vote until there is first defined a standard of reference as to what a vote should be worth. What is actually asked of the Court in this case is to choose among competing bases of representation—ultimately, really, among competing theories of political philosophy—in order to establish an appropriate frame of government for the State of Tennessee and thereby for all the States of the Union.

In such a matter, abstract analogies which ignore the facts of history deal in unrealities; they betray reason. This is not a case in which a State has, through a device however oblique and sophisticated, denied Negroes or Jews or redheaded persons a vote, or given them only a third or a sixth of a vote. . . . What Tennessee illustrates is an old and still widespread method of representation—representation by local geographical division, only in part respective of population—in preference to others, others, forsooth, more appealing. Appellants contest this choice and seek to make this Court the arbiter of the disagreement. They would make the Equal Protection Clause the charter of adjudication, asserting that the equality which it guarantees comports, if not the assurance of equal weight to every voter's vote, at least the basic conception that representation ought to be proportionate to population, a standard by reference to which the reasonableness of apportionment plans may be judged.

To find such a political conception legally enforceable in the broad and unspecific guarantee of equal protection is to rewrite the Constitution. . . . Certainly, "equal protection" is no more secure a foundation for judicial judgment of the permissibility of varying forms of representative government than is "Republican Form." Indeed since "equal protection of the laws" can only mean an equality of persons standing in the same relation to whatever governmental action is challenged, the determination whether treatment is equal presupposes a determination concerning the nature of the relationship. This, with respect to apportionment, means an inquiry into the theoretic base of representation in an acceptably republican state. For a court could not determine the equal-protection issue without in fact first determining the Republican-Form issue, simply because what is reasonable for equal protection purposes will depend upon what frame of government, basically, is allowed. To divorce "equal protection" from "Republican Form" is to talk about half a question.

The notion that representation proportioned to the geographic spread of population is so universally accepted as a necessary element of equality between man and man that it must be taken to be the standard of a political equality preserved by the Fourteenth Amendment—that it is, in appellants' words "the basic principle of representative government"—is, to put it bluntly, not true. However desirable and however desired by some among the great political thinkers and framers of our government, it has never been generally practiced, today or in the past. It was not the English system, it was not the colonial system, it was not the system chosen for the national government by the Constitution, it was not the system exclusively or even predominantly practiced by the States at the time of adoption of the Fourteenth Amendment, it is not predominantly practiced by the

States today. Unless judges, the judges of this Court, are to make their private views of political wisdom the measure of the Constitution—views which in all honesty cannot but give the appearance, if not reflect the reality, of involvement with the business of partisan politics so inescapably a part of apportionment controversies—the Fourteenth Amendment, "itself a historical product," . . . provides no guide for judicial oversight of the representation problem.

. . . .

. . . A federal court cannot provide the authority requisite to make a legislature the proper governing body of the State of Tennessee. And it cannot be doubted that the striking down of the statute here challenged on equal protection grounds, no less than on grounds of failure to reapportion decennially, would deprive the State of all valid apportionment legislation and—under the ruling in McCanless—deprive the State of an effective law-based legislative branch. . . .

Although the District Court had jurisdiction in the very restricted sense of power to determine whether it could adjudicate the claim, the case is of that class of political controversy which, by the nature of its subject, is unfit for federal judicial action. The judgment of the District Court, in dismissing the complaint for failure to state a claim on which relief can be granted, should therefore be affirmed.

Dissenting opinion of Mr. Justice HARLAN, whom Mr. Justice FRANKFURTER joins.

The dissenting opinion of Mr. Justice FRANKFURTER, in which I join, demonstrates the abrupt departure the majority makes from judicial history by putting the federal courts into this area of state concerns—an area which, in this instance, the Tennessee state courts themselves have refused to enter.

It does not detract from his opinion to say that the panorama of judicial history it unfolds, though evincing a steadfast underlying principle of keeping the federal courts out of these domains, has a tendency, because of variants in expression, to becloud analysis in a given case. With due respect to the majority, I think that has happened here.

Once one cuts through the thicket of discussion devoted to "jurisdiction," "standing," "justiciability," and "political question," there emerges a straightforward issue which, in my view, is determinative of this case. Does the complaint disclose a violation of a federal constitutional right, in other words, a claim over which a United States District Court would have jurisdiction . . . ? The majority opinion does not actually discuss this basic question, but, as one concurring Justice observes, seems to decide it "*sub silentio*." . . . However, in my opinion, appellants' allegations, accepting all of them as true, do not, parsed down or as a whole, show an infringement by Tennessee of any rights assured by the Fourteenth Amendment. Accordingly, I believe the complaint should have been dismissed for "failure to state a claim upon which relief can be granted." . . .

It is at once essential to recognize this case for what it is. The issue here relates not to a method of state electoral apportionment by which seats in the *federal* House of Representatives are allocated, but solely to the right of a State to fix the basis of representation in its *own* legislature. Until it is first decided to what extent that right is limited by the Federal Constitution, and whether what Tennessee has done or failed to do in this instance runs afoul of any such limitation, we need not reach the issues of "justiciability" or "political question" or any of the other considerations which in such cases as Colegrove v. Green, . . . led the

Court to decline to adjudicate a challenge to a state apportionment affecting seats in the federal House of Representatives, in the absence of a controlling Act of Congress. . . .

. . . .

I can find nothing in the Equal Protection Clause or elsewhere in the Federal Constitution which expressly or impliedly supports the view that state legislatures must be so structured as to reflect with approximate equality the voice of every voter. Not only is that proposition refuted by history, as shown by my Brother FRANKFURTER, but it strikes deep into the heart of our federal system. Its acceptance would require us to turn our backs on the regard which this Court has always shown for the judgment of state legislatures and courts on matters of basically local concern.

In the last analysis, what lies at the core of this controversy is a difference of opinion as to the function of representative government. It is surely beyond argument that those who have the responsibility for devising a system of representation may permissibly consider that factors other than bare numbers should be taken into account. The existence of the United States Senate is proof enough of that. To consider that we may ignore the Tennessee Legislature's judgment in this instance because that body was the product of an asymmetrical electoral apportionment would in effect be to assume the very conclusion here disputed. Hence we must accept the present form of the Tennessee Legislature as the embodiment of the State's choice, or, more realistically, its compromise, between competing political philosophies. The federal courts have not been empowered by the Equal Protection Clause to judge whether this resolution of the State's internal political conflict is desirable or undesirable, wise or unwise.

. . . The Federal Constitution imposes no limitation on the form which a state government may take other than generally committing to the United States the duty to guarantee to every State "a Republican Form of Government." And, as my Brother FRANKFURTER so conclusively proves, . . . no intention to fix immutably the means of selecting representatives for state governments could have been in the minds of either the Founders or the draftsmen of the Fourteenth Amendment.

In short, there is nothing in the Federal Constitution to prevent a State, acting not irrationally, from choosing any electoral legislative structure it thinks best suited to the interests, temper, and customs of its people. . . . A State's choice to distribute electoral strength among geographical units, rather than according to a census of population, is certainly no less a rational decision of policy than would be its choice to levy a tax on property rather than a tax on income. Both are legislative judgments entitled to equal respect from this Court.

The claim that Tennessee's system of apportionment is so unreasonable as to amount to a capricious classification of voting strength stands up no better under dispassionate analysis.

. . . .

A Federal District Court is asked to say that the passage of time has rendered the 1901 apportionment obsolete to the point where its continuance becomes vulnerable under the Fourteenth Amendment. But is not this matter one that involves a classic legislative judgment? Surely it lies within the province of a state legislature to conclude that an existing allocation of senators and representatives constitutes a desirable balance of geographical and demographical representation, or that in the interest of stability of government it would be best to defer for some further time the redistribution of seats in the state legislature.

Indeed, I would hardly think it unconstitutional if a state legislature's expressed reason for establishing or maintaining an electoral imbalance between its rural and urban population were to protect the State's agricultural interests from the sheer weight of numbers of those residing in its cities. A State may, after all, take account of the interests of its rural population in the distribution of tax burdens, . . . and recognition of the special problems of agricultural interests has repeatedly been reflected in federal legislation. . . . Does the Fourteenth Amendment impose a stricter limitation upon a State's apportionment of political representatives to its central government? I think not. These are matters of local policy, on the wisdom of which the federal judiciary is neither permitted nor qualified to sit in judgment.

The suggestion of my Brother FRANKFURTER that courts lack standards by which to decide such cases as this, is relevant not only to the question of "justiciability," but also, and perhaps more fundamentally, to the determination whether any cognizable constitutional claim has been asserted in this case. Courts are unable to decide when it is that an apportionment originally valid becomes void because the factors entering into such a decision are basically matters appropriate only for legislative judgment. And so long as there exists a possible rational legislative policy for retaining an existing apportionment, such a legislative decision cannot be said to breach the bulwark against arbitrariness and caprice that the Fourteenth Amendment affords. . . .

These conclusions can hardly be escaped by suggesting that capricious state action might be found were it to appear that a majority of the Tennessee legislators, in refusing to consider reapportionment, had been actuated by self-interest in perpetuating their own political offices or by other unworthy or improper motives. Since Fletcher v. Peck, 6 Cranch 87, was decided many years ago, it has repeatedly been pointed out that it is not the business of the federal courts to inquire into the personal motives of legislators. . . . The function of the federal judiciary ends in matters of this kind once it appears, as I think it does here on the undisputed facts, that the state action complained of could have rested on some rational basis. . . .

. . . .

From a reading of the majority and concurring opinions one will not find it difficult to catch the premises that underlie this decision. The fact that the appellants have been unable to obtain political redress of their asserted grievances appears to be regarded as a matter which should lead the Court to stretch to find some basis for judicial intervention. While the Equal Protection Clause is invoked, the opinion for the Court notably eschews explaining how, consonant with past decisions, the undisputed facts in this case can be considered to show a violation of that constitutional provision. The majority seems to have accepted the argument, pressed at the bar, that if this Court merely asserts authority in this field, Tennessee and other "malapportioning" States will quickly respond with appropriate political action, so that this Court need not be greatly concerned about the federal courts becoming further involved in these matters. At the same time the majority has wholly failed to reckon with what the future may hold in store if this optimistic prediction is not fulfilled. Thus, what the Court is doing reflects more an adventure in judicial experimentation than a solid piece of constitutional adjudication. . . .

In conclusion, it is appropriate to say that one need not agree, as a citizen, with what Tennessee has done or failed to do, in order to deprecate, as a judge, what the majority is doing today. Those observers of the Court who see it primarily as the last refuge for the correction of all inequality or injustice, no matter what its nature or source, will no doubt applaud this decision and its break with the past. Those who consider that continuing national respect for the Court's authority depends in large measure upon its wise exercise of self-restraint and discipline in constitutional adjudication, will view the decision with deep concern.

I would affirm.

[Mr. Justice HARLAN dealt with the subject of "The Inadequacy of Arithmetical Formulas as Measures of the Rationality of Tennessee's Apportionment" in an appendix, which, of course, may be found in the Supreme Court Reports.]

SWEEZY v. *NEW HAMPSHIRE*

UNITED STATES SUPREME COURT
354 U.S. 235 (1957)

By resolution, the New Hampshire legislature authorized the attorney general of the state, Wyman, to investigate subversive activities. Under this authority, the attorney general held several hearings in which he questioned Sweezy, a college professor, concerning his beliefs and activities as well as alleged Communist activity in the Progressive Party circa 1948. Sweezy answered some questions but refused to answer others on the grounds that those questions were either not pertinent to the subject under inquiry or transgressions of the limitations of the First Amendment of the United States Constitution. Among the specific questions which he refused to answer, one referred to a particular lecture he had given at the University of New Hampshire. The attorney general petitioned the appropriate state court to compel Sweezy to answer the questions. The court ruled that the questions were pertinent and found Sweezy guilty of contempt, when as a witness before the court, he persisted in his refusal to answer questions. Sweezy appealed to the state supreme court only to lose the case there. Consequently, he appealed to the Supreme Court of the United States alleging that the investigation deprived him of due process of law under the Fourteenth Amendment of the United States Constitution.

Mr. Chief Justice WARREN announced the judgment of the Court and delivered an opinion, in which Mr. Justice BLACK, Mr. Justice DOUGLAS, and Mr. Justice BRENNAN joined.

. . . .

THERE IS no doubt that legislative investigations, whether on a federal or state level, are capable of encroaching upon the constitutional liberties of individuals. It is particularly important that the exercise of the power of compulsory process be carefully circumscribed when the investigative process tends to impinge upon such highly sensitive areas as freedom of speech or press, freedom of political association, and freedom of communication of ideas, particularly in the academic community. Responsibility for the proper conduct of investigations rests, of course, upon the legislature itself. If that assembly chooses to authorize inquiries on its behalf by a legislatively created committee, that basic responsibility carries forward to include the duty of adequate supervision of the actions of the committee. This safeguard can be nullified when a committee is invested with a broad and ill-defined jurisdiction. The authorizing resolution thus becomes especially significant in that it reveals the amount of discretion that has been conferred upon the committee.

In this case, the investigation is governed by provisions in the New Hampshire Subversive Activities Act of 1951. The Attorney General was instructed by the legislature to look into violations of that Act. In addition, he was given the far more sweeping mandate to find out if there were subversive persons, as defined in that Act, present in New Hampshire. That statute, therefore, measures the breadth and scope of the investigation before us.

"Subversive persons" are defined in many gradations of conduct. Our interest is in the minimal requirements of that definition since they will outline its reach. According to the statute, a person is a "subversive person" if he, by any means, aids in the commission of any act intended to assist in the alteration of the constitutional form of government by force or violence. The possible remoteness from armed insurrection of conduct that could satisfy these criteria is obvious from the language. The statute goes well beyond those who are engaged in efforts designed to alter the form of government by force or violence. The statute declares, in effect, that the assistant of an assistant is caught up in the definition. This chain of conduct attains increased significance in light of the lack of a necessary element of guilty knowledge in either stage of assistants. The State Supreme Court has held that the definition encompasses persons engaged in the specified conduct "* * * whether or not done 'knowingly and willfully * * *.'" Nelson v. Wyman, 105 A. 2d 756.

The potential sweep of this definition extends to conduct which is only remotely related to actual subversion and which is done completely free of any conscious intent to be a part of such activity.

The statute's definition of "subversive organizations" is also broad. An association is said to be any group of persons, whether temporarily or permanently associated together, for joint action or advancement of views on any subject. An organization is deemed subversive if it has a purpose to abet, advise or teach activities intended to assist in the alteration of the constitutional form of government by force or violence.

. . . .

The nature of the investigation which the Attorney General was authorized to conduct is revealed by this case. He delved minutely into the past conduct of petitioner, thereby making his private life a matter of public record. The questioning indicates that the investigators had thoroughly prepared for the interview and were not acquiring new information as much as corroborating data already in their possession. On the great majority of questions, the witness was cooperative, even though he made clear his opinion that the interrogation was unjustified and unconstitutional. Two subjects arose upon which petitioner refused to answer: his lectures at the University of New Hampshire, and his knowledge of the Progressive Party and its adherents.

The state courts upheld the attempt to investigate the academic subject on the ground that it might indicate whether petitioner was a "subversive person." What he taught the class at a state university was found relevant to the character of the teacher. The

State Supreme Court carefully excluded the possibility that the inquiry was sustainable because of the state interest in the state university. There was no warrant in the authorizing resolution for that. . . . The sole basis for the inquiry was to scrutinize the teacher as a person, and the inquiry must stand or fall on that basis.

The interrogation on the subject of the Progressive Party was deemed to come within the Attorney General's mandate because that party might have been shown to be a "subversive organization." The State Supreme Court held that the "* * * questions called for answers concerning the membership or participation of named persons in the Progressive Party which, if given, would aid the Attorney General in determining whether that party and its predecessor are or were subversive organizations." . . .

The New Hampshire court concluded that the "* * * right to lecture and the right to associate with others for a common purpose, be it political or otherwise, are individual liberties guaranteed to every citizen by the State and Federal Constitutions but are not absolute rights * * *. The inquiries authorized by the Legislature in connection with this investigation concerning the contents of the lecture and the membership, purposes and activities of the Progressive Party undoubtedly interfered with the defendant's free exercise of those liberties." . . .

The State Supreme Court thus conceded without extended discussion that petitioner's right to lecture and his right to associate with others were constitutionally protected freedoms which had been abridged through this investigation. These conclusions could not be seriously debated. Merely to summon a witness and compel him, against his will, to disclose the nature of his past expressions and associations is a measure of governmental interference in these matters. These are rights which are safeguarded by the Bill of Rights and the Fourteenth Amendment. We believe that there unquestionably was an invasion of petitioner's liberties in the areas of academic freedom and political expression—areas in which government should be extremely reticent to tread.

The essentiality of freedom in the community of American universities is almost self-evident. No one should underestimate the vital role in a democracy that is played by those who guide and train our youth. To impose any strait jacket upon the intellectual leaders in our colleges and universities would imperil the future of our Nation. No field of education is so thoroughly comprehended by man that new discoveries cannot yet be made. Particularly is that true in the social sciences, where few, if any, principles are accepted as absolutes. Scholarship cannot flourish in an atmosphere of suspicion and distrust. Teachers and students must always remain free to inquire, to study and to evaluate, to gain new maturity and understanding; otherwise our civilization will stagnate and die.

Equally manifest as a fundamental principle of a democratic society is political freedom of the individual. Our form of government is built on the premise that every citizen shall have the right to engage in political expression and association. This right was enshrined in the First Amendment of the Bill of Rights. Exercise of these basic freedoms in America has traditionally been through the media of political associations. Any interference with the freedom of a party is simultaneously an interference with the freedom of its adherents. All political ideas cannot and should not be channeled into the programs of our two major parties. History has amply proved the virtue of political activity by minority, dissident groups, who innumerable times have been in the vanguard of democratic thought and whose programs were ultimately accepted. Mere unorthodoxy or dissent from the prevailing mores is not to be condemned. The absence of such voices would be a symptom of grave illness in our society.

Notwithstanding the undeniable importance of freedom in the areas, the Supreme Court of New Hampshire did not consider that the abridgment of petitioner's rights under the Constitution vitiated the investigation. In the view of that court, "the answer lies in a determination of whether the object of the legislative investigation under consideration is such as to justify the restriction thereby imposed upon the defendant's liberties." . . . It found such justification in the legislature's judgment, expressed by its authorizing resolution, that there exists a potential menace from those who would overthrow the government by force and violence. That court concluded that the need for the legislature to be informed on so elemental a subject as the self-preservation of government outweighed the deprivation of constitutional rights that occurred in the process.

We do not now conceive of any circumstance wherein a state interest would justify infringement of rights in these fields. But we do not need to reach such fundamental questions of state power to decide this case. The State Supreme Court itself recognized that there was a weakness in its conclusion that the menace of forcible overthrow of the government justified sacrificing constitutional rights. There was a missing link in the chain of reasoning. The syllogism was not complete. There was nothing to connect the questioning of petitioner with this fundamental interest of the State. Petitioner had been interrogated by a one-man legislative committee, not by the legislature itself. The relationship of the committee to the full assembly is vital, therefore, as revealing the relationship of the questioning to the state interest.

In light of this, the state court emphasized a factor in the authorizing resolution which confined the inquiries which the Attorney General might undertake to the object of the investigation. That limitation was thought to stem from the authorizing resolution's condition precedent to the institution of any inquiry. The New Hampshire legislature specified that the Attorney General should act only when he had information which "* * * in his judgment may be reasonable or reliable." The state court construed this to mean that the Attorney General must have something like probable cause for conducting a particular investigation. It is not likely that this device would prove an adequate safeguard against unwarranted inquiries. The legislature has specified that the determination of the necessity for inquiry shall be left in the judgment of the investigator. In this case, the record does not reveal what reasonable or reliable information led the Attorney General to question petitioner. The state court relied upon the Attorney General's description of prior information that had come into his possession.

The respective roles of the legislature and the investigator thus revealed are of considerable significance to the issue before us. It is eminently clear that the basic discretion of determining the direction of the legislative inquiry has been turned over to the investigative agency. The Attorney General has been given such a sweeping and uncertain mandate that it is his decision which picks out the subjects that will be pursued, what witnesses will be summoned and what questions will be asked. In this circumstance, it cannot be stated authoritatively that the legislature asked the Attorney General to gather the kind of facts comprised in the subjects upon which petitioner was interrogated.

Instead of making known the nature of the data it desired, the legislature has insulated itself from those witnesses whose rights may be vitally affected by the investigation. Incorporating by reference provisions from its subversive activities act, it has told the Attorney General, in effect to screen the citizenry of New Hampshire to bring to light anyone who fits into the expansive definitions.

Within the very broad area thus committed to the discretion of the Attorney General there may be many facts which the legislature might find useful. There would also be a great deal of data which that assembly would not want or need. In the classes of information that the legislature might deem it desirable to have, there will be some which it could not validly acquire because of the effect upon the constitutional rights of individual citizens. Separating the wheat from the chaff, from the standpoint of the legislature's object, is the legislature's responsibility because it alone can make that judgment. In this case, the New Hampshire legislature has delegated that task to the Attorney General.

As a result, neither we nor the state courts have any assurance that the questions petitioner refused to answer fall into a category of matters upon which the legislature wanted to be informed when it initiated this inquiry. The judiciary are thus placed in an untenable position. Lacking even the elementary fact that the legislature wants certain questions answered and recognizing that petitioner's constitutional rights are in jeopardy, we are asked to approve or disapprove his incarceration for contempt.

In our view, the answer is clear. No one would deny that the infringement of constitutional rights of individuals would violate the guarantee of due process where no state interest underlies the state action. Thus, if the Attorney General's interrogation of petitioner were in fact wholly unrelated to the object of the legislature in authorizing the inquiry, the Due Process Clause would preclude the endangering of constitutional liberties. We believe that an equivalent situation is presented in this case. The lack of any indications that the legislature wanted the information the Attorney General attempted to elicit from petitioner must be treated as the absence of authority. It follows that the use of the contempt power, notwithstanding the interference with constitutional rights, was not in accordance with the due process requirements of the Fourteenth Amendment.

The conclusion that we have reached in this case is not grounded upon the doctrine of separation of powers. In the Federal Government, it is clear that the Constitution has conferred the powers of government upon three major branches: the Executive, the Legislative and the Judicial. No contention has been made by petitioner that the New Hampshire legislature, by this investigation, arrogated to itself executive or judicial powers. We accept the finding of the State Supreme Court that the employment of the Attorney General as the investigating committee does not alter the legislative nature of the proceedings. Moreover, this Court has held that the concept of separation of powers embodied in the United States Constitution is not mandatory in state government. . . . Our conclusion does rest upon a separation of the power of a state legislature to conduct investigations from the responsibility to direct the use of that power insofar as that separation causes a deprivation of the constitutional rights of individuals and a denial of due process of law.

The judgment of the Supreme Court of New Hampshire is reversed.

Reversed.

Mr. Justice WHITTAKER took no part in the consideration or decision of this case.

Mr. Justice FRANKFURTER, whom Mr. Justice HARLAN joins, concurring in the result.

For me this is a very different case from Watkins v. United States, 354 U.S. 178. This case comes to us solely through the limited power to review the action of the States conferred upon the Court by the Fourteenth Amendment. Petitioner claims that respect for liberties guaranteed by the Due Process Clause of that Amendment precludes the State of New Hampshire from compelling him to answer certain questions put to him by the investigating arm of its legislature. Ours is the narrowly circumscribed but exceedingly difficult task of making the final judicial accommodation between the competing weighty claims that underlie all such questions of due process.

In assessing the claim of the State of New Hampshire to the information denied it by petitioner, we cannot concern ourselves with the fact that New Hampshire chose to make its Attorney General in effect a standing committee of its legislature for the purpose of investigating the extent of "subversive" activities within its bounds. The case must be judged as though the whole body of the legislature had demanded the information of petitioner. It would make the deepest inroads upon our federal system for this Court now to hold that it can determine the appropriate distribution of powers and their delegation within the forty-eight States. As the earlier Mr. Justice Harlan said for a unanimous Court in Dreyer v. People of State of Illinois, 187 U.S. 71:

> "Whether the legislative, executive and judicial powers of a State shall be kept altogether distinct and separate, or whether persons or collections of persons belonging to one department may, in respect to some matters, exert powers which, strictly speaking, pertain to another department of government, is for the determination of the State. And its determination one way or the other cannot be an element in the inquiry whether the due process of law prescribed by the Fourteenth Amendment has been respected by the State or its representatives when dealing with matters involving life or liberty."

Whether the state legislature should operate largely by committees, as does the Congress, or whether committees should be the exception, as is true of the House of Commons, whether the legislature should have two chambers or only one, as in Nebraska, whether the State's chief executive should have the pardoning power, whether the State's judicial branch must provide trial by jury, are all matters beyond the reviewing powers of this Court. Similarly, whether the Attorney General of New Hampshire acted within the scope of the authority given him by the state legislature is a matter for the decision of the courts of that State, as it is for the federal courts to determine whether an agency to which Congress has delegated power has acted within the confines of its mandate. . . . Sanction of the delegation rests with the New Hampshire Supreme Court, and its validation in Nelson v. Wyman, . . . is binding here.

. . . .

The questions that petitioner refused to answer regarding the university lecture, the third given by him in three years at the invitation of the faculty for humanities, were:

> "What was the subject of your lecture?"
>
> "Didn't you tell the class at the Uni-

versity of New Hampshire on Monday, March 22, 1954, that Socialism was inevitable in this country?"

"Did you advocate Marxism at that time?"

"Did you express the opinion, or did you make the statement at that time that Socialism was inevitable in America?"

"Did you in this last lecture on March 22 or in any of the former lectures espouse the theory of dialectical materialism?"

"I have in the file here a statement from a person who attended your class, and I will read it in part because I don't want you to think I am just fishing. 'His talk this time was on the inevitability of the Socialist program. It was a glossed-over interpretation of the materialist dialectic.' Now, again I ask you the original question."

In response to the first question of this series, petitioner had said at the hearing:

"I would like to say one thing in this connection, Mr. Wyman. I stated under oath at my last appearance that, and I now repeat it, that I do not advocate or in any way further the aim of overthrowing constitutional government by force and violence. I did not so advocate in the lecture I gave at the University of New Hampshire. In fact I have never at any time so advocated in a lecture anywhere. Aside from that I have nothing I want to say about the lecture in question."

The New Hampshire Supreme Court, although recognizing that such inquiries . . . "undoubtedly interfered with the defendant's free exercise" of his constitutionally guaranteed right to lecture, justified the interference on the ground that it would occur "in a limited area in which the legislative committee may reasonably believe that the overthrow of existing government by force and violence is being or has been taught, advocated or planned, an area in which the interest of the State justifies this intrusion upon civil liberties." According to the court, the facts that made reasonable the committee's belief that petitioner had taught violent overthrow in his lecture were that he was a Socialist, with a record of affiliation with groups cited by the Attorney General of the United States or the House Un-American Activities Committee and that he was co-editor of an article stating that, although the authors hated violence, it was less to be deplored when used by the Soviet Union than by capitalist countries.

When weighed against the grave harm resulting from governmental intrusion into the intellectual life of a university, such justification for compelling a witness to discuss the contents of his lecture appears grossly inadequate. Particularly is this so where the witness has sworn that neither in the lecture nor at any other time did he ever advocate overthrowing the Government by force and violence.

Progress in the natural sciences is not remotely confined to findings made in the laboratory. Insights into the mysteries of nature are born of hypothesis and speculation. The more so is this true in the pursuit of understanding in the groping endeavors of what are called the social sciences, the concern of which is man and society. The problems that are the respective preoccupations of anthropology, economics, law, psychology, sociology and related areas of scholarship are merely departmentalized dealing, by way of manageable division of analysis, with interpenetrating aspects of holistic perplexities. For society's good—if understanding be an essential need of society—inquiries into these problems, speculations about them, stimulation in others of reflection upon them, must be left as unfettered as possible. Political power must abstain from intrusion into this activity of freedom, pursued in the interest of wise government and the people's well-being, except for reasons that are exigent and obviously compelling.

These pages need not be burdened with proof, based on the testimony of a cloud of impressive witnesses, of the dependence of a free society on free universities. This means the exclusion of governmental intervention in the intellectual life of a university. It matters little whether such intervention occurs avowedly or through action that inevitably tends to check the ardor and fearlessness of scholars, qualities at once so fragile and so indispensable for fruitful academic labor. One need only refer to the address of T. H. Huxley at the opening of Johns Hopkins University, the Annual Reports of President A. Lawrence Lowell of Harvard, the Reports of the University Grants Committee in Great Britain, as illustrative items in a vast body of literature. Suffice it to quote the latest expression on this subject. It is also perhaps the most poignant because its plea on behalf of continuing the free spirit of the open universities of South Africa has gone unheeded.

. . . .

. . . in these matters of the spirit inroads on legitimacy must be resisted at their incipiency. This kind of evil grows by what it is allowed to feed on. The admonition of this Court in another context is applicable here. "It may be that it is the obnoxious thing in its mildest and least repulsive form; but illegitimate and unconstitutional practices get their first footing in that way, namely, by silent approaches and slight deviations from legal modes of procedure." . . .

Petitioner stated, in response to questions at the hearing, that he did not know of any Communist interest in, connection with, influence over, activity in, or manipulation of the Progressive Party. He refused to answer, despite court order, the following questions on the ground that, by inquiring into the activities of a lawful political organization, they infringed upon the inviolability of the right to privacy in his political thoughts, actions and associations:

> "Was she, Nancy Sweezy, your wife, active in the formation of the Progressive Citizens of America?"
>
> "Was Nancy Sweezy then working with individuals who were then members of the Communist Party?"
>
> "Was Charles Beebe active in forming the Progressive Citizens of America?"
>
> "Did he work with your present wife —Did Charles Beebe work with your present wife in 1947?"
>
> "Did it [a meeting at the home of one Abraham Walenko] have anything to do with the Progressive Party?"

The Supreme Court of New Hampshire justified this intrusion upon his freedom on the same basis that it upheld questioning about the university lecture, namely, that the restriction was limited to situations where the Committee had reason to believe that violent overthrow of the Government was being advocated or planned. It ruled:

> "* * * That he [the Attorney General] did possess information which was sufficient to reasonably warrant inquiry concerning the Progressive Party is evident from his statement made during the hearings held before him that 'considerable sworn testimony has been given in this investigation to the effect that the Progressive Party in New Hampshire has been heavily infiltrated by members of the Communist Party and that the policies and purposes of the Progressive Party have been directly influenced by members of the Communist Party.' " . . .

For a citizen to be made to forego even a part of so basic a liberty as his political autonomy, the subordinating interest of the State must be compelling. Inquiry pursued in safeguarding a State's security against threatened force and violence cannot be shut off by mere disclaimer, though of course a relevant claim may be made to the privilege against self-incrimination. (The New Hampshire Constitution guarantees this privilege.) But the inviolability of privacy belonging to a citizen's political loyalties has so overwhelming an importance to the well-being of our kind of society that it cannot be constitutionally encroached upon on the basis of so meagre a countervailing interest of the State as may be argumentatively found in the remote, shadowy threat to the security of New Hampshire allegedly presented in the origins and contributing elements of the Progressive Party and in petitioner's relations to these.

In the political realm, as in the academic, thought and action are presumptively immune from inquisition by political authority. It cannot require argument that inquiry would be barred to ascertain whether a citizen had voted for one or the other of the two major parties either in a state or national election. Until recently, no difference would have been entertained in regard to inquiries about a voter's affiliations with one of the various so-called third parties that have had their day, or longer, in our political history. This is so, even though adequate protection of secrecy by way of the Australian ballot did not come into use till 1888. The implications of the United States Constitution for national elections and "the concept of ordered liberty" implicit in the Due Process Clause of the Fourteenth Amendment as against the States, . . . were not frozen as of 1789 or 1868, respectively. While the language of the Constitution does not change, the changing circumstances of a progressive society for which it was designed yield new and fuller import to its meaning. . . . Whatever, on the basis of massive proof and in the light of history, of which this Court may well take judicial notice, be the justification for not regarding the Communist Party as a conventional political party, no such justification has been afforded in regard to the Progressive Party. A foundation in fact and reason would have to be established far weightier than the intimations that appear in the record to warrant such a view of the Progressive Party. This precludes the questioning that petitioner resisted in regard to that Party.

To be sure, this is a conclusion based on a judicial judgment in balancing two contending principles—the right of a citizen to political privacy, as protected by the Fourteenth Amendment, and the right of the State to self-protection. And striking the balance implies the exercise of judgment. This is the inescapable judicial task in giving substantive content, legally enforced, to the Due Process Clause, and it is a task ultimately committed to this Court. It must not be an exercise of whim or will. It must be an overriding judgment founded on something much deeper and more justifiable than personal preference. As far as it lies within human limitations, it must be an impersonal judgment. It must rest on fundamental presuppositions rooted in history to which widespread acceptance may fairly be attributed. Such a judgment must be arrived at in a spirit of humility when it counters the judgment of the State's highest court. But, in the end, judgment cannot be escaped—the judgment of this Court. . . .

And so I am compelled to conclude that the judgment of the New Hampshire court must be reversed.

Mr. Justice CLARK, with whom Mr. Justice BURTON joins, dissenting.

The Court today has denied the State of New Hampshire the right to investigate the extent of "subversive activities" within its boundaries in the manner chosen by its legislature. Unfortunately there is no opinion for the Court, for those who reverse are divided and they do so on entirely different grounds. Four of my Brothers join in what I shall call the principal opinion. They hold that the appointment of the Attorney General to act as a committee for the legislature results in a separation of its power to investigate from its "responsibility to direct the use of that power" and thereby "causes a deprivation of the constitutional rights of individuals and a denial of due process * * *." This theory was not raised by the parties and is, indeed, a novel one.

My Brothers FRANKFURTER and HARLAN do not agree with this opinion because they conclude, as do I, that the internal affairs of the New Hampshire State Government are of no concern to us. . . . They do join in the reversal, however, on the ground that Sweezy's rights under the First Amendment have been violated. I agree with neither opinion.

The principal opinion finds that "The Attorney General has been given such a sweeping and uncertain mandate that it is his decision which picks out the subjects that will be pursued, what witnesses will be summoned and what questions will be asked." The New Hampshire Act clearly indicates that it was the legislature that determined the general subject matter of the investigation, subversive activities; the legislature's committee, the Attorney General, properly decided what witnesses should be called and what questions should be asked. My Brothers surely would not have the legislature as a whole make these decisions. But they conclude, nevertheless, that it cannot be said that the legislature "asked the Attorney General to gather the kind of facts comprised in the subjects upon which petitioner was interrogated." It follows, says this opinion, that there is no "assurance that the questions petitioner refused to answer fall into a category of matters upon which the legislature wanted to be informed * * *." But New Hampshire's Supreme Court has construed the state statute. It has declared the purpose to be to investigate "subversive" activities within the State; it has approved the use of the "one-man" technique; it has said the questions were all relevant to the legislative purpose. In effect the state court says the Attorney General was "directed" to inquire as he did. Furthermore, the legislature renewed the Act in the same language twice in the year following Sweezy's interrogation. . . . In ratifying the Attorney General's action it used these words: "The investigation * * * provided for by chapter 307 of the Laws of 1953, as continued by a resolution approved January 13, 1955, is hereby continued in full force and effect, in form, *manner* and authority as therein provided * * *." (Emphasis added.) We are bound by the state court findings. We have no right to strike down the state action unless we find not only that there has been a deprivation of Sweezy's constitutional rights, but that the interest in protecting those rights is greater than the State's interest in uncovering subversive activities within its confines. The majority has made no such findings.

The short of it is that the Court blocks New Hampshire's effort to enforce its law. I had thought that in Commonwealth of Pennsylvania v. Nelson, 1956, 350 U.S. 497, we had left open for legitimate state control any subversive activity leveled against the interest of the State. I for one intended to suspend state action only in the field of subversion against the Nation and thus avoid a race to the courthouse door between federal and state prosecutors. Cases concerning subversive activities against the National Government have such interstate ramifications that individual state action might effectively destroy a prosecution on the national level. I thought we had left open a wide field for state action, but implicit in the opinions today is a contrary conclusion. They destroy the fact-finding power of the State in this field and I dissent from this wide sweep of their coverage.

The principal opinion discusses, by way of dictum, due process under the Fourteenth Amendment. Since the basis of the opinion is not placed on this ground, I would not think it necessary to raise it here. . . .

. . . .

Since the conclusion of a majority of those reversing is not predicated on the First Amendment questions presented, I see no necessity for discussing them. But since the principal opinion devotes itself largely to these issues I believe it fair to ask why they have been given such an elaborate treatment when the case is decided on an entirely different ground. It is of no avail to quarrel with a straw man. My view on First Amendment problems in this type of case is expressed in my dissent in Watkins, decided today. Since a majority of the Court has not passed on these problems here, and since I am not convinced that the State's interest in investigating subversive activities for the protection of its citizens is outweighed by any necessity for the protection of Sweezy I would affirm the judgment of the New Hampshire Supreme Court.

UPHAUS v. WYMAN

UNITED STATES SUPREME COURT

360 U.S. 72 (1959)

This case, like Sweezy, *involves a witness who had been summoned to testify before attorney general* Wyman *who was at the time investigating subversive activities in the state under authority granted him by the state legislature. You should, however, carefully note the difference in the facts of the two cases.*

Uphaus, the executive director of a summer camp was willing to testify about his own activities but refused to produce among other things the list of guests at the camp. Uphaus objected on the grounds (1) that the Smith Act precluded states from conducting this kind of investigation and (2) that this particular investigation violated his right to due process of law under the Fourteenth Amendment of the United States Constitution. To compel Uphaus to cooperate, Wyman *brought action in the appropriate state court. From decisions in that court and the state supreme court adverse to him, Uphaus appealed to the Supreme Court of the United States which sent the case back to the New Hampshire supreme court with instructions to review it in the light of United States Supreme Court's decision in* Sweezy. *This the New Hampshire court did, but once again it upheld the conviction of Uphaus for contempt. Again, Uphaus turned to the United States Supreme Court.*

Mr. Justice CLARK delivered the opinion of the Court.

. . . .

WE NOW pass to a consideration of the sole question before us, namely, the validity of the order of contempt for refusal to produce the list of guests at World Fellowship, Inc., [*the name of the camp*] during the summer seasons of 1954 and 1955. In addition to the arguments appellant made to the trial court, he urges here that the "indefinite sentence" imposed upon him constitutes such cruel and unusual punishment as to be a denial of due process.

Appellant vigorously contends that the New Hampshire Subversive Activities Act of 1951 and the resolution creating the committee have been superseded by the Smith Act, as amended. In support of this position appellant cites Com. of Pennsylvania v. Nelson. . . . The argument is that Nelson, which involved a prosecution under a state sedition law, held that "Congress has intended to occupy the field of sedition." . . . This rule of decision, it is contended, should embrace legislative investigations made pursuant to an effort by the Legislature to inform itself of the presence of subversives within the State and possibly to enact laws in the subversive field. The appellant's argument sweeps too broad. In Nelson itself we said that the "precise holding of the court * * * is that the Smith Act * * * which prohibits the knowing advocacy of the overthrow of the Government of the United States by force and violence, supersedes the enforceability of the Pennsylvania Sedition Act which proscribes the *same conduct*." (Italics supplied.) . . . The basis of Nelson thus rejects the notion that it stripped the States of the right to protect themselves. All the opinion proscribed was a race between federal and state prosecutors to the courthouse door. The opinion made clear that a State could proceed with prosecutions for sedition against the State itself; that it can legitimately investigate in this area follows *a fortiori*. In Sweezy v. State of New Hampshire, supra, where the same contention was made as to the identical state Act, it was denied *sub silentio*. Nor did our opinion in Nelson hold that the Smith Act had proscribed state activity in protection of itself either from actual or threatened "sabotage or attempted violence of all kinds." In footnote 8 of the opinion it is pointed out that the State had full power to deal with internal civil disturbances. Thus registration statutes, *quo warranto* proceedings as to subversive corporations, the subversive instigation of riots and a host of other subjects directly affecting state security furnish grist for the State's legislative mill. Moreover, the right of the State to require the production of corporate papers of a state-chartered corporation in an inquiry to determine whether corporate activity is violative of state policy is, of course, not touched upon in Nelson and today stands unimpaired, either by the Smith Act or the Nelson opinion.

Appellant's other objections can be capsuled into the single question of whether New Hampshire, under the facts here, is precluded from compelling the production of the documents by the Due Process Clause of the Fourteenth Amendment. Let us first clear away some of the underbrush necessarily surrounding the case because of its setting.

First, the academic and political freedoms discussed in Sweezy v. State of New Hampshire, supra, are not present here in the same degree, since World Fellowship is neither a university nor a political party. Next, since questions concerning the authority of the committee to act as it did are questions of state law, . . . we accept as controlling the New Hampshire Supreme Court's conclusion that "[t]he legislative history makes it clear beyond a reasonable doubt that it [the Legislature] did and does desire an answer to these questions." . . . Finally, we assume, without deciding, that Uphaus had sufficient standing to assert any rights of the guests whose identity the committee seeks to determine. . . . The interest of the guests at World Fellowship in their associational privacy having been asserted, we have for decision the federal question of whether the public interests overbalance these conflicting private ones. Whether there was "justification" for the production order turns on the "substantiality" of New Hampshire's interests in obtaining the identity of the guests when weighed against the individual interests which the appellant asserts. . . .

What was the interest of the State? The Attorney General was commissioned to determine if there were any subversive persons within New Hampshire. The obvious starting point of such an inquiry was to learn what persons were within the State. It is therefore clear that the requests relate directly to the Legislature's area of interest, i. e., the presence of subversives in the State, as announced in its resolution. Nor was the demand of the subpoena burdensome; as to time, only a few months of each of the two years were involved; as to place, only the camp conducted by the Corporation; nor as to the lists of names, which included about 300 each year.

Moreover, the Attorney General had valid reason to believe that the speakers and guests at World Fellowship might be subversive persons within the meaning of the New Hampshire Act. The Supreme Court of New Hampshire found Uphaus' contrary position "unrelated to reality." Although the evidence as to the nexus between World Fellowship and subversive activities may not be conclusive, we believe it sufficiently relevant to support the Attorney General's action. The New Hampshire definition of subversive persons was born of the legislative determination that the Communist movement posed a serious threat to the security of the State. The record reveals that appellant had participated in "Communist front" activities and that "[n]ot less than nineteen speakers invited by Uphaus to talk at World Fellowship had either been members of the Communist Party or had connections or affiliations with it or with one or more of the organizations cited as subversive or Communist controlled in the United States Attorney General's list." . . . While the Attorney General's list is designed for the limited purpose of determining fitness for federal employment, . . . and guilt by association remains a thoroughly discredited doctrine, it is with a legislative investigation—not a criminal prosecution—that we deal here. Certainly the investigatory power of the State need not be constricted until sufficient evidence of subversion is gathered to justify the institution of criminal proceedings.

The nexus between World Fellowship and subversive activities disclosed by the record furnished adequate justification for the investigation we here review. The Attorney General sought to learn if subversive persons were in the State because of the legislative determination that such persons, statutorily defined with a view toward the Communist Party, posed a serious threat to the security of the State. The investigation was, therefore, undertaken in the interest of self-preservation, "the ultimate value of any society," . . . . This governmental interest outweighs individual rights in an associational privacy which, however real in other circumstances, . . . were here tenuous at best. The camp was operating as a public one, furnishing both board and lodging to persons applying therefor. As to them, New Hampshire law requires that World Fellowship, Inc., maintain a register, open to inspection of sheriffs and police officers. It is contended that the list might be "circulated throughout the states and the Attorney Generals throughout the states have cross-indexed files, so that any guest whose name is mentioned in that kind of proceeding immediately becomes suspect, even in his own place of residence." . . . The record before us, however, only reveals a report to the Legislature of New Hampshire made by the Attorney General in accordance with the requirements of the resolution. We recognize, of course, that compliance with the subpoena will result in exposing the fact that the persons therein named were guests at World Fellowship. But so long as a committee must report to its legislative parent, exposure—in the sense of disclosure—is an inescapable incident of an investigation into the presence of subversive persons within a State. And the governmental interest in self-preservation is sufficiently compelling to subordinate the interest in associational privacy of persons who, at least to the extent of the guest registration statute, made public at the inception the association they now wish to keep private. In the light of such a record we conclude that the State's interest has not been "pressed, in this instance, to a point where it has come into fatal collision with the overriding" constitutionally protected rights of appellant and those he may represent. . . .

We now reach the question of the validity of the sentence. The judgment of contempt orders the appellant confined until he produces the documents called for in the subpoenas. He himself admitted to the court that although they were at hand, not only had he failed to bring them with him to court, but that, further, he had no intention of producing them. In view of appellant's unjustified refusal we think the order a proper one. . . .

. . . .

We have concluded that the committee's demand for the documents was a legitimate one; it follows that the judgment of contempt for refusal to produce them is valid. We do not impugn appellant's good faith in the assertion of what he believed to be his rights. But three courts have disagreed with him in interpreting those rights. If appellant chooses to abide by the result of the adjudication and obey the order of New Hampshire's courts, he need not face jail. If, however, he continues to disobey, we find on this record no constitutional objection to the exercise of the traditional remedy of contempt to secure compliance.

Affirmed.

Mr. Justice BRENNAN, with whom THE CHIEF JUSTICE, Mr. Justice BLACK and Mr. Justice DOUGLAS join, dissenting.

The Court holds today that the constitutionally protected rights of speech and assembly of appellant and those whom he may represent are to be subordinated to New Hampshire's legislative investigation because, as applied in the demands made on him, the investigation is rationally connected with a discernible legislative purpose. With due respect for my Brothers' views, I do not agree that a showing of any requisite legislative purpose or other state interest that constitutionally can subordinate appellant's rights is to be found in this record. Exposure purely for the sake of exposure is not such a valid subordinating purpose. Watkins v. United States, 354 U.S. 178. . . . This record, I think, not only fails to reveal any interest of the State sufficient to subordinate appellant's constitutionally protected rights, but affirmatively shows that the investigatory objective was the impermissible one of exposure for exposure's sake. I therefore dissent from the judgment of the Court.

I fully appreciate the delicacy of the judicial task of questioning the workings of a legislative investigation. A proper regard for the primacy of the legislative function in its own field, and for the broad scope of the investigatory power to achieve legislative ends, necessarily should constrain the judiciary to indulge every reasonable intendment in favor of the validity of legislative inquiry. However, our frame of government also imposes another inescapable duty upon the judiciary, that of protecting the constitutional rights of freedom of speech and assembly from improper invasion, whether by the national or the state legislatures. See Watkins v. United States . . . ; Sweezy v. State of New Hampshire. . . . Where that invasion is as clear as I think this record discloses, the appellant is entitled to our judgment of reversal.

Judicial consideration of the collision of the investigatory function with constitutionally protected rights of speech and assembly is a recent development in our constitutional law. The Court has often examined the validity under the Federal Constitution of federal and state statutes and executive action imposing criminal and other traditional sanctions on conduct alleged to be protected by the guarantees of freedom of speech and of assembly. The role of the state-imposed sanctions of imprisonment, fines and prohibitory injunctions directed against association or speech and their limitations under the First and Fourteenth Amendments has been canvassed quite fully. . . . And other state action, such as deprivation of public employment and the denial of admission to a profession, has also been recognized as being subject to the restraints of the Constitution. . . .

But only recently has the Court been required to begin a full exploration of the impact of the governmental investigatory function on these freedoms. Here is introduced the weighty consideration that the power of investigation, whether exercised in aid of the governmental legislative power, see Watkins v. United States, . . . or in aid of the governmental power to adjudicate disputes, . . . is vital to the functioning of free governments and is therefore necessarily broad. But where the exercise of the investigatory power collides with constitutionally guaranteed freedoms, that power too has inevitable limitations, and the delicate and always difficult accommodation of the two with minimum sacrifice of either is the hard task of the judiciary and ultimately of this Court.

It was logical that the adverse effects of unwanted publicity—of exposure—as concomitants of the exercise of the investigatory power, should come to be recognized, in certain circumstances, as invading protected freedoms and offending constitutional inhibitions upon governmental actions. For in an era of mass communications and mass opinion, and of international tensions and domestic anxiety, exposure and group identification by the state of those holding unpopular and dissident views are fraught with such serious consequences for the individual as inevitably to inhibit seriously the expression of views which the Constitution intended to make free. . . . [*In another case, we said:*] "This Court has recognized the vital relationship between freedom to associate and privacy in one's associations. * * * Inviolability of privacy in group association may in many circumstances be indispensable to preservation of freedom of association, particularly where a group espouses dissident beliefs." . . .

Of course, the considerations entering into the weighing of the interests concerned is different where the problem is one of state exposure in the area of assembly and expression from where the problem is that of evaluating a state criminal or regulatory statute in these areas. Government must have freedom to make an appropriate investigation where there appears a rational connection with the lawmaking process, the processes of adjudication, or other essential governmental functions. In the investigatory stage of the legislative process, for example, the specific interest of the state and the final legislative means to be chosen to implement it are almost by definition not precisely defined at the start of the inquiry, and due allowance must accordingly be made. Also, when exposure is evaluated judicially as a governmental sanction, there should be taken into account the differences between it and the more traditional state-inflicted pains and penalties. True it is, therefore, that any line other than a universal subordination of free expression and association to the asserted interests of the state in investigation and exposure will be difficult of definition; but this Court has rightly turned its back on the alternative of universal subordination of protected interests, and we must define rights in this area the best we can. The problem is one in its nature calling for traditional case-by-case development of principles in the various permutations of circumstances where the conflict may appear. But guide lines must be marked out by the courts. "This is the inescapable judicial task in giving substantive content, legally enforced, to the Due Process Clause, and it is a task ultimately committed to this Court." Sweezy v. State of New Hampshire, . . . (concurring opinion). On the facts of this case I think that New Hampshire's investigation, as applied to the appellant, was demonstrably and clearly outside the wide limits of the power which must be conceded to the State even though it be attended by some exposure. . . .

. . . .

One may accept the Court's truism that preservation of the State's existence is undoubtedly a proper purpose for legislation. But, in descending from this peak of abstraction to the facts of this case, one must ask the question: What relation did this investigation of individual conduct have to legislative ends here? If bills of attainder were still a legitimate legislative end, it is clear that the investigations and reports might naturally have furnished the starting point (though only that) for a legislative adjudication of guilt under the 1951 Act. But what other legislative purpose was actually being fulfilled by the course taken by this investigation, with its overwhelming emphasis on individual associations and conduct?

The investigation, as revealed by the report, was overwhelmingly and predominantly a roving, self-contained investigation of individual and group behavior, and behavior in a constitutionally protected area. Its whole approach was to name names, disclose information about those named, and observe that "facts are facts." The New Hampshire Supreme Court has upheld the investigation as being a proper legislative inquiry, it is true. . . . In evaluating this, it must be admitted that maintenance of the separation of powers in the States is not, in and of itself, a concern of the Federal Constitution. . . . But for an investigation in the field of the constitutionally protected freedoms of speech and assemblage to be upheld by the broad standards of relevance permissible in a legislative inquiry, some relevance to a valid legislative purpose must be shown, and certainly the ruling made below, that under the state law the Legislature has authorized the inquiry . . . does not conclude the issue here. The bare fact that the Legislature has authorized the inquiry does not mean that the inquiry is for a valid legislative end when viewed in the light of the federal constitutional test we must apply. Nor, while it is entitled to weight, is the determination by a state court that the inquiry relates to a valid legislative end conclusive. It is the task of this Court, as the Court recognizes in theory today, to evaluate the facts to determine if there actually has been demonstrated a valid legislative end to which the inquiry is related. . . . If an investigation or trial, conducted by any organ of the State, which is aimed at the application of sanctions to individual behavior is to be upheld, it must meet the traditional standards that the common law in this country has established for the application of sanctions to the individual, or a constitutionally permissible modification of them. . . . As a bare minimum there must be general standards of conduct, substantively constitutionally proper, applied to the individual in a fair proceeding with defined issues resulting in a binding, final determination. I had not supposed that a legislative investigation of the sort practiced here provided such a framework under the Constitution.

It is not enough to say, as the Court's position I fear may amount to, that what was taking place was an investigation and until the Attorney General and the Legislature had in all the data, the precise shape of the legislative action to be taken was necessarily unknown. Investigation and exposure, in the area which we are here concerned with, are not recognized as self-contained legislative powers in themselves. . . . Since this is so, it hardly fulfills the responsibility with which this Court is charged, of protecting the constitutional rights of freedom of speech and assembly, to admit that an investigation going on indefinitely in time, roving in subject matter, and cumulative in detail in this area can be in aid of a valid legislative end, on the theory that some day it may come to some point. Even the most abusive investigation, the one most totally committed to the constitutionally impermissible end of individual adjudication through publication, could pass such a test. At the stage of this investigation that we are concerned with, it continued to be a cumulative, broad inquiry into the specific details of past individual and associational behavior in the political area. It appears to have been a classic example of "a fruitless investigation into the personal affairs of individuals." . . . Investigation appears to have been a satisfactory end product for the State, but it cannot be so for us in this case as we evaluate the demands of the Constitution. Nor can we accept the legislative renewal of the investigation, or the taking of other legislative measures to facilitate the investigation, as being themselves the legislative justification of the inquiry. The report indicates that it so viewed them; in requesting legislation renewing the investigation and an investigation immunity statute, the Attorney General significantly stated that if the renewal legislation or some investigatory substitute were not passed, it "would mean no further investigation, no continuing check upon Communist activities * * *." This is just to admit the continuing existence of the investigation as a self-contained justification for the inquiry. However much the State may be content to rely on the investigation as its own sanction, I think it perfectly plain that it cannot be regarded as a justification here. . . .

. . . .

This Court's approach to a very similar problem in N.A.A.C.P. v. State of Alabama . . . should furnish a guide to the proper course of decision here. There the State demonstrated a definite purpose which was admittedly within its competence. That purpose was the ascertainment whether a foreign corporation was unlawfully carrying on local activities within Alabama's borders, because not qualified to do business in the manner required by state law. In a judicial proceeding having this as its express stated purpose, the State sought to obtain the membership list of the corporation. This Court carefully recognized the curbing of associational freedom that the disclosure called for by this inquiry would entail. It then analyzed the relationship between the inquiry and this purpose, and, concluding that there was no rational connection, it held the inquiry constitutionally impermissible. Here the situation is even more extreme; there is no demonstration at all of what the legislative purpose is, outside of the investigation of violations, suspicions of violations, and conduct raising some question of violation of an existing statute. It is anomalous to say, as I fear the Court says today, that the vaguer the State's interest is, the more laxly will the Court view the matter and indulge a presumption of the existence of a valid subordinating state interest. In effect, a roving investigation and exposure of past associations and expressions in the political field is upheld because it might lead to some sort of legislation which might be sustained as constitutional, and the entire process is said to become the more defensible rather than the less because of the vagueness of the issues. The Court says that the appellant cannot argue against the exposure because this is an investigation and the exposure may make the investigation lead somewhere, possibly to legislative action. But this is just to say that an investigation, once under state law it is classified as "legislative," needs no showing of purpose beyond its own existence. A start must be made somewhere, and if the principles this Court has announced, and to which the Court today makes some deference, are to have any meaning, it must be up to the State to make some at least plausible disclosure of its lawmaking interest so that the relevance of its inquiries to it may be tested. Then the courts could begin to evaluate the justification for the impact on the individual's rights of freedom of speech and assembly. But here not only has the State failed to begin to elucidate such an interest; it has positively demonstrated, it appears to me, through its Resolution, the Attorney General's and the state courts' interpretation of it, and the Resolution's re-enactment, that what it is interested in is exposure, in lieu of prosecution, and nothing definable else.

. . . .

. . . [*We*] have this in the context of an inquiry which was in practice being conducted in its overwhelming thrust as a vehicle of exposure, and where the practice had been followed of publishing names on the basis of a "not proven" verdict. We are not asked to hold that the State cannot carry on such fact-finding at all, with or without compulsory process. Nor are we asked to hold that as a general matter compulsory process cannot be used to amass facts whose initial relevance to an ultimate legislative interest may be remote. . . . We deal with a narrow and more subtle problem. We deal here with inquiries into the areas of free speech and assemblage where the process of compulsory disclosure itself tends to have a repressive effect. . . . We deal only with the power of the State to *compel* such a disclosure. We are asked, in this narrow context, only to give meaning to our statement in Watkins v. United States, . . . "that the mere semblance of a legislative purpose would not justify an inquiry in the face of the Bill of Rights." Here we must demand some initial showing by the State sufficient to counterbalance the interest in privacy as it relates to freedom of speech and assembly. On any basis that has practical meaning, New Hampshire has not made such a showing here. I would reverse the judgment of the New Hampshire Supreme Court.

Mr. Justice BLACK, and Mr. Justice DOUGLAS would decide this case on the ground that appellant is being deprived of rights under the First and Fourteenth Amendments. . . . But they join Mr. Justice BRENNAN'S dissent because he makes clear to them that New Hampshire's legislative program resulting in the incarceration of appellant for contempt violates Art. I, § 10 of the Constitution which provides that "No state shall * * * pass any bill of attainder." . . .

PRENTISS v. NATIONAL AIRLINES

UNITED STATES DISTRICT COURT
DISTRICT OF NEW JERSEY
112 F. SUPP. 306 (1953)

A New Jersey law provided that "the owner of every aircraft which is operated over the land or waters of this state is absolutely liable for injuries to persons or property on the land or water beneath, caused by ascent, descent, or flight of the aircraft, or the dropping or falling of any object therefrom, whether such owner was negligent or not, unless the injury is caused in whole or in part by the negligence of the person injured, or of the owner . . . of the property injured. . . ." In 1951–52, as a result of three plane crashes at Elizabeth, New Jersey, a host of cases were brought against the airline owners of the planes for deaths, personal injuries, and property damage caused to people and property on the ground where the planes crashed. In these suits, the airlines attempted to defend themselves chiefly on the basis that they had not been negligent. Since the language of the New Jersey statute made the owner liable whether he was negligent or not, such a defense by itself could hardly be effective. Consequently, in the Federal district court of New Jersey the airlines contended that the statute was invalid in that it violated the United States Constitution in two particulars (1) it deprived them of property without due process and (2) it constituted an attempt by a state to regulate interstate commerce. They also contended that the law violated a provision of the New Jersey constitution which states that all persons have an unalienable right "of acquiring, possessing, and protecting property."

Judge HARTSHORNE delivered the opinion of the court.

. . . .

IN DETERMINING the constitutionality of a legislative act, certain fundamental principles must be borne in mind: (a) the question is one, not of legislative policy, but of legislative power. . . . If the legislative branch of the state government has the power under the provisions of both the State and Federal Constitutions, to enact the statute in question, it is not for any court, a part of the judicial authority, co-equal with the legislative, to question such legislation or the wisdom of its exercise. Accordingly, the legislative authority has a wide discretion in the choice of policy to be applied in the governance of the citizenry. As long as this choice is supported by substantial reason and does not violate the fundamental requisites of fairness and justice, the courts cannot declare it invalid, as a violation of due process, even though the soundness of the reasons for such choice seem to the courts quite open to debate. . . .

(b) A statute is always presumed to be valid. . . .

(c) The police power of a state may "prescribe regulations to promote the health, peace, morals, education, and good order of the people, and to legislate so as to increase the industries of the state, develop its resources, and add to its wealth and prosperity." . . . On the other hand, the due process clause simply means procedurally the "law of the land," that is, not all procedural principles, but only those which are truly "fundamental." . . . Thus the interaction between the police power of a state and the due process clause of the Federal Constitution "demands only that the law shall not be unreasonable, arbitrary, or capricious, and that the means selected shall have a real and substantial relation to the object sought to be attained." . . . The inquiry in this regard is simply whether the measure "passes the bounds of reason and assumes the character of a merely arbitrary fiat." . . . Nor may a court invalidate statutes because the court might think that they fail of their purpose, nor because "it might seem to [the court] that they enforce an objectionable policy or inflict hardship in particular instances." . . .

(d) Since, in passing on the constitutionality of a legislative act, the Federal courts are vested with power to consider "cases" and "controversies" they have no power to consider facts other than those involved in the case at bar. Thus the Federal courts are not at liberty to consider purely suppositious facts, presented merely arguendo by counsel, as occurred here, any more than they are authorized to render advisory opinions. . . .

Bearing the above well settled principles in mind, we turn to the consideration of the validity of the above statutory provisions. As to these, defendant owners level their main attack on the ground that the liability of such owners is made absolute, rather than dependent upon negligence. This they claim takes the property of the owners, without due process of law.

In the first place, a reading of the act demonstrates defendants' claim to be too broad. The statute does not make the owner absolutely liable to aircraft passengers, but only "to persons or property on the land or water beneath." In the next place, contributory negligence by plaintiff bars recovery. Again, the "air man" or operator of the aircraft, if not the owner or lessee, is under no circumstances to be held absolutely liable. It is thus clear that the underlying purpose of the act was to place the cost of the dangers of the enterprise upon the industry itself,—a technique, the validity of which is well established by the nation-wide theory of workmen's compensation, for instance,—rather than upon a completely innocent third party, who had never embarked upon such enterprise as had the passenger and the owner, and had no interest in or benefit therefrom. In short, a mere reading of the provisions in question demonstrates not their departure from, but their adoption of, valid legislative techniques, and prima facie at least, reasonable consideration of the varying status of the parties involved.

We pass from this consideration of the statutory terms on their face to a closer scrutiny of the claim of defendant owners that "where a statute imposes absolute liability for an activity which is not extra hazardous, such a statute is invalid as a deprivation of property without due process of law." Taking this claim on its face, it is clearly incorrect. All we need do in this regard is again to turn our attention to the nation-wide policy of workmen's compensation. Here absolute liability is imposed upon practically all businesses, hazardous and non-hazardous alike.

However, not to quibble over mere words, but to go to the heart of the matter, defendants' argument in the present regard must in the end be based upon the proposition either that it is a deprivation of property without due process of law to impose absolute liability at all on any activity, or that it deprives of due process to impose the limited absolute liability set forth in the present statute on the aviation industry. We turn to these two contentions in turn.

From the very earliest records of the history of the common law—the times of Aethelbert and Alfred the Great,—absolute liability was imposed upon one who personally injured another. In fact, the inception of the doctrine of torts was that of absolute liability. On this, practically all common law historians agree. Indeed, the authorities show that negligence was unknown to the law till some thousand years later. Historically, therefore, at common law, absolute liability for torts was from the earliest times not merely recognized as due process of law, it was *the* due process of law.

Furthermore, that absolute liability is recognized today as due process of law, we have on the highest authority. In Crowell v. Benson, 1932, 285 U.S. 22, the highest court in the land said: "the power, under proper circumstances, to provide for liability without fault. * * * is beyond question." . . . the same court said: "liability without fault is not a novelty in the law. The common-law liability of the carrier, of the inn-keeper, or him who employed fire or other dangerous agency or harbored a mischievous animal, was not dependent altogether upon questions of fault or negligence. Statutes imposing liability without fault have been sustained. * * *." . . . The doctrine of absolute liability was well recognized in New Jersey long before the enactment of the statute in question. There can be no question, then, that absolute liability is not per se invalid.

Defendants' final contention on this ground must therefore be that, while absolute liability may at times be imposed, it is unlawful to impose it under the circumstances at bar.

The first question is, whether any action at all by the Legislature was requisite in order to create such liability. The American Law Institute, recognized throughout the United States as our outstanding association of jurists, has this to say as to the aviation industry, and as to those other than passengers who are harmed thereby, "although the utmost care is exercised (by the industry) to prevent the harm.": "Thus, aviation in its present state of development is ultrahazardous, because even the best constructed and maintained aeroplane is so incapable of complete control that flying creates a risk that the plane, even though carefully constructed, maintained and operated, may crash to the injury of persons, structures and chattels on the land over which the flight is made.

"* * * Thus, one of the risks of aviation is that the plane being flown at a high altitude and over a large area may encounter dangerous weather conditions which would be altogether abnormal on the surface of the earth. The chance that the aviator will encounter them is one of the risks which makes aviation an ultrahazardous activity. In this particular, aviation differs from activities which are carried on on the surface of the earth, the safety of which is rarely dependent upon unexpectable weather conditions."

. . . .

If then, limited absolute liability is valid as to aviation at common law, a fortiori such liability is valid when the legislative representatives of the people of the State have declared it to be the public policy and law of the State. For that is the very function entrusted by the Constitution to the keeping of the legislature, subject to the limitation that this determination shall not be a purely arbitrary one, but shall have reason in its support. In other words, to constitute a proper regulation of the rights of all affected by aviation—and this is what the entire statute in question does as to torts, contracts, crimes and property rights—the statute must have a reasonable relation to the public health, welfare and safety. Then, as seen above, it is a proper exercise of the police power. Then, by the same token, it does not deprive of property without due process of law, . . . as to statute covering even passengers on a railroad.

That the provisions of the statute in question do have a reasonable relation to the public welfare would seem clear from what has already been said. Certainly, the New Jersey Legislature, in view of the above evidence as to the ultrahazardous character of the aviation industry, had the right to reach the same conclusion, and to select as applicable to aviation, the very legal policy which the jurists of the American Law Institute, let alone the above legal aviation expert, deemed the soundest and fairest of all applicable policies.

Indeed, there are additional reasons why this choice of policy by the New Jersey Legislature bears a reasonable relation to the public welfare, thus validating the legislative choice as a proper exercise of the police power. . . . [*Dean John H. Wigmore has found*], after investigation as to aviation accidents, that "not in twenty per cent of the accidents which have thus far occurred would it have been possible for the plaintiff to find and produce provable evidence of the real cause of the accident." . . .

. . . .

In short, if the statute were not in effect—nor the common law rule above alluded to, and this rule differs in different states—plaintiffs could prove their right to recover in but one-fifth to one-third of their cases. In other words, in the great bulk of such cases, the injured plaintiffs, or their decedents in death cases, though innocent third parties, would be utterly unable to recover for the injury or death which befell them. Surely the Legislature had a right to provide a remedy for this. That such a decision by the Legislature bears a reasonable relation to the public welfare is too clear for argument. That the New Jersey Legislature did have this view and that the statutory provisions in question are considered valid by the State courts in New Jersey is indicated prima facie from the decision in the Bergen County Court of Common Pleas in the case of Kirschner v. Jones & White, 1932 U.S. Av.Rep. 278, where, after the enactment of the statute in question, the court sustained a verdict for plaintiff in a case where defendant's plane crashed on the roof of plaintiff's home—a situation practically on all fours with the cases at bar. This case is indeed the only known decision so far interpreting the statutory provisions in question.

Defendants' attack upon the validity of the above statutory provisions, as a deprival of property without due process, thus fails.

The provisions of the New Jersey Constitution, on which defendants rely, Art. I, § 1, are substantially identic today with the provisions of the New Jersey Constitution of 1844, immediately preceding the present State Constitution. These provisions were interpreted by the highest New Jersey State court to be equivalent to the due process clause of the Federal Constitution. . . . Hence defendants' reliance on the above provisions of the New Jersey Constitution is equally without merit.

Defendants further attack the validity of these statutory provisions as an invalid restraint upon interstate commerce. The statutory provisions in question clearly show that:

(1) They do not affect the actual movement of airplanes in interstate commerce.

(2) They do not affect the average airplane, even financially, as would a tax.

(3) They only affect an airplane owner financially on the occurrence of an accident. Such an accident the defendant owners will certainly agree is not the ordinary result of air travel.

(4) The benefit of the statutory provisions does not go to any one who in any wise participates in such air travel, such as passengers, but only to those who are, under ordinary circumstances, entire strangers to air travel, and who are totally without fault themselves.

It is obvious from the above that the effect of the above statutory provisions on interstate commerce is indirect and casual. It is equally obvious that the effect of such statutory provisions on the public welfare has the clearest of reason in its support, and is a rational exercise of the police power. The principle has been settled in a host of cases that if a statute is a proper exercise of the police power, and has but an indirect effect upon interstate commerce, it is not an invalid interference with interstate commerce.

The few authorities cited by defendants as in their support are so dissimilar in fact as not to be analogous. Nor do the statutory provisions in question conflict with Congressional control of interstate commerce. The field covered by them is entirely different from that covered by the Civil Aeronautics Act of 1938. . . .

Defendants' claim that the statutory provisions in question are invalid as an unreasonable burden on interstate commerce is thus insubstantial.

Since defendants' attack on the statutory provisions in question, as unconstitutional are found to be without merit, plaintiffs motion to strike the defenses barred by the New Jersey Act . . . is granted. On the motions for summary judgment . . . counsel will be heard further, on motion, if desired. Counsel will present forms of order accordingly in all cases here involved.

LAMBERT v. CALIFORNIA

UNITED STATES SUPREME COURT

355 U.S. 225 (1957)

A provision of the Los Angeles Municipal Code made it unlawful for "any convicted person" to be or remain in the city for more than five days without registering with the chief of police. Further, a provision of the Code made failure to register each day a separate offense.

When Virginia Lambert, who had been previously convicted for forgery, was arrested on suspicion for another offense, she was charged with violation of the registration law. Later, she was convicted in a California court, fined $250, and placed on probation for three years. She appealed the case to the appellate department of the superior court of California, asserting that the provision of the Code under which she had been convicted violated the due process clause of the United States Constitution. That court decided that there was no merit to her claim, and she then appealed to the United States Supreme Court.

Mr. Justice DOUGLAS delivered the opinion of the Court.

. . . .

THE registration provision, carrying criminal penalties, applies if a person has been convicted "of an offense punishable as a felony in the State of California" or, in case he has been convicted in another State, if the offense "would have been punishable as a felony" had it been committed in California. No element of willfulness is by terms included in the ordinance nor read into it by the California court as a condition necessary for a conviction.

We must assume that appellant had no actual knowledge of the requirement that she register under this ordinance, as she offered proof of this defense which was refused. The question is whether a registration act of this character violates due process where it is applied to a person who has no actual knowledge of his duty to register, and where no showing is made of the probability of such knowledge.

We do not go with Blackstone in saying that "a vicious will" is necessary to constitute a crime, . . . for conduct alone without regard to the intent of the doer is often sufficient. There is wide latitude in the lawmakers to declare an offense and to exclude elements of knowledge and diligence from its definition. . . . But we deal here with conduct that is wholly passive—mere failure to register. It is unlike the commission of acts, or the failure to act under circumstances that should alert the doer to the consequences of his deed. . . . The rule that "ignorance of the law will not excuse" . . . is deep in our law, as is the principle that of all the powers of local government, the police power is "one of the least limitable." . . . On the other hand, due process places some limits on its exercise. Engrained in our concept of Due Process is the requirement of notice. Notice is sometimes essential so that the citizen has the chance to defend charges. Notice is required before property interests are disturbed, before assessments are made, before penalties are assessed. Notice is required in a myriad of situations where a penalty or forfeiture might be suffered for mere failure to act. . . . These cases involved only property interests in civil litigation. But the principle is equally appropriate where a person, wholly passive and unaware of any wrongdoing, is brought to the bar of justice for condemnation in a criminal case.

Registration laws are common and their range is wide. . . . Many such laws are akin to licensing statutes in that they pertain to the regulation of business activities. But the present ordinance is entirely different. Violation of its provisions is unaccompanied by any activity whatever, mere presence in the city being the test. Moreover, circumstances which might move one to inquire as to the necessity of registration are completely lacking. At most the ordinance is but a law enforcement technique designed for the convenience of law enforcement agencies through which a list of the names and addresses of felons then residing in a given community is compiled. The disclosure is merely a compilation of former convictions already publicly recorded in the jurisdiction where obtained. Nevertheless, this appellant on first becoming aware of her duty to register was given no opportunity to comply with the law and avoid its penalty, even though her default was entirely innocent. She could but suffer the consequences of the ordinance, namely, conviction with the imposition of heavy criminal penalties thereunder. We believe that actual knowledge of the duty to register or proof of the probability of such knowledge and subsequent failure to comply are necessary before a conviction under the ordinance can stand. As Holmes wrote in The Common Law, "A law which punished conduct which would not be blameworthy in the average member of the community would be too severe for that community to bear." . . . Its severity lies in the absence of an opportunity either to avoid the consequences of the law or to defend any prosecution brought under it. Where a person did not know of the duty to register and where there was no proof of the probability of such knowledge, he may not be convicted consistently with due process. Were it otherwise, the evil would be as great as it is when the law is written in print too fine to read or in a language foreign to the community.

Reversed.

Mr. Justice BURTON, dissents because he believes that, as applied to this appellant, the ordinance does not violate her constitutional rights.

Mr. Justice FRANKFURTER, whom Mr. Justice HARLAN and Mr. Justice WHITTAKER join, dissenting.

The present laws of the United States and of the forty-eight States are thick with provisions that command that some things not be done and others be done, although persons convicted under such provisions may have had no awareness of what the law required or that what they did was wrongdoing. The body of decisions sustaining such legislation, including innumerable registration laws, is almost as voluminous as the legislation itself. The matter is summarized in United States v. Balint, 258 U.S. 250: "Many instances of this are to be found in regulatory measures in the exercise of what is called the police power where the emphasis of the statute is evidently upon achievement of some social betterment rather than the punishment of the crimes as in cases of *mala in se*."

Surely there can hardly be a difference as a matter of fairness, of hardship, or of justice, if one may invoke it, between the case of a person wholly innocent of wrongdoing, in the sense that he was not remotely conscious of violating any law, who is imprisoned for five years for conduct relating to narcotics, and the case of another person who is placed on probation for three years on condition that she pay $250, for failure, as a local resident, convicted under local law of a felony, to register under a law passed as an exercise of the State's "police power." * Considerations of hardship often lead courts, naturally enough, to attribute to a statute the requirement of a certain mental element—some consciousness of wrongdoing and knowledge of the law's command—as a matter of statutory construction. Then, too, a cruelly disproportionate relation between what the law requires and the sanction for its disobedience may constitute a violation of the Eighth Amendment as a cruel and unusual punishment, and, in respect to the States, even offend the Due Process Clause of the Fourteenth Amendment.

But what the Court here does is to draw a constitutional line between a State's requirement of doing and not doing. What is this but a return to Year Book distinctions between feasance and nonfeasance—a distinction that may have significance in the evolution of common-law notions of liability, but is inadmissible as a line between constitutionality and unconstitutionality. One can be confident that Mr. Justice Holmes would have been the last to draw such a line. What he wrote about "blameworthiness" is worth quoting in its context:

> "It is not intended to deny that criminal liability, as well as civil, is founded

on blameworthiness. Such a denial would shock the moral sense of any civilized community; or, to put it another way, a law which punished conduct which would not be blameworthy in the average member of the community would be too severe for that community to bear." (This passage must be read in the setting of the broader discussion of which it is an essential part. Holmes, The Common Law, at 49–50.)

If the generalization that underlies, and alone can justify, this decision were to be given its relevant scope, a whole volume of the United States Reports would be required to document in detail the legislation in this country that would fall or be impaired. I abstain from entering upon a consideration of such legislation, and adjudications upon it, because I feel confident that the present decision will turn out to be an isolated deviation from the strong current of precedents—a derelict on the waters of the law. Accordingly, I content myself with dissenting.

IN RE OPINION OF THE JUDGES

NEW HAMPSHIRE SUPREME COURT

114 A. 2D 514 (1955)

The legislature of New Hampshire by resolution requested the state supreme court to render an advisory opinion concerning the constitutionality of a bill which would establish an Industrial Park Authority. The following opinion defines the considerable powers which the bill would grant to the Authority. Notice particularly that some of the powers which would have been granted are of a "legislative" nature.

The following answer was returned in a *per curiam* opinion.

. . . .

THE JUSTICES of the Supreme Court make the following reply to your request for advice upon the question of whether the provisions of section 9 of House Bill 424 appear to be in conflict with the Constitution.

House Bill 424 provides for the creation of an Industrial Park Authority, "a body corporate and politic as an agency of the state" through which areas suitable for the development of additional industries and known as industrial parks, together with necessary facilities such as transportation, water and sewage, would be developed, maintained and operated. The authority would have power to acquire, hold and dispose of personal property, to acquire, sell and lease real property, and to collect fees for services made available within the parks. . . . It would also be authorized to expend money to develop, as an industrial park, real property owned by any local development organization having as its primary function the promotion, encouragement and development of industrial growth; and to construct upon any such property not more than one "suitable industrial building." All property owned by the Authority would be exempt from levy and sale on execution and from taxation.

The section to which your inquiry relates would empower the Industrial

Park Authority, in the financing of its development of industrial areas and facilities, to "issue to the state treasurer its notes * * * in an amount outstanding at any one time sufficient to enable the authority to carry out its functions under the act" and authorize the state treasurer "to purchase the notes of the authority," using therefor "any funds over which the state has exclusive control."

An appropriation of public money for a private purpose is forbidden. Legislation resulting in or leading to taxation for such a purpose is equally invalid. A loan of public money, like a pledge of the public credit, creates an obligation which requires or may require money to be raised by taxation and "stands on equal footing with one that is certain to do so." . . . The validity of section 9 depends upon "the essential character of the direct object of the expenditures which must determine [the bill's] validity." . . . The question is whether the expenditures will be primarily of benefit to private persons or private uses, which is forbidden, or whether they will serve public purposes for the accomplishment of which public moneys may properly be used.

The first section of the proposed act declares that there is a state-wide need for the development of additional industry and areas suitable for such development "for the preservation and betterment of the economy of the state and its inhabitants"; that the purpose of the act is to provide such areas "so as to provide and encourage orderly industrial development in the best interests of the state"; and that "the purposes of this act are public." Such legislative declarations would be entitled to weight in construing the statute and in determining whether it promoted a public purpose, even though they would "have no magical quality to make valid that which is invalid." . . . It is the essential characteristics of the bill which must determine its validity, rather than its declared purpose. . . .

The proposed act presents a double aspect in that in some respects it would confer a benefit upon the public and in others would result in benefits to private individuals. Such legislation is not necessarily invalid because individuals as such may profit, nor is it necessarily valid because of benefits provided for the public. . . . As above stated, the question is whether it bears directly and immediately or only remotely and circumstantially upon the public welfare.

The direct object of this bill is to encourage new industrial development in this state by providing suitable areas, buildings and facilities on such terms as will prove attractive to persons wishing to engage in private enterprise. However, under the bill in its present form, "the preservation and betterment of the economy of the state and its inhabitants" which it also seeks to provide might prove to be merely incidental and subsidiary to assistance rendered to private industry, rather than "a promotion of the general welfare which incidentally benefits certain individuals and which is proper." . . . In such a case the public purpose accomplished would be no more than the indirect public advantage which accompanies industrial welfare and general prosperity. The expenditure of public funds under such circumstances, "even if the public advantage takes specific form * * * [would be] a violation of the constitutional principle against taxation for private purposes." . . .

We find in the bill no standard or guide to control the action of the Authority in exercise of its delegated powers in furtherance of the general policy laid down by the Legislature. . . .

. . . .

House Bill 424 makes no provision for determination that particular undertakings by the Authority will serve the public purpose. No method is provided for establishing in a particular instance the fact that the public is not "already adequately served," so that a proposed undertaking will actually be "for the public use and purpose." . . . In the absence of standards to guide and control the action of the Authority in the exercise of its powers, . . . and of provision for "authoritative finding" that a particular undertaking will be within the stated purpose of the act, . . . and not primarily for the benefit of private users. . . . the bill is open to constitutional objection. Hence the provisions of section 9 of the bill must be considered in conflict with the Constitution.

Our opinion is requested and given with respect to the bill in its present form. Consequently it should not be taken to necessarily imply that the bill is incapable of revision to meet constitutional requirements. The need for the proposed legislation and the wisdom of its adoption are matters for the Legislature to determine. . . .

It is our present judgment that section 9, if enacted as a part of House Bill 424 in its present form, would conflict with the Constitution.

STATE v. TRAFFIC TELEPHONE WORKERS' FEDERATION OF NEW JERSEY

NEW JERSEY SUPREME COURT

66 A. 2D 616 (1949)

A highly complex New Jersey law aimed at eliminating strikes in certain public utilities defined, among other things, procedures for compulsory arbitration in management-labor disputes in those industries. Consequently, when members of the Traffic Telephone Workers' Federation went on strike and refused to comply with the provisions of the law on the grounds that the law was for a variety of reasons unconstitutional, the attorney general filed suit in the appropriate state court for a declaratory judgment as to the constitutionality of the law. The lower court held that it was constitutional. The case was brought to the state supreme court for certification of the judgment of the lower court. Although there were several constitutional questions raised in the case, we have only reproduced here those parts of the opinion dealing with the state constitutional question of delegation of power and the non-constitutional question of whether or not telephone companies are public utilities.

Justice VANDERBILT delivered the opinion of the court.

. . . .

. . . IT IS contended that telephone companies are not properly classified with the other public utilities. In the economic and social life of today, however, communication by telephone is a vital and indispensable essential to the health, safety and welfare of the public. Without the almost instantaneous means of communication that the telephone alone furnishes, our system of fire and police protection would be rendered relatively ineffective and the health, safety and indeed the life of the individual citizen would be gravely endangered. It is unrealistic in this day and age to suggest that if the telephone is not available one may send a telegram or a messenger for a physician or a policeman or a fire truck. Any such line of reasoning pressed to its logical conclusion would require the State to surrender all of the advances of modern science for a return to the Stone Age. . . .

. . . .

It is contended . . . that the provisions in the statute providing for compulsory arbitration are unconstitutional, because they delegate legislative power to an administrative agency, without setting up adequate standards to guide the administrative agency in the exercise of the powers delegated to it. The argument has great force. While there is no doubt that the legislature may delegate to an administrative body the exercise of a limited portion of its legislation power with respect to some specific subject matter, such delegation of legislative power must always prescribe the standards that are to govern the administrative agency in the exercise of the powers thus delegated to it. As was said in State Board of Milk Control v. Newark Milk Company, 179 A. 116: "The Legislature indubitably has power to vest a large measure of discretionary authority in the agency charged with the administration of a law, enacted in pursuance of the police power, to secure the health and safety of the people. This authority is one of common exercise; it invokes the principle that sustains rate making laws, and the authority vested in examining and control boards created to regulate the professions, trades, businesses, and other callings, deemed by the law-making body to be the proper subjects of governmental supervision. It is only necessary that the statute establish a sufficient basic standard—a definite and certain policy and rule of action for the guidance of the agency created to administer the law."

. . . If no standards are set up to guide the administrative agency in the exercise of functions conferred on it by the legislature, the legislation is void as passing beyond the legitimate bounds of delegation of legislative power and as constituting a surrender and abdication to an alien body of a power which the Constitution confers on the Senate and General Assembly alone. Nowhere in this act is there any guide furnished to the board of arbitration other than that it shall arbitrate "any and all disputes then existing between the public utility and the employees." . . .

The personnel of the board of arbitration under the statute will vary with each strike. There is no permanence or continuity in the various boards of arbitration which may be constituted in successive cases. There is, thus, an even greater need of specific standards than there would be in the case of a continuous administrative body which might gather experience as it went along. Furthermore, in the absence of standards, the very term "board of arbitration" carries with it the implication that the board will act in the way that arbitrators customarily act, not according to established criteria but according to the ideas of justice or of expedience of the individual arbitrators. Anyone who has had experience with arbitration realizes that this is the inherent weakness of arbitration as a remedy. Unless standards are set up in any submission to arbitration the tendency to compromise and be guided in part by expediency as distinguished from objective considerations and real right is inevitable. This is especially dangerous in the case of an arbitration where the rights of third parties, here the public, are concerned. Any increase in operating costs which may result from the arbitration will inevitably be charged to the public in increased rates. But the board of arbitration is nowhere directed to consider the rights of the public, which will ultimately be called upon to foot the bill. In these circumstances the need of legislative standards is peculiarly apparent.

Standards of delegation are peculiarly required, moreover, where the legislature is enacting a new pattern of social conduct. . . . In Fahey v. Mallonee, 332 U.S. 245 (1947), the United States Supreme Court held the Home Owners Loan Act . . . constitutional, but in doing so recognized that ampler legislative standards would have been desirable and that the absence of such standards would have rendered the act unconstitutional if the provisions under consideration there had been penal in character. In distinguishing the case from the Panama Refining Co. and Schechter cases the Court said: "Both cited cases dealt with delegation of a power to make federal crimes of acts that never had been such before and to devise novel rules of law in a field in which there had been no settled law or custom." . . . The provisions in the act relating to the powers of the board of arbitration are therefore unconstitutional.

The proceedings for compulsory arbitration through the board of arbitration go to the heart of the questioned legislation. Without them it cannot operate. It necessarily follows that the unconstitutional provisions of the statutes are inseparable from those which are otherwise valid. Accordingly, the entire act must be set aside and the judgment below reversed.

HEHER, J., Concurred in the result.

For reversal: Chief Justice VANDERBILT and Justices CASE, HEHER, OLIPHANT, WACHENFELD, BURLING and ACKERSON—7.

For affirmance: None.

COMMONWEALTH v. DIAZ

SUPREME JUDICIAL COURT OF MASSACHUSETTS SUFFOLK

95 N.E. 2D 666 (1950)

The facts in the case are set forth in detail in the opinion.

Justice SPALDING delivered the opinion of the court.

. . . .

ON an appeal from a District Court to the Superior Court the defendant was tried and convicted on a complaint charging a violation of regulations governing the Logan Airport and was sentenced to pay a fine of $25. The regulations involved, which were introduced in evidence, read as follows: "Section II (13). The operator of each taxicab or limousine in the proper line shall, at all times until engaged for hire, remain in the operator's seat and at the wheel of his vehicle, or outside and within six (6) feet of his vehicle, and shall, at no time while outside his vehicle, obstruct vehicular or pedestrian traffic." "Section IV (3): Any person who violates the provisions of these rules and regulations, shall be subject to the penalty not exceeding five hundred

($500.00) dollars for any one offence." The regulations of which these are a part are entitled, "Rules and regulations for the operation of taxicabs, limousines, motor buses, and charter automobiles at General Edward Lawrence Logan Airport established by the State airport management board, pursuant to the provisions of chapter 637, acts of 1948."

The case comes here on the defendant's exception to the denial of his motion for a directed verdict. There was evidence which would warrant a finding that the defendant, an operator of a taxicab, violated the regulations in question. The defendant does not contend otherwise. The ground urged in support of his exception is that the statute from which these regulations stem is an unconstitutional delegation of legislative power. That statute so far as material reads as follows: "The commissioner shall make such rules and regulations, subject to the approval of the board, for the use, operation, and maintenance of state-owned airports as he may from time to time deem reasonable and expedient, which may provide penalties for the violation of said rules and regulations not exceeding five hundred dollars for any one offence." . . These provisions are part of . . . "An Act changing the laws relative to state-owned airports in respect to their management, operation and maintenance and otherwise." The board referred to in the statute is the State airport management board. The commissioner mentioned therein is the commissioner of airport management. The commissioner is appointed by the State board of airport management, with the approval of the Governor and Council, and is "responsible for general supervision of all state-owned airports." . . .

That the Legislature cannot under our Constitution delegate its general power to make laws is so well settled that a citation of authorities is not necessary. That is especially true with respect to its power to define crimes and establish penalties therefor. . . . But one of the exceptions to or qualifications of that doctrine is that the Legislature may delegate to a board or an individual officer the working out of the details of a policy adopted by the Legislature. . . . [As *stated in a previous case:*] "To deny this [power] would be to stop the wheels of government. There are many things upon which wise and useful legislation must depend which cannot be known to the law-making power, and must therefore be a subject of inquiry and determination outside of the halls of legislation." . . . It is on this principle that ordinances and by-laws of municipalities and the regulations of various boards have been upheld. . . . Of course such ordinances or regulations, to be valid, must be within the ambit of the enabling statute. . . . The defendant makes no contention that the substance of the regulations under consideration is not within the scope of the delegated authority. The gist of his argument is that the statute upon which the regulations are based exceeds the limits of what may be lawfully delegated. Here, it is argued, the statute went beyond authorizing the commissioner and the board to work out the details of a policy adopted by the Legislature, and attempted to delegate to them the power to declare what acts shall constitute a criminal offence and to fix the penalties therefor.

. . . we are of opinion that a sufficiently definite legislative mandate is laid down so that the commissioner and board may constitutionally fill in the details and that the authority delegated was not excessive. The power granted to them to make such rules and regulations "for the use, operation, and maintenance of state-owned airports as he may from time to time deem reasonable and expedient" is not essentially different from the power granted by statute to the board of metropolitan park commissioners which was upheld in Brodbine v. Revere, 66 N.E. 607. There the board were given authority to "make rules and regulations for the government and use of the roadways or boulevards under its care, breaches whereof shall be breaches of the peace, punishable as such in any court having jurisdiction of the same." . . .

The fact that the statute empowered the commissioner, subject to the board's approval, to provide penalties for the violation of the regulations did not render it invalid. This is not a case where the statute authorized the commissioner to fix such penalties as he saw fit. Had the statute attempted to do that we have no doubt that it would have been an excessive delegation of power. . . . But the statute here did not do that; it empowered the commissioner, subject to the board's approval, to "provide penalties for the violation of said rules and regulations not exceeding five hundred dollars for any one offence." While the commissioner could prescribe penalties he could do so only within limits definitely prescribed by the Legislature.

In some instances where a local governing body or board is authorized to make regulations the penalty is fixed by the statute itself. . . .

But penalties attaching to the violation of regulations are not always fixed in this manner. Frequently, as here, the local governing body or board is empowered to prescribe the penalties within limits prescribed by the Legislature. . . . Thus it would appear that the practice of authorizing a municipality or board to fix penalties within definite limits is one of long standing in this Commonwealth and we know of no case decided by this court where it has been held to be objectionable.

It is true that in the instances mentioned above the power to prescribe penalties was within narrower limits than those granted here. It is one thing to give to a board or municipality power to fix penalties not in excess of $20 or even $100 and quite another to empower it to fix them up to $500. The authority which may be granted to a local governing body to fix penalties, even when a maximum limit is prescribed, is not unrestricted. Such bodies cannot be granted a roving commission to establish within broad limits such penalties as they see fit. That is essentially a legislative power which cannot be delegated. The question is one of degree. The "use, operation, and maintenance of state-owned airports" could conceivably necessitate rules and regulations relating to much more hazardous activities than those arising from the operation of taxicabs and limousines. The power to determine penalties granted to the commissioner here goes to the very verge of what is permissible, but we are not prepared to say that it crosses the line.

While the statute is not invalid, for the reasons discussed above, we are disposed to hold otherwise with respect to the regulation here involved, or at least so much of it as prescribes the penalty. Where authority is granted to a local governing body to work out the details of a legislative policy—even the broad authority given here: to make such rules and regulations "as * * * [the commissioner] may from time to time deem reasonable and expedient" —the power must not be exercised arbitrarily. In other words, the rules and regulations must be reasonable. . . .

Here it cannot be said that that portion of the regulation which defines the offence is unreasonable. The vice of it lies in that part which fixes the penalty. Had the Legislature intended that a penalty not to exceed $500 was to attach to every violation of the regulations to be promulgated it would have said so and would not have delegated, as it did here, the power to provide the penalty. In view of the numerous types of activities that must necessarily be regulated, and the wide difference in the seriousness of the various offences, it is reasonable to suppose that the Legislature contemplated that the penalties would not be the same for all offences and that the commissioner and board would exercise a reasonable and sound discretion in prescribing punishment that would fit the crime. This duty was not discharged here. By section IV (3) of the regulation the commissioner and board have in effect said that every violation, irrespective of its seriousness, shall carry a penalty not exceeding $500. Thus the defendant in the case at bar, because he was more than six feet from his taxicab while it was in line, is subjected to that penalty. This we think is not reasonable and far exceeds penalties generally prescribed by the Legislature for cognate offences. . . . We do not undertake to say what penalty should be prescribed for the offence here involved. That duty rests with the commissioner and the board, and is not a judicial function. We hold only that the regulation under consideration by reason of the penalty attaching to it was in excess of the commissioner's authority and is invalid.

We recognize that the defendant here was fined $25 rather than the maximum of $500, but that does not validate the conviction. The reasonableness of the regulation is to be tested by what can happen under it rather than by what actually did happen. . . . The fortuitous circumstance that a reasonable penalty was imposed by the court did not render the regulation valid and deprive the defendant of his right to challenge it. We also recognize that the ground on which we have held the regulation invalid is not the ground urged by the defendant, but that is immaterial. In substance he has challenged the law under which he was convicted and he is entitled not to be sentenced on a law that is invalid.

It follows that the defendant's exception to the denial of his motion for a directed verdict must be sustained.

So ordered.

SOUTH CAROLINA STATE HIGHWAY DEPARTMENT v. HARBIN

SOUTH CAROLINA SUPREME COURT

86 S.E. 2D 466 (1955)

Under an act of the state legislature empowering it to refuse, suspend, or revoke a driver's license, the South Carolina highway department established a point system for driving violations. The department reserved the right, after a hearing, to suspend an offender's license for six months if he received a prescribed number of points. In the course of a few months, Harbin, the defendant in this case, garnered enough points through traffic violations to exceed the allowed maximum. When his license was suspended, he petitioned the appropriate state court for a review of his suspension contending that the department did not have the power to put the point system into effect. He was upheld in the lower court. The highway department then petitioned to the state supreme court to review the decision of the lower court.

Justice OXNER delivered the opinion of the court.

. . . .

THE DEPARTMENT contends that the broad authority to suspend or revoke a license for a period of not more than a year for any cause which it deems satisfactory, . . . together with the authority to promote rules and regulations . . . fully empowers it to set up the "Point System," which it says embodies reasonable criteria to be used in the exercise of its discretionary power. It argues that all of the violations mentioned therein have a direct bearing on safety in the use of the highways and that the "Point System" is in accordance with the legislative policy.

Harbin asserts that [*the law*] fixes no standard and lays down no intelligible guide to which the Department must conform but leaves the right to revoke or suspend in its unrestricted and uncontrolled discretion, rendering said section void as an unconstitutional delegation of legislative power. In addition to attacking the constitutionality of the provision empowering the Highway Department to suspend a license "for cause satisfactory" to it, he challenges the reasonableness of some of the points and says that several others are contrary to legislative enactments. He points out that under this regulation a license may be suspended for five "warnings" given by a traffic officer, with no opportunity on the part of the driver to contest the justification for such warnings or to be heard on the question as to whether he has violated a traffic regulation, thereby making it possible to revoke a license at the whim or caprice of such officer. Attention is also called to the fact that for driving under the influence of intoxicants, a charge of 10 points is made, enabling the Department to suspend for a period of one year for a first offense, while the statute, . . . limits the suspension for a first offense to six months. Further illustrating his contention that the "Point System" goes beyond legislative sanction, it is said that the Department may suspend for one year for two acts of reckless driving, while . . . the 1952 Code limits the suspension to three months for the second offense of reckless driving.

Although there may be considerable merit in the attack on the reasonableness and validity of several of the items in the "Point System," we find it unnecessary to pass upon this phase of the matter and will proceed to decide the basic question of whether the power given the Department by [*the law*] is unconstitutional upon the ground that suspension or revocation is left to the absolute, unregulated, and undefined discretion of the Department.

The question of delegation of legislative power has confronted the courts with many perplexing problems, particularly during recent years when the complexities of government have been constantly on the increase. It is well settled that while the legislature may not delegate its power to make laws, in enacting a law complete in itself, it may authorize an administrative agency or board "to fill up the details" by prescribing rules and regulations for the complete operation and enforcement of the law within its expressed general purpose. . . . [*As another court said:*] "However, it is necessary that the statute declare a legislative policy, establish primary standards for carrying it out, or lay down an intelligible principle to which the administrative officer or body must conform, with a proper regard for the protection of the public interests and with such degree of certainty as the nature of the case permits, and enjoin a procedure under which, by appeal or otherwise, both public interests and private rights shall have due consideration." . . .

The difficulty is in the application of these general principles, for there is no fixed formula for determining the powers which must be exercised by the legislature itself and those which may be delegated to an administrative agency. The degree to which a legislative body must specify its policies and standards in order that the administrative authority granted may not be an unconstitutional delegation of its own legislative power is not capable of precise definition. . . .

A license to operate a motor vehicle is not a property right but a mere privilege which is subject to reasonable regulations under the police power in the interest of public safety and welfare. Such privilege is always subject to revocation or suspension for any cause having to do with public safety, but cannot be revoked arbitrarily or capriciously.

When the authority of the State Highway Department to suspend or revoke a license for any cause which it deems satisfactory is considered in the light of the foregoing principles, said provision must be declared invalid as an unlawful delegation of legislative power. It sets up no standard to guide the Department and contains no limitations. As a general rule, "A statute which in effect reposes an absolute, unregulated, and undefined discretion in an administrative body bestows arbitrary powers and is an unlawful delegation of legislative powers." 42 Am.Jur., page 343. We have held invalid ordinances attempting to vest such arbitrary powers in municipal authorities. . . .

It is suggested that there is no reason to suppose that the Department will revoke a license arbitrarily or capriciously and that it may fairly be assumed that this will only be done when necessary for the safety of the public. But this constitutes no answer to the question of whether there is an unlawful delegation of legislative power. "When courts are considering the constitutionality of an act, they should take into consideration the things which the act affirmatively permits, and not what action an administrative officer may or may not take." Northern Cedar Co. v. French, 230 P. 837. "The presumption that an officer will not act arbitrarily but will exercise sound judgment and good faith cannot sustain a delegation of unregulated discretion." 42 Am.Jur., Public Administrative Law, Section 45.

In oral argument counsel for the Department conceded that there was considerable doubt as to the validity of the power granted by [*the law*] if considered alone, but contended that the act as a whole establishes a clear legislative policy governing the Highway Department in the exercise of its discretionary power to suspend or revoke a license. It is said that the general purpose of the Act is to deny a driver's license to those who by reason of physical or mental affliction are unfit to operate a motor vehicle, and to revoke the licenses of those who by their negligent or reckless acts indicate a disregard for the safety of others on the highways, from which it is argued that the discretion given the Department can only be exercised for a cause having to do with public safety. But we are not at liberty to add such a limitation to the clear and unambiguous language of . . . [*the law*]. [*In the law*] . . . suspension is made mandatory for certain causes. Discretionary authority is then given the Department to suspend or revoke a license for certain other causes, including physical or mental infirmities, negligent operation of a motor vehicle causing death or injury to any person or serious damage to property, and habitual negligent or reckless driving. . . . it was evidently intended to give the Department the right to revoke for causes other than those which had been expressly provided for. And in the grant of this authority, there is no standard except the personal judgment of the administrative officers of the Department.

Our conclusion that . . . [*the law*] contains an unconstitutional delegation of legislative power is fully sustained by Thompson v. Smith, 154 S.E. 579. In a well considered opinion the Court there held invalid an ordinance of the City of Lynchburg which, after providing for mandatory suspension of licenses for certain causes, authorized the Chief of Police "to revoke the permit of any driver who, in his opinion, becomes unfit to drive an automobile on the streets of the city, * * *." The Court concluded that the right to drive an automobile may not be left to the arbitrary and uncontrolled discretion of the Chief of Police.

. . . .

Having concluded that the provision of the 1952 Code authorizing the Highway Department to suspend or revoke a driver's license "for cause satisfactory" to it, is an unconstitutional delegation of legislative power, it follows that the Department was without authority to adopt the "Point System." We are not now called upon to determine the difficult question of whether such power may be delegated to said agency. There can be no doubt that the Legislature, which under its police power has full authority in the interest of public safety to prescribe conditions under which the privilege to operate a motor vehicle may be granted and upon which such privilege will be revoked, may make the violation of traffic regulations, or other cause having to do with public safety, the basis for the revocation or suspension of a driver's license, and may prescribe the relative weight to be given to the violation of any statute or ordinance regulating traffic. But whether the power to evaluate such violation may be committed to an administrative agency presents a serious question not involved or argued on this appeal, and which we leave undecided.

We find no error in the order under review. It is affirmed.

BAKER, C. J., and STUKES, TAYLOR and LEGGE, JJ., concur.

CHAPTER FOUR

Executive Power

PARADOXICALLY, EVEN though the executive branch of our respective American governments has come to participate more and more in the lawmaking process, the traditional powers of the executive (to execute and administer the laws) have been sharply circumscribed by state constitutions, law, and judicial decisions. The office of governor in most states does not carry with it the same degree of executive power as resides in the office of the President. The reasons for this are largely historical. The office of governor was realized in the period after the Declaration of Independence and *before* the writing of the Constitution. During this period the prototype of a governor was the royal governor who represented an unpopular institution. It is no wonder that the earliest state constitutions, therefore, limited executive power markedly. In setting up state governments in later periods, there was a pronounced tendency to look upon the established state governments as models. Consequently, the office of governor has tended to be weak in most of our states.

Notice how we have stressed the constitutional limitations on the governor's office. The reason for this emphasis is that *in practice* some governors have been able to exercise vast executive power in spite of apparent limitations. This has been possible when either legislatures or courts have sanctioned such exercise specifically or, frequently, when no one with power or standing to do so saw fit to challenge such exercise of power. The important and complex point we are trying to make is that, although executive power tends to be broadened constantly, when it is challenged, the legal limitations on the state level are such that executive power can be thwarted more easily on that level than on the national level. Unfortunately, state courts do not act any more uniformly in these matters than they do in any other. Consequently, state court decisions dealing with executive power face in different directions. Again, the cases offered for your consideration are important not because they indicate with exactness what the law on the subject is, but rather because they indicate the important issues involved in determining the limits of executive power.

A. *The Writ of Mandamus in State and Federal Courts*

1. THE POWER OF STATE COURTS TO MANDAMUS THE GOVERNOR

If a government is to be a government of laws and not of men, it follows that officers of the government must execute and enforce the laws whether they want to or not. If this be the case, then the law must provide a way for forcing an official to carry out the provisions of a law even if the official does not want to do so. For example, if a state law provides that all veterans are to receive a bonus of $200 and the governor or state treasurer decides he is against it and will not authorize payment, should there not be a remedy at law to make the public officials do what the law provides? In the old common law, there grew up the concept that a person should be able to go to court and get a court order requiring a public official's performance of duty. To do so, under the common law, the person asked the court for a writ of *mandamus*, which was simply a writ issued to enforce the performance of some public duty. The common law use of such writs was carried over to American state law. But there has been one difficulty in the American political system which the British system did not and does not have to contend with—the concept of separation of powers. As you know, the British system does not pay the same reverence to the separation principle as ours does. Would not a decent respect for the principle of separation of powers preclude the judiciary from instructing officers of the executive branch how to perform their executive duties? In any case, state courts have uniformly held that the separation of powers principle does not prevent them from issuing a *mandamus* to all state executive officers save the governor. As to the power to *mandamus* a governor, the state courts go in two directions as the opinion in *Jenkins* v. *Knight* (p. 216) so well demonstrates.

In deciding whether or not to issue a writ of *mandamus* to any executive officer, the courts have traditionally made a distinction between "ministerial" and "discretionary" legal duties. A "ministerial" duty is simply, as the Supreme Court stated many years ago, "one in which nothing is left to discretion." Quite logically, a "discretionary" duty is one where the executive officer is expected to use some discretion about performance of the duty. The courts have held throughout our history that they can require an official by *mandamus* to perform a ministerial duty but not a discretionary one. When a state court feels it does have the power to *mandamus* a governor, it will not compel the governor to perform what it regards as a discretionary duty. Unfortunately, the distinction between ministerial and discretionary duties is not always clear-cut. As two renowned professors of law have stated:

> In mandamus it is said that the remedy lies only where the action to be commanded is "ministerial" or involves no element of "discretion." Another form of this idea is that the court can command the officer only if there is a "clear legal duty." The notion that each administrative act can be classified a priori either as

"ministerial" or "discretionary" is unsound and unworkable. If the mandamus cases in any one state are studied as a body, it will be found impossible to reconcile the decisions simply by assigning acts to one or the other class. The classification is illusory: it is apt to label the result rather than explain it. But in some cases its undiscriminating application excludes adequate judicial control. The short of the matter is this. Discretion is the power to make a choice between competing considerations. All powers to act admit on the one hand some elements of choice if only as to the manner of detail. On the other hand, nearly all powers to act, however numerous and broad the considerations relevant to choice, exclude and deny the legality of other elements as factors of choice.[1]

2. MANDAMUS AND THE FEDERAL COURTS

Because so many misconceptions about the use of *mandamus* on the state level arise from faulty knowledge about the use of *mandamus* in Federal courts, we feel it is important to deal briefly with the use of *mandamus* in the Federal courts. From 1813 until 1962, it was held that the Federal district courts except the district court for the District of Columbia did not have the power under common law to issue a writ of *mandamus*. The reason historically employed for such a finding was that the Federal government was a government of limited and enumerated powers and that the Federal courts have only the specific powers granted to them by the Constitution and Congress. The Constitution contains no provision granting Federal courts the power to issue writs of *mandamus* or granting them powers which state courts derive from the common law. Congress had at times in our earlier history given other Federal courts the power in certain types of cases. The reason that the district court for the District of Columbia was held to have the power to issue the writ was because that court inherited the power from the Maryland courts, whose common law remained in force in that part of its territory which became the District of Columbia. In 1948, Rule 81(b) of the Federal Rules of Civil Procedure was adopted which abolished specifically the writ of *mandamus* but the rule provided that: "Relief here-to-fore available by mandamus . . . may be obtained by appropriate motion under the practice prescribed in these rules." And in 1962, Congress granted *all* district courts "original jurisdiction at any action in the nature of *mandamus* to compel an officer or employee of the United States . . . to perform a duty owed the plantiff." Therefore, although it is technically correct to state that most Federal courts could not from 1813 to 1962 issue writs of *mandamus* and that since 1948 the writ has been abolished as to Federal courts, these courts have actually and still do prescribe remedies, such as the mandatory injunction, which are not technically writs of *mandamus* but do serve nearly the same purpose. The subject of the Federal courts' power in this respect is too complex to investigate fully at this point. However, it is important to know that despite the specific prohibition against the use of the writ, Federal

[1] Louis L. Jaffe and Nathaniel L. Nathanson, *Administrative Law* (Boston: Little, Brown and Co., 1961), p. 790. Reprinted with permission.

courts do at times provide remedies which accomplish the same result as they would by use of the writ.

Throughout our history, appropriate Federal courts have compelled all manner of Federal executives, except the President himself, to perform duties the courts regarded as ministerial, the concept of separation of powers to the contrary.

It is important to emphasize that no Federal court has ever tried to *mandamus* the President. At least since the hallmark case of *Mississippi* v. *Johnson,* 4 Wall. 475 (1867), it has been accepted as a matter of law that courts cannot compel the President to act or to keep him from acting even though his acts once performed may in proper cases be subject to judicial review. In that case, in which an action was sought to *restrain* President Johnson from carrying out acts of Congress, the Supreme Court specifically indicated that it was not deciding the question of whether courts could *mandamus* the President: "We shall limit our inquiry to the question presented by the objection, without expressing any opinion on the broader issues discussed by the argument, whether, in any case, the President of the United States may be required by the process of this court to perform a purely ministerial act under a positive law, or may be held amenable, in any case, otherwise than by impeachment for a crime." But in reaching its decision the Court said: "The Congress is the legislative department of the government; the President is the executive department. Neither can be restrained in its action by the judicial department; though the acts of both when performed, are, in proper cases, subject to its cognizance. The impropriety of such interference will be clearly seen upon consideration of its possible consequences. . . ." By way of dicta, the Court indicated that the same principle would hold were a *mandamus* involved. In short, it would seem safe to assert that courts cannot, or at least will not, attempt to *mandamus* the President. This has led some people to believe that by analogy state courts cannot *mandamus* a governor. As already pointed out, the courts of a substantial number of our states do not accept this view.

At this point, the question arises as to whether or not Federal courts can *mandamus* state officials. The answer is that where Federal law gives state officials ministerial duties to perform and they fail to perform them, redress may be sought in the appropriate Federal court and a remedy in the nature of a *mandamus* may be granted. By the nature of things, this rarely happens because very few Federal statutes prescribe duties for state officers. This discussion may raise the further question in your mind as to whether or not the appropriate Federal court could *mandamus* a governor. The Supreme Court in 1861 decided in *Kentucky* v. *Dennison,* 24 How. 66, that the law passed by Congress requiring governors to deliver up fugitives from justice placed only a moral duty on the governors, for the national government "has no power to impose on a State officer, as such, any duty whatever, and compel him to perform it." Since that time, Federal courts have found occasion to *enjoin* governors on the ground that what they were doing violated the national Constitution. This would suggest that there is no reason on the grounds of federalism or separation of powers to prevent a Federal court from reaching a governor with its processes in an appropriate case as in the situation involving Governor Barnett of Mississippi in 1962. Yet it is difficult to conceive of a practical situation wherein a Federal court would have occasion to compel a governor to perform a ministerial duty which Federal law constitutionally confers upon him. Could a Federal court order a governor himself to integrate the schools in order to achieve compliance with the Supreme Court's decision? Undoubtedly, the answer is no, because no law Federal or state confers responsibility on the governor of any state to run the school system. But Federal courts can order and have ordered appropriate state officials to *refrain from* doing something in such a way as to constitute, practically, an order *to do* something. The best example of this is the order which the United States Court of Appeals for the Fifth Circuit issued to keep Mississippi officials *from* preventing James Meredith from attending classes at the University of Mississippi:

> It is ordered that the State of Mississippi, Ross R. Barnett . . . [and a number of other state officials] their agents, employees, officers, successors, and all persons in active concert or participation with them, be temporarily restrained from:
>
> 1. Arresting, attempting to arrest, prosecuting or instituting any prosecution against James Howard Meredith under any statute, ordinance, rule, or regulation whatever, on account of his attending, or seeking to attend the University of Mississippi;
>
> 2. Instituting or proceeding further in any civil action against James Howard Meredith or any other persons on account of James Howard Meredith's enrolling or seeking to enroll, or attending the University of Mississippi;
>
> 3. Injuring, harassing, threatening, or intimidating James Howard Meredith in any other way or by any other means on account of his attending or seeking to attend the University of Mississippi;
>
> 4. Interfering with or obstructing by any means or in any manner the performance of obligations or the enjoyment of rights under this court's order of July 28, 1962, and the order of the United States District Court for the Southern District of Mississippi entered September 13, 1962, in this action; and
>
> 5. Interfering with or obstructing, by force, threat, arrest or otherwise, any officer or agent of the United States in the performance of duties in connection with the enforcement of, and the prevention of obstruction to, the orders entered by this court and the District Court . . . relating to the enrollment and attendance of James Howard Meredith at the University of Mississippi. . . .

A few days later, after Governor Barnett issued two proclamations, one ordering state law enforcement officials "to do all things necessary that the peace and security of the people of the State of Mississippi are fully protected," and another to Meredith proclaiming that "I Ross R. Barnett . . . do hereby finally deny you admission to the University of Mississippi," the court found the governor in contempt of the restraining order. But note carefully that the order directed officials as to what they must refrain from doing, that it was not an order in the nature of a *mandamus* directing them to take positive action of some kind. Legally, there is a difference, but do you see any difference in fact? [2]

Despite the fact that we have ranged far and wide in our discussion to acquaint you with the many issues involved, we want you, when reading *Jenkins* v. *Knight* (p. 216), to address yourself to this question, Should a governor be amenable to *mandamus* by state courts even as to ministerial duties?

B. Problems Arising from a Governor's Disability

One of the most fascinating questions in American government is what can be done practically to replace a governor when he is unable to perform his duties because of illness or injury. Generally, constitutions provide for a succession to office when the governor is disabled, but they do not specify a procedure for determining when the governor is disabled. If a governor admits he is disabled and provides for interim relief, there is no great difficulty. But, what would happen if the governor or those around him were unwilling to concede that he is disabled? Not too long ago, we were provided with the spectacle of a governor who apparently was mentally ill but unable to discern his own illness. He remained in office until the end of his term. You might well wonder how such a thing could happen. What you must remember is that to some the stakes are very high when it comes to who controls the office of governor. There may be politically powerful persons who believe that it is in their own interests (and, as they see it, in the public interest) to retain a disabled governor rather than have the officer in line succeed, particularly if they feel the successor will be unsympathetic to their objectives. For those who would seek to relieve a disabled governor, there are all kinds of political pitfalls. Suppose they charge accurately that the governor is mentally ill; shrewd politicians may be able to make it appear that the charge is a scurrilous attack not meriting serious consideration and refuse to permit examination. Or, if the governor is physically ill, they can minimize the seriousness of the illness and make it appear that heartless political enemies are just attempting to force the man out of office. Consequently, we have never discovered a successful method of determining when a governor should be replaced for disability. To get a perspective on these difficulties, recall the problem we have had with some of our Presidents. In the present century, four Presidents have lain gravely ill, Wilson, Harding, Franklin Roosevelt, and Eisenhower. In each case, nothing was done to replace the President while he was unable to function. After his illness, President Eisenhower drew up an agreement with his Vice-President indicating under what conditions Mr. Nixon would take over for Mr. Eisenhower and under what conditions Mr. Eisenhower would take back the reins. President Kennedy has followed suit and made essentially the same agreement with Vice-President

[2] For an excellent discussion which will help you to answer this question, see Kenneth C. Davis, *Administrative Law Text* (St. Paul: West Publishing Company, 1959), pp. 429–432.

Johnson. If you stop and reflect upon this method, you will realize that this is a curious way to handle the problem. The implication is that only the two individuals involved have a stake in what is done. Secondly, the specific agreements really leave too much discretion to the President who conceivably could be sicker than he knows. The fact that there has been no earnest attempt on the part of Congress to pass legislation or to bring about a constitutional amendment to provide machinery to determine presidential disability (despite much soul-searching on the topic) suggests the immense practical difficulties inherent in the problem.

Finding a means for determining disability and deciding when the officer in line would succeed does not end the matter. By what procedure will it be determined that the disability has ended? Second, what is the status of the officer serving for the governor? Is he governor or acting governor? If he is governor, can he be removed constitutionally when the "former" governor gets well? If he is only the acting governor, does he have the same constitutional powers as the "former" governor? In trying to answer these questions, examine closely your own state constitution to see what constitutional difficulties you would encounter in your own state, if your governor became incapacitated, and it appeared that he should be replaced, particularly when he did not want to be.

The cases offered here deal with very interesting aspects of the disability problem. *Barnhard* v. *Taggart* (p. 219) raises the question of what should be done when the governor feeling that he is too ill to perform his job wants the person next in line to succeed and that person refuses to do so until it is settled in a judicial proceeding that he has the right to do so. *Johnson* v. *Johnson* (p. 222) involves a claim by a lieutenant governor that he should be given a part of the governor's salary for performing his job when the governor was temporarily out of the state. The governor was not disabled in this case, but examination of the issue sheds some light on a question raised earlier, What is the status of a person succeeding the governor on a temporary basis? *Thompson* v. *Talmadge* (p. 224) deals with a very special kind of disability problem. What if a man is elected governor and dies before he ever takes office and the constitution is not clear on what should be done on such an occasion? Just as in former times there were several claimants to the throne whenever there was ambiguity over the accession, you can wager there will be contending parties for a vacant governor's chair when there is ambiguity as to who will fill it.

C. Problems Arising from Attempts to Remove Subordinate Administrative Officials

Unquestionably, in the name of efficiency it is desirable for executive officers to be able to remove subordinate officers who do not perform their duties adequately. At the same time, we, as a people, have come to recognize that if dismissals can be made too easily, a political spoils system results. It is not easy to devise a system which will at one and the same time make it easy to remove incompetents from government service and spare us from the spoils system. To avoid the evils of a spoils system, we have made extensive use of the classified civil service concept. We attempt to choose most of the employees of the executive branch of our various governments on the basis of merit, usually employing written and sometimes oral examinations. At the same time, we prescribe by law how employees so selected may be removed. In such provisions, an attempt is made to safeguard the employee covered in the classified civil service from loss of his job for anything short of compelling reasons and to provide procedural protections as well. But, in addition to employees in the classified service, we have a group of employees who are regarded as political executives who should not be covered in the classified service. These are generally people who occupy posts which, it is believed, should be held by people who are political partisans. For example, we would all probably agree that the principal officers of the administration should be people who are responsive to the mandate of the voters. In some states the governor chooses his principal subordinates, the theory being that the governor should be able to surround himself with aides who are in sympathy with his goals. In other states, however, some of the chief officers are elected. Where this is so, governors have difficulty in demanding their officers' full allegiance, for they can justifiably feel that they have their own exclusive mandate to serve the people without depending upon the governor. In any case, there will in every state be some high-ranking executive officers who are appointed by the governor and who are not in the classified service. This raises the question, Should a governor be free to remove such an officer, if he is not satisfied with his performance? *State* v. *Young* (p. 245) deals with a situation wherein the governor appointed a liquor commissioner for a set term and then felt compelled to remove him before the term was up. When reading the case, pay particular attention to how the Nebraska constitution restricts the governor's power to remove even though the court declares that in principle: "The power to remove an officer or employee in the executive branch of the government is an executive function." *State* ex rel. *Kelly* v. *Sullivan* (p. 249) deals with another kind of problem. Can a governor reinstate a suspended official after the suspension has been lifted, when there is no constitutional provision giving the governor power to reinstate? Still another type of problem is treated in *State* v. *District Court* (p. 253). When an executive officer by law has the power to appoint a subordinate and remove him after a hearing, can the employee seek redress in the courts? Under what circumstances will the courts help him? As you read these cases, ask yourself, Do the courts grant too much or too little power to executives over their subordinates?

There is a widely held belief that employees in the classified civil service in any of our jurisdictions are so well insulated by law and procedure as to make it too difficult, if not impossible, to remove them. As illustration, there was a popular story several years ago, when we were running into difficulties launching missiles. The question was asked: "Why are the missiles at Cape Canaveral like civil servants?" And the answer was, "They won't work because you can't fire them." The fact remains that despite protections from arbitrary dismissals, civil servants can be dismissed. *Gremillion* v. *Department of Highways* (p. 257) and *King* v. *Department of Public Safety* (p. 260) demonstrate that employees in the classified civil service may indeed be removed for cause. The question which is raised by these cases is, Do these employees have too little or too much protection for the efficient administration of governmental business?

D. The Governor and the National Guard

Every time the Army or the Department of Defense suggests cutting back on the strength of the National Guard, we are reminded how very important the Guard is to our governors. One of the important functions of the National Guard has been to provide a governor with a force capable of maintaining law and order when there is a real or potential danger that law and order will break down. There have been times when it has been alleged that a governor has employed the Guard in such a way as to deprive parties of rights guaranteed by the United States Constitution. In such situations, the parties have been able to seek redress in the Federal courts. Courts are generally reluctant to question a governor's decision that it was necessary to call out the Guard in order to preserve order. But, at the same time, courts have insisted that when the governor calls out the Guard, he must use the weight of that force to preserve constitutional rights. In the famous case, *Cooper* v. *Aaron*, 385 U.S. 18 (1958), which dealt in part with Governor Faubus' use of the Arkansas National Guard to keep Negro children out of the schools, the United States Supreme Court said: "The constitutional rights of respondents are not to be sacrificed or yielded to the violence and disorder which have followed upon the actions of the Governor and Legislature. . . . Thus law and order are not here to be preserved by depriving the Negro children of their constitutional rights." The Court went on to suggest that the Guard could have been used to prevent violence *and* to compel the children to attend school. In *Wilson and Co.* v. *Freeman* (p. 263), note that the Federal court actually questioned the governor's judgment as to whether or not there was enough evidence of violence to justify calling out the Guard even as it decided that he should have upheld the Wilson Company's constitutional rights. This raises an important question for your consideration. Who is in a better position to determine whether or not the Guard should be used, the governor or a court? If your answer is the governor, the question which logically follows is, What protection is there then from the arbitrary use of the National Guard by a governor? In that connection, a Supreme Court decision is very instructive, *Sterling* v. *Constantin*, 287 U.S. 378 (1932).

JENKINS v. KNIGHT

SUPREME COURT OF CALIFORNIA IN BANK
293 P. 2D 6 (1956)

The constitution of California requires that, when vacancies occur in the state legislature, the governor shall issue a call for special elections. In addition, the California election code provides that he shall issue the call "at once." When three vacancies developed during his tenure as governor, Goodwin Knight decided on considerations of economy to delay the call and schedule the elections to coincide with the forthcoming regular primary. Jenkins et al. *in original proceedings before the California supreme court sought a* mandamus *to compel the governor to call the special elections earlier.*

Judge GIBSON delivered the opinion of the court.

. . . .

THESE PROCEEDINGS raise questions involving the power of the court to require the Governor to act, and the extent, if any, to which he has discretion with respect to calling and fixing the date for special elections to fill legislative vacancies.

There is a conflict of authority in this country as to whether a governor is amenable to mandamus with respect to any of his duties. . . . Kumm, Mandamus to the Governor in Minnesota (1924), 9 Minn.L.Rev. 21; cases collected in Holcomb, Mandamus to the Chief Executive of the State (1922), 3 S.W. Pol.Sci.Q. 25. In some jurisdictions courts refuse to issue the writ against a governor under any circumstances, on the theory that interference with his action constitutes a violation of the doctrine of separation of powers or upon the ground that the issuance of a writ is inexpedient because of possible difficulty in enforcing it. . . . This reasoning has been rejected in many jurisdictions, including California where it has been consistently held for more than three quarters of a century that the writ will issue to compel a governor to perform ministerial acts required by law. Stuart v. Haight, 39 Cal. 87. . . .

These decisions are based on the fundamental principle that under our system of government no man is above the law. Chief Justice Stephen Field, speaking for the court in the early case of McCauley v. Brooks, 16 Cal. 11, 54–55, stated that where no discretion exists and a specific legal duty is imposed, ministerial in its character, an officer of the executive department of government, like any other citizen, is subject to judicial process and that, if this were not so, the government would cease to deserve the "high appellation" of being a government of laws. In the leading cases of Harpending v. Haight, 39 Cal. 189, 211–213, and Elliott v. Pardee, 86 P. 1087, it was held that the Governor should not be exempted from judicial process solely because he is the chief executive and that, like subordinate officers, he is amenable to mandamus to compel the discharge of a ministerial-duty which a body of citizens has a right to have performed. The duties whose performance was compelled in the cited cases were enjoined by statute, but there is no indication that a different result would have been reached had they been imposed by the Constitution. Although the courts in a few jurisdictions have held that they will not enforce ministerial duties imposed upon a governor by a constitution, we can see no logical basis for this classification. It would seem just as important to enforce duties directed by the people through the Constitution as those prescribed by the Legislature. . . .

Many acts of the Governor are, of course, inherently executive or political in nature, such as granting pardons, calling special sessions of the Legislature and signing or vetoing bills. . . . They require the exercise of judgment or discretion, and for this reason the courts will not interfere with their performance. Unfortunately, the terms "political" and "executive" have been used loosely in some jurisdictions as an explanation for denying the writ in cases where the courts failed to make a proper analysis of the nature of the duty to be performed. The critical question in determining if an act required by law is ministerial in character is whether it involves the exercise of judgment and discretion.

It is clear that the duty imposed upon the Governor to issue writs of election to fill vacancies in the Legislature is ministerial in character. The Governor has no discretion to determine whether an election should be called; he is commanded by the Constitution to issue a proclamation. Const. art. IV, § 12. The provisions of our Constitution are mandatory and prohibitory unless expressly declared to be otherwise, see Cal.Const. art. I § 22, and the duty to call elections to fill legislative vacancies is mandatory.

In related cases where officers enjoined by law to call a special election failed to act, it has been established that the duty is ministerial and that its performance may be compelled by mandamus. . . . The authority of these cases with respect to the ministerial character of the function is not lessened by the fact that they involve local officials. "It is not by the office of the person to whom the writ is directed, but the nature of the thing to be done, that the propriety or impropriety of issuing a mandamus is to be determined." Marbury v. Madison, 1 Cranch 137. . . .

The attorney general argues that, since no time is fixed in the Constitution within which the Governor must act after a vacancy occurs, his action involves an element of discretion. The answer to this argument is found in section 1773 of the Government Code which provides that, when vacancies occur, the Governor shall issue writs of election "at once." Shortly after the vacancy occurred in January 1955, the Governor stated that he then saw no necessity for calling a special election to fill the office in the absence of an expression of policy from the county board of supervisors. It is apparent that the Governor wished to avoid requiring the taxpayers to bear the expense of holding a special election unless the supervisors were of the view that the expenditure would be warranted under the circumstances. However, the exercise of the duty enjoined upon the Governor by the Constitution cannot be made dependent upon whether a board of supervisors considers an election to fill a vacancy in the Legislature to be in the public interest. The policy in this field has been determined by the people in section 12 of article IV of the Constitution. The importance of the duty to call special elections to fill vacancies in the Legislature is evident from the fact that failure to comply with the constitutional mandate would vitally affect the membership and operation of a coordinate branch of government as well as the basic right of the people to representation.

The question remains whether the Governor, when he issued the proclamations on January 4, 1956, acted in accordance with the law in fixing June 5, 1956 as the date on which the special elections are to be held. Petitioners argue that since the budget session of the Legislature will convene on March 5 and last for not more than 30 days, the elections should have been set at the earliest possible date so that the districts would be represented for at least a part of that session. The statutes do not fix a maximum time within which such elections must be held but specify that a minimum of 70 days' notice must be given, Elections Code, § 1001. The Governor therefore has discretion to set the election for some date after the expiration of the 70-day period, but it must, of course, take place within a reasonable time after the issuance of the proclamation. For example, if the Governor had issued a proclamation promptly after the first vacancy occurred on January 3, 1955, and had then fixed the date of the special election for June 5, 1956, a serious question would have arisen as to whether his action constituted a reasonable exercise of discretion. We are not, however, confronted with that problem. The delay in issuing the proclamations cannot be remedied now; we are limited to the question of whether the Governor has abused his discretion in setting the date of the elections for June 5, 1956. The earliest possible date on which the elections could be held after January 4, 1956, the date the proclamations were issued, is March 14, and 16 additional days would have to be allowed for counting the absentee ballots. . . . Were the election to be held on March 14, and were the budget session to last the full 30 days, the session would be nearly over before the person elected could qualify. In these circumstances it certainly cannot be said that the Governor acted unreasonably in fixing the date at June 5 to coincide with the presidential primary, thus sparing the counties involved the expense of holding two elections within a three-month period.

. . . .

[*The court denied the writ.*]

SHENK, CARTER, TRAYNOR, SCHAUER, SPENCE, and McCOMB, JJ., concur.

BARNHARD v. TAGGART

NEW HAMPSHIRE SUPREME COURT

29 A. 1027 (1890)

When Governor Goodell of New Hampshire became too ill to continue his work, he wrote a letter to Barnhard the attorney general asking him to "take such steps as . . . you think necessary to cause the President of the Senate to exercise the power of governor during the vacancy caused by my illness . . . [for] I am not able to perform the duties of the office, and the public should not suffer from my inability."

Taggart, the president of the senate, refused to assume the duties of governor because to him it was not clear that he could constitutionally do so. Consequently, Attorney General Barnhard petitioned the New Hampshire supreme court for a writ of mandamus *to compel Taggart to exercise the powers of governor. In his answer to the petition, Taggart made it clear that he was ready "to do his duty when he has authoritative evidence as to what it is" and that he was very willing to submit to the judgment of the court.*

Chief Justice Doe delivered the opinion of the court.

. . . .

"Whenever the chair of the governor shall become vacant, by reason of his death, absence from the state, or otherwise, the president of the senate shall, during such vacancy, have and exercise all the powers and authorities which, by this constitution, the governor is vested with when personally present; but when the president of the senate shall exercise the office of governor, he shall not hold his office in the senate." Const. art. 49. From 1784 to 1792 the governor (then styled the "President of the State of New Hampshire") was president of the senate. Instead of his present power of vetoing or approving bills passed by the senate and house, he had "a vote equal with any other member" of the senate, and also "a casting vote in case of a tie," and when his office was vacant all his powers were exercised by "the senior senator." When the constitution took effect, and the legislature met for the inauguration of the new government, June 2, 1784, Meshech Weare, the governor elect, was unable to be present. In brief periods of his illness and absence, in June, 1784, and February, 1785, his duties were performed by Woodbury Langdon, senior senator, acting as governor pro tem. On both occasions Langdon presided in the senate, by virtue of his provisional tenure of the governor's office; and on the 8th of June, 1784, as governor, he sat with the council, and exercised the governor's power (with the required advice and consent of the council) of signing warrants for the payment of money out of the state treasury. The authority of this precedent has not been shaken, and it does not appear that the soundness of the contemporaneous construction has ever been doubted. " 'Where a word having a technical as well as a popular meaning is used in the constitution, the courts will accord to it its popular signification, unless the very nature of the subject indicates, or the text suggests, that it is used in its technical sense.' . . . Words used in a constitution should be construed in the sense in which they were employed. They 'must be taken in the ordinary and common acceptation, because they are presumed to have been so understood by the framers, and by the people who adopted it. * * * It * * * owes its whole force and authority to its ratification by the people, and they judged of it by the meaning apparent on its face, according to the general use of the words employed, where they do not appear to have been used in a legal or technical sense.' . . ." "The terms 'jury' and 'trial by jury' are, and for ages have been, well known in the language of the law. They were used at the adoption of the constitution, and always, it is believed, before that time, and almost always since, in a single sense. * * * At that date * * * no such thing as a jury of less than twelve men, or a jury deciding by less than twelve voices, had ever been known, or ever been the subject of discussion, in any country of the common law." Opinion of the Justices, 41 N. H. 551, 552. A similar narrowness of meaning has not been attached to "vacant by reason of his death, absence from the state, or otherwise." And, if the public service could be thrown into disorder by a rule of construction with which the people who adopted the constitution were not familiar, the law would not apply a rule which they did not apply, but would carry into effect the understanding and intent of the voters who enacted article 49 for cases of necessity, and used "otherwise" in its comprehensive and usual sense. In the connection in which the word here occurs, "otherwise" includes the governor's physical disability, as equivalent, for the provisional purpose of this article, to his death or absence from the state. . . .

The primary and leading object of article 49 is evidence tending to show that the construction adopted in the first year of the constitution is correct. The mischief designed to be prevented was the suspension of executive government by the governor's death, absence from the state, or disability. . . . Opinion of the Court, 60 N. H. 585. The prescribed remedy is the duty of a substitute to act in cases of necessity. The services of a substitute may be necessary when the governor's absence or disability is temporary as well as when it is permanent. When there is an office to which no one has a title, and which is in fact held by no one, there is a vacancy. Johnston v. Wilson, 2 N. H. 202, . . . But, in article 49, "vacant, by reason of his death, absence from the state, or otherwise," has a broader signification if due weight is given to the evidential force of the primary and leading purpose that the executive work shall go on without interruption. An intermittent vacancy, such as occurred in the time of Governor Weare, may occur again; and the evils of an interregnum, which article 49 was intended to prevent, are not to be introduced by technical reasoning or arbitrary rules. "If, from the imperfection of human language, there should be serious doubts respecting the extent of any given power, * * * the objects for which it was given * * * should have great influence in the construction." Gibbons v. Ogden, 9 Wheat. 1, 189. The general object of article 49 forbids a construction that would sometimes cripple the government, and render it powerless in a department in which the public safety requires constant readiness for action.

It is proved by medical testimony that the governor is still in the physical condition stated in his letter to the attorney general, and that his disability may be reasonably expected to last a few weeks, and perhaps a few months. It is proved by the testimony of the secretary of state and the state treasurer that there is executive business demanding immediate attention, and that the governor's duties should no longer remain unperformed. The case being one of necessity, article 49 directs the president of the senate to exercise executive powers until the governor resumes them. The defendant being reluctant to act without an adjudication or some conclusive evidence of an emergency contemplated by that article, the governor requested the attorney general to take the steps needed for the protection of public interests. There might be a case in which the attorney general would intervene without such request. While a determination of the question of vacancy on a petition of this kind is not legally requisite to call the president of the senate to the executive chair, it may be a convenient mode of avoiding embarrassment that might sometimes arise from doubt and controversy in regard to his authority, and the validity of his acts. The existence of an executive vacancy is a question of law and fact within the judicial jurisdiction. If the defendant exercised executive power without a previous judgment on that question, the legality of his acts could be contested and determined in subsequent litigation, and the judicial character of the question does not depend upon the time when it is brought into court. With adequate legal process, the consideration and decision of such a question may be prospective as well as retrospective.

. . . .

In this case the inquiry is not whether the defendant can be compelled by mandamus to exercise the governor's powers in a particular manner (approve and sign a bill passed by the senate and house, concur with the council in the appointment of a justice of the peace and the pardon of a convict, or perform a ministerial act requiring no exercise of judgment), or whether the independence of each branch of the government shall be maintained in matters of law or fact which it is exclusively authorized to determine . . . but whether there is a vacancy, during which it is the defendant's right and duty to act, under article 49, and whether the state shall have the executive service to which it is entitled. Between the governor's and the defendant's right to "exercise all the powers" of the governor's office, there is no difference that excludes this case from the jurisdiction in which the title of the office could be determined, if it were disputed. The duty of jurors may be made as imperative as that of conscripts (Bowles v. Landaff, 59 N. H. 191); and the state's right to the executive service of the president of the senate, under article 49, is no less enforceable than its right to the judicial service of a juror. There is no express or implied exemption of the executive substitute from the compulsion of legal process. "The court will not interfere by mandamus with the executive officers of the government in the exercise of their ordinary official duties. * * * the court having no appellate power for that purpose, but when they refuse to act in a case at all * * * a mandamus may be issued to compel them." U.S. v. Black, 128 U.S. 40. The law generally authorizes coercion when a public officer refuses to act in a particular case in which it is his duty to act. . . . His refusal to act in all cases is not an exception to the rule applicable to his refusal in a single case.

If the defendant were exempt from mandamus, there would be another question. . . . Judgment for the plaintiff.

All concurred.

JOHNSON v. JOHNSON

NEBRASKA SUPREME COURT

3 N.W. 2D 414 (1942)

William E. Johnson, while lieutenant governor of Nebraska, had from time to time performed the duties of the governor while Governor Cochran was temporarily absent from the state. Johnson presented a claim for a share of the governor's salary proportionate to the time he devoted to performing the governor's duties. The state auditor (also a Johnson, by name) to whom the lieutenant governor had presented his claim, refused to approve it and the state treasurer joined him in this decision. Lieutenant Governor Johnson then took his claim to the appropriate state court. Rebuffed there, he appealed to the state supreme court.

Justice ROSE delivered the opinion of the court.

. . . .

THE CLAIM of the lieutenant governor is based on the following provisions of the Constitution: "In case of the death, impeachment and notice thereof to the accused, failure to qualify, resignation, absence from the state, or other disability of the Governor, the powers, duties and emoluments of the office for the residue of the term or until the disability shall be removed shall devolve upon the Lieutenant Governor." Const. art. IV, sec. 16.

Under these provisions it is argued on behalf of plaintiff that the framers of the Constitution intended to provide additional compensation for the lieutenant governor for service performed by him as governor during the absences of the governor from the state; that during such absences the lieutenant governor was de jure governor; that the powers, duties and emoluments of the governor devolved on the lieutenant governor during the former's absences. These propositions are argued at length with references to court decisions and textbooks. In ruling on the claim of plaintiff, other provisions of the Constitution should be considered under the Nebraska system of government. The salary of the governor is fixed by the Constitution at $7,500 a year. . . . The salary of the lieutenant governor is twice the salary of a state senator. . . . The governor and lieutenant governor shall receive such salaries as are provided by law. . . . The salary of a state officer was intended for a qualified and acting incumbent of a particular office. The salary fixed by the Constitution for the compensation of the governor and appropriated by law for that purpose was never meant to shuttle between the governor and the lieutenant governor.

The constitutional provisions upon which plaintiff relies for the allowance of his claim deal with disabilities "in case of the death, impeachment and notice thereof to the accused, failure to qualify, resignation, absence from the state, or other disability of the Governor." These are all disabilities within the meaning of the Constitution. Death, failure to qualify and resignation are permanent disabilities. Impeachment is a disability at least until trial and acquittal and permanent in the event of conviction. Absence from the state is a permanent disability if the governor abandons the office and becomes a nonresident, but mere temporary absence from the state for the performance of official duty or for recreation or for business of a personal nature not interfering with the interests of the public does not vacate the office of governor and instate the lieutenant governor therein with all the powers, duties and emoluments thereof. "Absence from the state," to entitle the lieutenant governor to the emoluments of the office of governor, is an absence amounting to a permanent disability or to a temporary disability creating a vacancy or to a disability which prevents the governor from holding the office. A governor does not lose his office by stepping over the boundary line of the state for a purpose or for a time that does not disqualify him from holding the office. During such an interval the lieutenant governor does not become governor. The Constitution does not provide for two governors at the same time. When the lieutenant governor performs duties in the executive office during a temporary, nondisqualifying absence of the governor, he still acts as lieutenant governor and his compensation during such an interval is the lawful salary for that officer. In Nebraska a public officer must perform all the duties of his office for the compensation allowed by law and if none is authorized the services are gratuitous. . . .

If the lieutenant governor was the de jure governor during the intervals enumerated in his claim, with all the powers, duties and emoluments thereof, as argued by counsel, he was, during these periods, clothed by the Constitution with powers as follows: "The Governor shall have power to remove any officer, whom he may appoint, in case of incompetency, neglect of duty, or malfeasance in office, and he may declare his office vacant, and fill the same as herein provided in other cases of vacancy." Const. art. IV, sec. 12.

Under this authority, the lieutenant governor, while temporarily performing executive duties, if a de jure governor in the office of governor during the latter's absence, could have removed all the appointees of the governor for cause and could have filled their places with appointees of his own selection. By virtue of the same authority, if de jure governor, he could have taken possession of the governor's mansion. In construing a provision of the Constitution, statesmanship should be imputed to the framers thereof, if permissible, rather than absurdity. When the purposes of the constitutional provisions under consideration are considered with other provisions throwing light on the same subjects, the more reasonable and better interpretation is the one adopted by defendants.

In this view of the law the claim in issue was properly disallowed by the auditor of public accounts, by the secretary of state and by the district court.

Affirmed.

THOMPSON v. TALMADGE

GEORGIA SUPREME COURT

41 S.E. 2D 883 (1947)

After he was elected governor and before his term of office began, Eugene Talmadge died. Because of ambiguities in the constitution, it was not clear what should be done under the circumstances. Consequently, there followed an interesting contest for power. The legislature elected Herman Talmadge governor. Ellis Arnall, who had been serving as governor and whose term had expired, refused to recognize Herman Talmadge as governor. He asserted that he was the legitimate governor until he was succeeded by a legitimate successor. Arnall then resigned and the man who had been serving with him as lieutenant governor, Melvin E. Thompson, took the oath of office. (Evidently, Arnall felt that resigning might be good strategy, since a governor of Georgia may not normally succeed himself.) In short, both Talmadge and Thompson claimed to be governor at the same time. Three law suits were taken to state courts in an attempt to ascertain who was the rightful governor. Ultimately the issue had to be resolved by the state supreme court.

Justice DUCKWORTH delivered the opinion of the court.

. . . .

THAT THE trial courts had jurisdiction in each of these cases to adjudicate all questions there raised that are collateral to the main question as to which of the contending parties is entitled to perform the duties of Governor of this State can not be seriously questioned. But it is stoutly maintained by counsel for Mr. Talmadge that the courts were without jurisdiction to adjudicate the principal question as to whether or not Mr. Talmadge is the lawful Governor of this State. The grounds upon which this contention is predicated are that it is a purely political question; that it has been determined by the General Assembly which under the Constitution has exclusive jurisdiction; and that the action of that body is not subject to review by the courts.

In the oral argument in this court counsel expressly waived all procedural questions, thus enabling us to move at once to a consideration of the main and controlling questions, the first of which is jurisdiction as just above stated. That the judiciary under the Constitution is wholly without jurisdiction to adjudicate a purely political question is not an open question. Also, it is the settled law of this State that actions of the General Assembly taken in virtue of a power conferred by the Constitution and in conformity with the provisions of the Constitution are not subject to review by the courts. The law is equally as well settled that the judiciary is by the Constitution given the power and jurisdiction to adjudicate any and all justiciable questions presented to it in litigation, and that this jurisdiction of the courts is neither ousted nor impaired by the fact that there may be involved in such cases political questions, or actions by the General Assembly. Counsel on each side have filed in this court exhaustive briefs on the question of jurisdiction to adjudicate the principal issue as to the title of Herman Talmadge to the office of Governor and have cited a number of decisions from courts of other jurisdictions, some of which involved the question as to who was the lawful Governor. The cases cited will not here be extensively discussed. We think it sufficient to state that they, in a general way, tend to support the respective positions of the parties citing them. . . . While it appears from an examination of all of the cited cases that a majority of those courts have exercised jurisdiction in cases similar in some respects to the cases we are now called upon to decide, yet it can not be said that those decisions are sufficient to settle the question of the jurisdiction of our courts to adjudicate the ultimate issue here made. We, therefore, look to the law of this State as embodied in the Constitution and the decisions of this court in arriving at a decision on such jurisdictional question, bearing in mind, however, the decisions of courts of other jurisdictions in so far as they may shed light upon the question.

The Constitution vests all legislative power in the General Assembly. . . . It vests all judicial power in the courts. . . . It commands that these powers remain forever separate and distinct. . . . This court in McCutcheon v. Smith, 35 S.E.2d 144, citing in the opinion a number of older decisions supporting its ruling, held that construing the Constitution and the statutes is the function of the judiciary, and that the General Assembly has no power to make such construction. By this was meant that determining the meaning of the Constitution, which is binding upon everyone, was the exclusive function of the courts in the adjudication of cases properly brought before them for decision. Therefore, it must be held that if in the present cases a construction of the Constitution is involved, that is a justiciable question which the courts have the exclusive jurisdiction to adjudicate in determining such cases. While there is presented here no law enacted by the General Assembly, the constitutionality of which is drawn in question, there is a formal resolution which followed publication of the election returns, and this is challenged and must be construed. The power of the judiciary to declare void unconstitutional "acts" of the legislature is expressed in . . . the Constitution. Whether or not this provision has reference solely to laws enacted by that body, it is indicative of the supreme power of the judiciary in its field of construction as between parties litigant, and certainly no action of the General Assembly is of higher dignity or importance, or would require greater constitutional power, than that of solemnly enacting the laws of this State. Manifestly a department of the State government vested with the power to declare void laws enacted by the Legislature has a power broad enough to declare void other actions of that department, which are of less dignity, if they are found to have violated the Constitution and to be an infringement of right.

In Beall v. Beall, 8 Ga. 210, this court, after stating that in measures exclusively of a political, legislative, or executive character, the supreme authority belongs to the legislative and executive departments, and that the mode of executing such powers could never become the subject of inquiry and investigation by the courts, further said: "But were this or any other question of a different nature, and capable of judicial inquiry and decision, then it would admit of a very different consideration—the action of either of the other departments, whether legislative or executive, being capable, in its own nature, of being brought to a judicial test, is subject to judicial review. It is, in all such cases, as we conceive, that the judicial authority is the final and common arbiter, provided by the constitution itself, and to whose decisions all others are subordinate," citing Story on the Constitution.

In Low v. Towns, 8 Ga. 360, this

court, speaking of the question of the validity of the title to a public office, said: "The validity of the title to an office created by law, is a judicial question—one which it is not only the duty of the courts to decide, but one which, in our judgment, it is the exclusive province of the judiciary department to determine, notwithstanding the Governor may have commissioned one of the claimants." In State ex rel. Mayor, etc., of City of Savannah v. Dews, R. M. Charlt. 397, it was said at page 400: "Legislative power is that which declares what the law shall be; judicial is that which declares what law is, and applies it to past transactions and existing cases; the one makes the law, the other expounds and judicially administers it; the one prescribes a rule of civil conduct, the other interprets and enforces it in a case in litigation." We have in this State a government of laws under a written Constitution. It requires the full discharge of their respective functions by each of the three coordinate departments of government to effectually operate the government and administer the laws. There is provided in this governmental scheme no other authority for the orderly adjudication and settlement of justiciable cases except the judicial department. Failure on the part of the judiciary to function would leave all such matters unsettled, and anarchy would prevail. This is not to say that the judiciary does or can control either of its coequals, the executive and the legislative departments, but in virtue of the power vested in it by the Constitution the judiciary can and must, when called upon in a case before it, adjudicate and decide all justiciable questions, whether they relate to the action of the other departments or not. If any department of the government, including the judiciary, acts beyond the bounds of its authority, such action is without jurisdiction, is unconstitutional, and is void. It is declared in the Code, § 89–903, that the public is not estopped by the acts of an officer done in the exercise of a power he never had. See also Motes v. Davis, 4 S.E.2d 597. "The judgment of a court having no jurisdiction of the person or subject-matter, or void for any other cause, is a mere nullity, and may be so held in any court when it becomes material to the interest of the parties to consider it." Code, § 110–709. And so it must be with any action of the General Assembly that is without the realm of its jurisdiction.

In the field of enacting laws general and broad power is given to the legislative department. If in the exercise of this power, which is unquestionably conferred upon it, the General Assembly merely fails to observe certain rules of internal procedure, the judiciary would not be authorized to review such action; and the same would be true as to any action of the officers of that body within the sphere of their jurisdiction. . . . There is however, a marked and fundamental difference between instances of incorrectly exercising unquestioned power and of exercise of a power never possessed.

The cases here presented do not involve an election contest, but they do involve questions as to the title to the highest office in the State government, including construction of the Constitution as to the jurisdiction of the General Assembly to elect a Governor under provisions of the Constitution, quoted infra, and the courts have jurisdiction to decide such questions.

As to the election of a Governor the Constitution of 1945 contains the following provisions: "The first election for Governor, under this Constitution, shall be held on Tuesday after the first Monday in November of 1946, and the Governor-elect shall be installed in office at the next session of the General Assembly. An election shall take place quadrennially thereafter, on said date, until another date be fixed by the General Assembly. Said election shall be held at the places of holding general elections in the several counties of this State, in the manner prescribed for the election of members of the General Assembly, and the electors shall be the same." . . . "The returns for every election of Governor shall be sealed up by the managers, separately from other returns, and directed to the President of the Senate and Speaker of the House of Representatives, and transmitted to the Secretary of State, who shall, without opening said returns, cause the same to be laid before the Senate on the day after the two houses shall have been organized, and they shall be transmitted by the Senate to the House of Representatives." . . . "The members of each branch of the General Assembly shall convene in the Representative Hall, and the President of the Senate and Speaker of the House of Representatives shall open and publish the returns in the presence and under the direction of the General Assembly; and the person having the majority of the whole number of votes, shall be declared duly elected Governor of this State; but, if no person shall have such majority, then from the two persons having the highest number of votes, who shall be in life, and shall not decline an election at the time appointed for the General Assembly to elect, the General Assembly shall immediately, elect a Governor viva voce; and in all cases of election of a Governor by the General Assembly, a majority of the members present shall be necessary to a choice." . . . The Constitution also provides: "Contested elections shall be determined by both houses of the General Assembly in such manner as shall be prescribed by law." . . .

In view of these provisions, did the General Assembly have power to elect a Governor under the circumstances that existed when they proceeded to elect Mr. Talmadge? . . . the General Assembly opened and published the returns of the election for Governor held on November 5, 1946. While it declares that no person at that time had a majority of the votes, it shows that the one and only reason for such conclusion was the fact that Eugene Talmadge who received the highest number of votes cast had departed this life. There is nowhere in the resolution a statement of fact that the election returns did not show that some person received a majority of the votes cast in the election.

It is well at this point to decide definitely whether, in publishing the returns and announcing the result, the members of the General Assembly acted in a capacity of higher or lower dignity and responsibility than is commonly possessed by other persons, officials, or boards designated by the law or Constitution as canvassers of state elections returns. To our minds there is no escape from the conclusion that in publishing the returns and declaring the results the members of the General Assembly were performing a strict and precise duty identical in character with that which rests upon any and all persons who are merely authorized to canvass. They were not, while performing that duty, exercising or authorized to exercise any discretion, but were simply performing the ministerial act of disclosing to the public the official election returns that had been prepared by the election managers. By using the simple mathematical process of adding the number of votes appearing thereon for the persons named and seeing whether any person named therein had a majority, they could know whether any person was elected, and, if so, it was their duty to declare that such person had been duly elected Governor. This canvassing of the returns and declaration of the result were constitutional directives to the General Assembly, and its failure to observe them ought not to defeat the right of the person elected or the franchise of the voters who elected him. This court clearly indicated in

Wood v. Arnall, 6 S.E.2d 722, that the will of the people could not be thus defeated. The question in that case was whether the June general election, as provided for by the act of 1937, Ga. L. 1937, p. 712, was intended by the act to apply to the office of attorney-general. It was held that the regular method of electing an attorney-general would include ascertainment and declaration of the result by the General Assembly as provided by the Constitution for election of Governor, and that since the statute relating to such June election did not provide for election of attorney-general according to such regular method, it should be construed as not applying to that office. It was not held that the General Assembly had any power or discretion to vary the result as shown by the election returns, but on the contrary the following was stated, at page 727 of 6 S.E.2d: "The question here involved is not whether an official regularly elected by the people at the time and place prescribed by law could be deprived of his office by virtue of the mere failure of the General Assembly to canvass and declare the result as directed by the constitution, for manifestly the will of the people could not be thus defeated."

The General Assembly, as canvassers of the election returns in this case, were subject to the general, if not indeed the universal, rule of law applicable to election canvassers. That rule is that they are given no discretionary power except to determine if the returns are in proper form and executed by the proper officials and to pronounce the mathematical result, unless additional authority is expressed. They can neither receive nor consider any extraneous information or evidence, but must look only to the contents of the election returns. . . .

. . . .

. . . we may say the universal rule so far as we are aware, show beyond reasonable doubt that the General Assembly, as canvassers, went beyond any authority conferred upon them, and hence, outside their legal jurisdiction, when they gave consideration to and made a finding of fact that the majority candidate had died after the election of November 5, 1946. It necessarily follows that all such action beyond the jurisdiction of the General Assembly was null and void and must be disregarded entirely.

It has been urged by counsel for Mr. Talmadge that two reasons why the General Assembly, in making such a canvass and announcing the result, were more than mere canvassers are (1) that the Constitution, . . . confers power upon the General Assembly to determine contested elections "in such manner as shall be prescribed by law" and (2) that since the Governor has no commission it is necessary to publicly recognize and authoritatively announce his election. We can not accept this argument as being tenable. The first reason is unsound because the matter of determining a contest is wholly independent of and apart from the canvassing of returns, which is merely consolidating the election returns and declaring the result. In this case there was no contest whatever, and the General Assembly had no right to exercise their power to determine contests in the performance of an entirely different duty as canvassers. The second reason is completely answered by the fact that the Secretary of State, the Attorney General, the State School Superintendent, the Comptroller General, the State Treasurer, the Commissioner of Agriculture, and the Commissioner of Labor receive commissions evidencing their election and title to their respective offices, and yet the Constitution . . . declares that all of these officers shall be elected at the same time and in the same manner as the Governor, and that "The provisions of the Constitution as to the transmission of the returns of the election, counting the votes, declaring the results, deciding when there is no election, and when there is a contested election, applicable to the election of Governor, shall apply to the election of the above named executive officers; they shall be commissioned by the Governor and hold their offices for the same time as the Governor." This demonstrates that the act of canvassing the returns and announcing the result is not designed for the purposes argued by counsel. The election of the officers last referred to is conducted in the same manner as that for Governor. As evidence of their election and title to the office, they are given a commission by the Governor. This evidence in behalf of the Governor is his public inauguration.

This case might be decided without giving consideration to the authority and function of the General Assembly in publishing the returns and announcing the result, since the resolution adopted by that body clearly shows that it made no statement to the effect that the election returns show that no person received a majority of the votes, which fact, as will be pointed out later, is an indispensable condition precedent to its power to elect a Governor. However, we think that either the constitutional limitation on its powers as to publishing the returns, or the inability to show that in fact no one received a majority of the votes in the general election, would constitute a sufficient or valid reason why the General Assembly acted without authority and without power. Together they constitute an insuperable barrier to the exercise of such power.

In this State all power and sovereignty repose in the people. The departments of the State government have and can exercise only such power as the people have conferred upon them by the Constitution. . . . More than 120 years ago the people of this State recaptured for themselves the general power to elect a Governor. By an amendment to the Constitution of 1798, adopted in 1824, art. 2, sec. 2, which conferred upon the General Assembly the power to elect a Governor, was expressly repealed, and in lieu thereof a new section reserving the power of electing a Governor in the people was adopted. That amendment, without material change, has been retained as a part of every subsequent Constitution, and is now found in the Constitution of 1945 as art. 5, sec. 1. . . . That portion of the provision over which the present litigation arose is paragraph 4, which is as follows: "The members of each branch of the General Assembly shall convene in the Representative Hall, and the President of the Senate and Speaker of the House of Representatives shall open and publish the returns in the presence and under the direction of the General Assembly; and the person having the majority of the whole number of votes, shall be declared duly elected Governor of this State; but, if no person shall have such majority, then from the two persons having the highest number of votes, who shall be in life, and shall not decline an election at the time appointed for the General Assembly to elect, the General Assembly shall immediately, elect a Governor viva voce; and in all cases of election of a Governor by the General Assembly, a majority of the members present shall be necessary to a choice."

By the terms of the Constitution, full and complete power to elect a Governor is reserved to the people, but if the voters fail to elect because they do not cast a majority of their votes for one person, then and then only is the power given to the Legislature to elect a Governor.

From what has been said it is evident that the *general* power or jurisdiction to elect a Governor remains in the people under the present Constitution, and that as related to the election of such an officer by the General Assembly that body is an agency or tribunal of special or limited jurisdiction. As to courts, it is a well settled principle that every presumption will be indulged in favor of judgments of a court of general jurisdiction, but that a judgment of a court of special or limited jurisdiction must show upon its face such facts as are necessary to give the court rendering such judgment jurisdiction of the person and the subject matter, otherwise the whole proceeding is coram non judice [*suit brought and determined in a court which has no jurisdiction in the matter*] and void. . . . Like principles are applicable to the General Assembly, so that in electing a Governor it would necessarily act as an agency or body of *special and limited* jurisdiction, and the facts essential to the existence of its jurisdiction in such matter should affirmatively appear. . . .

Much has been said by counsel on both sides regarding the word "person" and other words and phrases as they appear in the provision under consideration. The contentions urged by counsel for Mr. Talmadge, if sustained, would have the effect of isolating a few words from the entire paragraph and giving to them a refined definition without due consideration of the context in which they are used. This, under all the recognized rules of construction, can not be done. The true meaning of such words can be ascertained in no other way except by a consideration inter alia, of the subject matter to which they relate as disclosed by the entire paragraph. Of course, the words "person having" standing alone and independent of the subject matter would indicate a person alive at the time of his *having,* and the words "if no person shall have," considered in the same manner, would indicate the present tense as of the time the returns are canvassed, but when these words are considered, as they must be, in connection with and as a part of the entire paragraph, which discloses the plan for publication of the returns and declaring the results as to elections to be held in the future, but which will already have occurred at the time of such publication and declaration, it is very apparent that they refer to elections by the people that have already taken place at the time of such prescribed action by the General Assembly. It is equally plain that all mention of a person who received votes refers only to such past election by the people and to the person who receives the votes at that time. We can not insert by implication the phrase "who shall be in life" immediately following the word "person" as it appears in this paragraph twice before the word "person," which is followed by that phrase. . . . When thus construed, the word "person," as used in the first two clauses refers to a living person as of the time of the election by the people, and his subsequent death is immaterial, so far as any power of election by the General Assembly is concerned. By the subsequent use of the words "who shall be in life," the Constitution marks the first and only time when the General Assembly shall take note of or consider the fact that a person voted for at the election by the people might have subsequently died. The reason for this is obvious. At this point, the General Assembly is not concerned with the election returns further than to ascertain whether there are any two persons from whom it may effectually elect a Governor within the terms of the Constitution, but it is now concerned with the performance of such constitutional duty, that is, in a case where no person received a majority of the votes, and it is here informed by the Constitution that although a person might be one of two who received the highest number of votes, it should not be required to do the perfectly futile thing of electing as Governor one who is not still in life. Hence, it would thus finally become material for the General Assembly to ascertain the two persons (if there be such) having the highest number of votes "who shall be in life."

Much argument has been offered to the effect that since Eugene Talmadge died before his election was declared, it would have been futile for the General Assembly to declare that he had been duly elected Governor since it would have been impossible for him to assume the duties of that office. We will not here depart from the central, controlling question for the purpose of discussing whether or not the General Assembly should have followed the direction of the Constitution and declared that the man who was elected Governor but later died had been duly elected Governor of this State, but some reference to that question will be made later. If on publication of the returns it is disclosed that the voters have cast a majority of their votes for some person for Governor, the Constitution means that such person has been duly elected Governor of this State and directs the General Assembly to so declare. When this has been done the question is closed, so far as any present election is concerned. The constitutional provision for conferring *conditional and limited* power upon the General Assembly to elect a Governor remains dormant, does not come into operation, and can not become effective. "If no person shall have such majority," then and in no other event, "from the two persons having the highest number of votes, who shall be in life, and shall not decline an election at the time appointed for the General Assembly to elect, the General Assembly shall immediately, elect a Governor viva voce." Thus the General Assembly was limited not only to a specified event, but also to the two persons receiving the highest number of votes, who were still in life. If it had not been the very definite and clear intention that in every case the matter of electing a Governor must be as completely as possible governed by the expressed choice of the people, would it be reasonable to limit and restrict the General Assembly specifically to a choice between the two persons who receive the greatest number of votes, who are still in life? Is such manifest purpose to effectuate the will of the people reconcilable with the election by the General Assembly of one of two persons who receive some small number of votes, while the voters gave an overwhelming majority to another person who was in life on the date of the election?

Referring again to the meaning of the word "person" it may not be amiss to observe that just because this word may be defined in dictionaries as a living human being does not necessarily mean that it should be so construed in the foregoing provision of the Constitution or any other document or instrument. Everyone concedes that there was a living person who received a majority of the votes cast in the election of November 5, 1946. If the word "person" in the foregoing provision must be construed in all instances to mean a living human being, then it was pure surplusage to interpolate the phrase "who shall be in life" as a part of the clause referring to "the two persons" having the highest number of votes. If it was necessary to insert these words in this part of the provision in order to make the intention of the framers of the Constitution absolutely clear, then why was it not used in the preceding clause referring to the person receiving a majority? The answer is that the phrase was not intended to be even implied in the preceding clause.

There are two settled rules of construction that are applicable. One is that where a qualifying word or phrase is found in one provision and not in some other provision, the presumption is that the other provision was not intended to have such qualification. This seems to be universally recognized as a sound rule of construction. The other rule is that qualifying words are presumed to apply to the immediate antecedent and not to apply to a remote antecedent, where they are omitted from the latter. Both rules, of course, are subject to the general rule that instruments must be considered as a whole, and there are doubtless other qualifications and variations, but it seems to us that both rules are applicable here. . . . The clause "the person having a majority of the whole number of votes, shall be declared duly elected Governor," is not absurd as applied to the present situation. Its true meaning is, that the General Assembly shall declare such person to have been duly elected Governor. That is what it means under any and all circumstances, for it refers always to a past fact.

Moreover, we are authorized, if indeed not required, to give consideration to the history of elections for Governor over a period of approximately half a century before the drafting and submission of the present Constitution, and its ratification by the voters in 1945. Throughout that period there had been one and only one dominant political party in this State. That party was and is the Democratic party. Every Governor throughout that period was a Democrat, nominated by the Democrats of Georgia in a Democratic primary, after a campaign in which vital issues were discussed throughout the State and embodied in a platform of principles upon which he sought nomination. The only opposition in the general election that any Democratic nominee had ever encountered throughout such period was an "Independent," or a member of some minor opposing party, and some write-in votes for persons who were not candidates. Such opposition candidates were not only opposing the choice of the Democrats of Georgia, but were opposing the platform of principles upon which he had been nominated. It could not, therefore, in reason be asserted that any person, whether a member of the Constitutional Commission, a member of the General Assembly, or a voter who had a part in the adoption of the present Constitution, desired or intended that in the event the person nominated by the Democratic party as a candidate for Governor, and overwhelmingly elected in the general election, should thereafter die before the result is declared, the General Assembly must thereupon under language of the Constitution, ignore all qualified Democrats of the State and limit themselves to a choice between two persons for whom votes were cast in opposition to the Democratic nominee for Governor. To attribute such an intention to the great hosts of Georgians who had a part in adopting the Constitution when the language they employed does not imperatively demand it would be unreasonable, if not unthinkable. It would mean that they were willing and intended that all concern about the qualifications of the chief executive and principles for which he should stand may be wholly disregarded and abandoned. This conclusion is inescapable if it be admitted that a person who did not appear before the people, or who was a member of some minor opposing political party, or whose name had been written in, should be elevated to the high office of Governor, to the exclusion of all other Georgians eminently qualified to occupy that exalted office.

There are still other rules of interpretation that have been established by experience and which we think should be applied in this instance. In 11 Am.Jur. 684, § 67, it is said: "Framers of a new Constitution who adopt provisions contained in a former Constitution, to which a certain construction has been given, are presumed as a general rule to have intended that these provisions should have the meaning attributed to them under the earlier instrument. The embodiment in a Constitution, without change of verbiage, of provisions found in previous constitutions, precludes the court from giving their language a meaning different from that ascribed to the previous constitutional provisions, notwithstanding the construction referred to is that placed on the old Constitution by the legislature and not by the judicial department of government." It may be that the rule just quoted is stated more strongly than we would be willing to put it. It is unnecessary to go that far here. We would prefer to say that the meaning placed upon the language by such legislative construction will be presumed to have been the meaning intended by those who adopted a constitution, rather than that, as the quoted rule states, the courts are precluded by such construction. The rule is perhaps more correctly stated in 16 C.J.S., Constitutional Law, § 35, p. 76, as follows: "It is an established rule of construction that, where a constitutional provision has received a settled judicial construction, and is afterward incorporated into a new or revised constitution, or amendment, it will be presumed to have been retained with a knowledge of the previous construction, and courts will feel bound to adhere to it. Prior legislative construction is, likewise, presumed to have been adopted by subsequent adoption of the provision so construed. The language of an existing statute adopted into a constitution is presumed to be taken with its established construction."

What was the situation confronting the drafters of this Constitution as related to legislative interpretation of the language here employed? The provision of the Constitution, as stated above, was made a part of the Constitution of 1798 by amendment, and has constituted a part of every Constitution since that time. It was, without change in any respect, written into the present Constitution exactly as it appeared in the Constitution of 1877. There had at no time been a judicial construction of this language, but there had been legislative interpretation which, under either of the above rules, presumably shows the meaning intended by the framers of the present Constitution. By an act approved November 22, 1871, . . . providing for a special election for Governor, it was required that the election be held in the same manner, and the returns published and the result declared, as provided in the Constitution. Section 4 of the act declared that "if no person be found to have received a majority of the whole number of votes cast at said election, then from the two persons having the highest number of votes, who shall be in life, and shall not decline an election," the legislature shall elect a Governor. We repeat, for emphasis, the words, "if no person be found to have received a majority of the whole number of votes cast at said election," since it unmistakably refers to the date of the election. Under the rule above cited, the framers of the Constitution of 1877 presumably intended that its language, "if no person shall have such majority," which was taken from the constitution in force on the date of the above legislative enactment, meant precisely what the legislative construction had said it meant. After the adoption of that constitution, by an act of July 22, 1879, . . . which provided for an election to fill a vacancy in the office of Governor, it was provided that the General Assembly should canvass the returns of such special election and declare the result, or elect a Governor "in case no person shall receive a majority of the whole number of votes cast at such special election." Thus it appears that the language in the present Constitution about which this controversy arose had its meaning declared by legislative construction prior to its incorporation in the Constitution of 1877. Also, the meaning as thus stated was given to the same language as it appeared in the Constitution of 1877, by a subsequent act of the legislature construing the same; hence, when it was lifted from that Constitution and inserted in the present Constitution, presumably it was intended to have the same meaning.

In Massenburg v. Commissioners, 23 S.E. 998, this court said: "Where the constitution prescribes the manner in which a particular public functionary is to be elected, or prescribes the term during which he shall hold office, the legislature is thereafter powerless to modify, enlarge, or diminish that which is established by the constitution. * * * If, therefore, the people in their sovereign capacity, in convention assembled, do by the terms of an organic law, established by them and for them, reserve unto themselves the right of election to particular offices, the legislature cannot thereafter interfere with this reserved right, and provide other means than those established by the constitution for the election of incumbents to such offices, even though there be no negation of this right of legislative interference expressly stated in the terms of the constitution. The reservation of the right itself is a sufficient safeguard against the encroachment of legislative power, inasmuch as such reservation of itself operates as a denial to the legislature of the right of interference." There this court was announcing a fundamental principle of our State government under the Constitution. A departure from that high principle might well endanger the stability of the entire governmental structure. It declares a rule of law that denies any implied or inherent right or power in the legislative department to exercise any power that has not by the sovereign people, through that Constitution, been reposed in the legislative department of government. At the very point where any department of the State government fails to recognize the truth asserted in the first paragraph of the Constitution, to the effect that in this State the people are the masters and the officials the servants, liberty is imperiled. Since the duty and the responsibility to construe the Constitution has by the people been laid upon the judicial department in cases involving the rights of litigants, the constitutional limitation upon the power of each coordinate branch of the government must be adjudicated by the courts in cases calling that matter in question. Until such an adjudication has been made, neither the legislature nor the executive may be presumed to have intended to exceed its power, but they should welcome and willingly abide by the limitation when fixed by an adjudication. This court spoke again in Morris v. Glover, 49 S.E. 786, as follows: "In those governments where the lawmaking power is not fettered by a written Constitution limiting its authority, offices may be created, consolidated, or abolished at legislative will. * * * But where an office is created or guarded by express constitutional provision, its scope cannot be enlarged or lessened by statute, *nor can the office be filled in any manner other than that prescribed by the Constitution.*" (Italics ours.)

It would not necessarily cause a governmental breakdown, if, at the time fixed for the election of a Governor, no one was chosen Governor. The constitutional arrangement, while not sufficient to insure that there could not possibly occur a vacancy in that office, nevertheless makes reasonably sure that it shall be lawfully occupied at all times. Paragraph 1 of art. 5, sec. 1, fixes the term of the office of Governor at four years and until his successor shall be chosen and qualified. The phrase "until his successor shall be chosen and qualified," has a recognized and definite meaning, as declared by numerous decisions of this court. . . . That time in excess of the four year period which a Governor may be required to serve is a part of his constitutional term. His installation in office is for a term embracing, not only the four years mentioned, but such additional time as may be required for his successor to be chosen and qualified. The further provision rendering him ineligible to succeed himself has no bearing whatever upon the duration of his term. Its primary object is to prevent the necessity of the Governor engaging in a political campaign during his term. Certainly it is not for this court to fix the policy and the law about choosing a Governor. We merely construe the law which the people have adopted. A construction of the Constitution that would sustain the election of Mr. Talmadge by the legislature would place a controlling meaning upon the pertinent portion of the Constitution, which might compel some future General Assembly to elect as Governor a person wholly undesirable, because of his communistic or other alien philosophies of government, in any case where the majority candidate died before the returns were published by the legislature and where two of such undesirable persons received the next highest number of votes. It would not constitute a worthy solution of the stated hypothetical case to suggest that the General Assembly in such a case may simply make no election. Those members are under the solemnity of an oath, obligating them to obey the Constitution. In a case where the Constitution authorizes the General Assembly to elect a Governor, it declares that if the condition precedent exists "the General Assembly *shall* immediately, elect a Governor viva voce." (Italics ours.) Such a construction as that above mentioned would mean that the General Assembly when acting as canvassers of the election returns, are supreme, and their action is not subject to review. To thus hold would mean that had Mr. Eugene Talmadge been living, and despite the knowledge of everyone of his overwhelming election, the canvassers of those election returns could with immunity and finality assert that some other person was elected, and the people's right, together with the right of Eugene Talmadge to have his election recognized, could be thus destroyed, leaving them without any recourse whatever. This hypothetical case may never arise, and indeed we are all hopeful that it will never arise, but it is within the realm of future possibility and can not be ignored or overlooked when a construction of the Constitution is being made by a court.

From what has been said we must hold that in the circumstances appearing the General Assembly had no jurisdiction to elect the Honorable Herman Talmadge or any other person as Governor.

Under the Constitution, art. 5, sec. 1, par. 1, above cited, Governor Arnall was authorized to occupy the office of Governor until his successor was chosen and qualified. A successor was chosen, but his death prevented him from qualifying at the time fixed by law, thus creating the necessity for Governor Arnall to continue in office. But Mr. Thompson was elected in the general election in 1946 as Lieutenant Governor of this State, and he is required, in case of a vacancy in the office of Governor, to perform the duties of Governor. Constitution, art. 5, sec. 1, par. 7. The voluntary resignation of Governor Arnall on January 18, 1947, immediately imposed upon the Lieutenant Governor the duties of Governor. He is now entitled to perform all of the duties and exercise all the authority which by the Constitution and laws are imposed upon the Governor of this State.

. . . .

All the Justices concur, except JENKINS, C.J., and CANDLER, J., who dissent.

JENKINS, Chief Justice (dissenting).

The determination of the controlling legal question involved in these cases is a matter of great public concern, gravity, and importance. Laws and constitutions in a government of law as distinguished from an autocracy are not decreed and administered to fit some special occasion after *it has happened;* but being fashioned in advance to meet all future contingencies, they are more like ready made garments, and for this very reason do not always by specific, as distinguished from general, language fit unusual future contingencies as perfectly as we can afterwards see that they might possibly have been made to do. But there are few indeed in all this land who would exchange their liberty under a government of law for any other system where rights and liberties, if any, are doled out as a matter of grace from some malevolent or even benevolent autocrat.

I would much prefer, if it were possible to do so in a case of such great importance, to join in the majority opinion of my learned colleagues rather than dissent from the conclusions of law at which they have arrived. However, having resolved the questions as best I could, and having reached a decided conviction contrary to that expressed by the majority, with due modesty I trust as one of two dissenters, and with all deference to my majority brethren, I feel it incumbent upon me to state for the record, as briefly as I can but as fully as is necessary, the reasons which have impelled me to arrive at a different legal conclusion. While it is true that the majority opinion is the judgment of the court and therefore becomes the law of the land, it is also true that in the development of American jurisprudence the dissenting opinion is believed to have ofttimes played a useful part.

1. *The Lieutenant Governor cannot claim, nor does he in fact seek to claim under or by virtue of the death of Hon. Eugene Talmadge, but as conceded by his counsel of record and as shown by his pleadings, he bases his claim solely by virtue of the resignation in his favor of the incumbent Governor. The incumbent Governor, on account of the election having failed, was legally holding over after his regular term had expired, until, but only until, his successor could be legally chosen.*

The Lieutenant Governor, thus claiming under and by virtue of the holdover Governor's resignation in his favor, and having by his pleading in fact asked to be made a party to the suit originally instituted by the incumbent Governor holding over, does not, therefore, even claim to stand in the shoes of the late Hon. Eugene Talmadge; but, claiming as he does under the resignation of the holdover Governor, puts himself squarely in *his* shoes, and not only manifestly cannot but does not even seek to assert any claim to the office other than that which the resignation of the holdover Governor might give him. Unquestionably, when the election by the people failed, the incumbent Governor was constitutionally authorized to hold over beyond his regular term and for the next four years until the next election as provided for by the Constitution, unless it be that the Constitution, after disqualifying any incumbent Governor to succeed himself, goes further to provide for the termination of his holdover tenure by making provision for a special intermediate election by the General Assembly under such a contingency.

It is quite impossible, however, to so completely close one's eyes and ears as to be wholly unaware of the troubled state of mind of many of the citizens of this State, who appear to reason that, since on the same ticket at the last general election in November there appeared the name of a successful candidate for Governor, and of a successful candidate for Lieutenant Governor, the death of the former, although he did not become Governor, left the latter to succeed him. While this is not the contention of Mr. Thompson or his attorneys of record, since it is suggested and insisted upon by some of the briefs filed in his behalf by attorneys, amicus curiae, it is thought proper to refer to it. This too is the idea that has actually troubled me more than anything else—not as a matter of law, but because at first blush it might seem that way. It is doubtless true that to many the question presented is just that simple and just that plain. It would indeed have been so if the Constitution had declared, as it could have done, that, upon the failure of an election by the people by reason of the death of the successful candidate before being installed, the Lieutenant Governor would take over, and had it not on the contrary provided otherwise, that is, that under such circumstances the incumbent Governor and not the Lieutenant Governor shall hold over until a Governor can be chosen and qualified. A provision for the succession of the Vice President when the successful candidate for President shall die before taking office is contained in the Federal Constitution. The Georgia Constitution, however, not only failed thus to declare, not only does it limit the right of the Lieutenant Governor to succeed to the duties of Governor upon "the death, resignation, or disability of the *Governor*," not only does it preclude his right to do so by declaring that upon the failure of an election it is the incumbent Governor, not the Lieutenant Governor, who shall hold over "until his successor shall be chosen and qualified," but to make assurance doubly sure, the Constitution after prohibiting any Governor to succeed himself, although providing that he should hold over until his successor is chosen and qualified, goes on to expressly limit his holdover tenure by providing for a special election for Governor by the General Assembly when it shall appear when the returns are canvassed that the election has failed in that no person shall then have a majority of the votes cast. It is thus easy enough to see why it is that the Lieutenant Governor bases his claim, not by reason of the death of the successful candidate, but wholly under and by virtue of the resignation in his favor of the incumbent Governor holding over.

Courts must construe the provision of the Constitution creating the office of Lieutenant Governor as it is written and not as it might have been framed. We are dealing not with "subjunctives" that is, not as to what our Constitution "may, can, must, might, could, would, or should" contain, but only with that which it actually does contain. To do so is not resorting to technicalities. No layman, I am sure, much less a judge, would for one moment believe that it is the duty of courts to Gallop Poll their own minds in order to determine what they think the people think the Constitution *ought* to have contained. The office of Lieutenant Governor is indeed an exalted one, but since the right of the Lieutenant Governor to take over the duties of Governor has thus been positively limited by the Constitution creating the office in the three different ways which have been indicated to the one contingency set forth, he who takes the office takes only such office as the Constitution gives him, and it is not for courts by taking thought to add one cubit to its stature.

. . . .

3. *The Constitution by article* V, *section I, paragraph* IV, *delegates to the General Assembly the exclusive duty and authority to canvass the returns. This, as I understand, is not questioned by any one.*

This paragraph of the Constitution is in my opinion decisive as to that and other features of the case, but since it has been quoted in full in the majority opinion it will not be repeated here. Since, as stated, it not only seems manifest, but no one seems to question that the duty and responsibility of canvassing the returns is placed solely upon the

General Assembly, and that such action on their part is altogether conclusive, there is no need to give further consideration to this admittedly unambiguous phase of the case.

4. *Not only is authority clearly delegated to the General Assembly to canvass the votes; but to me it seems just as palpably clear that it is also made their duty to designate, that is adjudicate, the "person" "having" a majority of the votes cast, if any there be, and thus qualify him to take the oath of office.*

This proposition seems disputed by counsel for Mr. Thompson, inasmuch as they contend that the General Assembly acts only in a ministerial capacity in canvassing the returns and publishing the result. However, the very language of the Constitution says that the person so entitled "shall be declared duly elected Governor." This court by a unanimous bench has said that this function of the General Assembly constitutes an integral part of the election itself. Wood v. Arnall, 6 S.E.2d. 722. *Someone* ought to be empowered not only to publish the result of the figures, but to adjudicate authoritatively what it is that these figures mean, and who it is that has been "duly elected Governor." The Governor unlike other officers receives no commission. The Constitution in lieu thereof has very wisely committed to the General Assembly complete control of the election process. The Constitution provides that "the Governor-elect" (manifestly after being so declared) "*shall be installed in office at the next session of the General Assembly.*" It provides that the returns shall be opened and published by the President of the Senate and Speaker of the House "*in the presence and under the direction of the General Assembly,*" when the "person" "having" a majority of the votes cast shall be "*declared duly elected Governor of this State.*" The Constitution further provides the oath to be administered, which by statutory law perfectly consistent with the Constitution, Code, § 40–104, "shall be taken by the governor-elect in the presence of the General Assembly." All this constitutes the sole evidence of his right to execute the Executive power. It is not left for just anyone who might have the temerity to do so to seek to exercise the functions of the office. He must carry with him the authoritative credentials of the General Assembly. It is thus my view that the Constitution does not constitute the General Assembly mere administrative clerks or "tellers" to tabulate and publish the figures of the election. It was made something more than a mere animated adding machine. The figures merely furnish the basis that is the evidence on which the *declaration* required of the General Assembly by the Constitution is based. Just as with most officers it is the commission, so here it is the declaration followed by the installation, both by the General Assembly, which enables one actually elected governor to be recognized as such. While it was the Creator who embedded the granite within the mountain side which makes up the features of General Lee, it took the sculptor's hand to make it stand forth for men to recognize and acclaim.

5. *Under the Constitution, when the returns were canvassed it became the duty of the General Assembly to determine whether or not under the undisputed facts there was a person who did then have a majority of the votes cast, whom the General Assembly would properly designate as Governor-elect and thus qualify to appear before it and take the oath and be installed. Not only is the General Assembly entrusted with the duty of such a decision by the Constitution, but as I see it under the facts of this case, it correctly determined that the election by the people had in fact failed in that no "person" did then "have" a majority of the votes cast.*

Here it seems we arrive at a still

sharper line of demarkation between the opposing sides. This seems to be the crux of the case, for should it be held that under the facts of this case the General Assembly had the exclusive right to declare, and had in fact determined, that the election had failed, in that no "person" did then "have" a majority of the votes cast, it would follow almost as a matter of course that it thereupon became the duty and function of the General Assembly to proceed to elect a Governor. While the proposition just stated seems clear enough to me, it does involve a construction of the Constitution, which is not absolutely unambiguous, and therefore, as I see it, presents the first of the two justiciable points of controversy.

If the General Assembly, after canvassing the returns and publishing the result, should fail to declare any person "duly elected Governor" so as thus to qualify him to take the oath and be installed in office—should fail to do this and stop right there, without going to show *why* it had failed in its duty to do so by adjudicating the *absence* of any person whom it could qualify, there would seem to be a manifest dereliction of trust imposed upon it by the Constitution. The right of the General Assembly to determine when an election has failed and to declare that it has failed when such is the fact is not even a matter of necessary implication, for the language of the Constitution, not only provides that they shall declare who is elected Governor when there shall be a person who has a majority of the votes, but goes right on in the same connection to say what they shall do if no person shall have such a majority. It is conceded that under *some* circumstances they must proceed to elect a Governor. Would it not be an anomaly for them to do so without any determination as to why? To me, it does not seem possible to conceive that the General Assembly should be called upon to pass upon the *efficacy* of an election under one contingency, but not be called to pass upon the *failure* of an election upon the other contingency; especially so when it is given an alternative duty according to which contingency may actually exist. Not only does this paragraph of the Constitution thus speak for itself, but it has also been thus construed by another and different paragraph of the Constitution, Article V, section II, paragraph I, dealing with other State House officials, which says in just so many words that the General Assembly is given the same duty in those cases of "deciding when there is no election" as is "applicable to the election of Governor."

Moreover, it is well to stress here that it is by virtue of this same adjudication of the General Assembly that the election has failed that the incumbent Governor is authorized to constitutionally hold over beyond his regular term, and until his successor can be legally chosen. As already shown, it is only under and by virtue of such holdover tenure of the previous Governor, coupled with his resignation in favor of the Lieutenant Governor that the latter claims. If, as I see it, the Constitution has thus twice spoken for itself, and it seems that it has done so, not in specific terms but in a manner just about as plain as John Alden did ever speak for himself, the General Assembly has been given jurisdiction, not only to canvass the returns and publish the result of the ballots, not only to designate the Governor-elect, and thus qualify him to take the oath of office where there be some person who has a majority of the votes cast; but it seems just about as certain and just about as plain from the language of the Constitution itself that, if and when the election fails and there be no "person" who shall "have" a majority whom it can declare to be Governor-elect and proceed to install as Governor, it becomes its duty to adjudicate that fact. That the responsibility imposed upon the General Assembly is not a mere clerical formality confined to figuring up the votes, especially when the votes have become wholly ineffective, is shown with great uniformity in the rulings made by the courts of last resort in our sister States. See State ex rel. Morris v. Bulkeley, 23 A. 186; Dickson v. Strickland, 265 S.W. 1012; Carr v. Wilson, 9 S.E. 31, and Taylor v. Beckham, 56 S.W. 177. [*Cases decided in Connecticut, Texas, West Virginia, and Kentucky, respectively.*]

But it is urged and insisted by counsel for Mr. Thompson both in the written and oral arguments, that such cannot be the proper interpretation of the decisive paragraph, not only for the reason that the duties of the General Assembly are purely clerical in character, but, as I construe the effect of the argument, it has power to act in a reminiscent way only. That is, they say that the language of the paragraph forbids the General Assembly to do aught else than uselessly to show that "once upon a time" there *was* a person who prior to his death, *had* a majority of the votes cast, and who therefore, if he had not died, would still "have" a majority. Their more specific argument is that the paragraph provides with reference to electing a Governor that, if no person shall have a majority, then the General Assembly shall elect from the two persons having the highest vote *who shall be in life;* whereas the preceding portion of the paragraph merely declares that the person having the highest number of votes shall be declared duly elected Governor without including the italicized words *who shall be in life.* It is thus urged that the framers did not intend to require the successful candidate to be in life when the time should come for the General Assembly to declare him duly elected Governor. In other words, we seem to be asked to construe the quoted paragraph to mean that, when the successful candidate dies before qualifying, it is nevertheless the duty of the General Assembly to solemnly declare him to be "Governor-elect." There would seem to be no more reason to try to declare a deceased person Governor-elect than there would be to attempt to swear him in as Governor. The use of the words "who shall be in life" in one phrase and not in the other avails nothing. The provision in the Constitution is that the General Assembly shall declare the "person" "having" the majority vote as "duly elected Governor of this State." Why should the Constitution be expected to say that the person whom it shall name as Governor-elect so that it can install him in office should be in life? It *did* take the proper precaution of saying that, if and when the General Assembly came to elect a Governor itself, that deceased persons should not be counted in determining who had received the two highest votes from whom it was to elect. There is nothing strange about its language in either instance.

Before leaving this phase of the discusion, it might be proper to observe that from my viewpoint, that is, construing the Constitution as I have, to mean that the General Assembly did in fact have the delegated right and exclusive authority to declare whether or not under the circumstances existing in this case any person did then have a majority of the votes cast, the *execution* of that authority, that is, the determination of whether the election had or had not failed was a political function, of which the General Assembly was the sole arbiter. But in view of the holdings made by the majority opinion that it did not even have the power to say whether the election had or had not failed, I will seek to show, not only that it had the exclusive right and duty to declare whether or not the election had failed in that no one did then have a majority, but that its determination that it had failed was in fact correct, and therefore for that reason it had the right to elect.

If I be right as to both or right as to either of these propositions, the action of the General Assembly should be sustained.

Passing on then from the proposition that the General Assembly was exclusively authorized under the only reasonable interpretation of the language of the Constitution to adjudicate under the facts of this case whether or not the election had failed in that no person did then have a majority of the votes cast, let consideration now be given to the question as to whether or not the General Assembly was correct, in adjudicating that it had failed.

As I see this case, it does not hang solely upon the proper construction to be given to the word "person" and the word "have" when the Constitution says that the General Assembly shall proceed to elect a Governor when no "person" shall "have" a majority of the votes cast. To me the proper meaning and purport of the Constitution, as shown by all of its provisions, is that the General Assembly shall elect a Governor when at the time the returns are canvassed there shall be no "person" who shall "have" a majority of the votes cast whom the General Assembly can declare "duly elected Governor of this State" and whom it can proceed to install in office. But it is also true that the use of the words "person" and "have" are most highly significant and about as strongly indicative as any two words could be.

In determining the meaning of the word "person" as used in the quoted paragraph of the Constitution, the fact that the successful candidate though dead when the votes were canvassed was in life when the votes were cast by the people is, as I see it, a matter of historical interest only. This for the reason that he died, not only before becoming Governor, but even before the election itself was completed by a canvass of the returns by the General Assembly. This being true, it seems impossible to see how, when the time arrived for the returns to be canvassed, it could reasonably be said that any "person" did then "have" a majority of the votes cast. As to the construction of laws, our Code, § 102–102 (1) lays it down as a fundamental rule of construction that, except as applied to words of art, etc., "The ordinary signification shall be applied to all words." Webster's New International Dictionary (2d edition) defines the word "person" as "A being characterized by conscious apprehension." It in no way treats the word as referring to one who had become deceased. Giving then to the word "person" as used in the quoted paragraph of the Constitution its usual and natural interpretation, there is no obscurity. In the work entitled Words & Phrases, Perm. Ed., vol. 32, p. 204, in digesting a Wisconsin case with respect to a primary election law which provided that the *person* receiving the greatest number of votes at a primary should be declared the candidate of that party, the authors of the work mentioned quote that court as follows: "A dead man is not a 'person' within the statute; such word meaning a living human being," citing State ex rel. Bancroft v. Frear, 128 N.W. 1068. See also Brooks v. Boston & N. St. R. Co., 97 N.E. 760, where the Massachusetts court makes the somewhat gruesome statement that "A corpse is not a person." It would seem needlessly tedious and perhaps confusing to attempt too much analysis of this phrase of the paragraph in question. To seek to make that clear which is already clear can only lead to confusion. As someone once remarked, "The Scriptures often throw great light upon the commentaries." But before dismissing any further discussion as to whether in using the word "person" the Constitution really means a person whom the General Assembly could qualify to appear before it and take the oath of office, it might be helpful to briefly call attention to just one thing more. The paragraph says that the General Assembly shall elect when no "person" "shall have" a majority. Note the present tense of the words "shall have." What the Constitution actually says is therefore a far cry indeed from what it would have said had it been written that the General Assembly shall elect when no person shall have *and no deceased person ever did have a majority*. True enough that a person now deceased once had a majority of the votes, but his narrow cell of six feet of earth owns nothing now—rather be it said nothing akin to lands, goods, tenements, or offices.

6. *As I view the law as applied to the admitted facts, it was just as much the duty of the General Assembly, after correctly deciding, upon the returns being canvassed, that no "person" did then "have" a majority of the votes cast, to proceed to the election of a Governor as it would have been if no person had ever received such a majority.*

It is well to observe at the outset that the paragraph of the Constitution giving the General Assembly the right and duty to elect a Governor when the election by the people has thus failed, whether wise or unwise, antiquated or not, is not mere cast-up driftwood littering the shore line of today. It may in a way seem startling, but it cannot be doubted, and is in fact conceded on all sides, that there are contingencies when this may be done. Until the year 1824 the sovereign people had expressly given to their General Assembly the entire duty and responsibility of electing a Governor. While in general the method of election has been changed, one small remnant of this ancient authority clearly adheres in our Constitution of today. It is true that the application of this paragraph of the Constitution to the particular state of facts actually presented requires construction, for the reason that it is not so palpably and transparently clear as it would have been had no person, since deceased, ever received a majority of the votes cast; and it is true that it is only when the votes are canvassed and no "person" "shall have" a majority that the General Assembly is empowered to elect. But as already stated in discussing the preceding closely related phase of the case, the fact that there was a successful candidate who had received a majority of the votes cast, but who was dead when the General Assembly canvassed the returns, is a matter of historical interest only. If it be conceded, as I believe has been shown, that there was then no "person" who did then "have" a majority of the votes cast, the language of the Constitution seems explicit and direct that the General Assembly must proceed to elect, and this is true even though in doing so it may thus curtail the constitutionally extended tenure of the incumbent Governor who when an election fails holds over after his regular term has expired until, but only until his successor is chosen and qualified. Here again we get back to a fundamental principle of construction. Where the Constitution or constitutional statutes speak plainly, we must take them according to what they actually *say* and let them mean just that and nothing more. It is only when the *language* of the Constitution is in and of itself susceptible to two or more interpretations, each equally permissible, that courts are at liberty to consider the comparative reasonableness or unreasonableness of the two constructions in order to arrive at what must have been the true intent of such ambiguous language. . . . Where it speaks for itself, that is the end of the matter. The rule is thus a mandatory one, even though a different interpretation from that *actually expressed* might seem to better meet future contingencies, and thus afford a safer general rule to serve the public welfare.

Much has been said about changed conditions since the language of the quoted paragraph of the Constitution was embedded within our organic law in the year 1824. It is true many things have come to pass since then, but what has all this to do with the language of the Constitution requiring the General Assembly to elect a Governor under a named contingency? Language has not changed. Dictionaries were in vogue then just as they are now. The language under discussion has five times been carried forward and five times solemnly embedded within our organic law. The last time that this was done was but as yesterday, after the horses and buggies were mostly put away. There in clear cold print it stands, and there it should remain until the power that wrote it in shall write it out. Having, as I myself believe, construed the only possible ambiguities of the paragraph in the only way reasonably possible, the remainder, commanding the General Assembly to elect a Governor under the contingency stated, is as plain as language can make it, and is as plain now as it was in 1824. As it seems to me, the attack on the action taken by the General Assembly seems based, not so much on the theory that the Constitution fails to say what it means, as on the supposition that it does not mean what it says.

But it is insisted that the Legislature, by the now obsolete Code, § 40–102, has itself construed this paragraph of the Constitution, as it was contained in the old Constitution prior to its being carried forward to the present Constitution. The argument is that the people when carrying it forward into the present Constitution must have had in mind the interpretation previously made by the Legislature. It is urged that this Code section shows that the Legislature had construed the paragraph of the Constitution to mean that it did not have power to elect a Governor except when at the General Election no person did then receive a majority. It will be seen that the Legislature by this Code section was not dealing at all with the *General Election* dealt with by the paragraph of the Constitution, but was providing for a Special Election for Governor on account of a vacancy occurring in the office of Governor before the office of Lieutenant Governor had been created. This Special Election was under its own control, and it was privileged to depart from what the Constitution provided with respect to a failure under the General Election in any way it saw fit. Referring to this Special Election provided for by itself, the General Assembly declares that it shall elect when no person "shall receive a majority * * * at such special election, as provided in the Constitution." It is manifest that it did not cover the whole ground even as to such Special Election, as was done by the general language in the provision of the Constitution relating to the General Election. The language of the statute was apt enough as dealing with living persons who were concerned in the Special Election, but its language does not cover and does not take into account, as the Constitution does, the possibility of the successful candidate dying prior to taking office. So far as the statutory reference to the Constitution is concerned, it manifestly refers to the *manner and method* to be employed by the General Assembly when electing a Governor where such a Special Election shall fail. This reference is the means and the only means by which provision was made as to the method of procedure to be followed by the General Assembly. It would seem to be a strained construction to seek to make it apply as an interpretation as to *other* matters which the General Assembly evidently did not have in mind. It would therefore seem a slender thread indeed to hang an argument on, that the people in ratifying the present Constitution had this provision in mind as amounting in some sort of way to a vague and indefinite interpretation of the Constitutional provision now under review.

7. *The right and duty of the General Assembly to adjudge when an election by the people has failed not only being in the General Assembly under the facts here existing, but that body having not only adjudged, but correctly adjudged that such election had failed in this case, it follows that under such circumstances it was its duty to elect a Governor. Therefore, it is wholly unnecessary for us to speculate as to what the law would have been had the General Assembly sought to elect some person other than one of the two "persons" in life whom it had adjudicated had received the highest number of votes and who would not decline to serve. This is true for two reasons: first, because under the facts presented the question is purely academic and is not presented by the record, since the General Assembly after publishing the returns and declaring that the election had failed, then proceeded to follow the exact language written into the Constitution; and second, because the execution of its power, if it had the power, and I have sought to show that it did, was a purely political function concerning which courts are not privileged to interfere.*

I am unable to agree that a delegated political function ceases to be such even if in its *exercise* the Legislative branch of Government should find it necessary to construe the Constitution. The General Assembly and the Executive branch of government are given all political authority not actually inconsistent with the Constitution. The General Assembly no less than courts must support the Constitution of the people; but the people have entrusted to it and not the courts the duty of keeping itself within bounds in the administration of its actual political duties and powers. In this case not only did the General Assembly, in the performance of what I have sought to show was its political authority, keep within the exact letter of the Constitution, but since courts have no authority to intervene in the execution of an actual political authority, it would be fruitless for them to even speculate as to whether, under the special circumstances of this case, it would have correctly performed its political duties had it sought to do otherwise.

From all that has been said in this dissenting opinion, it will be seen: (a) Mr. Thompson could not possibly claim, nor does he in fact claim office by virtue of the death of Hon. Eugene Talmadge, since Mr. Talmadge at the time of his death had not become Governor, nor had Mr. Thompson become Lieutenant Governor. He bases his claim solely by virtue of the resignation in his favor of the incumbent Governor, who when the election became ineffective was entitled by the Constitution to hold over beyond his regular term until, but only until, his successor could be chosen and qualified. Mr. Thompson therefore stands in the shoes of the Governor holding over and could occupy no better position than he under whom he claims. (b) I am convinced that, when the General Assembly comes to canvass the returns of an election for Governor, it is made their duty, under the scheme of the Constitution of *this particular* State at least, to determine whether or not the election has failed. If there be any person having a majority of the votes cast, it is made their duty to declare him "duly elected Governor," and to proceed to "install" him in office. If, on the other hand, there shall be no "person" who shall then "have" a majority vote, whom it can declare "duly elected Governor" and whom it can proceed to install, it seems manifest to me that it should so declare. It is not a mere teller to tabulate the figures. (c) If no "person" shall "have" a majority of the votes cast, whom it can declare Governor-elect and proceed to install in office, it becomes the duty of the General Assembly under the mandate of the Constitution to proceed to elect a Governor in the manner therein prescribed. (d) Under ordinary circumstances, all this, though disputed, seems perfectly plain to me; but under the somewhat ambiguous language of the Constitution *as applied to the facts here presented* it was and is, as I believe, a *justiciable* question, that is, subject to court adjudication as to whether or not the General Assembly was authorized to determine whether the election had or had not failed; and whether, therefore, it should or should not proceed to elect a Governor under its delegated political authority. (e) The answer to these questions, as in this opinion I have sought to show, is that it does have the right to determine one way or another each of these questions as a part of its delegated political authority. (f) The General Assembly thus having the right as a part of its political authority to determine whether or not under the facts here presented the election had or had not failed for the reason indicated, and it also having in my opinion the right to determine as a part of its political authority the question as to whether under the facts presented it must proceed to elect a Governor (both of these questions as to the right to decide at all being, as stated, justiciable and therefore subject to review by the courts)—it follows just as plainly that in each instance the *exercise* of this authority, if it had the authority, that is, the determination either that the election had failed or that it had not failed, and that the General Assembly must or must not elect a Governor, is not subject to review, the only question open to review being whether it had the right to decide the questions at all. (g) Accordingly, while I differ with my majority colleagues as to whether the General Assembly had political authority to adjudicate those questions at all, for I think that it did, while they by the controlling majority opinion have adjudicated that it did not, I do not differ with them on the proposition that authority to adjudicate must be first had before it can be exercised. My disagreement is that, on this justiciable question as to whether or not the General Assembly had the right and power to determine these questions, it not only had the exclusive political authority to do so, but in the *exercise* of such authority it in fact determined them correctly.

CANDLER, Justice (dissenting). In my view the cases do not present justiciable controversies. It is my opinion that they involve questions over which the General Assembly has been given exclusive jurisdiction, and whether it has acted correctly or incorrectly, the courts are given no power under the Constitution to interfere.

STATE v. YOUNG

NEBRASKA SUPREME COURT

48 N.W. 2D 677 (1951)

The governor of Nebraska, after notice and hearing, directed the removal of Young as liquor control commissioner for having accepted gifts and selling insurance to liquor licensees. Young refused to surrender the office contending that the governor did not have the power to remove him. On the order of the governor, the attorney general filed suit in the state supreme court on behalf of the state to determine by what warrant Young held the office of liquor control commissioner.

Justice CARTER delivered the opinion of the court.

. . . .

THE FACTS are not in dispute. The respondent for many years before becoming a member of the liquor control commission was engaged in the insurance business in Omaha. For some years he operated his own agency, but during the times here involved he was brokering his business with general agents. By this manner of handling he turned the insurance business that came to him to the general agency which issued the policy, collected the premium, and remitted his commission to him. A number of respondent's insurance clients were liquor licensees who operated under the control of the liquor control commission. When respondent became a member of the liquor control commission he discontinued the solicitation of liquor licensees for insurance. It appears, however, that approximately 30 liquor licensees purchased insurance from the general agencies and directed that the account of respondent be credited with the commissions. Respondent received approximately $2,400 in such commissions in 1949. It is the acceptances of these commissions that brought about the notice, hearing, and order of removal by the Governor.

The supreme executive power in the state is lodged in the Governor. Art. IV, section 6, Constitution. Except as limited by the Constitution itself the supreme executive power is to be exercised by the Governor and, under the division of powers devised by the Constitution, neither the Legislature nor the courts may exercise the powers thus conferred upon the executive branch. The power to remove an officer or employee in the executive branch of the government is an executive function. The lodging of the supreme executive power in the Governor by the Constitution reposes in the Governor the power to remove executive officers and employees of the government appointed by him, except as limited by the Constitution itself. The only limitation placed upon the executive power of the Governor in connection with the removal of executive officers and employees appointed by him is Article IV, section 12, of the Constitution, which provides: "The Governor shall have power to remove any officer, whom he may appoint, in case of incompetency, neglect of duty, or malfeasance in office, and he may declare his office vacant, and fill the same as herein provided in other cases of vacancy." Under this section of the Constitution we think it is clear that the Governor must specify charges against an officer or employee falling within its provisions, give notice and hearing, allege a ground of removal set forth in the constitutional provision, and produce evidence sufficient to sustain the action taken. Whether or not the provisions of Article IV, section 12, of the Constitution, have been complied with, is in the final analysis a question for the courts. As to all officers and employees in the executive department appointed by the Governor who do not fall within the class designated by Article IV, of the Constitution, section 12, they are removable at the will of the Governor by virtue of the grant of the supreme executive power to him by Article IV, section 6, of the Constitution.

One of the primary questions to be here determined is whether or not a member of the liquor control commission is within the classification of officers and employees designated in Article IV, section 12. It is clear, we think, that the latter provision was intended to include all officers and employees in the executive department which were appointed by the Governor for a definite term. If this were not so the power of the Legislature to fix the terms of offices which it creates would be form without substance. Although not an executive department, the liquor control commission is an executive agency and its members are subject to the provisions of Article IV, section 12, of the Constitution. . . .

We have not overlooked the early decision of State ex rel. Hastings v. Smith, 52 N.W. 700. We think that the holding of the fifth paragraph of the syllabus in that case correctly states the rule. It provides: "Where the incumbent is elected or appointed for a definite term, and is removable only for specified cause, the power of removal cannot be exercised until there has been preferred against him specific charges of which he shall have notice, and an opportunity afforded him to be heard in his defense." Such holding is pursuant to the limitation contained in Article IV, section 12, of the Constitution, rather than under the grant of the supreme executive power of the Governor by Article IV, section 6, of the Constitution, in which latter event removal would be wholly at the will of the Governor without notice or hearing. We disapprove that part of State ex rel. Hastings v. Smith, which purports to hold that Article IV, section 12, of the Constitution applies only to officers appointed by the Governor which are mentioned in the Constitution.

In creating the Nebraska Liquor Control Commission the Legislature provided in part as follows: "The Governor shall appoint three members of the commission, one of whom he shall designate as chairman. One member shall be appointed every two years and shall hold office for a period of six years. Any appointee may be removed by the Governor, after an opportunity to be heard, for malfeasance, misfeasance or neglect in office." . . . It further provided: "No commissioner, secretary or person appointed or employed by the commission shall solicit or accept any gift, gratuity, emolument or employment from any person subject to the provisions of this act, or from any officer, agent or employee thereof, nor solicit, request from or recommend, directly or indirectly, to any such person or to any officer, agent or employee thereof, the appointment of any person to any place or position; and every such person, every officer, agent or employee thereof, is hereby forbidden to offer to any commissioner, secretary, or to any person appointed or employed by the commission, any gift, gratuity, emolument or employment. If any commissioner, secretary or any person appointed or employed by the commission shall violate any of the provisions of this section, he shall be removed from the office or employment held by him. Every person violating the provisions of this section shall be deemed guilty of a misdemeanor, and upon conviction thereof shall be fined not more than five hundred dollars, or shall be imprisoned in the county jail not less than sixty days nor more than six months, or be both fined and imprisoned." . . .

The power of the Legislature in the creation of an office, admittedly a legislative function, is limited to those matters which are defined as ingredients of the office. The general rule is that the power to appoint carries with it the power to remove, and even if the occupant may be subject to impeachment, the power of the Governor to remove remains wholly unaffected by such fact. It is within the power of the Legislature to create an office, define its powers, limit its duration, and provide for the compensation of the occupant. The power of appointment and removal is in the Governor except as limited by Article IV, section 12, of the Constitution, and the legislative or judicial branches may not properly trench upon the executive power thus granted. Myers v. United States, 272 U.S. 52. . . .

. . . .

The charge here made is that respondent violated . . . a penal statute, by accepting insurance commissions on policies issued to persons subject to the regulation and control of the liquor control commission. The evidence shows, and the respondent admits, that he received such commissions. It being an offense subject to punishment under the penal provisions . . . [*of the statute*], it affords ample grounds for removal by the Governor, since the charge constitutes malfeasance within the meaning of Article IV, section 12, of the Constitution.

By . . . [*the words of the law*], the Legislature evidenced an intention to prohibit a member of the liquor control commission to deal with persons subject to the regulation and control of the commission. The pertinent language used is: "No commissioner * * * shall solicit or accept any gift, gratuity, emolument or employment from any person subject to the provisions of this act." The receiving of insurance commissions on policies issued to persons under the regulation and control of the liquor control commission is within the purview of the act. The purpose of the statute is to remove the temptation on the part of a commissioner to use his influence with those under the regulation and control of the commission for private gain. Experience shows that to permit such dealings has a tendency to create partiality and discrimination on the part of the officer in administering the functions of his office. It involves a question of public morals in the administration of government of which the supreme executive power could properly take cognizance in the performance of his constitutional duty to take care that the laws be faithfully executed and the affairs of the state efficiently and economically administered. This power flows from the Constitution itself and is self-executing. It exists whether or not the Legislature acts within its constitutional authority with reference to it. The right of the Governor to remove exists outside of the power of the Legislature to make the acts constituting the basis of the removal punishable under a penal statute.

The record shows that respondent had notice, a specification of charges, and a hearing. The specification of charges is sufficient and the evidence supports the charges made. The order of removal by the Governor is in all respects regular and binding. The respondent has not been an occupant of the office of liquor control commissioner since the issuance of the order of removal by the Governor. A judgment of ouster against respondent is hereby entered. The proper writ will be allowed to oust respondent from the office of liquor control commissioner if it be necessary in order to secure a vacation of the office of respondent.

Judgment of ouster.

STATE EX REL. *KELLY* v. *SULLIVAN*

FLORIDA SUPREME COURT

52 SO. 2D 422 (1951)

When Sullivan, sheriff of Dade County was charged with various crimes, he was suspended pending the outcome of his trial. To fill the vacancy, the governor appointed Kelly. When Sullivan was subsequently cleared by court action, the governor reinstated him. Thereupon Kelly filed on information in the Florida supreme court which in effect challenged Sullivan's right to the office of sheriff. Kelly claimed that the governor in reinstating Sullivan had usurped the powers granted the senate in the constitution.

Justice FABISINSKI delivered the opinion of the court.

. . . .

THE SOLE issue raised by the pleadings is the right of the Governor to reinstate a suspended officer at a time when the Senate is in session. It is conceded that the Governor had the constitutional power to reinstate Sullivan if he had done so before the Senate convened.

The answer to this question turns upon a construction of Section 15, Article IV, of our Constitution, the pertinent parts of which are as follows: "officers * * * may be suspended from office by the Governor * * * and the cause of suspension shall be communicated * * * to the Senate at its next session. * * * Every suspension shall continue until the adjournment of the next session of the Senate * * * but the Governor may reinstate the officer * * * upon satisfactory evidence that the * * * charges against him are untrue. If the Senate * * * fail[s] to take action before its adjournment, the officer suspended shall resume the duties of the office."

Section 15 of Article IV of the Constitution sets forth three separate, distinct and independent grants of power: (1) power to suspend, (2) power to reinstate, and (3) power to remove. The first two are granted exclusively to the Governor without any restrictions or restraint, except that the power to *suspend* ceases when the Senate convenes. The power to remove is granted to the Governor with the limitation that the removal shall not become effective except upon the consent of the Senate, and may be exercised only while the Senate is in session.

Counsel for the respective parties have exhausted all the available authorities in excellent briefs, upon the question of the power of the Governor to suspend or remove public officers, and the power and function of the Senate in respect thereto. They have presented their views ably in oral argument. As a result, counsel and the Court are, for the purposes of this case, in agreement as to every phase of the application of our Constitutional provisions to the present controversy, except the single question stated. The applicable principles of law which are, for the purposes of this case, conceded, may accordingly be summarized without the necessity of citing numerous authorities.

We have held, and counsel agree that for the purposes of this case it is a settled principle of our law, that the power of the Governor to suspend an officer may not be exercised while the Senate is in session, although he may recommend the removal of such officer *to the Senate* at such time. . . .

As long ago as 1892 this Court, speaking through Chief Justice George P. Raney, discussing the power of the Governor in the matter of suspensions and removal from office, held that the Governor is the exclusive judge, insofar as the Courts are concerned, of the sufficiency of the proof of the charges advanced against an officer, not merely because the Courts have been given no power of review, but for the further reason that the Senate has been granted such power. And it is as much the duty of the Governor to reinstate an officer against whom a charge warranting suspension has been made, and who has been by him suspended, if the evidence does not sustain the charge, as it is to suspend him in the first instance. And the courts may not inquire into the factual basis for reinstatement, any more than they may inquire as to the sufficiency of the evidence for suspension. . . .

It has also been held that the power of review exists in the Senate only upon recommendation by the Governor that the officer be removed. The fact that the Governor has suspended the officer, without making such recommendation, leaves nothing for determination by the Senate, even though the suspension continues throughout the entire session. . . .

It is the contention of Kelly that since under settled law, the Governor may not suspend an officer while the Senate is in session, he may not, while the Senate is in session, reinstate an officer who was suspended by him at a time prior to the convening of the Senate.

Kelly also contends that once an officer has been suspended, such suspension, if it continues to a time when the Senate has convened, must continue in effect until the adjournment of the Senate.

We reject the validity of both of these contentions.

The Governor alone has the power to suspend a public officer. He has the power and it is his duty to reinstate a public officer suspended by him upon satisfactory evidence that the charges against the officer are untrue. The Governor may not suspend an officer while the Senate is in session, but may recommend his removal to the Senate, and if the Senate concurs, the removal is effected. It is the duty of the Governor to communicate the fact and cause of the suspension to the Senate, but this may be done at any time while the Senate is in session. If the Governor communicates the fact and cause of the suspension to the Senate, together with a recommendation for removal, and the Senate fails to take action before its adjournment, the officer is entitled to resume the duties of his office immediately. It is the function of the Senate, and never that of the Courts, to review the evidence upon which the Governor suspends an officer in the event the Governor recommends his removal from office.

If the Governor suspends an officer, and communicates the fact and cause of the suspension to the Senate, but fails to recommend his removal, the Senate has no power to remove the officer. Removal from office must be the result of the joint action of the Governor and Senate —the Governor recommending, and the Senate consenting. There is no specific provision of the Constitution restricting the right of the Governor to reinstate an officer suspended by him to a time when the Senate is not in session. There *is* a specific provision to the effect that suspension shall continue until the adjournment of the Senate, unless before that time the Governor recommends, and the Senate consents to, his removal. There is also a specific provision that the Governor may reinstate the officer upon satisfactory evidence that the charges against him are untrue; and if the Governor avails himself of this provision to reinstate an officer removed by him before the Senate convenes, the Senate has no right, power, or voice in relation to the matter.

Assuming the principles stated in the last two paragraphs as conceded, we turn now to the question which arises in the instant case: Has the Governor, while the Senate is in session, the constitutional power and authority to reinstate an officer suspended by him prior to the convening of the Senate, when he has determined that the charges upon which he was suspended are untrue? Or must the Governor (and the officer) await the adjournment of the Senate?

Although there is no specific provision of the Constitution which in terms forbids the Governor from exercising his right of suspension while the Senate is in session, this Court, in 1915, in an advisory opinion, rendered to the then Governor, decided that the power of the Governor to suspend an officer exists only between sessions of the Senate, and that while the Senate is in session he cannot, during such session, suspend an officer, but can during such time only recommend to the Senate then in session a permanent removal of such officer. . . .

It is the argument of the relator, Kelly, that because it was held in the foregoing advisory opinion that the Governor might not *suspend* an officer during a session of the Senate it now should be held that he is precluded from *reinstating* an officer during a session of the Senate.

We find nothing either in the spirit or the context of the constitutional provision involved to warrant us in reaching such a conclusion. In State ex rel. Attorney General v. Johnson, 11 So. 845, decided in 1892, it was pointed out by this Court that it is just as much the duty of the Governor to reinstate an officer who has been suspended, if the evidence does not sustain the charge, as it is to suspend him in the first instance. For us now to hold that the Governor was restricted in this duty so that he could not perform it while the Senate is in session would be a pronouncement in direct violation of an apparently clear mandate of the Constitution.

In addition, it is clear from what has already been said that the Senate is granted no power to *remove* an officer. That power is vested solely in the Governor. It is true that the Senate must *concur* in the recommendation of the Governor before the officer may be removed, but beyond that it may not go. How can it be successfully maintained that any power of the Senate is usurped when by the fact of reinstatement itself, the Governor has manifested his determination not to recommend removal?

Under our Constitution, public officers may be removed by two methods. For certain offices, impeachment is prescribed. For all other appointive and elective officers removal is effected by the joint action of the Governor and Senate—the governor being the initiator and movant, and the Senate the reviewing and consenting body. There is a striking resemblance in the two methods, in the respect that in neither instance has the Senate the slightest power to initiate the proceedings. In the case of impeachment, the House of Representatives prefers the charges, and prosecutes the proceedings before the Senate. In all other cases, the Senate may not adjudicate removal except on the express recommendation of the Governor. In neither case has the Senate any power, right or prerogative to exercise its functions as a reviewing body upon its own motion or initiative. The potential power of the Senate to hear and adjudicate the merits of a charge against a public officer can only be invoked by a formal charge in impeachment proceedings, or a formal recommendation of removal by the Governor, and such potential power is not activated by an order of suspension standing alone.

The words in the Article, "and the cause of suspension shall be communicated * * to the Senate at its next session. * * * Every suspension shall continue until the adjournment of the next session of the Senate" are not so compelling in nature and effect as to require that these words be taken out of their context with the section as a whole, and justify us in relieving the Governor of his constitutional duty to reinstate an officer when he has ascertained that the charges made against such officer are untrue. And, as we have already pointed out, the good faith of a Governor, or lack thereof, in making his findings and acting thereon, cannot be questioned by the courts. Under our system of government, and the theory of checks and balances in its administration, certain responsibilities are cast upon the executive, others upon the legislative, and still others upon the judicial, departments, with the intention and purpose, at least in part, that the responsibility for the performance of their respective functions may be ascertained, and each made accountable therefor to the forum of public opinion. By the action of the Governor in reinstating Sullivan, the Senate has lost no prerogative or function vested in it by the Constitution, and hence its powers have not been usurped by the Governor's action.

. . . .

Of what is the Senate itself deprived by the reinstatement of the officer while it is in session? It has no function, power, or prerogative in the case of the communication to it of a suspension, absent a recommendation of removal. It can only receive the communication—it may not take any action thereon recognized by law or the Constitution. If we assume that it might at least desire to take measures to satisfy itself of the good faith of the Governor in suspending the officer, it may do this after the event of reinstatement as well as before.

We can conclude only that the power to reinstate a suspended officer is not abrogated by the intervention of a session of the Senate, and it necessarily follows that the demurrer to the information should be sustained, and the writ quashed.

. . . .

SEBRING, C. J., TERRELL, CHAPMAN and ADAMS, JJ., and PARKS, Associate Justice, concur.

THOMAS, J., dissents.

TERRELL, Justice (concurring).

. . . .

A fair consideration of one coordinate branch of the government for another would require that the Governor transmit all suspension orders to the Senate in ample time for it to give them due consideration before it adjourns, but there is no limitation on his power to do so. Any time the Governor comes into possession of "satisfactory evidence that the charge or charges" against the suspended officer are not true, he may reinstate him. Such evidence may be submitted to the Governor any time before the suspension order goes to the Senate. Even if he receives it after the suspension order goes to the Senate, it would not be inappropriate for the Governor to request the Senate to return the order for further action. As a member of the Senate I have known this request to be made and met with compliance. It is a courtesy unusually extended the Governor by the Senate.

. . . .

There is positively no reason in logic why the power of the Governor to reinstate a suspended officer should not extend through the session of the Senate. The Governor and the Senate are both bound by the evidence to support the grounds of suspension, it has nothing more to stand on. This fact accounts for the language of Section 15, Article IV. The makers of the Constitution took this view of it, this Court has so construed it and the Senate has adjudicated suspensions for 65 years, guided by this interpretation.

For the reasons so stated I concur in the majority opinion.

STATE v. DISTRICT COURT

MINNESOTA SUPREME COURT

107 N.W. 2D 307 (1960)

Commissioner Turnbladh, the head of the Minnesota state department of corrections charged Rigg, warden of the state prison, with misconduct in office arising out of excessive food withdrawals. Following a long private conference between the two officers, the commissioner scheduled a formal administrative hearing to act on the charges. Rigg filed suit in the appropriate state district court to enjoin the commissioner from holding the proposed hearing. He alleged that, in their conference, the parties had arrived at a "settlement and adjudication" of the charges and that the matter was now res judicata *(a matter already adjudged; there is a good discussion of the doctrine of* res judicata *in the opinion of the court). Consequently, Rigg argued, the commissioner "has been divested of jurisdiction over the person of the warden with relation to such subject matter . . ." The court granted a temporary injunction. At that point, the commissioner took the matter to the state supreme court, to prevent the district court from making the injunction permanent.*

Justice LOEVINGER delivered the opinion of the court.

. . . .

THE ONLY question for the courts at this time is whether the commissioner has jurisdiction to determine that the warden shall or shall not be retained in the state service, or whether the commissioner has been deprived of such jurisdiction by the informal proceedings mentioned above. If the commissioner has jurisdiction, it is improper, under our decisions and under generally recognized principles of law, for the courts to interfere with the administrative proceeding prior to the making of such a determination.

The first issue that arises is whether the doctrine of res judicata is applicable in the present proceeding at all. Although there is some authority to the effect that this doctrine does not apply to administrative proceedings, the sounder view appears to be that stated in 2 Davis, Administrative Law Treatise, § 18.02, as follows:

> "As a matter of principle, it is completely clear that the reasons behind the doctrine of res judicata as developed in the court system are fully applicable to *some* administrative proceedings. * * * The sound view is therefore to use the doctrine of res judicata when the reasons for it are present in full force, to modify it when modification is needed, and to reject it when the reasons against it outweigh those in its favor."

Rigg's entire theory as to the application of res judicata to the present proceedings is constructed on the basis of a sentence appearing in Minn.St. 15.0418 relating to the hearing of contested cases in administrative proceedings. After stating the requirements for notice, specification of issues, opportunity to be heard, preparation of a record, and other matters, this section contains the following provision:

> "* * * Informal disposition may also be made of any contested case by stipulation, agreed settlement, consent order or default."

In any rational view of what actually occurred, it does gross violence to common sense to assert that a private conference between a department head and a subordinate executive relating to the conduct of that department constitutes a "hearing" in the sense that this term is used in statutes or decisions by lawyers familiar with legal procedure. It further does gross violence to common sense to assert that an announcement to newspaper reporters constitutes a "stipulation, agreed settlement, consent order or default." There are numerous opinions and statements by lawyers and judges decrying "trial by newspaper." It is significant in the present case that Rigg seeks to establish the alleged informal disposition of this matter by putting newspaper reports and the affidavit of a newspaper reporter before the court. It is no reflection on these publications or the reporters involved to say that it would be a travesty of legal process to accept newspaper reports of statements by public officials as the equivalent of a formal judgment or administrative adjudication.

However, even were the newspaper reports accepted as the equivalent of a formal administrative order, it is still clear that under the authorities this is not the kind of proceeding to which the doctrine of res judicata is properly applicable. As indicated in the quotation from Davis above, there is no authority anywhere to the effect that res judicata is applicable to *all* administrative proceedings regardless of their nature. The only authority for the application of this doctrine in such proceedings goes no further than to assert that the doctrine should be applied to administrative proceedings which are essentially quasijudicial in nature. It is clear, however, that this does not include proceedings relating to removal from employment of a public employee.

This precise question was presented in New York in the case of Evans v. Monaghan, 123 N.Y.S.2d 662. In that case a New York policeman was accused of accepting bribes from a professional gambler and of protecting the gambler against arrest. A formal hearing on these charges was held before a judge specially authorized as a hearing commissioner. The principal witness refused to testify. Other evidence was taken, and a formal written finding was made that the policeman was not guilty of the charges. Four months later the same charges were again filed against the policeman. The principal witness by this time had changed his mind and agreed to testify. A hearing was held on the new charges, and the policeman was found guilty. An appeal was taken to the courts alleging that the second trial was a violation of the policeman's rights, and that the first trial and formal findings constituted res judicata. In rejecting the plea of res judicata and sustaining the finding against the policeman and the order for discharge, the appellate division of the New York supreme court said. . . .

> "The rule has never prevented the court itself from being moved to reopen the case and to re-examine the basis of its judgment for a cause which the court would regard as sufficient. While the judges developed a set of their own

limitations on the sufficiency of the grounds which would move them to reopen, the rules related to the circumstances of exercise of power rather than to the power itself.

"A rule of law which would always treat as an analogue to the judgment of a court the determination of an administrative officer in the discipline of public employees would have to have a guarded acceptance and be taken with some considerable reservation. The theory of the enlargement of the court rule of finality to take in administrative determinations is that the administrator has acted 'judicially,' but that analogy in such a case rests very largely upon the fact that he conducts a hearing.

"His determination of what to do about the charges, if he finds them sustained, is essentially an administrative function, for in that phase of his authority he carries out the duty to administer the public agency in the direction of the public service it performs.

* * * * * *

"We would hesitate, too, to apply to this kind of a determination, involving discipline of public employees, the full effect of court judgments between litigating parties. The general rule has been stated that while the doctrine of res judicata applies to a judicial determination of a board or officer, it does not apply 'to a decision made while acting ministerially or administratively.' Such a determination, if 'not recognized by the law of the forum as a judgment,' is 'no bar to further proceedings in relation to the same matter.'"

On appeal this decision was affirmed, . . . with the court of appeals saying:

"* * * it would be beyond the spirit as well as beyond the letter of the doctrine of res judicata, as that doctrine is applied in court procedure, to bar the second departmental trial of petitioners."

. . . Further, there is a long line of cases in this court which expressly approves that rationale by holding that the decision of an administrative body in determining whether or not to discharge an employee is an administrative function. . . . These decisions go so far as to hold that, in view of the constitutional division of the powers of government, jurisdiction cannot be conferred upon the courts, either directly or indirectly, to pass upon or interfere with this administrative function; and, therefore, that any judicial review of such a matter must be a limited review. Thus, the holdings of this court are that in exercising the function at issue here an administrator is acting in an executive or administrative capacity, and the basis for the application of the doctrine of res judicata does not, therefore, exist.

. . . .

Thus, accepting all the well-pleaded facts of Rigg's complaint and affidavits and giving him the benefit of all reasonable inferences therefrom, it is clear that the doctrine of res judicata does not prevent a prospective determination now by the commissioner as to whether Rigg should be retained as warden. Therefore it is improper to grant Rigg any of the relief prayed for in the court below on the face of his pleadings. . . .

A second, equally important, point is that in such a situation as presented here an administrative agency has a well-established right to reopen, rehear, and redetermine the matter even after a determination has been made. This is a rule of general application. . . .

. . . .

What the commissioner of corrections will or may do with respect to the present situation is not before us and is not now our concern. The commissioner has the continuing responsibility for administration of the state prison, as well as other institutions. By a formal notice, the sufficiency of which is not challenged, he has proposed to hold a hearing upon specified charges, as well as upon any other charges that may properly be filed, on Rigg's qualifications to continue to hold the office of warden. The administrative action with which we are concerned here relates to prospective matters. Neither this court nor the district court can, constitutionally, be entrusted with the responsibility for determining or controlling those administrative matters. . . . There is certainly no logical basis for the court's undertaking to prevent the administrator who has this responsibility from exercising his judgment with respect to it. It requires emphatic repetition that the matter before us does not involve any question of penalty or civil liability, but only the future continuance in a responsible public position of an employee whose qualifications are formally challenged by his superior—regardless of the basis or merits of that challenge, which we are not in a position to pass upon.

In the third place, regardless of the applicability of the doctrine of res judicata, and regardless of the power of the administrator to reopen and rehear this matter, it should be clear that on any view the plea of res judicata does not, as Rigg asserts, operate to divest the administrative agency of jurisdiction. The statutory authority of the commissioner with respect to Rigg cannot, on the facts pleaded, be "exceeded or exhausted," as suggested in the dissenting opinions. Since there are no facts pleaded which would, if true, divest the commissioner of either jurisdiction or responsibility to make the determination proposed to be made, there is no "fact issue" for determination by the lower court. All that is required for determination of the instant case is a careful application of well-established principles of law.

. . . .

This court has held that the only exceptions to the long-settled rule that no one is entitled to an injunction against the actual or threatened acts of an administrative agency until the administrative remedies and the remedies by direct review have been exhausted are in case of a showing of the imminence of actual irreparable harm from action beyond the agency's jurisdiction or contrary to constitutional principles. . . .

This court has most recently applied that rule in the case of State ex rel. Sheehan v. District Court, 93 N.W.2d 1, certiorari denied Standard American Life v. Sheehan, 359 U.S. 909. In that case the commissioner of insurance proposed to hold a hearing to determine whether an insurance company was engaging in unfair competition or deceptive practices. The insurance company sought and secured from the district court a restraining order preventing the holding of the hearing by the commissioner on the grounds that he was proposing to act beyond his statutory jurisdiction and in such a manner as to deprive the insurance company of due process of law. This court issued a writ of prohibition to the district court directing it to refrain from further proceedings in that matter. . . .

. . . .

In the situation presented here, the commissioner has the power of appointment, of removal, and of hearing and determining charges upon which removal may be based. . . . The commissioner is charged with the responsibility for the control and supervision of the institution and the department within which the warden is employed. Minn. St. 243.01. It has been repeatedly held by this court, in cases cited above, that such administrative responsibility for the effective functioning of departments and institutions cannot be transferred from the administrator to the courts. . . .

This court cannot, therefore, consistently with its own prior decisions, and particularly with the decision in the Sheehan case, permit the district court to interfere with the administrative process prior to a final determination by the commissioner as to the fitness of the warden to continue in the position he holds in the public service. . . .

. . . .

Thus, confining our decision to the legal issues necessarily presented by this proceeding, as we must, it is clear that the writ of prohibition should issue to prevent judicial interference with administrative responsibility for determination of the continuing qualifications of the executives in the public service. The doctrine of res judicata is not applicable here because the confidential conference between the commissioner and the warden cannot in any realistic sense be called a hearing, nor can a newspaper report of a public statement be called an adjudication. By both reason and precedent the doctrine of res judicata is not applicable to proceedings involving the continuance in office of public employees. The commissioner, as any other administrator, clearly has the right to reopen, rehear, and redetermine a matter involving prospective action, regardless of the character of a previous determination, at least within the very short time interval involved here. In any event, res judicata is only a plea in bar and does not operate to deprive a tribunal of jurisdiction. Finally, under the clear decision of this court in the Sheehan case, the district court has no right to interfere with an administrative agency which is proposing to act in a matter properly within the scope of its general responsibility until final action has been taken by the administrative agency.

The writ is made absolute.

DELL, C. J., took no part in the consideration or decision of this case.

FRANK T. GALLAGHER, Justice (concurring specially).

[*Justice Nelson and Justice Knutson both wrote dissenting opinions.*]

GREMILLION v. DEPARTMENT OF HIGHWAYS

LOUISIANA COURT OF APPEAL FIRST CIRCUIT

129 SO. 2D 805 (1961)

Gremillion, a foreman in the department of highways of Louisiana and a member of the state classified civil service, was discharged by his superior for alleged misconduct. It was charged that he engaged in political activity, which is unlawful for a member of the classified civil service. He appealed to the Civil Service Commission which concluded that he had in fact engaged in the alleged unlawful activity and dismissed his appeal. From here, Gremillion appealed to the state supreme court which transferred the matter to the court of appeals, as it has the power to do.

Judge HERGET delivered the opinion of the court.

. . . .

ARTICLE 14, Section 15(N) (7) of the Louisiana Constitution reads as follows:

"No employee in the Classified Service of the State or a city, and no member of a State or City Commission shall be a member of any national, state, or local committee of a political party, or an officer or member of any factional, political club or organization, or a candidate for nomination or election to any public office, or shall make any political speech or public political statement in behalf of any candidate, faction, or party, as a part of any political campaign for the nomination or election of public officers, or shall *take any part* in the management or affairs of any political faction or party or *in any political campaign, except to exercise his right as a citizen to express his opinion privately, to serve as a commissioner or official watcher at the polls in any election, and to cast his vote for whom he pleases.*" (Emphasis ours).

This article of the Constitution is clear and not ambiguous and specifically the Civil Service employee is denied the right to "take *any* part * * * in any political campaign, except to exercise his right as a citizen to express his opinion privately, to serve as a commissioner or official watcher at the polls in any election, and to cast his vote for whom he pleases."

Learned counsel for appellant argue with great force the charge under which appellant was dismissed does not state a cause of action for the reason the action denounced on the part of a Civil Service employee is public activity on the part of the employee, such as headquarters work, telephone work, aiding in raising funds or the doing of something of an organized nature with a definite pattern of signification of clear intent to take part in a political campaign. It is the contention of counsel for appellant the request by a foreman of his employees to vote for a certain candidate in an election is permissible and is not encompassed within the restrictions of the Constitution. Therefore such activity on the part of a Civil Service employee is insufficient to warrant his discharge.

In the case of Norris v. United States, 86 F.2d 379, the Court said:

"* * * The word 'campaign' is in the public domain. It has no technically legal use. If it had, many of the cases cited to us by appellant might well be in point. The meaning of the word 'campaign,' when applied to a candidacy for an office, is known of all men. True, its constituent elements—the things which are done in a campaign—differ from zero to infinity. The word means, when applied to a personal political candidacy, all of the things and necessary legal and factual acts done by the candidate *and his* adherents, in an effort to obtain a majority, or plurality of the votes to be cast in any election for a public office. * * *" (Emphasis ours).

In the case of State ex rel. Green et al. v. City of Cleveland et al., Ohio App., 33 N.E.2d 35, an Ohio decision, a classified Civil Service employee of the City of Cleveland brought a declaratory judgment action to determine whether such an employee of Cleveland was prohibited by the Cleveland Charter (. . . reading in part as follows: "* * * No person in the service of the city shall use his official authority to influence or coerce the political action of any person or body, or to interfere with any nomination or election to public office.") from campaigning at an election for or against a bond issue, a special tax levy, amendments to the city charter, or in favor of or against any issue submitted to the electorate of the City of Cleveland. In resolving the question, the Court . . . concluded:

"It is the conclusion of the majority of this court that any election in which the voters are asked to pass judgment on candidates for office or on issues, is political in its purpose and result, and when an employee in the classified service of the city takes part in the campaign preceding such election he is taking part in a 'political campaign' contrary to the prohibition contained in § 140 of the city charter."

There is a strong dissenting opinion in the case to the effect that a political campaign had the meaning of only party or partisan organization or campaign and did not contemplate public questions such as bond issues, tax levies and charter amendments.

In our opinion the meaning of "political campaign" contemplates every effort made to insure the election of a nominee or the success of a political issue submitted to the people for determination by voting at an election. It encompasses the filing of intention to become a candidate, the financing of the campaign, the checking of poll lists, the placing of advertising in the newspapers, television and radio, and staffing and arrangement for headquarters and above all the solicitations of the voters by adherents of the candidate. It incorporates the actions of all parties, organized or unorganized, to accomplish the desired result. The purpose of a political campaign insofar as an individual is concerned is to stimulate the adherents of a candidate to join the individual in securing the election of a candidate. Any effort by an adherent to accomplish this result is of necessity a taking part in a political campaign. There is no requirement that one joining in the effort to elect a candidate participate therein only as an organized worker. The ultimate objective of the political campaign is to secure the election of the individual candidate by the effort of all adherents whether organized or unorganized. Much of the success of a political campaign by an individual results from the solicitation by adherents of the office-seeker of the electorate.

The purpose of the Civil Service law is to insure the employee the right to retain his position on the merit of his work and not because of his political partisanship. To accomplish this purpose, of necessity, restrictions had to be placed upon the activity of a Civil Service employee in a political campaign. We are not called upon to determine what these restrictions should be but our duty is simply to apply those restrictions placed in the Constitution by the people. By the clear provisions of the Constitution any political activity of the Civil Service employee in a political campaign was prohibited with the exception of the three specifically provided for activities. The use of the language "any part * * * in any political campaign" is all-inclusive and denies to the Civil Service employee any participation in a political campaign, not excepted in the Constitution.

At the hearing there was offered evidence which the Commission accepted as true that appellant requested employees under his supervision to vote for the candidate of his choice for governor, Mr. Preaus. This action on the part of appellant was, in our opinion, a taking part in a political campaign prohibited by the Constitution. While a Civil Service employee is permitted to express his private opinion as to his choice of candidates in a political campaign, he is denied the right to solicit votes on behalf of the candidate of his choice, and especially is this reprobated when the evidence shows that the requests are made by a foreman of those employees under his supervision.

. . . .

In the case of Konen v. New Orleans Police Department, 226 La. 739, 77 So.2d 24, the [*state*] Supreme Court in its opinion used the language that the Court would not disturb the decision of the Civil Service Commission unless the action of the Board or Commission was arbitrary and where the decision was based on substantial evidence the Court would not consider the weight or sufficiency of the evidence. Though the use of the words "substantial evidence" were used in the opinion, it is noteworthy the holding of the Court was predicated upon the fact that, as there was some evidence in the record to substantiate the charge, it was not within the province of the Court to consider the weight or sufficiency thereof and the appellate jurisdiction was limited to questions of law alone.

. . . .

In order to make crystal clear our view of the jurisdiction vested in this Court by the Constitution of Louisiana on appeals from decisions of the Commission, we emphasize that under the plain provisions of the Constitution the decision of the Civil Service Commission is final on the facts and this Court is limited in its jurisdiction to the resolution or determination of questions of law only. We are powerless to inquire into the weight or sufficiency of the evidence on which the decision of the Commission is based and in this respect if there is any evidence produced before the Commission in support of the charge, then the weight and sufficiency thereof is peculiarly within the province of the Civil Service Commission. We are not concerned with the determination of whether the evidence is substantial or probative so long as there is evidence in the record on which a finding of fact might be determined by the Civil Service Commission. The findings of facts by the Commission must be based on evidence in the record and it is only in those instances where the record is barren of any evidence to support the findings of facts by the Commission the invalidity of action of the Commission is apparent, presents a question of law, the jurisdiction of which is vested in this Court.

. . . .

[*The decision of the Civil Service Commission dealt with in the opinion was affirmed.*]

KING v. DEPARTMENT OF PUBLIC SAFETY OF LOUISIANA

LOUISIANA SUPREME COURT
108 SO. 2D 524 (1959)

King, an employee of the Louisiana department of public safety and a member of the classified civil service, was dismissed by the director of his department who was upheld in his action in a subsequent hearing before the Civil Service Commission. When King first appealed to the supreme court of Louisiana, he alleged that the commission had arbitrarily refused to hear evidence that his dismissal had been politically motivated. The supreme court remanded the case to the Civil Service Commission in effect directing them to hear the evidence regarding the alleged political motivation for the dismissal. This the commission did and found that there was no substance to the allegation. King once again turned to the state supreme court.

Judge Ponder delivered the opinion of the court.

. . . .

In the letter of dismissal, the appellant was charged:

"1. That during the latter part of January, 1957, your request to the Director of the Department of Public Safety that certain filing cabinets of the Department be worked on was denied by the Director of the Department, and despite this denial you did negotiate with personnel of the Remington Rand Company to make such repairs on said filing cabinets at an uncertain price and that said unauthorized repairs were actually being made when discovered by the Director of the Department of Public Safety, and that said complete disregard of the express order of the Director of the Department of Public Safety, amounts to insubordination in the highest degree."

"4. That during the first two weeks of January, 1957, you did exhibit extremely poor supervision over one of your subordinate personnel namely, Henry Mudd, Driver's License Examiner of Cameron Parish, and that said poor supervision was due to the fact that the Drivers' License Examiner's office in the Parish of Cameron, State of Louisiana, had been closed for two weeks and that many people in that area were unable to secure drivers' licenses or renew drivers' licenses and that due to this office closure the Department of Public Safety received complaints from the local authorities, namely Sheriff O. B. Carter of Cameron Parish who telephoned the Director's office on January 16, 1957, and informed the Director that the Drivers' License Office in Cameron had been closed for two weeks, and that when you were contacted by Colonel Forrest C. Pendleton in reference to said situation on January 16, 1957, you stated that you had no knowledge of the office being closed until January 15, 1957, despite the fact that you had or should have had reports from your Drivers' License Supervisor of that District, as to the activities carried on by the Drivers' License office in the Parish of Cameron, and that your complete ignorance of this situation amounts to gross incompetence and severely impeded the efficiency of the services rendered to the public in that area by the Department of Public Safety."

As to the charges and causes for dismissal the Commission concluded:

"The facts found and stated in the original opinion herein are fixed and final. They were never subject to review (Constitution Article XIV, Section 15(O) (1) [LSA]). They cannot now be constitutionally reviewed by this Commission or by any other tribunal. If they could be re-examined, the evidence adduced at this second hearing only reaffirms the finding that appellant's discharge for insubordination and for neglect of duty was legal, and constituted a reasonable exercise of the duty imposed upon employing authorities by law and particularly by Rule 12.1 of the Rules of this Commission.

"The suggestion of appellant's counsel that one of the causes for his client's discharge was the insignificant circumstance that he caused filing cabinets to be repaired which needed repairing is incorrect. The cause was the insubordination implicit in having the repairs made despite the order not to do so.

"Insubordination and neglect of duty have always been recognized as valid causes for the removal of civil service employees. Insubordination disrupts orderly administration of any organization wherein there is gradation of authority, and neglect of any assigned duty destroys the unity of effort required for the accomplishment of any enterprise depending on concerted action. Such delinquencies are necessarily detrimental to the efficiency of public service and cannot be condoned when committed by employees in the classified service, particularly by those occupying positions of importance. The security provided by law to classified employees imposes upon them the reciprocal obligation of a high degree of loyalty and efficiency, in both of which appellant was deficient.

"Appellant's derelictions expressed in the letter of dismissal and numbered 1 and 4, examined in the light of all the evidence, are again deemed to be sufficiently detrimental to the efficiency of the State service as to justify the action of the appointing authority in dismissing him therefrom."

On appeal to this Court, appellant contends that the evidence does not justify or support the penalty of dismissal and to impose the extreme penalty of discharge is so inequitable, arbitrary, capricious and unreasonable as to disclose a wanton abuse of the discretion vested in the Civil Service Commission; that the findings of fact by the Commission on charges Nos. 1 and 4 do not constitute acts of a substantial nature directly affecting the public interest; that the Commission's conclusion of law on charge No. 4 violated the concept of the "classification plan" provided for in Section 15(I) (b), Article 14 of the Constitution and Chapter 5, Rules 5.1–5.6 of the Civil Service Rules; that the evidence at the two hearings preponderantly shows that the appointing authority would not have taken the disciplinary action of dismissing appellant except for political reasons or prejudices; that the Commissions' conclusions of law are inconsistent with the charges made in No. 1 and No. 4; that the findings of fact do not support the allegations of charge No. 4.

Suffice it to say, without categorically answering the contentions of appellant, there is evidence in the record to support the charges and there is no evidence of political motivation. The contention that the charges were not substantial is without merit and the reasons given by the Commission in its findings quoted heretofore are well founded, viz.: that the insubordination is substantial enough to support dismissal.

There is no merit in the contention that the punishment is inequitable since the insubordination is of such a nature that it is highly detrimental to the efficiency of the service. This Court held in Cottingham v. Department of Revenue, State of Louisiana, 94 So.2d 662, that where there is a real and substantial relation between the assigned cause for dismissal and the qualification for the position, the sufficiency of the cause assigned for dismissal is a question of fact which the Civil Service Commission has the exclusive right to determine. Where the decision of the Commission is based on evidence, the court may not consider the weight or sufficiency of the evidence. . . .

The attorney for the Department of Public Safety cogently answered appellant's complaints urged against charge No. 4 in his brief, viz.:

> "Under the rules set forth by this Honorable Court in the Cottingham, Domas and Konen cases, cited supra, and applying the 'substantial relation' test enunciated in those authorities, the following becomes self evident. There is a real and substantial relation between the assigned cause for dismissal and appellant's qualifications for the public work in which he was engaged. His utter disregard of and complete indifference to the operation of the Cameron office could well affect the matter of his reliability and competence to continue to perform the duties of Drivers License Administrator, a position which requires careful and thorough supervision and checks of the various Examiners and their offices throughout the State of Louisiana. Since this substantial relation exists, the Commission did not act arbitrarily in upholding the dismissal of appellant. As pointed out in the Cottingham case, cited supra, whether the cause was sufficient and reasonable for removing appellant from service is a question of fact which this Court is without jurisdiction to decide."

We conclude that the decision of the Commission was not arbitrary or capricious. There is evidence in the record to support the conclusions reached by the Commission. So long as there is any evidence in the record to support the findings of the Commission we are without jurisdiction to determine the sufficiency of the evidence or the reasonableness of the cause. It is only where there is no evidence in the record to support the findings of the Commission that we are authorized to consider the evidence.

For the reasons assigned, the judgment is affirmed at appellant's cost.

WILSON AND COMPANY v. FREEMAN

UNITED STATES DISTRICT COURT MINNESOTA DISTRICT

179 F. SUPP. 520 (1959)

The case grew out of a protracted labor-management dispute between Wilson and Company (meat packers) and the United Packinghouse Workers of America. As a consequence of violence between the strikers and non-strikers (in and around the Wilson Company, Albert Lea, Minnesota Plant), local law enforcement officers called upon the governor for help. Governor Freeman responded by calling out some detachments of the National Guard, declaring the area to be under limited martial law, and ordering the Wilson Company plant closed. The Company (a Delaware corporation) applied to the United States district court for the district of Minnesota for an injunction to restrain state officials from interfering with the operation of the plant, arguing that the Governor's action violated the Company's property rights safeguarded by the Fourteenth Amendment of the United States Constitution.

Per curiam.

. . . .

PLAINTIFF IS engaged in the operation of a meat packing plant in the City and Township of Albert Lea, Freeborn County, Minnesota. It employs in the production end of its business some 1,100 employees, together with some 200 supervisory or staff officials. In the operation of its business it maintains the customary buildings and facilities usually required in the meat packing industry. For many years the production employees have been represented by the United Packinghouse Workers of America, commonly referred to as U.P.W.A. A local union of a similar name is generally referred to as Local Union No. 6.

Since on or about October 29, 1959, a strike has existed as between the production employees represented by Local Union No. 6 and plaintiff at the latter's Albert Lea plant, and the plant has been picketed. Plaintiff attempted to continue its operations with some of its supervisory and maintenance employees. Later on, however, plaintiff began to employ and solicit the employment of new workers, with the public announcement that, if its striking employees did not return to work, their positions would be filled by new employees. The new employees were recruited generally from the rural areas in Freeborn County and contiguous counties and a number from the State of Iowa. Albert Lea is situated about twenty miles from the Iowa state line. The new employees from Iowa, however, did not substantially exceed the number of Iowa residents employed before the strike. Beginning in November, 1959, the employees increased in number so that by December 8, 1959, plaintiff's plant was operating at about one-half capacity with approximately 500 production employees in addition to plaintiff's regular supervisory and maintenance staff. In the meantime, however, there were some acts of violence on the picket line by the pickets which led to an order issued by the District Court of Freeborn County enjoining the local union from interfering with free access to plaintiff's plant and enjoining the strikers from acts of violence or threatened violence. Subsequently, certain alleged violators on the picket line were cited for contempt of court, the citation being returnable on December 15, 1959. On December 8, 9 and 10, 1959, the number of pickets on the picket line increased. Large crowds estimated on December 10th to be over 1,000 persons gathered in and about plaintiff's plant attempting to block the entrance to the plant so that the production employees could not leave the plant. Rocks were thrown by the crowd at the cars carrying the production employees to and from the plant. Windows of automobiles were broken and cars damaged. Non-striking workers were threatened with bodily harm. Police, as well as union officials, unsuccessfully attempted to quell the acts of violence and the massing of pickets by pleading with the pickets to disperse, to refrain from violence, and to return to their homes. However, such pleas were of no avail. No attempts were made by the police to arrest any of the mob indulging in the acts of violence. The District Court of Freeborn County, on December 10, 1959, did issue a supplemental restraining order, which among other matters limited the number of pickets to four at any one entrance. This order, however, was not served by reason of the Governor's subsequent decree of martial law and the suspension of all restraining orders issued by the District Court in a proclamation promulgated by the military authorities acting under the decree of martial law. Moreover, the District Court was forbidden by the military to issue any further orders in the labor dispute between plaintiff and the striking workers. In addition to the mob violence at the plant, there were acts of vandalism, principally at the farms of some of the non-union production workers, all of which apparently were carried on by the strikers for the purpose of intimidating those who continued to work at plaintiff's plant.

It was shortly after midnight on December 11, 1959, that the law enforcement officials of the City of Albert Lea and Freeborn County addressed a letter to Orville L. Freeman, Governor of the State, requesting that he act under his powers under Article V, Section 4, of the Minnesota Constitution, . . . and assume responsibility for the maintenance of law and order in the City and County, and that he temporarily close the Wilson & Co. plant. . . . Within hours after receiving this communication, the Governor made a finding that a state of insurrection existed in the City of Albert Lea and County of Freeborn, and proclaimed that martial law prevailed in said City and County. . . . In pursuance of the proclamation of the Governor, the Major General of the Minnesota National Guard issued a proclamation in which he declared that the continued operation of plaintiff's plant would precipitate riots and other acts of violence, and ordered the suspension of any operation of the plant, and further ordered that no person should be permitted ingress to or egress from the plant except as permitted by the military. Moreover, he forbade any person to loiter, congregate or assemble in the vicinity of the plant, and declared that "The civil jurisdiction of all legally constituted courts of law in the jurisdiction concerned in this Proclamation shall continue to operate with full force and effect except that any and all court orders pertaining to the dispute between the Wilson Company Packing Plant at Albert Lea and the labor union representing the striking workers are hereby suspended and all courts shall be without jurisdiction to issue any further orders or decrees pertaining thereto until further order." . . .

. . . .

At the threshold of this proceeding, we are met with the question as to the Governor's right to place the City of Albert Lea and the County of Freeborn under martial law. He purports to act under the Constitution of the State of Minnesota under Article V, Section 4, which provides that "He shall be commander-in-chief of the military and naval forces, and may call out such forces to execute the laws, suppress insurrection and repel invasion." This same Article provides that the Governor "shall take care that the laws be faithfully executed, * * *." There is no language in the Constitution which specifically empowers the Governor to declare martial law. But obviously where there is actual war in a community, or where insurrection or revolt occurs so that the duly constituted government is usurped and overcome by the insurrectionists or mobs, the Governor is impliedly authorized to declare martial law. But where any disturbance caused by a strike or otherwise presents a situation with which the local police or other local law enforcement agencies are not able to cope, it does not follow that, without more, the drastic and oppressive rule of martial law can be imposed upon any community. The Governor has the power to call out the National Guard to aid the local authorities in suppressing violence in labor disputes and he is under the sworn duty to enforce the laws with the use of such powers as the law affords. Under martial law, the rights of citizens may be abridged and greatly restricted. In fact, the basis for martial law assumes that local government has completely broken down and is, or is about to be taken over by the forces of a mob. No one will disagree that a serious situation existed at or near plaintiff's plant at Albert Lea when strikers and their sympathizers sought by mob violence to prevent some 500 persons from carrying on their lawful employment with plaintiff. Obviously, however, plaintiff was within its rights notwithstanding the strike in attempting to keep its plant in production and to afford employment to those persons who were willing to work. Plaintiff is protected by the Constitution of the United States in its right to possess its property and to use it in any lawful manner that it may desire to pursue. Plaintiff cannot be held responsible for mob violence which was allegedly precipitated by its attempt to keep its plant open. A strike by union workers does not prevent the employer from employing non-union workers in its plant. That the laws of Minnesota are enacted for the express purpose of curbing violations of law of the kind herein recounted is clear from the following statutes:

> "When three or more persons, having assembled for any purpose, shall disturb the public peace by using force or violence to any other person or to property, or shall threaten or attempt to commit such disturbance, or to do any unlawful act by the use of force or violence, accompanied by the power of immediate execution of such threat or attempt, they shall be guilty of a riot." M.S.A. § 615.02.
>
> "When three or more persons shall assemble with intent:
>
> "(1) To commit any unlawful act by force;
>
> "(2) To carry out any purpose in such a manner as to disturb the public peace; or
>
> "(3) Being assembled, shall attempt to threaten any act tending toward a breach of the peace or an injury to persons or property, or any unlawful act—
>
> "Such an assembly is unlawful, and every person participating therein, by his presence, aid, or instigation, shall be guilty of a misdemeanor." M.S.A. § 615.04.
>
> "Every person who shall remain present at the place of an unlawful assembly, after having been warned to disperse by a magistrate or public officer, unless as a public officer or at the request of any such officer he is assisting in dispersing the same, or in protecting persons or property or in arresting offenders, shall be guilty of a misdemeanor." M.S.A. § 615.05.
>
> "Every person who enters into a combination with another to resist the exe-

cution of any legal process or other mandate of a court of competent jurisdiction, under circumstances not amounting to a riot, shall be guilty of a gross misdemeanor." M.S.A. § 615.07.

"Every person who shall * * * throw any deadly missile, in a public place, or in any place where there is any person to be endangered, although no injury actually results, shall be guilty of a misdemeanor." M.S.A. § 615.09.

"Any person who shall use in reference to and in the presence of another, or in reference to or in the presence of any member of the family of another, abusive or obscene language, intended, or naturally tending to provoke an assault or any breach of the peace, shall be guilty of a misdemeanor." M.S.A. § 615.15.

At the time the Governor declared martial law, the local government of the City of Albert Lea and the County of Freeborn was functioning. The courts were open, the citizens were moving freely in and about their daily pursuits without danger, except those who desired to continue with their work for plaintiff. The District Court of Freeborn County had issued restraining orders against mass picketing and violence, and contempt citations by reason of the violation of such orders had been set for hearing before the court, but without any attempt to call out the National Guard in aid of the civil authorities in maintaining peace and order in the suppression of mob violence, the Governor summarily declared martial law for the City of Albert Lea and the entire county of Freeborn. The rights of the courts to proceed against members of the mob by way of contempt were enjoined. The workers who desired to return to their work at the plant were forbidden to return, and plaintiff's right under the Federal Constitution to operate its plant was abrogated by the decree of the military.

We are not unmindful of the discretion which must necessarily rest in the Governor of a State in determining whether martial law, with the resulting deprivation of constitutional rights, shall be imposed upon any community. Moreover, we recognize that courts should proceed cautiously before interfering with the acts of a Governor of a sovereign State in determining that martial law is necessary in the State of which he is the chief executive and commander-in-chief of the armed forces of the State. We are also mindful of the necessity of preventing bloodshed and that property rights must at times be sacrificed in order to prevent the spilling of blood. But a free people do not surrender to mob rule by the expediency of martial law until all means available to the City, County and State to enforce the laws have proved futile. The imposition of the drastic action and the curtailment of constitutional rights of citizens of a State resulting from a declaration of martial law, cannot be sustained except in situations of dire necessity. We are convinced that that situation has not as yet arisen in Freeborn County.

The Governor possesses no absolute authority to declare martial law. Military rule cannot be imposed upon a community simply because it may seem to be more expedient than to enforce the law by using the National Guard to aid the local civil authorities. As this Court stated in Strutwear Knitting Company v. Olson, 13 F.Supp. 384, 390,

"The state has no more important interest than the maintenance of law and order. * * * It is as much the duty of the state to protect property from destruction by mob violence and to preserve the liberty of the citizen to use his property lawfully as it is to protect the same property from theft or arson. No official intrusted with the enforcement of the law can select the laws which he will enforce or the citizens that he will protect. He has sworn to enforce all laws and to protect all citizens, and there is no escape for him

> 'from the paramount authority of the Federal Constitution.' Sterling et al. v. Constantin et al., supra. 287 U.S. 378, * * *.
>
> "The fact that a large group of individuals may have a grievance, just or unjust, against an owner of property will not warrant a resort to violence to remedy that grievance, nor will the hazard, inconvenience, and expense involved in suppressing the violence justify the state in refusing to enforce the law or in depriving the owner of his property or his right to enjoy it. To say that, because the lawful use of property will incite lawless persons to commit crimes and to destroy life and property, such lawful use must be suppressed, is to say that the will of a mob, and not the Constitution of the United States, has become the supreme law of the land."

But it is urged that the Governor's judgment as to the measures necessary to be taken to suppress the mob should not be questioned by the Courts and in absence of arbitrary, capricious conduct on his part in declaring martial law, the Courts are impotent to stay his hand. However, there is an utter absence of any persuasive showing here that law enforcement could not be maintained in the City of Albert Lea and in the County of Freeborn by the National Guard available to the Governor in aid of the local authorities. Moreover, we cannot subscribe to the principle or doctrine that a Governor of a State may bow to the demands of a law-violating mob that a plant under strike shall be closed when neither the local nor State authorities have used all the means available to them to suppress the mob by invoking enforcement of the laws of the State enacted to be enforced under such circumstances. Peace and order may be restored by acceding to the demands of the mob, but at the sacrifice of law. Such expedient measures would encourage and breed mob rule and law violations in every labor dispute. No citizen would be secure in the peaceful possession of his property. By way of analogy, let us assume a situation that not infrequently arises in our country. Racial hatred, for instance, against so-called minority citizens moving into a community, with the resulting demand that such citizens leave the neighborhood, often incites mob action. If the violence could not be suppressed by local authorities, a Governor could impose martial law and the military could issue an order that the innocent citizens leave the neighborhood because if they did so, peace and tranquillity would prevail. Lawlessness in this manner could be suppressed, but it would be obtained by compelling the victims of such lawlessness to surrender their constitutional rights so precious to all freedom-loving people.

It is entirely understandable that the local officials of the City of Albert Lea and the County of Freeborn when they met on the evening of December 10th were greatly exercised and concerned as to what might happen on the following day in light of the mob violence which had already taken place at plaintiff's plant, and that that concern prompted the promulgation of the petition to the Governor for aid. But when the military moved into the City on the morning of December 11th, it must have been apparent that in this local labor dispute the State of Minnesota was not required to surrender to mob violence. Under the factual presentation herein, it would be a shocking reflection on the stability of our State Government if the State could not quell the mob action in Freeborn County without declaring martial law and decreeing the deprivation of constitutional rights of those who are the victims of the lawlessness.

This is the second time in the history of Minnesota that martial law has been declared by a Governor. A declaration of martial law connotes the disintegration of the local and State Government which has been created to maintain peace and order under civil rule. Under martial law, all constitutional rights could conceivably be abolished. There could be no freedom of the press, freedom of speech, freedom of assembly, freedom from unreasonable search and seizure, and all courts could be abolished except the military courts established by the military. The abdication of our civil form of government to military rule, with the seizure of private property in contravention of Federal constitutional rights, cannot be sustained on this record. In our opinion, the lawlessness and violence in Albert Lea and Freeborn County did not constitute either "insurrection" or "invasion" within the meaning of Article V, Section 4, of the Constitution of the State of Minnesota.

Reference has been made to Powers Mercantile Co. v. Olson, 7 F.Supp. 865, in which this Court, after a declaration by the Governor of martial law in the City of Minneapolis, declined to enjoin the enforcement of a military order denying to plaintiff the right to use their trucks on the streets of Minneapolis. We made no finding in that case as to the Governor's right to declare martial law. Admittedly, the factual situation there markedly differed from that with which we are now confronted. In any event, each case must be determined on its own facts. The refusal to grant a preliminary injunction in the Powers case was due to the peculiar circumstances of that case, and is no precedent here in support of defendants' position.

In closing, it may be noted that, if it can be successfully urged that during the early morning of December 11th the apparent exigencies of the situation seemed to justify the declaration of martial law, it must be apparent that, upon sober reflection, the situation at the time the complaint herein was filed impellingly justifies a finding that the need for martial law in Albert Lea and Freeborn County no longer exists. Certainly, the civil authorities, with the aid of the National Guard, can control any further disturbance in and around the plant of the plaintiff without the closing of the plant and without an order forbidding workers who desire to work the right of free ingress to and egress from their place of employment. We are convinced that present conditions no longer require denial to the plaintiff of its constitutional rights, and that the prayer for relief in its complaint should be granted.

The above is adopted as the Court's findings of fact herein, and as conclusions of law the Court finds that it has jurisdiction of this suit; that the several motions to dismiss should be, and hereby are, denied; that plaintiff is entitled to an interlocutory injunction during the pendency of this suit and until further order of the Court restraining the defendants, and each of them, and all persons acting under or for them, from in any way preventing plaintiff from possessing or using its plant and property in any lawful manner, and from interfering with the right of plaintiff, its officers, agents and employees, to have free and unlimited access to and egress from its said plant and property. Upon the giving of a bond in the usual form in the sum of $5,000, to be approved by a Judge of this Court, such a writ of injunction shall issue. It is so ordered. A stay until December 27, 1959, at 12:00 midnight, is hereby granted.

Exceptions are reserved.

CHAPTER FIVE

Judicial Power

BASICALLY, "judicial power" is the power to decide cases. More precise is the definition accepted by the United States Supreme Court in *Muskrat* v. *United States,* 219 U.S. 346 (1910): "Judicial power is the power of a court to decide and pronounce a judgment and carry it into effect between persons and parties who bring a case before it for decision." Judicial power should not be confused with "jurisdiction." Jurisdiction is the word used to describe the *kinds* of cases in which a particular court may exercise its judicial power. For example, Article III of the United States Constitution provides that "The judicial power of the United States, shall be vested in one supreme Court, and in such inferior Courts as the Congress may from time to time ordain and establish." The Article then stipulates the kinds of cases to which the judicial power of the Supreme Court shall extend. By the terms of Article III, Congress can limit extensively the Supreme Court's appellate jurisdiction but Congress cannot constitutionally limit in any way the Supreme Court's exercise of judicial power in cases where it does have jurisdiction. There have been cases in which it has been alleged that a particular act of Congress has limited the meaning or use of judicial power and the Court has upheld the law. But in these cases, the Court has held that the act did not actually affect judicial power as such. A good illustration of this point is the Supreme Court's decision in *Ex parte McCardle,* 7 Wallace 506 (1868). After the Supreme Court had heard argument and taken the case under advisement, Congress passed a law over a presidential veto taking away the Supreme Court's appellate jurisdiction in this type of case. Counsel for the appellant argued that Congress had interfered with the exercise of judicial power:

> . . . This case has been argued in this court, fully. Passing then from the domain of the bar, it was delivered into the sacred hands of the judges; and was in the custody of the court. For aught that was known by Congress, it was passed upon and decided by them. Then comes . . . this act of Congress. Its language is general, but, as was universally known, its purpose was specific. If Congress had specifically enacted "that the Supreme Court of the United States shall never publicly give judgment in the case of McCardle, already argued, and on which we anticipate that it will soon deliver judgment, contrary to the

> views of the majority in Congress, of what it ought to decide," its purpose to interfere specifically with and prevent the judgment in this very case would not have been more real or, as a fact, more universally known.
>
> Now, can Congress thus interfere with cases on which this high tribunal has passed, or is passing, judgment? Is not legislation like this an exercise by the Congress of judicial power?

Despite counsel's excellent argument, the Supreme Court held that Congress had not abridged *judicial power:*

> We are not at liberty to inquire into the motives of the legislature. We can only examine into its power under the Constitution; and the power to make exceptions to the appellate jurisdiction of this court is given by express words.
>
> What, then, is the effect of the repealing act upon the case before us? We cannot doubt as to this. Without jurisdiction the court cannot proceed at all in any cause. Jurisdiction is power to declare the law, and when it ceases, the only function remaining to the court is that of announcing the fact and dismissing the cause. And this is no less clear upon authority than upon principle.
>
> Several cases were cited by the counsel for the petitioner in support of the position that jurisdiction of this case is not affected by the repealing act. But none of them, in our judgment, afford any support to it. They are all cases of the exercise of judicial power by the legislature, or legislative interference with the courts in the exercising of continuing jurisdiction.

As a consequence of the power to decide cases properly brought before them, the courts have acquired a host of ancillary powers, that is, powers necessary to enable them to fulfill their basic function. To decide cases, courts must be able among other things to compel witnesses to testify and to punish for contempt. When the courts have felt that certain powers are essential to deciding cases, they have declared these powers to be part of judicial power and as such they do not have to be granted to the courts by acts of the appropriate legislature. Nonetheless, legislatures have sometimes passed legislation granting such powers to the courts. When legislatures have tried by legislation to strip courts of powers that courts feel are part of judicial power, the courts have struck down such legislation as a violation of the separation of powers principle which is operative in our state governments as well as the national.

It was through the process of judicial decision that ancillary powers were incorporated into judicial power, and thereby American courts acquired for themselves the power of judicial review. Nowhere does the United States Constitution give courts the power to declare acts of Congress or actions of the President unconstitutional. It has been argued vigorously that the Framers understood judicial power to include judicial review. Perhaps, they did. In any case, Chief Justice Marshall speaking for the Supreme Court in 1803 in *Marbury* v. *Madison*, 1 Cranch 137 (1803) settled the matter. He argued persuasively that in deciding a particular case it is sometimes necessary to interpret the Constitution and to find an act of Congress in violation of it, but that this was nothing more than the legitimate exercise of judicial power. But let Marshall speak for himself:

> If an act of the legislature, repugnant to the Constitution, is void, does it notwithstanding its invalidity, bind the courts, and oblige them to give effect? Or, in other words, though it be not law, does it constitute a rule as operative as if it was a law? This would be to overthrow in fact, what was established in theory; and would seem, at first view, an absurdity too gross to be insisted on. It shall, however, receive a more attentive consideration.
>
> It is, emphatically, the province and duty of the judicial department, to say what the law is. Those who would apply the rule to particular cases, must of necessity expound and interpret that rule. If two laws conflict with each other, the courts must decide on the operation of each. So, if a law be in opposition to the Constitution; if both the law and the Constitution apply to a particular case, so that the court must either decide the case, conformable to the law, disregarding the Constitution; or conformable to the Constitution, disregarding the law; the court must determine which of these conflicting rules governs the case; this is the very essence of judicial duty. If then, the courts are to regard the Constitution, and the Constitution is superior to any ordinary act of the legislature, the Constitution, and not such ordinary act, must govern the case to which they both apply.

Marshall later went on to add that "The judicial power of the United States is extended to all cases arising under the Constitution. Could it be the intention of those who gave this power, to say, that in using it, the Constitution should not be looked into? That a case arising under the Constitution should be decided, without examining the instrument under which it arises? This is too extravagant to be maintained. In some cases, then, the Constitution must be looked into by the judges. . . ."

Marshall's argument may seem so logical and so convincing that you may be surprised to learn that many of his distinguished contemporaries took issue with him. Jefferson, for example, felt that there was no question but what the Constitution was the supreme law of the land. He argued nevertheless that judicial review was not necessary to uphold the supremacy of the Constitution and that Congress and the President could be relied upon to uphold the Constitution, perhaps, better than the courts. Not only that, but, if the responsibility lay with Congress and the President in their appropriate spheres, the people had recourse to the ballot box to remedy their failure to pay proper respect to the Constitution. To really appreciate the difference between the respective positions of Marshall and Jefferson, one must understand one of the implicit basic assumptions Marshall made. He apparently assumed that upon occasion Congress and/or the President would patently and willfully violate the Constitution. Surely, if this was in prospect, it could logically be argued that judicial review was the only hope for preserving the Constitution. But, it was just as logical to believe as Jefferson did, that, practically, there would probably be no such situations and, in the unlikely event there was, the people could remedy the situation by ballot. Consequently, as Jefferson saw it, there was no need for the institution of judicial review. If one goes back over our history on the national level, there are precious few instances where it could be demonstrated that judicial review saved the Constitution from harm at the hands of Congress or the President. On the state level, the situation is different. Justice Holmes summed up this point well, years ago, when he said: "I do not think the United States would come to an end if we lost our power to declare an Act of Congress void. I do think the Union would be imperiled if we could not make that declaration as to the laws of the several states." Finally, it is pertinent to point out that Constitutions of other great democracies have been preserved without the institution of judicial review. England is the best, and best-known, example. Whatever the merits of the arguments for or against judicial review, it has remained an integral part of the American system since 1803.

It is no overstatement to say that as the keepers of "the judicial power" our courts have enormous responsibilities. In keeping with Shakespeare's observation that "Uneasy lies the head that wears a crown," our courts have manifested great concern over the role they are called upon to play in our system. They are at once jealous of their power and fearful of it. Despite their insistence that they have the power of review and woe to the legislature or executive who tries to deny it, the courts themselves at times have effectively limited themselves. We will explore that phenomenon directly.

In addition to their concern over the exercise of the power of judicial review, the courts, particularly in recent years, have demonstrated a marked concern over the procedures employed in apprehending and trying alleged criminals. Quite rightly, the courts have felt a heavy responsibility for seeing that criminal convictions are obtained in accord with a meticulous regard for fair procedures.

A. *Judicial Self-Restraint*

Although it is well-established that our courts have the power of judicial review, judges have traditionally manifested a self-consciousness about using it. When they have done so, they have often been apologetic about it. True, some courts at some time, like the Supreme Court during the early New Deal days, have shown little reluctance to declare acts of the legislatures and actions of the executives unconstitutional. But these are the exceptions not the rule. Usually, courts have demonstrated a marked deference toward their sister branches of government and, when it has been necessary to declare acts or actions unconstitutional, it has been done more in sorrow than with joy. It has become commonplace for courts to assert that they will assume the other branches have acted constitutionally unless it can be demonstrated clearly and convincingly that they have violated constitutional provisions. In a manner of speaking, the courts have viewed judicial review as a last resort, available for use but to be used infrequently. You have already read in the discussion of the reapportionment problem a demonstration of the reluctance of courts to exercise judicial review where they believed that constitutional questions can be better solved by the "political" branches of the government.

Despite the traditional reluctance of courts to exercise judicial review, a good statement providing a theoretical framework for its use was long in being formulated. It was in our own times that Justice Frankfurter consolidated and developed judicial thinking on self-restraint into such a statement. In a dissenting opinion in *Board of Education* v. *Barnette*, 319 U.S. 624 (1943), he wrote:

> Not so long ago we were admonished that the only check upon our own exercise of power is our own sense of self-restraint. For the removal of unwise laws from the statute books appeal lies not to the courts but to the ballot and to the processes of democratic government. We have been told that generalities do not decide concrete cases. But the intensity with which a general principle is held may determine a particular issue, and whether we put first things first may decide a specific controversy.
>
> The admonition that judicial self-restraint alone limits arbitrary exercise of our authority is relevant every time we are asked to nullify legislation. The Constitution does not give us greater veto power when dealing with one phase of "liberty" than with another. . . . In neither [no] situation is our function comparable to that of a legislature or are we free to act as though we were a super-legislature. Judicial self-restraint is equally necessary whenever an exercise of political or legislative power is challenged. There is no warrant in the constitutional basis of this Court's authority for attributing different roles to it depending upon the nature of the challenge to the legislation. Our power does not vary according to the particular provision of the Bill of Rights which is invoked. . . .
>
> When Mr. Justice Holmes, speaking for this Court, wrote that "It must be remembered that legislatures are ultimate guardians of the liberties and welfare of the people in quite as great a degree as the courts," he went to the very essence of our constitutional system and the democratic conception of our society. He did not mean that for only some phases of civil government this Court was not to supplant legislatures and sit in judgment upon the right or wrong of a challenged statute. He was stating the comprehensive judicial duty and role of this Court in our Constitutional scheme whenever legislation is sought to be justified on any ground, namely, that responsibility for legislation lies with legislatures, answerable as they are directly to the people, and this Court's only and very narrow function is to determine whether within the broad grant of authority vested in legislatures they have exercised a judgment for which reasonable justification can be offered.

Whether persuaded by Justice Frankfurter or the merits of the position itself or both, a majority of the Supreme Court was committed to the self-restraint approach for some years before Frankfurter's retirement. With the retirement of Justices Whittaker and Frankfurter, this approach apparently no longer commands the allegiance of a majority of the Court. Justice Goldberg appears to have joined Chief Justice Warren and Justices Black, Douglas, and Brennan in rejecting the approach of Justice Frankfurter. Most state judges are committed to the approach, however. This raises the interesting question, Why do a majority of the current Supreme Court justices and a significant number of state judges reject it? The quotation from Frankfurter points up the cause of contention. The libertarians on the Supreme Court: Warren, Black, Douglas, Brennan and Goldberg and their counterparts on the state courts are willing to exercise self-restraint in varying degrees with respect to legislative and executive action in the *economic* sphere, but they are not so willing to do so in situations where the other branches of government restrict civil liberties, primarily, the First Amendment freedoms. They believe that in our concept of government there are "preferred freedoms," i.e. speech, press, religion, and assembly. To buttress their belief, these justices have pointed out in appropriate cases that: (1) these freedoms have been asserted in the First Amendment in absolute terms, "Congress shall make no law . . ."; and (2) democracy cannot survive when these fundamental freedoms are denied. Consequently, they take the position that where these important freedoms are concerned, action by the legislative and executive branches which appears to destroy them will not be accorded the usual presumption of constitutionality and that it is important for the courts to very actively exercise their power of judicial review to safeguard First Amendment freedoms. Although the call to arms by the judicial "activists," as the libertarians are sometimes called, is sounded primarily for cases involving First Amendment freedoms, it is understandable why those who are aggressive about using judicial review in those cases will by inclination be more ready to find legislatures and executives guilty of arbitrariness in other areas. In a sense, by their position in First Amendment cases, in contrast to Frankfurter's, they have demonstrated that they are more willing to pass judgment on the actions of legislatures and executives. In the foregoing, we hope we have not conveyed the impression that the justices are so irrevocably and so absolutely committed that when there is a split decision involving the use of judicial review five are on one side and four on the other. Remember, that even the "activists" have a high regard for the idea of judicial self-restraint in most kinds of situations and remember that those advocating self-restraint are not ready to give up judicial review entirely. With this in mind, it is easy to see that alignments will vary depending upon the facts of a particular case.

We offer for your consideration two cases in which the Minnesota supreme court exercised judicial self-restraint in non-First Amendment cases. In *Naftalin* v. *King* (p. 128), the court refused to void an act which was patently unconstitutional. The majority was concerned about the unfortunate practical effect such an action on its part would have. Should a court in such a case concern itself with any other consideration but whether or not the law is unconstitutional? Which opinion seems more reasonable to you, the majority or dissenting opinion? In *State* v. *Meyer* (p. 279), it was alleged that the legislature had unconstitutionally abridged the courts' judicial power. The case, therefore, is not only instructive as to the issue of judicial review but also as to the concept of "judicial power" which we discussed earlier.

B. *Due Process in Criminal Cases*

A great number of American judges have in recent years strongly felt that one of their most important tasks was to insist that the procedures used in apprehending and attempting to convict alleged criminals be fair. Perhaps, the best explanation for such insistence was provided by Justice Jackson when he dissented in *Shaughnessy* v. *U.S.* ex rel. *Mezei,* 345 U.S. 206 (1953):

> Procedural fairness, if not all that originally was meant by due process of law, is at least what it most uncompromisingly requires. Procedural due process is more elemental and less flexible than substantive due process. It yields less to the times, varies less with conditions, and defers much less to legislative judgment. Insofar as it is technical law, it must be the specialized responsibility within the competence of the judiciary on which they do not bend before political branches of the Government, as they should on matters of policy which comprise substantive law.
>
> . . . Only the untaught layman or the charlatan lawyer can answer that procedures matter not. Procedural fairness and regularity are of the indispensable essence of liberty. Severe substantive laws can be endured if they are fairly and impartially applied. Indeed, if put to the choice, one might well prefer to live under Soviet substantive law applied in good faith by our common law procedures than under our substantive law enforced by Soviet procedural practices. Let it not be overlooked that due process of law is not for the sole benefit of the accused. It is the best insurance for the Government itself against those blunders which leave lasting stains on a system of justice but which are bound to occur on *ex parte* consideration. . . .

1. RIGHT-TO-COUNSEL PROBLEMS

We undoubtedly agree that the accused in a criminal trial *should* be entitled to have a lawyer represent him at the trial. But suppose the accused insists he does not want a lawyer. Should the court force counsel upon him? Suppose the accused just says "I'm guilty. Let's get the trial over with in a hurry. I do not care whether or not I have a lawyer." Should the court insist that he have a lawyer and furnish counsel? The Supreme Court of the United States has supplied partial answers to these questions which *state* courts are obliged to consider. An explanation of this statement is in order.

First, since the Bill of Rights by itself has been interpreted to apply only to the national government, the United States Constitution provides for "the assistance of counsel" in criminal cases only in Federal courts. Although there were those who argued that right-to-counsel should be specifically and completely read into the due process clause of the Fourteenth Amendment, for thirty years and until 1963, Supreme Court majorities did not accept that proposition. Instead, they held that the due process clause of the Fourteenth Amendment did not automatically provide right-to-counsel in all state cases but that it did require a fair trial. Therefore, if denial of counsel in a particular state case constituted unfairness, such a denial violated the due process requirement of the Fourteenth Amendment of the United States Constitution. In *Betts* v. *Brady*, 316 U.S. 455 (1942), Justice Roberts wrote for the majority:

> Due process of law is secured against invasion by the Federal Government by the Fifth Amendment and is safeguarded against state action in identical words by the Fourteenth. The phrase formulates a concept less rigid and more fluid than those envisaged in other specific and particular provisions of the Bill of Rights. Its application is less a matter of rule. Asserted denial is to be tested by an appraisal of the totality of facts in a given case. That which may, in one setting, constitute a denial of fundamental fairness, shocking to the universal sense of justice, may, in other circumstances, and in the light of other considerations, fall short of such denial.

From 1942 to 1963, the United States Supreme Court had occasion to define what they regard as situations wherein denial of counsel constituted unfairness to such a degree as to violate due process. Professor C. Herman Pritchett succinctly summarizes the Supreme Court decisions this way:

> State counsel cases continued to come to the Court in unusual numbers, well over twenty in the decade following *Betts* v. *Brady*. In a very considerable number of these cases the Court held that due process does require furnishing of counsel. This is very likely to be the holding, for example, when the offense is a capital one; where the conduct of the trial judge appears to be questionable; where the defendent is young or ignorant or otherwise handicapped; or where the points of law involved are too technical for a layman to grasp.[1]

Then, in a landmark case in 1963, the Supreme Court unequivocally rejected this approach and reversed *Betts* v. *Brady*. Mr. Justice Black speaking for the Court in *Gideon* v. *Wainwright*, 372 U.S. 335 (1963) said:

> We accept *Betts* v. *Brady*'s assumption, based as it was on our prior cases, that a provision of the Bill of Rights which is "fundamental and essential to a fair trial" is made obligatory upon the States by the Fourteenth Amendment. We think that the Court in *Betts* was wrong, however, in concluding that the Sixth Amendment's guarantee of counsel is not one of those fundamental rights.

In *Gideon*, the specific issue decided by the Court was that a state was required by the United States Constitution to supply counsel for a defendant in a criminal case, *if he wanted one* but could not afford to pay one. But Black's language leaves no doubt that the Sixth Amendment is now incorporated in the Fourteenth.

Since, as Black also pointed out, the Court has in the past construed the

[1] C. Herman Pritchett, *The American Constitution* (New York: McGraw-Hill Book Co., 1959), p. 543. Used by permission.

Sixth Amendment "to mean that in federal courts counsel must be provided for defendants unable to employ counsel unless the right is competently and intelligently waived," state courts are still left with the problem of deciding in most cases, when right-to-counsel is waived, whether it has been done "competently and intelligently." For the great bulk of criminal cases are tried in state courts initially, since most of our criminal law is state law. Even though the way may be open to a successful appeal to the United States Supreme Court later, state courts in most criminal cases will have the first opportunity (1) to determine whether or not to accept a waiver and (2) to determine, on appeal, whether or not the trial court erred in accepting a waiver.

The problem of waiver is not a new one for state courts; they have wrestled with it for years as *Willey* v. *Hudspeth* (p. 285), *Spiers* v. *Turner* (p. 290), *Johnson* v. *Mayo* (p. 293), *Gant* v. *Banmiller* (p. 295), and *People* v. *Easter* (p. 296) demonstrate. These cases are not presented as an indication of how all state courts have and will decide such cases, for, in truth, state courts differ markedly in their respective approaches. Rather, these cases have been selected to enable you to address yourself to two crucial questions which the problem of waiver raises, (1) Is it ever possible to have a fair trial, when the accused does not have the benefit of counsel? (2) Assuming that the answer to the first question is "yes," as our courts have held (by even permitting waiver), what are the legitimate criteria for deciding whether or not a waiver is competent and intelligent? Specifically, are youth, lack of intelligence, and mental and/or physical illness factors which should automatically compel courts to *require* counsel for the accused? In reading these cases, bear in mind that they were decided before the 1963 decision of the Supreme Court. Consequently, there are references to what was then an accurate assumption, that the Sixth Amendment had not been incorporated into the Fourteenth. Do not be confused by these references; the 1963 Supreme Court decision negates that assumption. But such references do raise an interesting question, Would the decision in any of these cases have been different, if the Supreme Court decision had come first? We are inclined to think so as to several cases.

Ex parte McCoy (p. 297) raises still another important right-to-counsel question. At what point in the process of apprehension and trial does an accused have a right to counsel? There are those who insist that at the earliest moment feasible after being apprehended, a person should be entitled to counsel. They argue that if counsel is not available before the trial, it may well nigh be impossible for a defense attorney in the trial to undo the damage an accused may have done to his cause by talking to law enforcement officials without the benefit of counsel. Others feel that it makes the job of law enforcement officials intolerably difficult, if at the early stages they must contend with counsel. They point out that in many cases involving the most heinous crimes, such as murder and rape, there are no witnesses and, unless the accused talks, it is impossible to convict him when he is guilty. It is a foregone conclusion that a lawyer would not permit his client in such a situation to talk. Further, they contend that, although an accused should be protected from third-degree methods, he should not be prevented from voluntarily unburdening himself as to his guilt. Bear in mind these contentions as you read *Ex parte McCoy* and determine for yourself whether or not the court decided wisely in that case. Also, take into account two recent decisions of the United States Supreme Court [*Hamilton* v. *Alabama*, 368 U.S. 52 (1961) and *White* v. *Maryland*, 373 U.S. 59 (1963)] in which the Court held that, at least in capital cases, the accused is entitled to counsel at "critical" stages in criminal proceedings such as the arraignment stage in Alabama and the "preliminary hearing" in Maryland. As the Court explained, "What happens there may affect the whole trial. Available defenses may be irretrievably lost, if not then and there asserted. . . ." 368 U.S. 52, 57 (1961). But note that the Court did not specify, however, what other stages of criminal proceedings they would regard as "critical" nor whether they would apply a different standard in non-capital cases.

2. OTHER DUE PROCESS PROBLEMS

Because fairness like beauty depends in part upon the perception of the beholder, it is not surprising that there have been an enormous number of litigants carrying cases to appeals courts alleging that procedures allowed or employed by lower courts and administrative agencies were lacking in fairness. The cases that follow are a very small sampling and are intended to be suggestive rather than exhaustive. *Wojculewicz* v. *Cummings* (p. 299) deals with this perplexing question, Does it violate due process to try someone who is not in good health? In *Powell* v. *Commonwealth* (p. 303) it was contended that it was unfair to allow a jury to announce its verdict while the defendant's counsel was temporarily absent from the courtroom. The Supreme Court of the United States decided in *Griffin* v. *Illinois* (p. 307) that it was unfair for an Illinois court not to provide convicted robbers who claimed to be indigent a transcript of the trial. In *Thompson* v. *City of Louisville* (p. 314), the United States Supreme Court reviewed the record of a conviction in a Louisville, Kentucky police court case and determined that Thompson had been convicted on insufficient evidence, hence unfairly. In your opinion, were the procedures, found wanting by the courts in the decisions you read, so unfair as to constitute a deprivation of due process? An interesting and very important sidelight to the *Griffin* case is how much the decision disturbed the Conference of State Chief Justices. In a highly controversial report issued in the Conference's behalf in 1958, it was stated that there was "danger of swamping some state appellate courts under the flood of appeals which may be loosed by *Griffin* and *Eskridge*" the latter, another case involving the failure to furnish a free transcript, wherein the Supreme Court held that the petitioner was denied his constitutional rights, 357 U.S. 214 (1958). But the Supreme Court has maintained its stand. In March 1963, in *Draper* v. *Washington*, 372 U.S. 487 (1963), a case raising questions about the kind of record which had to be provided an indigent criminal defendant seeking an appeal, the Court reaffirmed its decision in *Griffin*.

STATE v. MEYER

MINNESOTA SUPREME COURT

37 N.W. 2D 3 (1949)

One of the major provisions of the Minnesota Youth Conservation Act of 1947 is the requirement that district courts in sentencing minors were to commit these young offenders to state training schools rather than to state penal institutions. When Meyer, who was 18 years old, pleaded guilty to a third degree burglary charge, his attorney asked the court if it proposed to sentence Meyer under the Youth Conservation Act of 1947. The court replied that it had no alternative. Whereupon Meyer's counsel moved to arrest the judgment on the grounds that the act was unconstitutional. The court sustained the objection and, with the consent of the state and Meyer, certified to the state supreme court questions as to the constitutionality of the act. The case raised several interesting issues which are too important and interesting to omit. However, we urge you to pay special attention to the contention that the legislature was usurping judicial power and the court's reaction to it.

Justice KNUTSON delivered the opinion of the court.

. . . .

A BRIEF description of the act may be helpful to an intelligent understanding of its validity. Under the act there is created a youth conservation commission, . . . consisting of five persons, including the director of the division of public institutions, the chairman of the state board of parole, and three others appointed by the governor with the consent of the senate. One of the appointed members is designated as chairman by the governor. Such chairman is the full-time director of the commission. . . . The act provides for a salary for the director . . . and per diem compensation for the other two appointive members, but no additional compensation for the director of the division of public institutions or the chairman of the state board of parole. . . .

The act applies to two distinct groups: Those found delinquent by juvenile courts, . . . and those convicted of a felony or a gross misdemeanor in the district courts who are under the age of 21 years. . . .

The act does not affect the procedure governing trial or hearing. It applies only when there has been a conviction or a plea of guilty and affects only the disposition that may be made of the offender after such conviction. It does not affect the power of the trial court to grant a new trial or set aside its judgment by reason of surprise, fraud, perjury, or otherwise, nor does it affect the right of appeal. . . .

With respect to juvenile court cases, the principal change introduced by the act consists of eliminating the power of the juvenile court to commit a minor to the state training school for boys at Red Wing or to the home school for girls at Sauk Center, and requires the court instead to commit the youth to the commission. . . . The juvenile court retains authority to place the youth on probation or to make such other disposition of the case as the court may decide, not involving commitment to a state school.

The district court cannot commit a youth under the age of 21 years to a penal institution, but must sentence him to the commission. The court retains authority to place the youth on probation on any terms it sees fit after a presentence investigation has been made. Unless the court places the youth on probation, the court must commit the offender to the commission for the maximum term prescribed by the statute creating the crime for which the youth was committed. . . .

Upon commitment by a juvenile court, the commission has the right to retain control of the youth until he or she reaches the age of 21 years. At that time the offender must be discharged in any event. . . . The commission may confine the youth in the state training school for boys or the home school for girls or place him or her on probation, or, after confinement, on parole on such terms as it may prescribe, having in mind the best interests of the youth and society. . . . It cannot confine the youth in a penal institution. . . . It may discharge the youth from its control entirely before the age of 21 is reached. . . .

When commitment is from a district court upon conviction of a felony or gross misdemeanor, the commission is given authority to confine the youth in a penal institution or place him on probation or, after confinement, on parole, on such terms as it may prescribe. . . . The youth must in any event be discharged on the expiration of the term for which the court sentenced him. . . . If before that time he reaches his 25th birthday, he must then be discharged, unless the commission finds that to do so would be dangerous to the public, in which event he is turned over to the regular adult criminology agencies. . . .

Whether the commitment is from a juvenile court or district court, before treatment is prescribed by the commission it must make a study of the youth. . . .

. . . .

Tested by these rules, we have no difficulty in finding that the act meets the requirements of Minn.Const. art. 4, § 27.

Defendant . . . contends that the act is in violation of Minn.Const. art. 3, § 1, and art. 6, §§ 1, 2, and 5, in that it violates the separation of powers of the three branches of our government, and that it is an invasion of the judicial powers vested in the courts by our constitution, and also that it deprives the supreme court and district courts of their "inherent powers." These claims will be considered together.

We fully recognize that it is as important today as it ever was to maintain an impartial and independent judiciary as one of the three coordinate branches of our government, but in determining whether the legislative branch is encroaching upon the judicial it is fundamental that we keep in mind the distinction between those functions which are inherently judicial in their nature and those acts which the judiciary perform within the limits prescribed by the legislature.

The legislature can, and always has, fixed and determined the punishment that shall be imposed for a violation of law and the limits of discretion vested in the courts in the imposition of the sentence. It determines whether the law violator shall be committed to a penal institution at all, or if some other form of punishment, such as a fine, shall apply. It may determine the minimum as well as the maximum sentence; it may permit the court to fix the length of the sentence within the maximum term prescribed or it may prescribe a minimum which is mandatory and permit the court to fix the maximum, or it may provide a maximum and permit an administrative body to determine how long the violator shall serve; it may require the court to sentence violators to certain penal institutions or grant the court authority to determine which of such institutions such violator may be committed to, or it may vest in an administrative official the power to determine which institution shall be used; and it may grant an administrative board the authority to supervise a convicted person, either within or without a penal institution. It may also grant the court power to suspend a sentence and may limit such power to certain cases and deny it as to others. These are but a part of the functions performed by the courts within the limits prescribed by the legislative branch of the government.

A good statement of the law on this subject is found in State v. Dugan, 89 A. 691, where the court, in upholding the constitutionality of the New Jersey indeterminate sentence law, said:

"* * * The pronouncing of a sentence is undoubtedly a judicial act; but the punishment which the sentence pronounces comes from the law itself. As Blackstone truly expressed it, under head of 'Judgment and its Consequences': 'The court must pronounce that judgment which the law hath annexed to the crime.' It is further said that the statute in effect curtails the judicial discretion to be exercised by the judge. Granting that it does, it is, nevertheless, the valid exercise of legislative power under the Constitution over crimes." . . .

. . . [*In a previous case*] we said:

"It is the exclusive province of the Legislature to declare what acts, deemed by the lawmakers inimical to the public welfare, shall constitute a crime, to prohibit the same and impose appropriate penalties for a violation thereof. With the wisdom and propriety thereof the courts are not concerned." . . .

The constitutionality of the California act, which is in most respects similar to ours, was upheld against contentions identical to those raised here in Re Herrera, 143 P.2d 345, where the court said:

"There is no unconstitutional delegation of legislative or judicial power, as petitioners contend, in thus vesting power in the Authority to determine, within the limits prescribed, how long convicted persons shall be detained and how they shall be treated after commitment. The standards governing the Authority in determining the kind of treatment and release of such persons are well within constitutional requirements."

The present act is similar in many respects to the indeterminate sentence law, under which the state board of parole determines how long a convicted offender must serve within statutory limits prescribed by the legislature or the maximum sentence imposed by the court in those cases where the legislature has conferred a discretionary power upon the courts to fix the maximum. The constitutionality of laws establishing indeterminate sentences has long since been established. . . .

. . . .

We long ago abandoned the ancient doctrine of compensatory punishment for crime and adopted the more modern theory under which one of the primary aims of sentences imposed upon law violators is to ultimately reform and rehabilitate the offender so that he can be returned to society as a useful and law-abiding citizen. Establishment of our juvenile court, our system of indeterminate sentences with supervision vested in the state board of parole or our system of suspended sentences and probation, and other laws of this kind are intended to accomplish that purpose. We recognized this change in State ex rel. Kelly v. Wolfer, . . . where we said, 138 N.W. 317:

"* * * It is long since that criminology gave us our modern conception of criminality, from which has arisen an ever-increasing tendency to regard 'punishment' for crime as being not so much compensatory as reformatory, and from this tendency, in turn, have sprung laws greatly amplifying and extending the administrative functions incident to the execution of the penalties prescribed by law for crime and imposed by the courts upon those who have incurred the same. It is not at all strange, then, that, in the course of legislative attempts in the various states of the Union to meet the requirements of this extended administrative system, laws should sometimes be passed which at least seem to attempt to vest administrative officers with powers properly appertaining to the judicial or executive departments of the government. Bitter attacks have been made upon some of these laws, most notably upon the so-called indeterminate sentence system, with its credits for good behavior, upon the parole system, and upon the prison transfer system; such attacks being grounded variously upon the contentions that the legislation assailed attempts to vest administrative officers with the judicial power of sentence or the executive power of pardon, or else is an unauthorized delegation of legislative powers. . . ."

The Youth Conservation Act is only another attempt to find the most effective method of accomplishing the desirable object of rehabilitating and reforming youthful offenders. It recognizes that the formative years of youth offer the greatest opportunity for reformation and that youthful offenders often can be handled more effectively by some method other than commitment to a penal institution, and still it safeguards society by providing means whereby those who are a menace may be confined the same as under prior law.

Defendant confuses the function of the court in imposing sentence with the function of determining what the sentence shall be. It has always been a legislative function to determine what the sentence shall be. Here, the sentence is commitment to the commission. The act does not become operative as to district court cases until after conviction by trial or plea of guilty. It does not encroach upon those functions which are inherently judicial, and it is not violative of the articles of our constitution mentioned in this paragraph.

Defendant further contends that the act is repugnant to Minn.Const. art. 5, § 4. This claim rests largely upon the provision of subd. 31 of the act, which reads:

"Whenever a person committed to the Commission upon conviction of a crime is discharged from its control other than by expiration of the maximum term of commitment as provided under this section, or under the provisions of subdivision 27, such discharge shall, when so ordered by the Commission restore such person to all civil rights and shall have the effect of setting aside the conviction and nullifying the same and of purging such person thereof."

Whether the salutary purpose of removing the stigma which follows the conviction of a crime from the life of a young person who has been reformed and rehabilitated and is about to be returned to society may be accomplished without resort to the constitutional board of pardons we need not now determine. Defendant is in no position to raise that question. As a general rule, the courts will not pass upon the constitutionality of a law unless a decision on that very point becomes necessary.

"* * * a litigant may be heard to question the constitutionality of a statute only when and so far as it is being or is about to be applied to his disadvantage." State ex rel. Clinton Falls Nursery Co. v. County of Steele, 232 N.W. 737.

. . . .

It is also the contention of defendant that subds. 10 and 19 of the act infringe upon the constitutional powers of the state board of pardons.

Acts such as our Youth Conservation Act are comparatively new in the field of criminology. However, exactly the same questions regarding constitutionality frequently have been raised against the constitutionality of laws creating parole boards or other administrative bodies having control over persons convicted of crime. These laws have been upheld almost unanimously. The argument that laws vesting in administrative boards the authority to determine how a convict should be handled after conviction interfere with the pardoning power vested in the executive or a pardon board most frequently stems from the failure to distinguish between a pardon or reprieve and a parole or probation. A pardon is the exercise of executive clemency. It completely frees the offender from the control of the state and relieves him of all legal disabilities resulting from his conviction. As a practical matter, it wipes out the conviction itself. Commonwealth ex rel. Banks v. Cain, 28 A.2d 897, where the distinction is pointed out as follows:

"* * * A pardon is the exercise of the sovereign's prerogative of mercy. It completely frees the offender from the control of the state. It not only exempts him from further punishment but relieves him from all the legal disabilities resulting from his conviction. It blots out the very existence of his guilt, so that, in the eye of the law, he is thereafter as innocent as if he had never committed the offense: * * * A parole, on the other hand, does not obliterate the crime or forgive the offender. It is not an act of clemency, but a penological measure for the disciplinary treatment of prisoners who seem capable of rehabilitation outside of prison walls. It does not set aside or affect the sentence; the convict remains in the legal custody of the state and under the control of its agents, subject at any time, for breach of condition, to be returned to the penal institution. Neither is a parole a commutation of sentence within the meaning of that term in the constitutional provision."

In Ware v. Sanders, 124 N.W. 1081, the constitutionality of the Iowa statute creating a board of parole was challenged. In upholding it, the court said: "* * * The constitutional objection is grounded upon the thought that it in some manner trenches upon the power vested in the Governor of the state to grant pardons, reprieves, and commutations. The objection is unsound. The power of the Governor to pardon or reprieve a criminal, or to commute a sentence pronounced by a court, is in no manner abrogated, restricted, or removed by this statute. Whether punishment may be imposed at all, and, if so, its character and extent, is a matter of statute alone; and, if the Legislature in its wisdom concludes it to be sound policy to offer a premium to good conduct and reform in a prisoner by tendering him an amelioration of the rigor of his punishment, we are unable to see in what manner this constitutes the slightest interference with the exercise of executive clemency."

In State v. Duff, 122 N.W. 829, the court said in upholding the indeterminate sentence as against the claim that it infringes upon the pardoning power of the executive:

"* * * That the parole of prisoners under the provisions of the indeterminate sentence law does not infringe the constitutional right of the Governor to grant pardons, reprieves, etc., is supported by the undoubted weight of authority." This is the almost unanimous holding of the courts. . . .

The act does not prevent the governor or the state board of pardons from granting a pardon or a reprieve. We therefore hold that the act, insofar as its constitutionality is now before us, does not violate Minn.Const. art. 5, § 4.

Lastly, defendant claims that the act violates Minn.Const. art. 1, §§ 2, 6, 7, and 8, and U.S.Const. Amend. XIV.

. . . .

Defendant's arguments respecting the . . . constitutional provisions mentioned in this paragraph may be summarized as follows:

(a) That a defendant committed to the commission under the act is deprived of his right to credits for good conduct available to older offenders . . . and consequently there is such discrimination as to violate the due process clause.

The answer to this is that the act is intended for his benefit, not his detriment. There is always some discrimination when classification is based on age, but so long as the classification has some reasonable basis it cannot be held unconstitutional on that account. The same argument could be made against the constitutionality of our juvenile court act. . . . juveniles over the age of 12 years may, upon order of the juvenile court, be proceeded against as adult offenders. Those under 12 may not be. Those under 18 come within the jurisdiction of the juvenile court; those older do not. . . Prior to L.1917, c. 397, jurisdiction extended only to persons under 17 years of age. . . . Prior to L. 1933, c. 184, jurisdiction of the juvenile court continued only until the child reached the age of 19 years. . . . By the 1933 act, the age limit was extended to 21 years. Undoubtedly, the legislature could have extended the jurisdiction of the juvenile court to persons under 21 if it saw fit to do so. The youth act has for its primary purpose the reformation and rehabilitation of youthful offenders. It has for its very foundation provisions beneficial to those who come within its operation. Laws providing different punishments and methods of supervision for persons of different ages are not violative of constitutional due process. . . .

The equal protection of the law is secured if the law operates in the same way on all who belong in the same class. . . . [*For example, a Kansas case held that a*] law providing for differences in the method of handling offenders of opposite sexes does not violate the due process clause.

(b) That it deprives a person committed to the commission of the right to petition for a parole . . . or a pardon . . . and that it is therefore discriminatory.

There is nothing in the act to prevent the submission of a petition to the pardon board. The commission is vested with the power to parole now vested in the state board of parole. While it may be true that the operative methods for granting paroles may vary, there is no denial of the right to petition the commission for a parole. A similar classification based on age is found in . . . [*a law*], permitting a person convicted of a crime who is under 21 years of age at the time of the commission of the crime to petition for a pardon extraordinary. This right is conferred on youthful offenders by the legislature, not the constitution. The classification based on age is no doubt as valid in one case as in the other.

(c) That defendant is denied his constitutional right of a definite sentence and a full, complete, and speedy trial.

The act does not affect any rights concerning trial. The sentence prescribed by the legislature is at least as definite as it is under an indeterminate sentence. In addition, it affects only the administrative supervision of the convicted person after conviction. We see no merit in this contention.

(d) That it deprives defendant of the right to notice, hearing, the right to be represented by counsel, and the right of appeal or review.

None of these rights now existing are taken away. All rights of appeal, new trial, stay of sentence, or bail previously existing are preserved by the act. Subd. 30. The same questions regarding a right to a hearing have been raised and rejected in cases involving the revocation of suspensions of sentence and revocation of parole or probation and conditional pardons. There is no constitutional right to a hearing in proceedings subsequent to conviction and the imposition of sentence. . . . Neither is there any constitutional right to assistance of counsel after the completion of the trial and such appeal therefrom as may be provided by law. . . . Neither is there any constitutional right to a hearing before revocation of probation.

In all these arguments, defendant seeks to confuse the administrative supervision of convicted offenders after the imposition of sentence with proceedings that take place prior to the imposition of sentence. The trial terminates when the defendant is convicted. No rights of the defendant are affected by the act in any way up to that time. The court must then impose such sentence as the legislature has prescribed. In this case, the mandatory sentence is commitment to the commission unless the court places defendant on probation. Supervision of defendant after commitment may be vested in an administrative board without violating any constitutional rights of defendant. That is what the act does. "* * * This commitment is a judicial determination of the fact of defendant's conviction and a pronouncement of the sentence for the offense, namely, commitment to the Authority for the term prescribed by law, and is therefore the court's judgment and sentence of the convict * * * and is appealable." In re Herrera, 143 P.2d 345. . . .

We conclude that the act does not violate any provision of the state or federal constitutions insofar as it is now before us. The decision of the trial court is reversed with instructions to proceed with the imposition of sentence in accordance with the law.

So ordered.

WILLEY v. HUDSPETH

KANSAS SUPREME COURT

178 P. 2D 246 (1947)

Willey, a seventeen-year-old boy, was charged with breaking and entering a grocery store and with stealing articles amounting to $25.25. At the time of arraignment, Willey entered a plea of guilty and was given a sentence to be served in a state reformatory. Later, while on parole from the reformatory, he was convicted of a felony in Missouri. He was sent back to Kansas and placed in the Kansas State Penitentiary to serve out his term. Committing a felony is, of course, a violation of parole.

Willey subsequently petitioned the Kansas supreme court for a writ of habeas corpus *naming Hudspeth, the warden of the state penitentiary, the respondent. He alleged that his constitutional rights had been violated in the original Kansas conviction in that he had not been given assistance of counsel during his trial. (He also contended that he should have been returned to the reformatory where he had originally been sentenced to serve. But in a part of the opinion not reproduced below, the court quickly dismissed that contention as being without merit.)*

Justice BURCH delivered the opinion of the court.

. . . .

THE PETITION for a writ of habeas corpus filed in this case sets forth that the petitioner was denied his constitutional rights to have the assistance of counsel; that the court did not grant the petitioner the right to consultation of a counselor; that the petitioner did not desire to plead guilty as charged; that he did not waive the right of counsel, either orally or in writing; that he was coerced and intimidated by authorities and was unjustly held incommunicado from the date of his arrest on the 2nd of November until the date he was sentenced on the 7th day of November and further that the respondent, who is the warden of the Kansas State Penitentiary at Lansing, has no authority to detain the petitioner in custody because he was sentenced to the reformatory and not to the penitentiary.

The answer of the respondent denies all of the allegations contained in the petition. In support of the answer several affidavits have been filed. One of them is the affidavit of Ben L. Humphreys, who was the county attorney of Crawford County at the time the petitioner pleaded guilty and was sentenced. Such affidavit specifically denies the statements of the petitioner as to his being coerced and intimidated by authorities and held incommunicado and declares that such statements are untrue; that the petitioner was not abused, coerced or threatened in any way for the purpose of causing him to plead guilty or to influence him in his actions; that the plea of guilty was made voluntarily and that the petitioner was not induced by any threats or coercion by any one. Such affidavit concludes by stating that the petitioner "did not at that time express any desire for counsel or intimate by any expression or action that he desired counsel to advise with him or represent him." In addition, the respondent has filed the affidavit of August Dorchy, who was the sheriff of Crawford County at the time the petitioner was awaiting trial. His affidavit also is to the effect that the petitioner was not threatened, coerced or influenced by the sheriff or by other officers in any way to plead guilty while the petitioner was in the custody of the sheriff. The contentions of the petitioner as to his being coerced or held incommunicado are not corroborated in any manner and consequently, we have no hesitancy in holding that he has not sustained the burden of proof required to establish that he was coerced into entering his plea or held incommunicado and that his petition cannot be allowed for such reasons. See Hill v. Hudspeth, 168 P.2d 922, and cases therein cited.

. . . .

The foregoing brings us to consideration of the serious question involved in the case—should this 17-year-old boy have been given the benefit of counsel before he was permitted to enter his plea of guilty to the felony charges filed against him? We are not concerned with the career of crime which the petitioner may have followed since he was first sent to the reformatory by the State of Kansas. We are gravely concerned, however, with the perplexing problem presented as to whether a 17-year-old boy should be permitted to enter a plea of guilty in a felony case without being required to confer with counsel. Counsel for the respondent call our attention to the fact that at the time the proceedings referred to herein occurred, G.S. 1935, 62-1304, was in effect, and as was said in Hill v. Hudspeth, supra, such statute only required that it was the duty of the court to assign counsel for an accused "at his request." Such counsel also state that this court has held a recital in a journal entry that an accused was without counsel is not the equivalent of showing that the accused was denied counsel. . . . Respondent's counsel suggest also that the instant case should be governed by the reasoning followed in Fairce v. Amrine, 121 P.2d 256, and Hill v. Hudspeth, supra. In such cases affidavits of the respective judges of the district courts were filed which, in substance, disclosed that it was always the custom of the judges, when an accused was brought into court charged with a felony, to inform the defendant fully of his constitutional rights and ask him if he had a lawyer and if he had none, the defendant was advised of his right to have one and that the court would appoint one for him. An affidavit to such effect was filed in this case by the Honorable L. M. Resler, who was judge of the district court in which the proceedings occurred. The affidavit, in addition to setting forth the foregoing, also states that it was the custom of the court to explain the charge in the information so that the accused would understand it and inform him what the penalty was. The affidavit contained the following statement, "All this [referring to the above custom] was done before defendant was asked to plead and I am positive this procedure was followed in this case." The assertion by the respondent that we have refused to issue a writ of habeas corpus under similar circumstances in the cited cases is correct. We have, but in none of the cited cases and in none which our research has disclosed, has this court approved the practice of permitting a 17-year-old boy to enter a plea of guilty to a felony without consulting with counsel. We do not question the information contained in the affidavit of the judge. The question still remains undecided, however, whether a court should always require that a 17-year-old boy consult with counsel. In justification of the action taken in the present case counsel for the respondent have filed a second affidavit of the Honorable L. M. Resler which, in substance, sets forth that upon reflection he recalls and remembers that when the petitioner entered his plea of guilty the father of the petitioner was present in the district court room at Pittsburg, Kansas, and further that the father was also present when the petitioner was sentenced to the State Reformatory. The affidavit continues by stating that "the affiant remembers and recalls that when the affiant left the bench, after the sentence of the said James Willey, that the said Floyd Willey [the father] talked to the affiant in the back of the court room about the sentence of James Willey [petitioner]. That at no time during said conversation, nor at any other time, did said Floyd Willey, father of said James Willey, ever make any objection to this affiant about the plea or sentence of his son, James Willey."

The respondent suggests further that the showing relative to the father having been present mitigates, minimizes and negatives any possible imposition upon the petitioner's rights which may have arisen by reason of his being only 17 years old at the time. It is submitted, in behalf of the respondent, that since the petitioner stood before the court, with his father in the court room, the father could have counseled with the petitioner and advised him of his rights; that therefore, the petitioner was in effect afforded the benefit of the mental capacities of a mature man and that consequently, there was no actual imposition upon the petitioner's rights merely because he was young and inexperienced at the time he entered his plea of guilty. There is no showing in this record, however, that the father did confer with his son about the entering of the plea. The father has filed an affidavit to the effect that he knew nothing about the matter. His affidavit, in part, reads as follows: "Your affiant further states that he was never notified, or informed through any channel that his son, James Willey, had been arrested, convicted, or committed to the Kansas State Industrial Reformatory until some time after the entire matter had transpired." If we assume, however, that the father was present at the time his son pleaded guilty and was sentenced, the question still remains unanswered whether the petitioner should have been required to confer with counsel. In other words, the court is of the opinion that the absence or presence of the petitioner's father in the court room should not control determination of the proper answer to the question.

When the petitioner, as a boy only 17 years of age, stood before the court, under the laws of this state he could not have entered into a valid contract obligating himself; he could not have voted; he could not have married without the consent of a parent; he could not alone, without a guardian or next friend, have been heard to say anything in the court room in a civil action which would have been binding him. Should we say, in such circumstances, that about the only thing he could have done alone, with legal significance, was to have pleaded guilty to a felony in a court of law? In the case of State v. Oberst, 273 P. 490, we said: "It is part of our fundamental law that a person on trial for a crime is entitled to the assistance of counsel for his defense. Bill of Rights, Const. Kan. § 10. This right is intended to be adequately secure by our Penal Code (R.S. 62-1304), and the same doctrine is as thoroughly emphasized in our criminal jurisprudence as any one matter treated in the 125 volumes which chronicle the judicial deliberations of this court."

From the same opinion the following is quoted: "* * * In the case before us the defendant was a 17 year old boy * * *. The one thing this youngster needed more than anything else before pleading guilty to such a horrifying accusation was consultation with and the advice of a good lawyer, * * *." . . .

The opinion continues: " * * * It is suggested that there are many prisoners incarcerated in our penal institutions on pleas of guilty given without advice of counsel. We doubt that, and would be sorry, indeed, if it were true, particularly, if they are 17 year old lads, who without legal advice pleaded guilty to murder in the first degree. Certainly we are not anxious to share the responsibility for such a lamentable situation. We are well assured that the common practice in the district courts of this state is not to accept a plea of guilty *in any felony case*, except on the well-considered advice of counsel for the prisoner, and some careful judges take other precautions to avoid miscarriage of justice which need not now be discussed." (273 P. at page 494.) (Emphasis supplied.)

In the Oberst case, supra, the defendant was accused of having committed much more infamous crimes than those involved in the present case. But the decision did not turn upon that point alone. Burglary in the second degree and grand larceny certainly are serious offenses and this court is of the opinion that no distinction necessarily arises in considering the general question because the defendant in one case is accused of murder and in another case is accused of some other felony.

The fundamental question involved is whether the petitioner in this case can be said to have intelligently, understandingly and in a comprehending manner entered his plea of guilty. In the often-quoted and followed case of Johnson v. Zerbst, 304 U.S. 458, the opinion reads as follows: "* * * 'courts indulge every reasonable presumption against waiver' of fundamental constitutional rights and that we 'do not presume acquiescence in the loss of fundamental rights.' A waiver is ordinarily an intentional relinquishment or abandonment of a *known right or privilege*. The determination of whether there has been an intelligent waiver of the right to counsel must depend, in each case, upon the particular facts and circumstances surrounding that case, including the background, *experience*, and conduct of the accused." (Emphasis supplied.)

The opinion continues: "The purpose of the constitutional guaranty of a right to counsel is to protect an accused from conviction resulting from his own ignorance of his legal and constitutional rights, and the guaranty would be nullified by a determination that an accused's ignorant failure to claim his rights removes the protection of the Constitution."

The opinion in Johnson v. Zerbst also develops the significant fact that where there has been no intelligent and comprehensive waiver of constitutional rights that the court is without jurisdiction to accept the plea. It reads: "Since the Sixth Amendment constitutionally entitles one charged with crime to the assistance of Counsel, compliance with this constitutional mandate is an essential jurisdictional prerequisite to a federal court's authority to deprive an accused of his life or liberty."

The opinion continues: "* * * If the accused, however, is not represented by counsel and has not competently and intelligently waived his constitutional right, the Sixth Amendment stands as a jurisdictional bar to a valid conviction and sentence depriving him of his life or his liberty. A court's jurisdiction at the beginning of trial may be lost 'in the course of the proceedings' due to failure to complete the court—as the Sixth Amendment requires—by providing counsel for an accused who is unable to obtain counsel, who has not intelligently waived this constitutional guaranty, and whose life or liberty is at stake. [citing Frank v. Mangum, 237 U.S. 309.] If this requirement of the Sixth Amendment is not complied with, the court no longer has jurisdiction to proceed. The judgment of conviction pronounced by a court without jurisdiction is void, and one imprisoned thereunder may obtain release by habeas corpus. [citing In re Nielsen, 131 U.S. 176.]" We realize that the Sixth Amendment to the Federal Constitution may not be binding upon the states but by the same reasoning the same results are reached under the Fourteenth Amendment thereto and under the due process clause of a state constitution. . . .

The record in the present case is silent as to the degree of intelligence which the petitioner may have possessed when he stood before the court. We cannot gather therefrom any knowledge pertaining to his educational attainments, general mental alertness or lack thereof. We assume, therefore, that he possessed average intelligence for a boy of his age. Upon such an assumption we reach the conclusion that ordinarily a 17-year-old boy is not possessed of sufficient comprehension of his constitutional rights in a felony case to waive them and that he should be given the benefit of consultation with counsel. We are of the opinion, also, that the possible presence of his father in the court room did not assure the petitioner of his constitutional rights. In such connection, it is interesting to note that the Supreme Court of Georgia has held that an accused is deprived of his right to be represented by counsel in violation of his constitutional right where the attorneys appointed by the court to represent him are ignorant and inexperienced. . . . Since the failure to appoint counsel for the petitioner in the present case and to require that the petitioner consult with such counsel deprived the court of jurisdiction to render judgment, it follows that the judgment entered upon the plea of guilty was void. It also follows that the failure to appoint counsel was not a mere trial error or irregularity and that the judgment can be attacked and set aside on a petition for a writ of habeas corpus.

In reaching the foregoing conclusion,

this court is cognizant of the great amount of juvenile delinquency which appears to be prevalent in the country at the present time. We are not holding that in every case where the plea of a minor has been accepted without his having been compelled to consult with counsel, the judgment and sentence entered thereafter necessarily is void. As hereinbefore set forth, the question whether one accused of crime has waived his right to the assistance of counsel must depend in each case upon the particular facts and circumstances. We hold only that in the present case the petitioner is unlawfully restrained in the penitentiary.

It does not follow, however, that he is entitled to be released from the custody of the law enforcement officers of this state. As we said in Davis v. Hudspeth, 167 P.2d 293, at page 295: "* * * Not all of the proceedings in the district court were void. Such court had general jurisdiction of the subject matter by reason of the information having been filed therein. According to the allegations of the information reasons exist for the proper detention of the prisoner and the peace and dignity of the state demand that he be dealt with according to law." (See citations set forth therein.)

The petitioner is not entitled to his absolute freedom and, therefore, the writ will be denied but it is ordered that the judgment and sentence entered on his plea of guilty be set aside; that he be discharged from his confinement under such illegal sentence and judgment; that he be placed in the custody of the sheriff of Crawford County, Kansas in order that appropriate proceedings against him may be taken in the district court of such county.

SPIERS v. TURNER

UTAH SUPREME COURT

361 P. 2D 509 (1961)

Spiers, a nineteen-year-old, petitioned the appropriate state court for a writ of habeas corpus *naming Turner, warden of the state prison, as defendant. He alleged that the proceeding in which his probation was revoked violated his constitutional right to due process because he was not represented by counsel. Note carefully, however, that Spiers had waived right-to-counsel.*

Justice WADE delivered the opinion of the court.

. . . .

ON JULY 28, 1960, Spiers and two other boys were taken before a magistrate and charged with committing a felony of second degree burglary by entering a building at night through an open door with intent to commit larceny. The complaint was read and each defendant given a copy. The magistrate informed them of their right to counsel at every stage of the proceeding, their right to and time for preliminary hearing, all of which they waived and were bound over to the district court and placed on bail.

Thereafter, on August 15, 1960, Spiers was arraigned before District Judge Norseth in Ogden, Utah. The information was read and he was furnished with a copy and informed that he was entitled to counsel and allowed time before entering his plea. He stated that he desired to waive both counsel and time for entering his plea, and to plead then, which the court allowed him to do. Thereupon the court referred his case to Mr. Tite of the Adult Probation Department to investigate whether he was suitable probation material and fixed August 29 as the day for report. The court warned: "That doesn't mean you're going to get probation * * *. It will depend on what the report indicates. But I want to warn you now if I put you on probation and you foul up again * * * if you fail to keep your commitments, I'll send you to the penitentiary."

On August 29, Spiers appeared before Judge Norseth to hear the report of the probation officer and for the court to decide whether to place him on probation or send him to prison. After such hearing the court suspended sentence, placed him on probation and ordered him to report to the court on October 3, 1960.

On September 6, Officer Tite brought Spiers into District Judge Wahlquist's court at Ogden for violation of his probation. He reported that on September 1, Spiers had pleaded guilty in the city court to reckless driving on August 31, contrary to his signed probation agreement to "violate no penal law." On questioning, Spiers admitted that he drove more than 80 miles per hour on Wall Avenue in a 40-mile-per-hour zone.

He said: "I got panicky when an officer wanted to stop me. There was another car that was by me, and we were going down Washington Avenue and the officer was following us and he told me to turn out. I went down on 25th Street to Wall."

Judge Wahlquist asked if he wanted a lawyer, and he answered, "No, I am not able to afford one."

The matter was then set over until two o'clock. The judge directed the clerk to make certain that his parents knew where he was and to give him an opportunity to talk with his parents or any lawyer or friend he wanted to talk this matter over with. When the court reconvened at two o'clock his mother was present in court, and Brent Spiers stated to the judge that he had talked with her, but Mrs. Spiers stated she hadn't really talked to him. The court then said, "You don't want to talk to anyone further about it?" Spiers answered: "No." After some further questioning, Judge Wahlquist said, "Eighty miles an hour in city traffic is a more serious matter than if you had robbed a gas station. It's more dangerous. It threatens more people. Do you have anything else you want to tell me about this? Do you have any reason why I shouldn't put you in prison?" Spiers answered: "I just got panicky."

After considerable discussion about his juvenile court record and city court record, the judge sentenced him to a term of not less than one nor more than 20 years in the Utah State Penitentiary.

Spiers was thereupon sent to the state prison and on September 16, 1960, through his present attorney, petitioned the Salt Lake District court for a writ of habeas corpus. After hearing, that court found that appellant had sufficient mental capacity throughout all of the proceedings against him to understand such proceedings and his right to counsel, and to waive such right, which he did.

The determining factor of whether appellant was convicted without due process of law is whether there has been an intelligent waiver of his right to counsel. This must depend upon the facts and circumstances of each case, including the background, experience and conduct of the accused.

It is argued that the evidence shows that Spiers was only 19 years old, that he was immature for his age, that his I. Q. was only 75, that he graduated from high school with low grades and was obviously somewhat immature for his age. The burden is upon the defendant to show that he has been denied his constitutional rights. The trial court, after hearing the witnesses and seeing appellant give his testimony, was in much better position than we to judge his intelligence. There was no evidence of fear or coercion, or any other reason why he was induced to waive his rights other than that he thought the course he took was for his best good. There was nothing to indicate that at any stage of the proceedings he did not understand what was going on, the questions asked, or the effect of his waiver of counsel. In view of this situation we conclude that the trial court's finding that he intelligently waived his right to counsel must be sustained.

Did the trial court err in revoking Spiers' probation? The main argument of Spiers' counsel is that he was not informed when he pleaded guilty of second degree burglary, that it was a felony and that such plea might subject him to a term in the state prison. A study of the record indicates that the above-stated claim is erroneous, for both in the complaint and the statements of the magistrate and the district judge it was made clear that he was charged with a felony, and Judge Norseth, as above quoted at the time of referring the matter to the probation department, warned him that if he was placed on probation but failed to keep his commitments, "I will send you to the penitentiary." Counsel further argues that the statements by Judge Wahlquist previously quoted that driving at 80 miles per hour is a more serious matter than if you had robbed a gas station is incorrect. While opinions may differ on the seriousness of robbing a gas station and driving at 80 miles per hour at eleven o'clock at night, still Spiers clearly violated his probation agreement, and this statement by the court does not show an abuse of discretion in revoking his probation.

There are no set rules by which that question can be determined. The mere fact that Spiers violated his probation agreement and was guilty of reckless driving does not necessarily require that his probation be revoked. In each case all the surrounding facts and circumstances should be, and usually are, carefully considered by the trial court, keeping in mind that rehabilitation of the person on probation is the most important objective. We should further keep in mind that the trial court is in a better position to determine this question than we are since he heard and saw the witnesses, had the advice and counsel of the probation officer and the advantages of observing the defendant and his advisers who appeared before the court.

Spiers was unstable, panicky and lacking in his determination to keep his probation agreement. He apparently had a wrong instinct to run from officers and not work with them. In the offense to which he pleaded guilty in the city court he exposed himself and the public to great danger in trying to speed from the officers rather than to do what they directed and cooperate with them. On the other hand, he seems ready to admit his crimes after he is caught. In other words, he seems to be a type that may be easily led and greatly in need of wise counsel and guidance. I hope that his experience in the state prison will be beneficial and increase his determination for rehabilitation rather than to influence him to follow hardened criminals, that his record there will be good so that he will be paroled at the earliest possible date.

From a careful consideration of the above facts, we conclude that the evidence does not justify us in holding that there was an abuse of discretion by the trial judge in revoking the probation.

Affirmed.

HENRIOD, McDONOUGH and CROCKETT, JJ., concur.

CALLISTER, J., concurs in result.

JOHNSON v. MAYO

FLORIDA SUPREME COURT SPECIAL DIVISION B

40 SO. 2D 134 (1949)

Johnson was tried, convicted, and sentenced for larceny. He petitioned the appropriate state court for a writ of habeas corpus *naming Mayo, the state custodian of prisoners, the respondent. Johnson alleged that he was denied due process by virtue of the fact that he was not represented by counsel during his trials. Dealing with the petition for writ of* habeas corpus *on two separate occasions, the lower court at length denied the petition, and Johnson appealed to the state supreme court.*

Justice SEBRING delivered the opinion of the court.

. . . .

ON OCTOBER 16, 1945, John R. Johnson was tried and convicted in the Circuit Court of Madison County, Florida, for the larceny of an automobile and sentenced to serve five years in the State penitentiary. A few weeks later he was tried and convicted in the Circuit Court of Jefferson County, Florida, for the larceny of another automobile and sentenced to serve five years in the State penitentiary, the sentence to commence upon the expiration of the Madison County sentence.

In August 1948 Johnson filed his petition in habeas corpus representing that he was being unlawfully deprived of his liberty by virtue of the judgments entered in the above stated cases, because of the fact that at the time of the trial of the aforementioned cases he was a person of little formal education, was penniless, knew nothing about court practice and procedure and was forced to trial in both cases without the aid of counsel after his request of the trial court that counsel be furnished to him.

. . . .

The finding of the judge who presided at the habeas corpus hearing that no request was ever made by the petitioner that counsel be furnished him in the Jefferson County trial is amply supported by the great weight of the evidence. Under the facts disclosed by the record, the failure of the petitioner to make this request clearly operated as a waiver of his right to object to the judgment on this ground, in any subsequent proceeding.

The finding of the presiding judge that the petitioner made a request for, and was denied, court-appointed counsel in the Madison County case is also supported by the great weight of evidence.

The real question on the appeal is whether the failure of the court to appoint counsel in the Madison County case operated as a denial of the constitutional rights of the petitioner under Florida or Federal law.

Though the courts of this state doubtless have the inherent power to appoint defense counsel in any criminal prosecution where such course seems proper in the interest of fairness and justice, there is no requirement under Florida law that counsel be furnished an insolvent defendant, except in a prosecution involving a capital offense. Johnson v. Mayo, 28 So.2d 585. Such duty as may rest upon the Florida courts to furnish counsel in criminal cases less than capital arises by virtue of the Fourteenth Amendment to the United States Constitution, and it imposes no absolute requirement that counsel be furnished unless the accused is incapable of representing himself adequately at the trial on account of age, ignorance or lack of mental capacity. Whether any such incapacity exists is purely personal and is a factual issue which can be determined only by an examination and observation of the individual in question. Where a trier of the facts has made a finding on the issue his finding will not be disturbed if supported by competent credible evidence. . . .

There is ample evidence in the record to show that the petitioner was not incapable of adequately defending himself at the trials by reason of age, ignorance, mental incapacity, or any other disability or infirmity. He was approximately 30 years of age at the time of the trials. Though he had had but seven grades of public school education he had worked as a salesman for years and had also been employed by the Federal Government as group director of C.C.C. laborers building trails in the mountains; hence, he had acquired broad general experience. He was no stranger to criminal law or procedure. In 1933 he was tried and convicted in Jackson County, for breaking and entering and received a two-year sentence in the Florida State Prison. In 1939 he was convicted in the United States District Court for the Eastern District of Tennessee for a violation of the internal revenue laws and received a four months sentence. In 1944 he was convicted in the United States District Court for the Eastern District of Kentucky for unlawful possession of distilled spirits and sentenced to serve a period of 30 days in the county jail. In the same year he was convicted in Tennessee for felonious assault and sentenced to serve a term of one to three years in the State Penitentiary. According to the record, the Supreme Court of Tennessee dismissed the appeal and ordered that he be subjected to said sentence if ever again he should be brought within the jurisdiction of the Courts of Tennessee.

As found by the judge who conducted the hearing, the Madison County and Jefferson County trials in which the petitioner was convicted seem to have been of a relatively simple nature. The petitioner's sole defense in each of the trials was that of alibi and this defense appears to have been fully and completely presented by defense witnesses. In the Madison County case the petitioner cross-examined State witnesses, produced defense witnesses and took the stand in his own behalf. In the Jefferson County case he cross-examined state witnesses, put defense witnesses on the stand, and at the conclusion of this evidence announced to the court that he did not care to testify in his own behalf.

The circuit judge who presided at the habeas corpus hearing had the opportunity to observe the petitioner, to hear him testify, and to judge of his mental capacity, his maturity and his intelligence. The finding of the trial judge based upon the evidence adduced and on his observation of the petitioner was that "the petitioner was fully capable of properly looking after his defenses in these cases, and that his constitutional rights have not been denied him."

We find no basis in the record for any disagreement with the findings and conclusions of the able circuit judge who conducted the hearing. He had the opportunity not afforded any other tribunal of examining and observing the petitioner during the course of the habeas corpus proceeding. The order entered by him was clearly supported by the great weight of the evidence.

We hold that the petitioner was not denied due process of law in either of the criminal prosecutions and hence that the order appealed from should stand affirmed.

It is so ordered.

ADAMS, C. J., CHAPMAN, J., and WHITE, Associate Justice, concur.

GANT v. BANMILLER

PENNSYLVANIA SUPERIOR COURT
171 A. 2D 603 (1961)

Gant, pleading guilty, was convicted and sentenced for burglary. Later, he petitioned the appropriate state court for a writ of habeas corpus *naming Banmiller, warden of the state penitentiary in which Gant was incarcerated, as defendant. He alleged that among other things he had been denied the right-to-counsel at his trial. Eventually, he carried an appeal to the state superior court.*

Judge RHODES delivered the opinion of the court.

. . . .

IN THE present petition relator states that he was arrested in Brooklyn, New York, and returned to Philadelphia to stand trial on burglary charges. The instant petition alleges further that relator was not given a magistrate's hearing; that he was not advised of his rights in extradition proceedings; that there was a lack of counsel in New York; and that he was detained on his return to Philadelphia in a police station for seventy-two hours. It is settled that questions of the sufficiency and regularity of proceedings prior to indictment cannot be raised by a petition for a writ of habeas corpus unless . . . [*Gant*] can show that the alleged irregularities caused the failure of due process. . . .

Even if [*Gant*] had been brought into Pennsylvania without extradition proceedings, he has no standing to question the jurisdiction of the Pennsylvania court to accept a plea of guilty to an indictment regularly found charging crimes committed in this state. . . .

The main contention of relator's petition is that he was not represented by counsel at the trial and upon his plea of guilty to the burglary charges. A review of the record does not show any assertion of innocence by relator, or a request for counsel, or any ingredient of unfairness which actively operated in the process leading to his plea of guilty and sentence. In Pennsylvania there is no absolute right to counsel in a noncapital case. . . . Lack of counsel at state noncapital trials denies federal constitutional protection only when the absence results in a denial to accused of the essentials of justice. . . . The burden is upon the one who avers denial of due process because of failure to provide counsel to demonstrate that for want of benefit of counsel an ingredient of unfairness operated in the process that resulted in his confinement. . . . The court below properly dismissed the petition since it contained no averments cognizable on habeas corpus and did not raise any matters requiring factual determination. . . .

The order is affirmed.

PEOPLE v. EASTER

ILLINOIS SUPREME COURT

75 N.E. 2D 688

Easter pleaded guilty to a charge of armed robbery and was accordingly sentenced to jail for a term of one year to life. Easter petitioned for a writ of error in the state supreme court alleging primarily that he had been denied due process because he was not represented by counsel.

Justice GUNN delivered the opinion of the court.

. . . .

THE POINTS raised in this case, presented in the same manner on the common-law record only, have been before us many times. When no bill of exceptions is filed the only questions which this court can consider on writ of error are those appearing in the common-law record. . . . And defendant cannot complain of the failure of the court to appoint counsel for him where the common-law record fails to show he asserted his right to have an attorney appointed to represent him. . . . It is well settled that there is no duty imposed upon the court to appoint counsel for an accused unless he states upon his oath his inability to procure legal assistance. . . . The application of these principles does not operate to deny due process. Foster v. People of the State of Illinois, 67 S.Ct. 1716. . . .

We have specifically held that a failure of the record to show that counsel was appointed to defend persons charged with crime does not constitute denial of due process of law. The record in this case shows that the plaintiff in error was arraigned in open court, was furnished with a copy of the indictment and a list of the jurors by whom he would be tried, and upon such arraignment pleaded guilty to the crime of armed robbery and waived in writing a trial by jury. The record further discloses that the court admonished the plaintiff in error as to the effect of his plea, but he persisted in his plea of guilty, and thereupon was sentenced by the court for the commission of the crime of armed robbery. The record also shows the age of the plaintiff in error to be twenty-seven years. All of the requirements of the statute with regard to arraignment and plea appear to have been complied with in this record.

The plaintiff in error argues he was threatened by the State's Attorney, and that the witnesses against him were all policemen, and would do him bodily harm if he did not plead guilty; that he was threatened and awed by the court, and did not know of his right to have an attorney to represent him, and because of these things was deprived of his constitutional right. None of these matters appear in a bill of exceptions; they are only the arguments of plaintiff in error long after the proceeding in the circuit court. If they were entitled to the dignity of being considered, there is still no claim he is not guilty of the crime charged. The plaintiff in error does not present any valid reason upon the record submitted justifying a reversal, and the other matters alleged in his argument cannot be considered for the reason they were either not before the trial court, or, if so, were not preserved in the manner required for our consideration.

The judgment of the Circuit court of Franklin County is affirmed.

Judgment affirmed.

EX PARTE McCOY

CALIFORNIA SUPREME COURT

194 P. 2D 531 (1948)

The facts of the case are succinctly set forth in the opinion. We call your special attention to the fact that here the court deals with this question: Is an accused entitled to counsel before trial?

Justice EDMONDS delivered the opinion of the court.

. . . .

ALBERT WILLIE McCoy pleaded guilty to a misdemeanor charge and was sentenced to a term in the county jail. This court granted a writ of habeas corpus upon his petition which alleged that he was denied counsel and not advised of his legal rights. The state concedes that the judge of the police court by whom he was sentenced did not inform McCoy as to his right to counsel. By stipulation, the other issues have been submitted for decision upon affidavits and the prior testimony of McCoy and certain other persons.

In an affidavit, McCoy states that after his arrest upon a Saturday night, he asked the officer, who was operating the elevator in the Oakland city jail, if he could "get in touch with his people." The officer said "No." He noticed some of the prisoners using the telephone, and asked one of the jailors if he could "call some of his people, so they could get him a lawyer." The jailor refused to let him do so. Between the time he was placed in jail and the following Monday morning when he was taken before a police judge for arraignment, he asked "at least three different jailors could he call out or write a letter to his folks, so they could get him a lawyer." In each instance, permission was refused and the last jailor to whom he spoke told him he could not telephone or write a letter until after he appeared in court.

On Monday morning, en route to the court, he asked the officer in charge of him for an attorney and was told that he could not get one "until he went back upstairs [to the jail]."

In court, the clerk read the complaint to him and "he again said in a soft voice to the officer, couldn't he get a lawyer; the officer motioned him to keep quiet, and said 'answer the Clerk'; the Clerk in the meantime had asked affiant, was he guilty or not guilty; the Clerk again repeated the question, and affiant answered in the affirmative; the officer motioned affiant to return to the prisoner's dock, and as affiant started to same, he again asked the officer, could he get a lawyer, and said officer, as he nudged affiant to speed him back in the stock, replied that affiant could get a lawyer when he got out."

After these proceedings, the affidavit concludes, in the city jail, before he was taken to the county jail, he asked the officer, who later took him there, if he could get a lawyer. This officer took him to a desk and he was shown a yellow sheet with the names of a number of lawyers on it, and he "was told to sign a slip for the lawyer he wanted." He picked the name of one of them "at random" and immediately after signing the request he was taken to the county jail. He never heard from nor saw the lawyer whose name he selected. He had never been arrested before and knew nothing about jail rules.

By affidavit the chief jailor explained the general custom of the institution. He declared that during the time when McCoy was in custody "no prisoner who requested an attorney was denied an opportunity to obtain the services of an attorney; that all prisoners are informed that those desiring the services of an attorney may request the same by signing a book maintained for such purpose" and such record shows the request made by McCoy after he was returned to the jail following his appearance in the police court. The bailiff and clerk of the police court who were on duty at the time of McCoy's arraignment and sentence each deny that any defendant who requested counsel was told by an officer of the court "that he would have to answer guilty or not guilty to the charge or that he could see a lawyer when he got out."

From these affidavits, it reasonably may be concluded that, prior to his arraignment and plea of guilty, the petitioner made several requests for counsel which were refused by the officers who had him in custody. By Penal Code section 686, the California Constitution (Art. I, sec. 13), and in accordance with the due process clause of the Fourteenth Amendment of the United States Constitution, a defendant in a criminal action is entitled to counsel. . . . The conduct of an officer of a state court constitutes state action within the meaning of the due process clause, even where the act violates a special command of state law such as the requirement of the Penal Code . . . therefore, the refusal to grant petitioner's request for counsel clearly constituted a denial of fundamental civil rights.

A writ of habeas corpus may not be used as a substitute for an appeal . . . but a "violation of the defendant's constitutional rights during the trial leading to his conviction is ground for attack on the judgment in a habeas corpus proceeding if the petitioner has no other adequate remedy to test the constitutionality of the proceeding resulting in his conviction." In re Wallace, 152 P.2d 3. In the present case, the time for appeal had expired before petitioner finally was able to obtain legal aid and the record upon an appeal would not show the violation of his right to counsel.

The state contends that if this court determines that McCoy should be discharged from custody of the sheriff of Alameda County "he should be sent back to the Police Court, be permitted to withdraw his plea, given the right to engage counsel and proceed with his defense." This presents the question as to whether or not a petitioner who is wrongfully imprisoned may be remanded to the trial court for correction of procedural errors.

Section 1484 of the Penal Code provides that in a proceedings on habeas corpus "* * * The court or judge must * * * dispose of such party as the justice of the case may require * * *." So a petitioner will not necessarily be discharged merely because the judgment and commitment are void, if there is valid process under which he may be held. . . . The petition of McCoy shows that he was arrested upon the charge of the commission of a misdemeanor. Subsequent action of the court officers, depriving the trial court of jurisdiction to convict and sentence McCoy, did not acquit him of the offense, and he is still subject to be tried upon any valid charge made against him in the complaint.

In the case of In re Bouchard, 176 P. 692, the court did not hold the judgment and sentence to be void, but the petitioner was discharged because he had already served over twelve months, and "the 'justice of the case' does not require that the prisoner be remanded." . . . However, in both Matter of Smith, . . . and In re Dal Porte, . . . although the court held that the judgments of conviction were void and the imprisonments illegal, the prisoners were remanded to the custody of the sheriff to await further action of the trial court.

No reason appears for treating a case where the defendant is deprived of his right to counsel differently from one in which other procedural error or irregularity has occurred. Accordingly, the writ is discharged and the petitioner is remanded to the custody of the sheriff for further proceedings in the police court of the city of Oakland, in conformity with his constitutional right to counsel.

GIBSON, C. J., and SHENK, CARTER, TRAYNOR, SCHAUER, and SPENCE, JJ., concur.

WOJCULEWICZ v. *CUMMINGS*

CONNECTICUT SUPREME COURT OF ERRORS

138 A. 2D 512 (1958)

In prison, after having been convicted for murder, Wojculewicz began a series of court tests alleging that he did not have a fair trial, largely, but not exclusively, on the grounds that he had not been well enough physically to look after his interests adequately in the trial. At one point Wojculewicz discharged the public defender, who served as his counsel, to argue his own case before the supreme court of appeals, not successfully, however. In the following case, Wojculewicz was once more before the supreme court of appeals seeking a writ of habeas corpus *naming Cummings, the warden of the state prison, as defendant. He was still alleging that his trial had been unfair. This time he was represented by a special public defender appointed to represent him.*

Justice BALDWIN delivered the opinion of the court.

. . . .

THE FACTS found by the trial court may be stated in summary as follows: In the fusilade at the scene of the robbery on November 5, 1951, the plaintiff suffered gunshot wounds, one of which transected his spinal cord and injured his kidneys and spleen. The lower part of his body, below the umbilicus, was paralyzed. He lost control of his bowels and bladder, and his weight dropped below 100 pounds. He sustained no injury to his brain. He had been brought from the scene of the robbery to the New Britain Hospital in shock. After an examination an operation was performed, his spleen was removed, his torn kidney was sutured, and the ruptured intercostal arteries and blood vessels in his chest were tied. A spinal tap was done and, later, bullets were removed from his chest and arm. He remained in the New Britain Hospital until December 27, 1951, when he was taken to the McCook Memorial Hospital in Hartford, where he was kept until his trial ended on March 18, 1952. On January 8, 1952, a physical and neurological examination revealed that he was not suffering from any psychiatric abnormality and that the severing of his spinal cord had not affected his mental capabilities. On February 20, 1952, a second examination, which lasted the most of the forenoon and was made by two psychiatrists, showed the plaintiff to be a man of average intelligence who understood the nature of the charges against him and was not suffering from any mental disorders which affected his responsibility. The plaintiff did not make any complaint of pain or any request that the interview be postponed. He gave a complete and detailed history of his life and activities up to the time of the crime charged. It was determined that he was mentally and physically able to maintain his defense in court. While at the McCook Memorial Hospital, he was directly under the care of the senior resident in surgery. The plaintiff was allowed to confer with his counsel whenever he requested. All the medication administered to him was recorded in a hospital chart except three one-half-grain codeine pills and three five-grain aspirin tablets which were given to a policeman who accompanied the plaintiff to the courthouse on March 10, 1952. Nothing in the hospital records reveals whether the plaintiff received this medication, and there is no other order in these records reciting the administration of medication to the plaintiff during the trial. The plaintiff expressed a wish, and made an attempt, to commit suicide.

The plaintiff's trial began on the 4th day of March, 1952, and continued until the 18th. Each day he was brought on a stretcher from the hospital to the courtroom in the County Building at Hartford. During court sessions the stretcher, with the plaintiff lying on his back on it, was placed in front of the jury. The plaintiff was well cared for by attendants. His bladder and bowel requirements were served during recesses in a room adjoining the courtroom. On no single day did the amount of drugs given to him exceed three one-half-grain codeine pills and three five-grain aspirin tablets, which are relatively mild dosages. During the trial the plaintiff suffered considerable pain and discomfort, but he made no complaints regarding the care he was receiving. During recesses in the trial and at other times he was visited by friends and relatives, including his wife, his mother and his father-in-law.

In the course of the trial, on Friday, March 14, 1952, at noon, after a recess, the plaintiff's counsel made an oral motion that court be adjourned until the next court day, which was the following Tuesday, claiming that the plaintiff was in such pain that he could not continue with the trial. The physician who had the plaintiff under his care examined the plaintiff and reported his condition to be such that he could continue to stand trial. The motion was denied. Shortly thereafter, the trial was recessed until the following Tuesday. The denial of this motion was considered and disposed of as a ground of appeal in State v. Wojculewicz, 119 A.2d 913.

Throughout the trial the plaintiff was alert, assisted counsel in the selection of the jury, and frequently and continuously conferred with him during the trial. The plaintiff recalls vividly the events of the trial, where he was in the courtroom, where he was taken and who visited him during recesses, and who took care of him. He instructed his counsel privately on March 18, 1952, not to offer any evidence in his behalf. He himself did not testify. The fact that the plaintiff lay on his back on a stretcher before the jury during the trial did not cause him degradation or seriously interfere with his defense. He lay on his back on a stretcher during the hearing of the present habeas corpus proceeding.

He was not prevented mentally or physically from making his defense at his trial. None of the persons who visited him at the courthouse during the trial appeared at the habeas corpus hearing to testify that his physical and mental condition at the time of his trial was as he claims. At no time during the trial, except on Friday, March 14, as previously noted, did the plaintiff make any objection to the court that he was unable to proceed because of pain or physical discomfort. The trial court in the present proceeding concluded that the plaintiff at his trial was not so mentally distraught as to be unable to understand the nature of the proceedings against him and to make his defense, and that he had a fair trial.

The plaintiff's claims of error are not directed to the subordinate facts in the finding but to the conclusions which the court has drawn from them. The plaintiff asserts that because of his mental and physical condition, which was due to the injuries from which he was suffering and the medication which he was required to take to relieve this pain and discomfort, and because it was necessary for him to lie on a stretcher before the jury without control of his bladder and bowels, he was denied a fair trial in violation of the due process provisions of the federal and state constitutions. U.S.Const. Amend. XIV, § 1; Conn.Const. Art. I, § 9. The first time the plaintiff raised this claim was on the reargument of his appeal in this court on December 8, 1955, three years and nine months after the original trial. This fact, as pointed out by the state, is significant in considering the sincerity of his claims. But it was a fact for the trial court to weigh, and it is of consequence on this appeal only so far as it may tend to support the conclusions reached by the court. We do not consider it in any sense as a waiver or an estoppel [*a bar to plaintiff's bringing up alleged facts*].

A fair trial is implicit in the term "due process of law." A denial of due process divests the trial court of jurisdiction and is properly raised upon an application for a writ of habeas corpus. Wojculewicz v. Cummings, 124 A.2d 886. The requirements of due process are met in the trial of a person accused of crime if he has been given the benefit of a fair and impartial trial in accordance with the settled course of judicial proceedings in this state. . . . A fair trial is one conducted in all material things in substantial conformity to law, before an impartial judge and an unprejudiced jury in an atmosphere of judicial calm. . . . This rule carries the obvious implication that no accused should be put to trial when he is insane or his mental capabilities are so affected by drugs or physical pain that he cannot maintain his defense. . . .

The plaintiff's reasons for his claim that he was denied a fair trial fall into three general categories, and they are so treated in his brief. First, there are his severe and disabling injuries. He sustained these on November 5, 1951. The trial began approximately four months later, on March 4, 1952. The trial court has found that psychiatric and physical examinations were made on January 8, 1952, and again on February 28, 1952. In the opinion of medical experts, whose competency is unchallenged, the plaintiff was not suffering from any mental or physical disabilities which would prevent him from standing trial. No request for an adjournment or continuance was made although, as we have noted in a prior opinion, the plaintiff was represented by competent counsel. . . .

Second, the plaintiff asserts that his intellect was clouded by drugs administered to relieve his pain. This feature of the case was fully reviewed, as the meticulous care given to details in the trial court's finding abundantly shows. At no time, the court found, were dosages of drugs to relieve the plaintiff's pain and discomfort administered in sufficient quantities to becloud his perceptions.

Third, the plaintiff complains because he was placed in front of the jury lying on a stretcher without control of his bladder and bowels. This, he charges, degraded and humiliated him. As to the care for his physical discomforts resulting from the lack of bladder and bowel control, the trial court found that his needs were well cared for by the attendants and that he made no complaint. Further, the court found that these infirmities did not interfere with the plaintiff's ability to conduct his defense. The placing of the stretcher in front of the jury was not harmful or improper. The plaintiff had a right to be where he could hear and see the witnesses and the jury and where they could see him. . . . The control of the proceedings in a courtroom is necessarily within the discretion of the trial court. . . . No complaint was made by the plaintiff or his counsel concerning his position in the courtroom during the trial. We take judicial notice of the arrangement of the witness and jury boxes in our courtrooms and assume that the accused was placed as he was to enable him to hear the witnesses and to see and be seen, which was his right. The conclusion that he was not prejudiced in this regard in conducting his defense is a proper one.

The plaintiff contends that if any one of the foregoing claims might not of itself be sufficient to prevent a fair trial, their cumulative effect when considered together rendered him unfit to stand trial. Where the accused, as in this case, is severely injured in the perpetration of the crime for which he is charged, the fixing of the time for his trial requires the exercise of a sound discretion, in the first instance by the state's attorney and counsel for the accused, and, ultimately, by the trial court. Under our constitution an accused is entitled to a speedy trial. Conn.Const. Art. I, § 9. This means that the state must proceed with the prosecution without undue delay. The finding of the trial court discloses that the plaintiff received prompt and competent medical and surgical treatment for his injuries and that he was examined before trial on two different occasions, some considerable time apart, to determine whether his condition was such that he could stand trial. When the date for the trial was fixed, neither the plaintiff nor his counsel made any objection to the court or asked for any adjournment, so far as the record discloses. Because of the nature of the plaintiff's injuries, the probability of his recovery or of his further improvement was remote. . . .

The question whether a criminal trial should be postponed or continued because of the mental or physical condition of the accused rests in the sound discretion of the trial court. Most of the cases deal with the review of the court's action on a motion. The issue is fundamentally the same, whether it arises on a motion or on a writ of habeas corpus as in the case at bar. An abuse of discretion in denying a motion for a continuance could result in forcing the accused to trial to the prejudice of his right to a fair trial. The cases cited in the footnote sustain the trial court's denial of such a motion. Had the plaintiff made a motion for a postponement, the court would have acted within its legal discretion in denying it. In Felts v. Murphy, 201 U.S. 123, . . . the accused, charged with murder, was almost totally deaf. Upon an application for a writ of habeas corpus, he claimed that he had been denied a fair trial because the testimony of the witnesses had not been repeated to him. The Supreme Court of the United States sustained a judgment denying the writ. . . .

The determination whether an accused has been denied a fair trial because of his mental and physical condition rests, in a case such as this, upon factual determinations and the conclusions to be drawn therefrom. The physical infirmities of the plaintiff did not prevent him from conferring with his counsel before or during his trial. He was alert and remembered all of the details of the trial. His condition did not hinder him from securing witnesses or from testifying in his own behalf, which he freely decided not to do. The prospect that his condition would improve was extremely remote. His physical infirmities, although they were inflicted while he was committing an armed robbery, were such as could arouse the sympathy of the jury rather than work against him. The trial court's conclusion that he had been accorded a fair trial was reasonably and properly drawn from all the facts.

There is no error.

In this opinion the other Judges concurred.

POWELL v. COMMONWEALTH

KENTUCKY COURT OF APPEALS

346 S.W. 2D 731 (1961)

After Powell was tried, convicted, and sentenced to death for the murder of his wife, he sought a new trial on the grounds that he was denied due process of law in the first trial. His lawyer had not been in the courtroom when the jury returned to announce its verdict. When the lower court overruled Powell's motion, he appealed to the state court of appeals.

Commissioner STANLEY delivered the opinion of the court.

. . . .

Section 267 of the Criminal Code (as did § 263 of the 1854 Code) provides:

> "Upon a verdict being rendered, the jury may be polled, at the instance of either party, which consists of the clerk or judge asking each juror if it is his verdict, and if one answers in the negative, the verdict can not be received."

Long ago (1879) in Temple v. Commonwealth, 77 Ky. 769, where a verdict in a murder case was received during the absence of the defendant and his counsel, in commenting on their right to be present when the verdict was received and to poll the jury, the court wrote:

> "[A]t no time in the whole course of the trial is this right more valuable than at the final step when the jury are to pronounce that decision which is to restore him to the liberty of a citizen, or to consign him to the scaffold or to a felon's cell in the state prison. He has a right not only to see and know that the whole jury is present assenting to the verdict, but by polling to demand face to face of each juror whether the verdict is his verdict, and to object to it unless each member of the jury shall answer for himself that the verdict is his.
>
> "The right to poll the jury in criminal causes has in this state always been deemed an essential part of the right of trial by jury. It is guaranteed by both the constitution and the statute, and ought to be maintained and preserved by the courts as essential to the protection of the rights of the citizen."

The present case is distinguishable in part from the Temple case since here the defendant was present in person, but the statements regarding the importance of the right to poll the jurors in the manner defined in the Code are pertinent. It may well be assumed that the defendant did not know he had the right. But his counsel knew it. The temporary absence of the attorney in the present case was with the tacit approval of the court. He was, we may assume, within call at his nearby office. True, the poll of the jurors is a permissive right which may be waived. . . . But it is a substantial legal right and to deny it without waiver is prejudicial error in a felony case. . . .

In the Carver case the defendant's attorney was temporarily absent from the courtroom but in the courthouse when the verdict was received and the jury dismissed. We reiterated that the right to poll the jury in criminal cases is an essential part of the right of trial by jury and held denial to be prejudicial error. In the present case the judge polled the jury as a body but not the individual jurors, as the Code, above quoted, provides. Had the defendant's counsel been present, he may have deemed this to be sufficient. But that is speculative.

Too much emphasis upon the subordinate point of polling the jury may lead to misconceiving or missing altogether the primary and more fundamental point involved.

Since the court substantially polled the jury and the attorney might have waived it altogether had he been present, the importance of the technical omission or deviation from the literal Code provision lies in the fact that it is indicative or symbolic of the need of the defendant to have had his lawyer present when the verdict of death was returned. Many and perhaps more vital occurrences are conceivable where the accused would have greater need for having his lawyer by his side to advise him and to protect his rights, particularly in a case of capital crime. The court may not speculate, in a matter that is so vital, that nothing will occur that might require the attorney's presence. We quote from Carver v. Commonwealth, 256 S.W.2d 375.

> "This court has long recognized the importance of the constitutional right of the accused to be present with his counsel at all stages of a trial. In Temple v. Commonwealth . . . we said:
>
> " 'The right to be heard by himself and counsel necessarily embraces the right to be present himself and to have a reasonable opportunity to have his counsel present also at every step in the progress of the trial. * * * The presence of the accused is not mere form. It is of the very essence of a criminal trial not only that the accused shall be brought face to face with the witness against him, but also with his triers.' "

. . . .

It is a primary right of a person accused of a felonious crime, especially where a death penalty may be imposed, that he shall be represented by counsel at every stage of his trial—from its beginning to its end. The return of the verdict is crucial and the need for counsel may be greater, as stated in the above quotations from the Temple and Wilcher cases, supra. This right of counsel throughout the trial is firmly rooted in our criminal jurisprudence. It is cherished as one of the most important safeguards against an unfair trial. Like the right of the defendant to be present himself, his right to the effective assistance of counsel is a requirement of our Bill of Rights, § 11, Ky.Const., and the presence of both is a condition of due process of law assured by the Fourteenth Amendment to the Federal Constitution. True, the right may be waived, but in such a case the waiver should be so clear and unequivocal as to indicate a conscious intent. There was no such waiver in this case.

This court and the Supreme Court

have been sedulous in maintaining that right. Both courts have declared it to be of the essence of an opportunity to defend one's self that he have the advice of counsel throughout, and to deprive him of it violates his constitutional rights. If that has been done, it is prejudicial where a man's life is to be forfeited. Powell v. State of Alabama, 287 U.S. 45. . . .

Two juries have imposed the severest penalty provided by the law upon the appellant. But, as the late Mr. Justice Cardozo, when a judge of the New York Court of Appeals, wrote, "A criminal, however shocking his crime, is not to answer for it with forfeiture of life or liberty till tried and convicted in conformity with law." People v. Moran, 158 N.E. 35, 37.

The court is of opinion that the judgment must be and it is

Reversed.

MONTGOMERY, STEWART and WILLIAMS, JJ., dissenting.

MONTGOMERY, Judge (dissenting).

The majority opinion deals with the second ground urged for reversal of the death sentence. As stated by appellant's counsel, it is that he "was denied his constitutional and statutory rights when his counsel was not present at the time the verdict was returned by the jury which resulted in a denial of his right to have the jury polled." There are two answers to this contention: (1) The accused was not denied "a reasonable opportunity to have his counsel present," and (2) the accused waived his right to have the jury polled.

The majority opinion rests its holding upon a statement from Carver v. Commonwealth, Ky., 256 S.W.2d 375, and, in particular, upon a quotation in that case from Temple v. Commonwealth. . . .

> " 'The right to be heard by * * counsel * * * embraces the right * * * to have a reasonable opportunity to have his counsel present * * *.' "

The Temple case quotation also appears in the Lett and Kokas cases cited in the majority opinion.

Powell was represented by eminent and able counsel of his own choice, not court appointed counsel. He had placed his cause in the hands of counsel whom he believed to be capable of protecting his rights on trial. The conduct of his defense was a matter entrusted to the skill and discretion of this counsel. In what way then, if any, was this accused denied a reasonable opportunity to have his counsel present?

It is unquestioned that the counsel absented himself voluntarily by going to his office to keep an appointment. The record discloses no communication between counsel and trial judge concerning counsel's departure and return except the statement by counsel that he was leaving. There is no hint that counsel desired, requested, or expected to be called to the courtroom when the jury returned a verdict. So far as the record shows, accused's counsel and the prosecuting attorney both left the courtroom without any apparent intention of returning when the jury retired to consider its verdict.

On this point alone, the present case is distinguishable from the Carver case. There, counsel left the courtroom for a brief visit to the men's restroom in the same building, while here, counsel left the courthouse and went to his office in another building. The jury returned a verdict within thirty to forty-five minutes and was discharged before appellant's counsel returned. The record does not show when he returned. It was not the duty of the trial judge to require accused's counsel to be present at all times any more than it was his duty to require counsel to cross examine a witness or to do other things in the exercise of his discretion in conducting the defense of the accused. Under the circumstances of this case, it cannot be said that the accused was denied "a reasonable opportunity to have his counsel present."

The real question presented is: Did the accused waive his right to have the jury polled? Criminal Code, § 267, quoted in the majority opinion, provides that "* * the jury may be polled, at the instance of either party, * * *." The accused had no right to have a jury polled except by request. In Asher v. Commonwealth, 299 S.W. 568, the record did not show any request had been made. The right to poll was held to have been waived by the failure to make a request. Dietzman, J., wrote: "* * * the Code only requires the jury to be polled 'at the instance of either party.'" The rule was stated in State v. Vaszorich, 98 A.2d 299, by Mr. Justice Brennan, now of the United States Supreme Court, then a member of the New Jersey Supreme Court, thus:

> "Although a poll of the jury is the right of the accused, it is not a necessary ingredient of his conviction, but must be requested by timely request, Rule 2:7–9(d), and may be waived by a failure to make such request. . . ."

May the accused not waive this privilege by sitting silently by and permitting his counsel to depart from the courtroom to his office in another building without hint or suggestion of his return?

. . . .

It, therefore, is concluded that the accused was afforded a reasonable opportunity to have his counsel present, that he waived the privilege of having the jury polled, and that it was not error for the verdict to be received in the absence of his counsel.

I am strengthened in these conclusions by a record which shows that the polling of the jury was an afterthought. Counsel first made such a claim by filing an amended motion and grounds for a new trial on November 17, 1959, thus indicating that the poll of the jury was not contemplated by accused's counsel on the day the verdict was rendered, October 13, 1959, or on October 22, 1959, when he filed his motion for a new trial. Had accused's counsel intended other than to waive the polling of the jury, he would have raised the question sooner. Further strengthening my conclusions are the statements in the majority opinion that "the court substantially polled the jury" and doubtless, "had the defendant's counsel been present, he would have deemed it sufficient." . . .

I would affirm the judgment.

STEWART and WILLIAMS, JJ., join in the dissent.

GRIFFIN v. ILLINOIS

UNITED STATES SUPREME COURT

351 U.S. 12 (1956)

Griffin was tried and convicted of armed robbery. Immediately following conviction, he filed a motion in the trial court "asking that a certified copy of the entire record . . . be furnished . . . without cost. . . ." It was alleged that poverty prevented the purchase of the stenographic record of proceedings. Counsel for Illinois acknowledged petitioner's indigence and the necessity of obtaining a formal record of alleged trial errors if there was to be an appellate review. Under Illinois law there was, however, no obligation to provide such records at public expense in non-capital criminal cases. Griffin appealed to the Illinois supreme court on the grounds that failure to provide the records constituted a denial of due process and equal protection. The Illinois court decided otherwise. Consequently, Griffin appealed to the United States Supreme Court.

Mr. Justice Black announced the judgment of the Court in an opinion in which Chief Justice Warren, Mr. Justice Douglas, and Mr. Justice Clark joined.

Providing equal justice for poor and rich, weak and powerful alike is an age-old problem. People have never ceased to hope and strive to move closer to that goal. This hope, at least in part, brought about in 1215 the royal concessions of Magna Charta: "To no one will we sell, to no one will we refuse, or delay, right or justice. * * * No free man shall be taken or imprisoned, or disseised, or outlawed, or exiled, or anywise destroyed; nor shall we go upon him nor send upon him, but by the lawful judgment of his peers or by the law of the land." These pledges were unquestionably steps toward a fairer and more nearly equal application of criminal justice. In this tradition, our own constitutional guaranties of due process and equal protection both call for procedures in criminal trials which allow no invidious discriminations between persons and different groups of persons. Both equal protection and due process emphasize the central aim of our entire judicial system—all people charged with crime must, so far as the law is concerned, "stand on an equality before the bar of justice in every American court." Chambers v. Florida, 309 U.S. 227. . . .

Surely no one would contend that either a State or the Federal Government could constitutionally provide that defendants unable to pay court costs in advance should be denied the right to plead not guilty or to defend themselves in court. Such a law would make the constitutional promise of a fair trial a worthless thing. Notice, the right to be heard, and the right to counsel would under such circumstances be meaningless promises to the poor. In criminal trials a State can no more discriminate on account of poverty than on account of religion, race, or color. Plainly the ability to pay costs in advance bears no rational relationship to a defendant's guilt or innocence and could not be used as an excuse to deprive a defendant of a fair trial. Indeed, a provision in the Constitution of Illinois of 1818 provided that every person in Illinois "ought to obtain right and justice freely, and without being obliged to purchase it, completely and without denial, promptly and without delay, conformably to the laws."

There is no meaningful distinction between a rule which would deny the poor the right to defend themselves in a trial court and one which effectively denies the poor an adequate appellate review accorded to all who have money enough to pay the costs in advance. It is true that a State is not required by the Federal Constitution to provide appellate courts or a right to appellate review at all. . . . But that is not to say that a State that does grant appellate review can do so in a way that discriminates against some convicted defendants on account of their poverty. Appellate review has now become an integral part of the Illinois trial system for finally adjudicating the guilt or innocence of a defendant. Consequently at all stages of the proceedings the Due Process and Equal Protection Clauses protect persons like petitioners from invidious discriminations. . . .

All of the States now provide some method of appeal from criminal convictions, recognizing the importance of appellate review to a correct adjudication of guilt or innocence. Statistics show that a substantial proportion of criminal convictions are reversed by state appellate courts. Thus to deny adequate review to the poor means that many of them may lose their life, liberty or property because of unjust convictions which appellate courts would set aside. Many States have recognized this and provided aid for convicted defendants who have a right to appeal and need a transcript but are unable to pay for it. A few have not. Such a denial is a misfit in a country dedicated to affording equal justice to all and special privileges to none in the administration of its criminal law. There can be no equal justice where the kind of trial a man gets depends on the amount of money he has. Destitute defendants must be afforded as adequate appellate review as defendants who have money enough to buy transcripts.

The Illinois Supreme Court denied these petitioners relief under the Post-Conviction Act because of its holding that no constitutional rights were violated. In view of our holding to the contrary the State Supreme Court may decide that petitioners are now entitled to a transcript, as the State's brief suggests. . . . We do not hold, however, that Illinois must purchase a stenographer's transcript in every case where a defendant cannot buy it. The Supreme Court may find other means of affording adequate and effective appellate review to indigent defendants. For example, it may be that bystanders' bills of exceptions or other methods of reporting trial proceedings could be used in some cases. The Illinois Supreme Court appears to have broad power to promulgate rules of procedure and appellate practice. We are confident that the State will provide corrective rules to meet the problem which this case lays bare.

The judgment of the Supreme Court of Illinois is vacated and the cause is remanded to that court for further action not inconsistent with the foregoing paragraph. Mr. Justice FRANKFURTER joins in this disposition of the case.

Vacated and remanded.

Mr. Justice FRANKFURTER, concurring in the judgment.

The admonition of de Tocqueville not to confuse the familiar with the necessary has vivid application to appeals in criminal cases. The right to an appeal from a conviction for crime is today so established that this leads to the easy assumption that it is fundamental to the protection of life and liberty and therefore a necessary ingredient of due process of law. "Due process" is, perhaps, the least frozen concept of our law—the least confined to history and the most absorptive of powerful social standards of a progressive society. But neither the unfolding content of "due process" nor the particularized safeguards of the Bill of Rights disregard procedural ways that reflect a national historic policy. It is significant that no appeals from convictions in the federal courts were afforded (with roundabout exceptions negligible for present purposes) for nearly a hundred years; and, despite the civilized standards of criminal justice in modern England, there was no appeal from convictions (again with exceptions not now pertinent) until 1907. Thus, it is now settled that due process of law does not require a state to afford review of criminal judgments.

. . . .

Law addresses itself to actualities. It does not face actuality to suggest that Illinois affords every convicted person, financially competent or not, the opportunity to take an appeal, and that it is not Illinois that is responsible for disparity in material circumstances. Of course a State need not equalize economic conditions. A man of means may be able to afford the retention of an expensive, able counsel not within reach of a poor man's purse. Those are contingencies of life which are hardly within the power, let alone the duty, of a State to correct or cushion. But when a State deems it wise and just that convictions be susceptible to review by an appellate court, it cannot by force of its exactions draw a line which precludes convicted indigent persons, forsooth erroneously convicted, from securing such a review merely by disabling them from bringing to the notice of an appellate tribunal errors of the trial court which would upset the conviction were practical opportunity for review not foreclosed.

To sanction such a ruthless consequence, inevitably resulting from a money hurdle erected by a State, would justify a latter-day Anatole France to add one more item to his ironic comments on the "majestic equality" of the law. "The law, in its majestic equality, forbids the rich as well as the poor to sleep under bridges, to beg in the streets, and to steal bread." . . .

The State is not free to produce such a squalid discrimination. If it has a general policy of allowing criminal appeals, it cannot make lack of means an effective bar to the exercise of this opportunity. The State cannot keep the word of promise to the ear of those illegally convicted and break it to their hope. But in order to avoid or minimize abuse and waste, a State may appropriately hedge about the opportunity to prove a conviction wrong. When a State not only gives leave for appellate correction of trial errors but must pay for the cost of its exercise by the indigent, it may protect itself so that frivolous appeals are not subsidized and public moneys not needlessly spent. The growing experience of reforms in appellate procedure and sensible, economic modes for securing review still to be devised, may be drawn upon to the end that the State will neither bolt the door to equal justice nor support a wasteful abuse of the appellate process.

. . . .

We must be mindful of the fact that there are undoubtedly convicts under confinement in Illinois prisons, in numbers unknown to us and under unappealed sentences imposed years ago, who will find justification in this opinion, unless properly qualified, for proceedings both in the state and the federal courts upon claims that they are under illegal detention in that they have been denied a right under the Federal Constitution. It would be an easy answer that a claim that was not duly asserted—as was the timely claim by these petitioners—cannot be asserted now. The answer is too easy. Candor compels acknowledgement that the decision rendered today is a new ruling. Candor compels the further acknowledgement that it would not be unreasonable for all indigent defendants, now incarcerated, who at the time were unable to pay for transcripts of proceedings in trial courts, to urge that they were justified in assuming that such a restriction upon criminal appeals in Illinois was presumably a valid exercise of the State's power at the time when they suffered its consequences. Therefore it could well be claimed that thereby any conscious waiver of a constitutional right is negatived.

The Court ought neither to rely on casuistic arguments in denying constitutional claims, nor deem itself imprisoned within a formal, abstract dilemma. The judicial choice is not limited to a new ruling necessarily retrospective, or to rejection of what the requirements of equal protection of the laws, as now perceived, require. For sound reasons, law generally speaks prospectively. More than a hundred years ago, for instance, the Supreme Court of Ohio, confronted with a problem not unlike the one before us, found no difficulty in doing so when it concluded that legislative divorces were unconstitutional. . . . In arriving at a new principle, the judicial process is not impotent to define its scope and limits. Adjudication is not a mechanical exercise nor does it compel "either/or" determinations.

We should not indulge in the fiction that the law now announced has always been the law and, therefore, that those who did not avail themselves of it waived their rights. It is much more conducive to law's self-respect to recognize candidly the considerations that give prospective content to a new pronouncement of law. That this is consonant with the spirit of our law and justified by those considerations of reason which should dominate the law, has been luminously expounded by Mr. Justice Cardozo, shortly before he came here and in an opinion which he wrote for the Court. See Address of Chief Judge Cardozo, 55 Report of New York State Bar Ass'n, 263, 294 et seq., and Great Northern R. Co. v. Sunburst Oil & Refining Co., 287 U.S. 358. Such a molding of law, by way of adjudication, is peculiarly applicable to the problem at hand. The rule of law announced this day should be delimited as indicated.

Mr. Justice BURTON and Mr. Justice MINTON, whom Mr. Justice REED and Mr. Justice HARLAN join, dissenting.

While we do not disagree with the desirability of the policy of supplying an indigent defendant with a free transcript of testimony in a case like this, we do not agree that the Constitution of the United States compels each State to do so with the consequence that, regardless of the State's legislation and practice to the contrary, this Court must hold invalid state appellate proceedings wherever a required transcript has not been provided without cost to an indigent litigant who has requested that it be so provided. It is one thing for Congress and this Court to prescribe such procedure for the federal courts. It is quite another for this Court to hold that the Constitution of the United States has prescribed it for all state courts.

In the administration of local law the Constitution has been interpreted as permitting the several States generally to follow their own familiar procedure and practice. In so doing this Court has recognized the widely differing but locally approved procedures of the several States. Whether approving of the particular procedures or not, this Court has treated them largely as matters reserved to the States and within the broad range of permissible "due process" in a constitutional sense.

Illinois, as the majority admit, could thus deny an appeal altogether in a criminal case without denying due process of law. McKane v. Durston, 153 U.S. 684. To allow an appeal at all, but with some difference among convicted persons as to the terms upon which an appeal is exercised does not deny due process. It may present a question of equal protection. The petitioners urge that point here.

Whether the Illinois statute denies equal protection depends upon whether, first, it is an arbitrary and unreasonable distinction for the legislature to make, between those convicted of a capital offense and those convicted of a lesser offense, as to their right to a free transcript. It seems to us the whole practice of criminal law teaches that there are valid distinctions between the ways in which criminal cases may be looked upon and treated without violating the Constitution. Very often we have cases where the convicted seek only to avoid the death penalty. As all practicing lawyers know, who have defended persons charged with capital offenses, often the only goal possible is to avoid the death penalty. There is something pretty final about a death sentence.

If the actual practice of law recognizes this distinction between capital and noncapital cases, we see no reason why the legislature of a State may not extend the full benefit of appeal to those convicted of capital offenses and deny it to those convicted of lesser offenses. It is the universal experience in the administration of criminal justice that those charged with capital offenses are granted special considerations. Examples of such will readily occur. All States allow a larger number of peremptory challenges of jurors in capital cases than in other cases. Most States permit changes of venue in capital cases on different terms than in other criminal cases. Some States require a verdict of 12 jurors for conviction in a capital case but allow less than 12 jurors to convict in noncapital cases. On the other side of the coin, most States provide no statute of limitations in capital cases. We think the distinction here made by the Illinois statute between capital cases and noncapital cases is a reasonable and valid one.

Secondly, certainly Illinois does not deny equal protection to convicted defendants when the terms of appeal are open to all, although some may not be able to avail themselves of the full appeal because of their poverty. Illinois is not bound to make the defendants economically equal before its bar of justice. For a State to do so may be a desirable social policy, but what may be a good legislative policy for a State is not necessarily required by the Constitution of the United States. Persons charged with crimes stand before the law with varying degrees of economic and social advantage. Some can afford better lawyers and better investigations of their cases. Some can afford bail, some cannot. Why fix bail at any reasonable sum if a poor man can't make it?

The Constitution requires the equal protection of the law, but it does not require the States to provide equal financial means for all defendants to avail themselves of such laws.

Mr. Justice BLACK's opinion is not limited to the future. It holds that a past as well as a future conviction of crime in a state court is invalid where the State has failed to furnish a free transcript to an indigent defendant who has sought, as petitioner did here, to obtain a review of a ruling that was dependent upon the evidence in his case. This is an interference with state power for what may be a desirable result, but which we believe to be within the field of local option.

Whether Illinois would permit appeals adequate to pass upon alleged errors on bills of exception, prepared by counsel and approved by judges, without requiring that full stenographic notes be transcribed is not before us. We assume that it would.

Mr. Justice HARLAN, dissenting.

Much as I would prefer to see free transcripts furnished to indigent defendants in all felony cases, I find myself unable to join in the Court's holding that the Fourteenth Amendment requires a State to do so or to furnish indigents with equivalent means of exercising a right to appeal. The importance of the question decided by the Court justifies adding to what Mr. Justice BURTON and Mr. Justice MINTON have written my further grounds for dissenting and the reasons why I find the majority opinions unsatisfying.

. . . I would decline to decide the constitutional question tendered by petitioner because the record does not present it in that "cleancut," "concrete," and "unclouded" form usually demanded for a decision of constitutional issues. . . . In my judgment the case should be remanded to the Illinois courts for further proceedings so that we might know the precise nature of petitioners' claim before passing on it.

. . . .

According to petitioners' tabulation, no more than 29 States provide free transcripts as of right to indigents convicted of non-capital crimes. Thus the sweeping constitutional pronouncement made by the Court today will touch the laws of at least 19 States and will create a host of problems affecting the status of an unknown multitude of indigent convicts. A decision having such wide impact should not be made upon a record as obscure as this, especially where there are means ready at hand to have clarified the issue sought to be presented.

. . . .

The Court thus holds that, at least in this area of criminal appeals, the Equal Protection Clause imposes on the States an affirmative duty to lift the handicaps flowing from differences in economic circumstances. That holding produces the anomalous result that a constitutional admonition to the States to treat all persons equally means in this instance that Illinois must give to some what it requires others to pay for. Granting that such a classification would be reasonable, it does not follow that a State's failure to make it can be regarded as discrimination. It may as accurately be said that the real issue in this case is not whether Illinois *has* discriminated but whether it has a duty *to* discriminate.

I do not understand the Court to dispute either the necessity for a bill of exceptions or the reasonableness of the general requirement that the trial transcript, if used in its preparation, be paid for by the appealing party. The Court finds in the operation of these requirements, however, an invidious classification between the "rich" and the "poor." But no economic burden attendant upon the exercise of a privilege bears equally upon all, and in other circumstances the resulting differentiation is not treated as an invidious classification by the State, even though discrimination against "indigents" by name would be unconstitutional. Thus, while the exclusion of "indigents" from a free state university would deny them equal protection, requiring the payment of tuition fees surely would not, despite the resulting exclusion of those who could not afford to pay the fees. And if imposing a condition of payment is not the equivalent of a classification by the State in one case, I fail to see why it should be so regarded in another. Thus if requiring defendants in felony cases to pay for a transcript constitutes a discriminatory denial to indigents of the right of appeal available to others, why is it not a similar denial in misdemeanor cases or, for that matter, civil cases?

It is no answer to say that equal protection is not an absolute, and that in other than criminal cases the differentiation is "reasonable." The resulting *classification* would be invidious in all cases, and an invidious classification offends equal protection regardless of the seriousness of the consequences. Hence it must be that the differences are "reasonable" in other cases not because the "classification" is reasonable but simply because it is not unreasonable in those cases for the State to fail to relieve indigents of the economic burden. That is, the issue here is not the typical equal protection question of the reasonableness of a "classification" on the basis of which the State has imposed legal disabilities, but rather the reasonableness of the State's failure to remove natural disabilities. The Court holds that the failure of the State to do so is constitutionally unreasonable in this case although it might not be in others. I submit that the basis for that holding is simply an unarticulated conclusion that it violates "fundamental fairness" for a State which provides for appellate review, and thus apparently considers such review necessary to assure justice, not to see to it that such appeals are in fact available to those it would imprison for serious crimes. That of course is the traditional language of due process. . . .

. . . .

Of course the fact that appeals are not constitutionally required does not mean that a State is free of constitutional restraints in establishing the terms upon which appeals will be allowed. It does mean, however, that there is no "right" to an appeal in the same sense that there is a right to a trial. Rather the constitutional right under the Due Process Clause is simply the right not to be denied an appeal for arbitrary or capricious reasons. Nothing of that kind, however, can be found in any of the steps by which Illinois has established its appellate system.

We are all agreed that no objection of substance can be made to the provisions for free transcripts in capital and constitutional cases. The due process challenge must therefore be directed to the basic step of permitting appeals at all without also providing an *in forma pauperis* procedure. But whatever else may be said of Illinois' reluctance to expend public funds in perfecting appeals for indigents, it can hardly be said to be arbitrary. A policy of economy may be unenlightened, but it is certainly not capricious. And that it has never generally been so regarded is evidenced by the fact that our attention has been called to no State in which *in forma pauperis* appeals were established contemporaneously with the right of appeal. I can find nothing in the past decisions of this Court justifying a holding that the Fourteenth Amendment confines the States to a choice between allowing no appeals at all or undertaking to bear the cost of appeals for indigents, which is what the Court in effect now holds.

It is argued finally that, even if it cannot be said to be "arbitrary," the failure of Illinois to provide petitioners with the means of exercising the right of appeal that others are able to exercise is simply so "unfair" as to be a denial of due process. I have some question whether the non-arbitrary denial of a right that the State may withhold altogether could ever be so characterized. In any event, however, to so hold it is not enough that we consider free transcripts for indigents to be a desirable policy or that we would weigh the competing social values in favor of such a policy were it our function to distribute Illinois' public funds among alternative uses. Rather the question is whether some method of assuring that an indigent is able to exercise his right of appeal is "implicit in the concept of ordered liberty," Palko v. Connecticut, 302 U.S. 319, so that the failure of a

State so to provide constitutes a "denial of fundamental fairness, shocking to the universal sense of justice." . . . Such an equivalence between persons in the means with which to exercise a right of appeal has not, however, traditionally been regarded as an essential of "fundamental fairness," and the reforms extending such aid to indigents have only recently gained widespread acceptance. Indeed, it was not until an Act of Congress in 1944 that defendants in federal criminal cases became entitled to free transcripts, and to date approximately one-third of the States still have not taken that step. With due regard for the constitutional limitations upon the power of this Court to intervene in State matters, I am unable to bring myself to say that Illinois' failure to furnish free transcripts to indigents in all criminal cases is "shocking to the universal sense of justice."

As I view this case, it contains none of the elements hitherto regarded as essential to justify action by this Court under the Fourteenth Amendment. In truth what we have here is but the failure of Illinois to adopt as promptly as other States a desirable reform in its criminal procedure. Whatever might be said were this a question of procedure in the federal courts, regard for our system of federalism requires that matters such as this be left to the States. However strong may be one's inclination to hasten the day when *in forma pauperis* criminal procedures will be universal among the States, I think it is beyond the province of this Court to tell Illinois that it must provide such procedures.

THOMPSON v. CITY OF LOUISVILLE

UNITED STATES SUPREME COURT

362 U.S. 199 (1960)

The facts in the case are succinctly set forth in the opinion.

Mr. Justice Black delivered the opinion of the Court.

Petitioner was found guilty in the Police Court of Louisville, Kentucky, of two offenses—loitering and disorderly conduct. The ultimate question presented to us is whether the charges against petitioner were so totally devoid of evidentiary support as to render his conviction unconstitutional under the Due Process Clause of the Fourteenth Amendment. Decision of this question turns not on the sufficiency of the evidence, but on whether this conviction rests upon any evidence at all.

The facts as shown by the record are short and simple. Petitioner, a long-time resident of the Louisville area, went into the Liberty End Cafe about 6:20 on Saturday evening, January 24, 1959. In addition to selling food the cafe was licensed to sell beer to the public and some 12 to 30 patrons were present during the time petitioner was there. When petitioner had been in the cafe about half an hour, two Louisville police officers came in on a "routine check." Upon seeing petitioner "out there on the floor dancing by himself," one of the officers, according to his testimony, went up to the manager who was sitting on a stool nearby and asked him how long petitioner had been in there and if he had bought anything. The officer testified that upon being told by the manager that petitioner had been there "a little over a half-hour and that he had not bought anything," he accosted Thompson and "asked him what was his reason for being in there and he said he was waiting on a bus." The officer then informed petitioner that he was under arrest and took him outside. This was the arrest for loitering. After going outside, the officer testified, petitioner "was very argumentative—he argued with us back and forth and so then we placed a disorderly conduct charge on him." Admittedly the disorderly conduct conviction rests solely on this one sentence description of petitioner's conduct after he left the cafe.

The foregoing evidence includes all that the city offered against him, except a record purportedly showing a total of 54 previous arrests of petitioner. Before putting on his defense, petitioner moved for a dismissal of the charges against him on the ground that a judgment of conviction on this record would deprive him of property and liberty without due process of law under the Fourteenth Amendment in that (1) there was no evidence to support findings of guilt and (2) the two arrests and prosecutions were reprisals against him because petitioner had employed counsel and demanded a judicial hearing to defend himself against prior and allegedly baseless charges by the police. This motion was denied.

Petitioner then put in evidence on his own behalf, none of which in any way strengthened the city's case. He testified that he bought, and one of the cafe employees served him, a dish of macaroni and a glass of beer and that he remained in the cafe waiting for a bus to go home. Further evidence showed without dispute that at the time of his arrest petitioner gave the officers his home address; that he had money with him, and a bus schedule showing that a bus to his home would stop within half a block of the cafe at about 7:30; that he owned two unimproved lots of land; that in addition to work he had done for others, he had regularly worked one day or more a week for the same family for 30 years; that he paid no rent in the home where he lived and that his meager income was sufficient to meet his needs. The cafe manager testified that petitioner had frequently patronized the cafe, and that he had never told petitioner that he was unwelcome there. The manager further testified that on this very occasion he saw petitioner "standing there in the middle of the floor and patting his foot," and that he did not at any time during petitioner's stay there object to anything he was doing. There is no evidence that anyone else in the cafe objected to petitioner's shuffling his feet in rhythm with the music of the jukebox or that his conduct was boisterous or offensive to anyone present. At the close of his evidence, petitioner repeated his motion for dismissal of the charges on the ground that a conviction on the foregoing evidence would deprive him of liberty and property without due process under the Fourteenth Amendment. The court denied the motion, convicted him of both offenses, and fined him $10 on each charge. A motion for new trial, on the same grounds, also was denied, which exhausted petitioner's remedies in the police court.

Since police court fines of less than $20 on a single charge are not appealable or otherwise reviewable in any other Kentucky court, petitioner asked the police court to stay the judgments so that he might have an opportunity to apply for certiorari to this Court (before his case became moot) to review the due process contentions he raised. The police court suspended judgment for 24 hours during which time petitioner sought a longer stay from the Kentucky Circuit Court. That court, after examining the police court's judgments and transcript, granted a stay concluding that "there appears to be merit" in the contention that "there is no evidence upon which conviction and sentence by the Police Court could be based" and that petitioner's "Federal Constitutional claims are substantial and not frivolous." On appeal by the city, the Kentucky Court of Appeals held that the Circuit Court lacked the power to grant the stay it did, but nevertheless went on to take the extraordinary step of granting its own stay, even though petitioner had made no original application to that court for such a stay. Explaining its reason, the Court of Appeals took occasion to agree with the Circuit Court that petitioner's "federal constitutional claims are substantial and not frivolous." The Court of Appeals then went on to say that petitioner

> "appears to have a real question as to whether he has been denied due process under the Fourteenth Amendment of the Federal Constitution, yet this substantive right cannot be tested unless we grant him a stay of execution because his fines are not appealable and will be satisfied by being served in jail before he can prepare and file his petition for certiorari. Appellee's substantive right of due process is of no avail to him unless this court grants him the ancillary right whereby he may test same in the Supreme Court."

Our examination of the record presented in the petition for certiorari convinced us that although the fines here are small, the due process questions presented are substantial and we therefore granted certiorari to review the . . . judgments. . . .

The city correctly assumes here that if there is no support for these convictions in the record they are void as denials of due process. The pertinent portion of the city ordinance under which petitioner was convicted of loitering reads as follows:

> "It shall be unlawful for any person * * *, without visible means of support, or who cannot give a satisfactory account of himself, * * * to sleep, lie, loaf, or trespass in or about any premises, building, or other structure in the City of Louisville, without first having obtained the consent of the owner or controller of said premises, structure, or building; * * *" §85-12, Ordinances of the City of Louisville.

In addition to the fact that petitioner proved he had "visible means of support," the prosecutor at trial said "This is a loitering charge here. There is no charge of no visible means of support." Moreover, there is no suggestion that petitioner was sleeping, lying or trespassing in or about this cafe. Accordingly he could only have been convicted for being unable to give a satisfactory account of himself while loitering in the cafe, without the consent of the manager. Under the words of the ordinance itself, if the evidence fails to prove all three elements of this loitering charge, the conviction is not supported by evidence, in which event it does not comport with due process of law. The record is entirely lacking in evidence to support any of the charges.

Here, petitioner spent about half an hour on a Saturday evening in January in a public cafe which sold food and beer to the public. When asked to account for his presence there, he said he was waiting for a bus. The city concedes that there is no law making it an offense for a person in such a cafe to "dance," "shuffle" or "pat" his feet in time to music. The undisputed testimony of the manager, who did not know whether petitioner had bought macaroni and beer or not but who did see the patting, shuffling or dancing, was that petitioner was welcome there. The manager testified that he did not at any time during petitioner's stay in the cafe object to anything petitioner was doing and that he never saw petitioner do anything that would cause any objection. Surely this is implied consent, which the city admitted in oral argument satisfies the ordinance. The arresting officer admitted that there was nothing in any way "vulgar" about what he called petitioner's "ordinary dance," whatever relevance, if any, vulgarity might have to a charge of loitering. There simply is no semblance of evidence from which any person could reasonably infer that petitioner could not give a satisfactory account of himself or that he was loitering or loafing there (in the ordinary sense of the words) without "the consent of the owner or controller" of the cafe.

Petitioner's conviction for disorderly conduct was under § 85–8 of the city ordinance which, without definition, provides that "[w]hoever shall be found guilty of disorderly conduct in the City of Louisville shall be fined * *." etc. The only evidence of "disorderly conduct" was the single statement of the policeman that after petitioner was arrested and taken out of the cafe he was very argumentative. There is no testimony that petitioner raised his voice, used offensive language, resisted the officers or engaged in any conduct of any kind likely in any way to adversely affect the good order and tranquillity of the City of Louisville. The only information the record contains on what the petitioner was "argumentative" about is his statement that he asked the officers "what they arrested me for." We assume, for we are justified in assuming, that merely "arguing" with a policeman is not, because it could not be, "disorderly conduct" as a matter of the substantive law of Kentucky. . . . Moreover, Kentucky law itself seems to provide that if a man wrongfully arrested fails to object to the arresting officer, he waives any right to complain later that the arrest was unlawful. . . .

Thus we find no evidence whatever in the record to support these convictions. Just as "Conviction upon a charge not made would be sheer denial of due process," so is it a violation of due process to convict and punish a man without evidence of his guilt.

The judgments are reversed and the cause is remanded to the Police Court of the City of Louisville for proceedings not inconsistent with this opinion.

Reversed and remanded.

GLOSSARY

Glossary

The following definitions are taken from *Black's Law Dictionary* (St. Paul, Minn., West Publishing Company, 4th Edition, 1951) with the kind permission of the West Publishing Company. We have endeavored to include in the Glossary words, phrases, and terms which are used in the cases and discussions contained in this book and which we thought would be unfamiliar to you. But since the Glossary is limited in scope and is no real substitute for a law dictionary, you are urged to familiarize yourself with *Black's Law Dictionary* and to use it when seeking definitions for words, phrases, and terms which are not contained here.

We should like to call your attention to two matters of detail. First, in *Black's*, whenever definitions are drawn from other sources, like court decisions, those sources are cited, as you will note below. Second, material enclosed in brackets is supplied by the authors and is not drawn from *Black's*.

a fortiori. With stronger reason; much more. A term used in logic to denote an argument to the effect that because one ascertained fact exists, therefore another, which is included in it, or analogous to it, and which is less improbable, unusual, or surprising, must also exist.

ad hoc. For this; for this special purpose.

An attorney ad hoc, or a guardian or curator ad hoc, is one appointed for a special purpose, generally to represent the client or infant in the particular action in which the appointment is made. Bienvenu v. Insurance Co., 33 La.Ann. 212.

ad valorem. According to value. Powell v. Gleason, Ariz., 74 P.2d 47, 50, 114 A.L.R. 838.

Duties are either *ad valorem* or *specific*; the former when the duty is laid in the form of a percentage on the value of the property; the latter where it is imposed as a fixed sum on each article of a class without regard to its value. The term *ad valorem* tax means a tax or duty upon the value of the article or thing subject to taxation. Arthur v. Johnston, 185 S.C. 324, 194 S.E. 151, 154.

amicus curiæ. Lat. A friend of the court.

A by-stander (usually a counsellor) who interposes and volunteers information upon some matter of law in regard to which the judge is doubtful or mistaken, Fort Worth & D. C. Ry. Co. v. Greathouse, Tex.Civ.App., 41 S.W.2d 418, 422; or upon a matter of which the court may take judicial cognizance. The Claveresk, C.C.A.N.Y., 264 F. 276, 279; In re Perry, 83 Ind.App. 456, 148 N.E. 163, 165. Implies friendly intervention of counsel to remind court of legal matter which has escaped its notice, and regarding which it appears to be in danger of going wrong. Blanchard v. Boston & M. R., 86 N.H. 263, 167 A. 158, 160.

Also a person who has no right to appear in a suit but is allowed to introduce argument, authority, or evidence to protect his interests. Ladue v. Goodhead, 181 Misc. 807, 44 N.Y.S.2d 783, 787.

appellant. The party who takes an appeal from one court or jurisdiction to another. Used broadly or nontechnically, the term includes one who sues out a writ of error. Widgins v. Norfolk & W. Ry. Co., 142 Va. 419, 128 S.E. 516, 518.

appellee. The party in a cause against whom an appeal is taken; that is, the party who has an interest adverse to setting aside or reversing the judgment.

Slayton v. Horsey, 97 Tex. 341, 78 S.W. 919. Sometimes also called the "respondent."

In a nontechnical sense, "appellee" may include a defendant in writ of error. Widgins v. Norfolk & W. Ry. Co., 142 Va. 419, 128 S.E. 516, 518.

. . . .

arguendo. In arguing; in the course of the argument. A statement or observation made by a judge as a matter of argument or illustration, but not directly bearing upon the case at bar, or only incidentally involved in it, is said (in the reports) to be made *arguendo*, or in the abbreviated form, *arg*.

bank. A bench or seat; the bench of justice; the bench or tribunal occupied by the judges; the seat of judgment; a court. The full bench, or full court; the assembly of all the judges of a court.

A "sitting *in bank*" is a meeting of all the judges of a court, usually for the purpose of hearing arguments on demurrers, points reserved, motions for new trial, and other law points, as distinguished from the sitting of a single judge at the assises or at *nisi prius* and from trials at bar to determine facts. 3 Bla. Comm. 28, n. But in this sense, *banc* is perhaps the more usual form of the word. "Sitting in bank" is also described as an official meeting of four of the judges of a common-law court. Wharton, Lex.

brief. A written document; a letter; a writing in the form of a letter. A summary, abstract, or epitome. A condensed statement or epitome of some larger document, or of a series of papers, facts and circumstances, or propositions.

In American practice. A written or printed document, prepared by counsel to serve as the basis for an argument upon a cause in an appellate court, and usually filed for the information of the court. It embodies the points of law which the counsel desires to establish, together with the arguments and authorities upon which he rests his contention. A brief, within a rule of court requiring counsel to furnish briefs, before argument, implies some kind of statement of the case for the information of the court. Gardner v. Stover, 43 Ind. 356. A "brief" is the vehicle of counsel to convey to the appellate court the essential facts of his client's case, a statement of the questions of law involved, the law he would have applied, and the application he desires made of it by the court. Bell v. Germain, 12 Cal.App. 375, 107 P. 630. The brief of evidence in connection with an auditor's report is considered a "brief" though it may embody the stenographic report of the testimony in full. McKenzie v. Perdue, 67 Ga.App. 202, 19 S.E.2d 765, 774.

. . . .

certiorari. Lat. (To be informed of, to be made certain in regard to.) The name of a writ of review or inquiry. . . .

Certiorari is an appellate proceeding for reexamination of action of inferior tribunal or as auxiliary process to enable appellate court to obtain further information in pending cause, Shapleigh Hardware Co. v. Brumfield, 159 Miss. 175, 130 So. 98. A writ directed only to an inferior tribunal, Stewart v. Johnston, C.C.A.Cal., 97 F.2d 548.

. . . .

In some states the writ has been abolished by statute so far as the common-law name is concerned, but the remedy is preserved under the new name of "writ of review"; Southwestern Telegraph & Telephone Co. v. Robinson, Tex., 1 C.C.A. 91, 48 F. 771.

compos mentis. Sound of mind. Having use and control of one's mental faculties.

coram non judice. In presence of a person not a judge. When a suit is brought and determined in a court which has no jurisdiction in the matter, then it is said to be *coram non judice*, and the judgment is void. Manufacturing Co. v. Holt, 51 W.Va. 352, 41 S.E. 351.

cujus est solum, ejus est usque ad cœlum et ad inferos. To whomsoever the soil belongs, he owns also to the sky and to the depths. The owner of a piece of land owns everything above and below it to an indefinite extent. Co.Litt. 4; Shell Oil Co. v. Manley Oil Corporation, D.C.Ill., 37 F.Supp. 289, 292.

de jure. Of right; legitimate; lawful; by right and just title. In this sense it is the contrary of *de facto.* . . . It may also be contrasted with *de gratia,* in which case it means "as a matter of right," as *de gratia* means "by grace or favor." Again it may be contrasted with *de œquitate;* here meaning "by law," as the latter means "by equity." . . .

[*de minimis.* Abbreviated form for *de minimus non curat lex.*]

de minimis non curat lex. The law does not care for, or take notice of, very small or trifling matters. The law does not concern itself about trifles. Cro.Eliz. 353. Thus, error in calculation of a fractional part of a penny will not be regarded. Hob. 88. So, the law will not, in general, notice the fraction of a day. Broom, Max. 142.

[*dicta, dictum.* See *obiter dictum.*]

[*en banc.* See *bank.*]

ex contractu. From or out of a contract.

In both the civil and the common law, rights and causes of action are divided into two classes,—those arising *ex contractu,* (from a contract,) and those arising *ex delicto,* (from a delict or tort.) See 3 Bl.Comm. 117; Mackeld. Rom.Law, § 384. See Scharf v. People, 134 Ill. 240, 24 N.E. 761; Federal Life Ins. Co. v. Maxam, 70 Ind.App. 266, 117 N.E. 801, 807.

If cause of action declared in pleading arises from breach of promise, the action is "ex contractu". Chambers v. Birmingham Trust & Savings Co., 232 Ala. 609, 168 So. 893.

ex delicto. From a delict, tort, fault, crime, or malfeasance. [See *ex contractu.*]

An action "ex delicto" is an action of tort; an action arising out of fault, misconduct, or malfeasance. Sayers & Muir Service Station v. Indian Refining Co., 266 Ky. 779, 100 S.W.2d 687, 689. If cause of action declared in pleading arises from breach of duty growing out of contract, it is in form "ex delicto" and case. Chambers v. Birmingham Trust & Savings Co., 232 Ala. 609, 168 So. 893.

ex parte. On one side only; by or for one party; done for, in behalf of, or on the application of, one party only.

A judicial proceeding, order, injunction, etc., is said to be *ex parte* when it is taken or granted at the instance and for the benefit of one party only, and without notice to, or contestation by, any person adversely interested. Janin v. Logan, 209 Ky. 811, 273 S.W. 531, 532; Van Alen v. Superior Court in and for Los Angeles County, 37 Cal.App. 696, 174 P. 672; Stella v. Mosele, 299 Ill.App. 53, 19 N.E.2d 433, 435.

In its primary sense, *ex parte,* as applied to an application in a judicial proceeding, means that it is made by a person who is not a party to the proceeding, but who has an interest in the matter which entitles him to make the application. Thus, in a bankruptcy proceeding or an administration action, an application by A. B., a creditor, or the like, would be described as made "*ex parte* A. B.," *i. e.,* on the part of A. B.

In its more usual sense, *ex parte* means that an application is made by one party to a proceeding in the absence of the other. Thus, an *ex parte* injunction is one granted without the opposite party having had notice of the application. It would not be called "*ex parte*" if he had proper notice of it, and chose not to appear to oppose it. Sweet.

"*Ex parte,*" in the heading of a reported case, signifies that the name following is that of the party upon whose application the case is heard.

ex post facto law. A law passed after the occurrence of a fact or commission of an act, which retrospectively changes the legal consequences or relations of such fact or deed. By Const. U. S. art. 1, § 10, the states are forbidden to pass "any *ex post facto* law." In this connection the phrase has a much narrower meaning than its literal translation would justify. . . .

. . . .

An "ex post facto law" is defined as a law which provides for the infliction of punishment upon a person for an act done which, when it was committed, was innocent; a law which aggravates a crime or makes it greater than when it was committed; a law that changes the punishment or inflicts a greater punishment than the law annexed to the crime when it was committed; a law that changes the rules of evidence and receives less or different testimony than was required at the time of the commission of the offense in order to convict the offender; a law which, assuming to regulate civil rights and remedies only, in effect imposes a penalty or the deprivation of a right which, when done, was lawful; a law which deprives persons accused of crime of some lawful protection to which they have become entitled, such as the protection of a former conviction or acquittal, or of the proclamation of amnesty; every law which, in relation to the offense or its consequences, alters the situation of a person to his disadvantage. State v. Rowe, 116 N.J.L. 48, 181 A. 706.

functus officio. Lat. A task performed. Board of School Trustees of Washington City Administrative Unit v. Benner, 222 N.C. 566, 24 S.E.2d 259, 263.

Having fulfilled the function, discharged the office, or accomplished the purpose, and therefore of no further force or authority. Applied to an officer whose term has expired, and who has consequently no further official authority; and also to an instrument, power, agency, etc., which has fulfilled the purpose of its creation, and is therefore of no further virtue or effect. Blanton Banking Co. v. Taliaferro, Tex.Civ. App., 262 S.W. 196.

in forma pauperis. In the character or manner of a pauper. Describes permission given to a poor person to sue without liability for costs.

in loco parentis. In the place of a parent; instead of a parent; charged, factitiously, with a parent's rights, duties, and responsibilities. Wetherby v. Dixon, 19 Ves. 412; Brinkerhoff v. Merselis, 24 N.J.L. 683; Howard v. United States, D.C.Ky., 2 F.2d 170, 174; Meisner v. United States, D.C.Mo., 295 F. 866, 868.

in terrorem. In terror or warning; by way of threat. Applied to legacies given upon condition that the recipient shall not dispute the validity or the dispositions of the will; such a condition being usually regarded as a mere threat.

infra. Lat. Below, under, beneath, underneath. The opposite of *supra,* above. . . .

. . . .

inter alia. Among other things. A term anciently used in pleading, especially in reciting statutes, where the whole statute was not set forth at length. *Inter alia enactatum fuit,* among other things it was enacted. Plowd. 65.

interregnum. An interval between reigns. The period which elapses between the death of a sovereign and the election of another. The vacancy which occurs when there is no government.

ipso facto. By the fact itself; by the mere fact. By the mere effect of an act or a fact. Barber Asphalt Paving Co. v. Hayward, 248 Mo. 280, 154 S.W. 140, 141.

. . . .

judgement. . . . The official and authentic decision of a court of justice upon the respective rights and claims of the parties to an action or suit therein litigated and submitted to its determination. People v. Hebel, 19 Colo.App. 523, 76 P. 550; Bullock v. Bullock, 52 N.J.Eq. 561, 30 A. 676, 27 L.R.A. 213, 46 Am.St.Rep. 528; State v. Brown & Sharpe Mfg. Co., 18 R.I. 16, 25 A. 246, 17 L.R.A. 856.

. . . .

A decree is a judgment. Fuller v. Fuller, 49 R.I. 45, 139 A. 662, 663; Knettle v. Knettle, 190 Wash. 395, 68 P.2d 218, 220; Spartan Mills v. Law, 186 S.C. 61, 194 S.E. 653, 655; National Surety Co. v. Mulligan, 105 N.J.L. 336, 146 A. 372, 375. As used in some statutes, judgment and decree are synonymous. Finnell v. Finnell, 113 Okl. 269, 230 P. 912, 913; Kline v. Murray, 79 Mont. 530, 257 P. 465, 467; Weeden v. Weeden, 116 Ohio St. 524, 156 N.E. 908, 909.

. . . .

mala in se. Wrongs in themselves; acts morally wrong; offenses against conscience. 1 Bl.Comm. 57, 58; 4 Bl.Comm. 8; Com. v. Adams, 114 Mass. 323, 19 Am.Rep. 362; Turner v. Merchants' Bank, 126 Ala. 397, 28 So. 469.

mandamus. Lat. We command. This is the name of a writ (formerly a high prerogative writ) which issues from a court of superior jurisdiction, and is directed to a private or municipal corporation, or any of its officers, or to an executive, administrative or judicial officer, or to an inferior court, commanding the performance of a particular act therein specified, and belonging to his or their public, official, or ministerial duty, or directing the restoration of the complainant to rights or privileges of which he has been illegally deprived. Lahiff v. St. Joseph, etc., Soc., 76 Conn. 648, 57 A. 692, 65 L.R.A. 92, 100 Am.St.Rep. 1012.

The action of *mandamus* is one, brought in a court of competent jurisdiction, to obtain an order of such court commanding an inferior tribunal, board, corporation, or person to do or not to do an act the performance or omission of which the law enjoins as a duty resulting from an office, trust, or station. Where discretion is left to the inferior tribunal or person, the *mandamus*, can only compel it to act, but cannot control such discretion. Rev.Code Iowa, 1880, § 3373 (Code 1931, § 12440).

Writ of "mandamus" is summary writ issued from court of competent jurisdiction to command performance of specific duty which relator is entitled to have performed. People v. Nelson, 346 Ill. 247, 178 N.E. 485, 487.

It is legal, not equitable, remedy, and, when issued, is an inflexible peremptory command to do a particular thing. State ex rel. Onion v. Supreme Temple Pythian Sisters, 227 Mo.App. 557, 54 S.W.2d 468, 469.

The writ of *mandamus* is either *peremptory* or *alternative*, according as it requires the defendant absolutely to obey its behest, or gives him an opportunity to show cause to the contrary. It is the usual practice to issue the alternative writ first. This commands the defendant to do the particular act, or else to appear and show cause against it at a day named. If he neglects to obey the writ, and either makes default in his appearance or fails to show good cause against the application, the peremptory *mandamus* issues, which commands him absolutely and without qualification to do the act.

[*modus operandi*. Method of operating.]

[*nexus*. Connection or link.]

obiter dictum. Words of a prior opinion entirely unnecessary for the decision of the case. Noel v. Olds, 78 U.S.App.D.C. 155, 138 F.2d 581, 586.

Statements in opinions wherein courts indulged in generalities that had no actual bearing on issues involved. Graham v. Jones. 198 La. 507, 3 So.2d 761, 774.

A remark made, or opinion expressed, by a judge, in his decision upon a cause, "by the way," that is, incidentally or collaterally, and not directly upon the question before him, or upon a point not necessarily involved in the determination of the cause, or introduced by way of illustration, or analogy or argument. . . .

pari materia. Lat. Of the same matter; on the same subject; as, laws *pari materia* must be construed with reference to each other. Bac.Abr. "Statute," I, 3; Dupont v. Mills, Del., 196 A. 168, 177, 119 A.L.R. 174.

pendente lite. Lat. Pending the suit; during the actual progress of a suit; during litigation. In re Morrissey's Will, 91 N.J.Eq. 289, 107 A. 70, 71.

per curiam. Lat. By the court. A phrase used in the reports to distinguish an opinion of the whole court from an opinion written by any one judge. . . .

petitioner. One who presents a petition to a court, officer, or legislative body. In legal proceedings begun by petition, the person against whom action or relief is prayed, or who opposes the prayer of the petition, is called the "respondent."

prima facie. Lat. At first sight; on the first appearance; on the face of it; so far as can be judged from the first disclosure; presumably; a fact presumed to be true unless disproved by some evidence to the contrary. State ex rel. Herbert v. Whims, 68 Ohio App. 39, 38 N.E.2d 596, 599.

prima facie case. Such as will suffice until contradicted and overcome by another evidence. Pacific Telephone & Telegraph Co. v. Wallace, 158 Or. 210, 75 P.2d 942, 947. A case which has proceeded upon sufficient proof to that stage where it will support finding if evidence to contrary is disregarded. In re Hoagland's Estate, 126 Neb. 377, 253 N.W. 416.

A litigating party is said to have a *prima facie* case when the evidence in his favor is sufficiently strong for his opponent to be called on to answer it. A *prima facie* case, then, is one which is established by sufficient evidence, and can be overthrown only by rebutting evidence adduced on the other side. In some cases the only question to be considered is whether there is a *prima facie* case or no. Thus a grand jury are bound to find a true bill of indictment, if the evidence before them creates a *prima facie* case against the accused; and for this purpose, therefore, it is not necessary for them to hear the evidence for the defense. Mozley & Whitley. And see State v. Hardelein, 169 Mo. 579, 70 S.W. 130; State v. Lawlor, 28 Minn. 216, 9 N.W. 698.

pro tanto. For so much; for as much as may be; as far as it goes. Donley v. Hays, 17 Serg. & R. (Pa.) 400.

pro tempore. For the time being; temporarily; provisionally.

pro rata. Proportionately; according to a certain rate, percentage, or proportion. According to measure, interest, or liability. Chaplin v. Griffin, 252 Pa. 271, 97 A. 409, 411, Ann.Cas.1918C, 787. According to a certain rule or proportion. 19 Am.L.Reg.N.S. 355, n. (U.S.D.C.-Cal.).

Thus, the creditors (of the same class) of an insolvent estate are to be paid *pro rata;* that is, each is to receive a dividend bearing the same ratio to the whole amount of his claim that the aggregate of assets bears to the aggregate of debts.

qua. Lat. Considered as; in the character or capacity of. For example, "the trustee *qua* trustee [that is, in his character as trustee] is not liable," etc.

quo warranto. In old English practice. A writ, in the nature of a writ of right for the king, against him who claimed or usurped any office, franchise, or liberty, to inquire *by what authority* he supported his claim, in order to determine the right. It lay also in case of non-user, or long neglect of a franchise, or misuser or abuse of it; being a writ commanding the defendant to show *by what warrant* he exercises such a franchise, having never had any grant of it, or having forfeited it by neglect or abuse. 3 Bl.Comm. 262.

In England, and quite generally throughout the United States, this writ has given place to an "information in the nature of a *quo warranto*," which, though in form a criminal proceeding, is in effect a civil remedy similar to the old writ, and is the method now usually employed for trying the title to a corporate or other franchise, or to a public or corporate office. Ames v. Kansas, 111 U.S. 449, 4 S.Ct. 437, 28 L.Ed. 482; People v. Londoner, 13 Colo. 303, 22 P. 764, 6 L.R.A. 444; An extraordinary proceeding, prerogative in nature, addressed to preventing a continued exercise of authority unlawfully asserted. Johnson v. Manhattan Ry. Co., N.Y., 53 S.Ct. 721, 289 U.S. 479, 77 L.Ed. 1331.

It is intended to prevent exercise of powers that are not conferred by law, and is not ordinarily available to regulate the manner of exercising such powers. State ex rel. Johnson v. Conservative Savings & Loan Ass'n, 143 Neb. 805, 11 N.W.2d 89, 92, 93.

remand. To send back.

Cause

The sending the cause back to the same court out of which it came, for purpose of having some action on it there.

Prisoner

After a preliminary or partial hearing before a court or magistrate, is to send him back to custody, to be kept until the hearing is resumed or the trial comes on. Ex parte Chalfant, 81 W.Va. 93, 93 S.E. 1032, 1033.

When a prisoner is brought before a judge on habeas corpus, for the purpose of obtaining liberty, the judge hears the case, and either discharges him or remands him.

res judicata. A matter adjudged; a thing judicially acted upon or decided; a thing or matter settled by judgment. A phrase of the civil law, constantly quoted in the books. Epstein v. Soskin, 86 Misc.Rep. 94, 148 N.Y.S. 323, 324; Rule that final judgment or decree on merits by court of competent jurisdiction is conclusive of rights of parties or their privies in all later suits on points and matters determined in former suit. American S. S. Co. v. Wickwire Spencer Steel Co., D.C. N.Y., 8 F.Supp. 562, 566. And to be applicable, requires identity in thing sued for as well as identity of cause of action, of persons and parties to action, and of quality in persons for or against whom claim is made. Freudenreich v. Mayor and Council of Borough of Fairview, 114 N.J.L. 290, 176 A. 162, 163. The sum and substance of the whole rule is that a matter once judicially decided is finally decided. Massie v. Paul, 263 Ky. 183, 92 S.W.2d 11, 14. . . .

. . . .

res nova. A new matter; a new case; a question not before decided.

respondeat superior. Let the master answer. This maxim means that a master is liable in certain cases for the wrongful acts of his servant, and a principal for those of his agent. Broom, Max. 843. Southern Paramount Pictures Co. v. Gaulding, 24 Ga.App. 478, 101 S.E. 311; Delaware, L. & W. R. Co. v. Pittinger, C.C.A.N.J., 293 F. 853, 855. Under this doctrine master is responsible for want of care on servant's part toward those to whom master owes duty to use care, provided failure of servant to use such care occurred in course of his employment. Shell Petroleum Corporation v. Magnolia Pipe Line Co., Tex.Civ.App., 85 S.W.2d 829, 832. Doctrine applies only when relation of master and servant existed between defendant and wrongdoer at time of injury sued for, in respect to very transaction from which it arose. James v. J. S. Williams & Son, 177 La. 1033, 150 So. 9, 11. Hence doctrine is inapplicable where injury occurs while servant is acting outside legitimate scope of authority. Rogers v. Town of Black Mountain, 224 N.C. 119, 29 S.E.2d 203, 205. But if deviation be only slight or incidental, employer may still be liable. Klotsch v. P. F. Collier & Son Corporation, 349 Mo. 40, 159 S.W.2d 589, 593, 595; Adams v. South Carolina Power Co., 200 S.C. 438, 21 S.E.2d 17, 19, 20.

Doctrine does not apply in relation between state officers and their subordinates, unless superior participates in or directs act. People v. Standard Accident Ins. Co., 42 Cal.App.2d 409, 108 P.2d 923, 925.

Municipalities are exempt from doctrine when officers are acting in exercise of governmental functions. Lemieux v. City of St. Albans, 112 Vt. 512, 28 A.2d 373, 374.

standing to sue doctrine. Doctrine that in action in federal constitutional court by citizen against a government officer, complaining of alleged unlawful conduct there is no justiciable controversy unless citizen shows that such conduct invades or will invade a private substantive legally protected interest of plaintiff citizen. Associated Industries of New York State v. Ickes, C.C.A.2, 134 F.2d 694, 702.

stare decisis. Lat. To abide by, or adhere to decided cases.

Policy of courts to stand by precedent and not to disturb settled point. Neff v. George, 364 Ill. 306, 4 N.E.2d 338, 390, 391. Doctrine that, when court has once laid down a principle of law as applicable to a certain state of facts, it will adhere to that principle, and apply it to all future cases, where facts are substantially the same. Moore v. City of Albany, 98 N.Y. 396, 410; Regardless of whether the parties and property are the same. Horne v. Moody, Tex.Civ.App., 146 S.W.2d 505, 509, 510. Under doctrine a deliberate or solemn decision of court made after argument on question of law fairly arising in the case, and necessary to its determination, is an authority, or binding precedent in the same court, or in other courts of equal or lower rank in subsequent cases where the very point is again in controversy. State v. Mellenberger, 163 Or. 233, 95 P.2d 709, 719, 720, 128 A.L.R. 1506. Doctrine is one of policy, grounded on theory that security and certainty require that accepted and established legal principle, under which rights may accrue, be recognized and followed, though later found to be not legally sound, but whether previous holding of court shall be adhered to, modified, or overruled is within court's discretion under circumstances of case before it. Otter Tail Power Co. v. Von Bank, 72 N.D. 497, 8 N.W.2d 599, 607, 145 A.L.R. 1343. Under doctrine, when point of law has been settled by decision, it forms precedent which is not afterwards to be departed from, and, while it should ordinarily be strictly adhered to, there are occasions when departure is rendered necessary to vindicate plain, obvious principles of law and remedy continued injustice. McGregor v. Provident Trust Co. of Philadelphia, 119 Fla. 718, 162 So. 323. The doctrine is a salutary one, and should not ordinarily be departed from where decision is of long standing and rights have been acquired under it, unless considerations of public policy demand it. Colonial Trust Co. v. Flanagan, 344 Pa. 556, 25 A.2d 728, 729.

The doctrine is limited to actual determinations in respect to litigated and necessarily decided questions, and is not applicable to dicta or obiter dicta. In re Herle's Estate, 165 Misc. 46, 300 N.Y.S. 103.

. . . .

[*stipulate, stipulating.* See stipulation.]

stipulation. A material article in an agreement.

Practice

The name given to any agreement made by the attorneys engaged on opposite sides of a cause, (especially if in writing,) regulating any matter incidental to the proceedings or trial, which falls within their jurisdiction. Such, for instance, are agreements to extend the time for pleading, to take depositions, to waive objections, to admit certain facts, to continue the cause. See Lewis v. Orpheus, 15 F.Cas. 492; Southern Colonization Co. v. Howard Cole & Co., 185 Wis. 469, 201 N.W. 817, 819.

Practice

An agreement between counsel respecting business before the court. It is not binding unless assented to by the parties or their representatives, and most stipulations are required to be in writing. Holland Banking Co. v. Continental Nat. Bank of Jackson County, Kansas City, Mo., D.C. Mo., 9 F.Supp. 988, 989.

. . . .

sub silentio. Under silence; without any notice being taken. Passing a thing *sub silentio* may be evidence of consent.

[*sub specie aeternitatis.* Under the aspect of eternity; in its essential or universal nature.]

supra. Lat. Above; upon. This word occurring by itself in a book refers the reader to a previous part of the book, like "*ante;*" it is also the initial word of several Latin phrases.

[*ultra vires*. Beyond, outside of, in excess of powers. A public officer alleged to be acting beyond his power is said to be acting *ultra vires*.]

vel non. Or not.

These words appear in the phrase "devisavit vel non" . . . meaning, literally, "did he devise or not." 26 C.J.S. p. 1296. Examples of their use by the courts may be seen in the following quotations: "So the sufficiency vel non of the order of publication is important" (Cone v. Benjamin, 27 So.2d 90, 97, 157 Fla. 800); "the negligence vel non of the owner was * * * for the jury" (Johnson v. Wood, 21 So.2d 353, 355, 155 Fla. 753); and "We come at last to the merits vel non of this appeal" (Hollywood, Inc., v. Clark, 15 So.2d 175, 185, 153 Fla. 501).

viva voce. Lat. With the living voice; by word of mouth. As applied to the examination of witnesses, this phrase is equivalent to "orally." It is used in contradistinction to evidence on affidavits or depositions. As descriptive of a species of voting, it signifies voting by speech or outcry, as distinguished from voting by a written or printed ballot.

The word "ballot" is used as a symbol of secrecy, while "viva voce" is used as a symbol of publicity. Day v. Walker, 124 Neb. 500, 247 N.W. 350, 351.

INDEX OF CASES

INDEX

INDEX

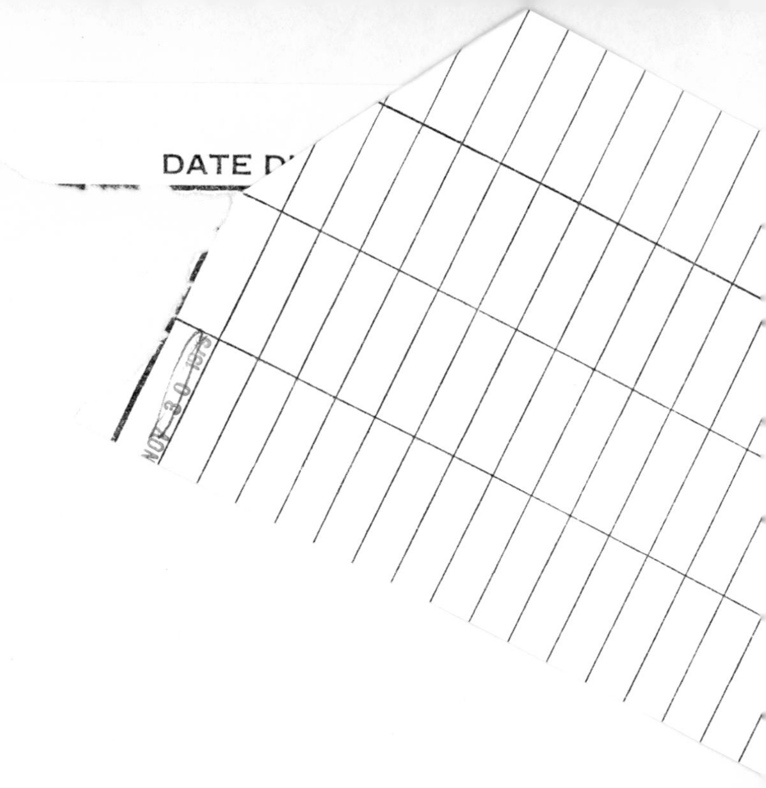
DATE D
NOV 3 0 1975